Kenneth Hein

Eucharist and
Excommunication
A study in early Christian doctrine
and discipline

European University Papers

Europäische Hochschulschriften
Publications Universitaires Européennes

Series XXIII
Theology

Reihe XXIII   Série XXIII

Theologie
Théologie

Vol./Bd. 19

Kenneth Hein

Eucharist and
Excommunication
A study in early Christian doctrine
and discipline

Herbert Lang Bern
Peter Lang Frankfurt/M.
1973

Kenneth Hein

Eucharist and Excommunication

A study in early Christian doctrine and discipline

Herbert Lang Bern
Peter Lang Frankfurt/M.
1973

ISBN 3 261 00882 2

FOREWORD

The growth and expansion of ecumenical sentiments among the
various Christian churches in recent years has given a totally new
character and urgency to the old question of <u>communicatio in
sacris</u>. It was inevitable that the Eucharist would become a major issue for ecumenical discussion and exploration very early in
the modern ecumenical movement. But Christianity's present efforts to achieve a unity which will overcome the ugly divisions of
several centuries are often hindered as much by the complex of
disciplinary traditions as by the diversity of doctrinal positions
adopted by the various Christian churches and communities. Up to
the present moment, this has proved to be especially true in regard to any consideration of the Eucharist in the present ecumenical dialogue.

Within the past few years, the varying eucharistic beliefs of
the Christian churches have been fairly well worked out and clearly stated. The outcome has been the realization that the differences lie more in the language than in the substance of the traditional eucharistic doctrines of the Christian churches. However, the remaining doctrinal differences that still separate
Christians have generally given rise, at least among those who
speak "officially" for the churches, to the feeling and disciplinary measure that the Eucharist may not be used as a <u>means</u> toward
achieving unity among the churches. That is, "intercommunion,"
"open communion," and "intercelebration" have been ruled out.
Rather, the Eucharist is to be the end and fruit of already accomplished doctrinal unity. But this attitude, while still often e-
nough "officially" reconfirmed, has become less and less pronounced
in recent years as the general consensus grows that it is utterly
utopian to expect such doctrinal unity before Christians of various confessions should be permitted to share the same table of

the Lord's Supper. This does not mean that the feeling or objective need for a solid theological basis for any changes in eucharistic discipline is absent. However, before a good theoretical foundation for any possible changes in this discipline can be layed, an intensive, in-depth look at the early Church's eucharistic discipline is necessary. It is hoped that this present study will prove a useful step in that direction. The scope of this work has been limited to the role which the Eucharist had in the first three centuries of the early Church's dealings with heretics and her own sinful members.

Special thanks and expressions of gratitutde go to various superiors and the members of Holy Cross Abbey, Canon City, Colorado for allowing me the opportunity to undertake extended theological studies in Europe. In addition, I wish to thank all those who have so kindly assisted me in the preparation of this dissertation, especially Professor Dr. Joseph Ratzinger, under whose direction this dissertation was written, Professor Dr. Johannes Neumann for his ready assistance and advice, Professor Dr. Otto Betz for his directions in regard to Qumran and New Testament studies, and the members of both the Protestant and Catholic theological departments at the University of Tübingen for their suggestions and encouragement. Also, grateful thanks go to the theologians and professors of Collegio di Sant' Anselmo, Rome, the University of Würzburg, and the University of Regensburg for their helpful advice. Finally, the members of the Archabbey of Beuron are to be most hightly recommended for the truly Christian charity shown toward me during the time I spent with them while using their fine theological library.

TABLE OF CONTENTS

FOREWARD.. iii

ABBREVIATIONS... xi

PART ONE

The Biblical Roots

Chapter One: CULTIC DISCIPLINE IN JUDAISM

1. Preliminary Remarks................................ 3
2. Forms of Cultic Discipline
   a. The curse and the ban......................... 4
   b. Purification rites............................ 7
   c. The arcane discipline......................... 10
3. Qumran and Similar Sects.......................... 10

Chapter Two: RELIGIOUS DISCIPLINE IN THE GOSPELS

1. Adoption and Adaptation of Jewish Discipline
   a. The curse and the ban......................... 13
   b. Purification rites............................ 17
2. Eucharist and Excommunication in the Fourth Gospel
   a. Eucharistic immanence......................... 23
   b. Immanence and excommunication................. 34

Chapter Three: EXCURSUS: JUDAS ISCARIOT AND THE LAST
SUPPER

1. Judas in the New Testament....................... 38
2. Judas in Early Christian Tradition............... 45

Chapter Four: THE EUCHARISTIC CHARACTER OF THE CHURCH

1. Preliminary Remarks............................... 51
2. The Church in Eucharistic Perspective
   a. The Christological aspect..................... 52
   b. The sacramental aspect........................ 54
   c. The eschatological aspect..................... 55

    d. The fraternal aspect.......................... 57

  3. The Nature of Eucharistic Unity.................. 64

Chapter Five: THE HISTORICAL BASIS OF ECCLESIAL
                 EXCOMMUNICATION

  1. The Theological Basis According to the Gospels.... 69

  2. The Practice of Excommunication in the Acts of the
    Apostles

    a. Discipline toward individuals................. 77

    b. Discipline toward Jews and gentiles........... 81

Chapter Six: DISCIPLINE IN THE PAULINE AND PASTORAL
                LETTERS

  1. Preliminary Remarks............................. 87

  2. The Pauline Epistles

    a. Letters before Paul's first imprisonment.

      a). Problems of moral-ethical discipline.

        1). Letters to the Thessalonians.......... 90

        2). The First Letter to the Corinthians.... 92

      b). Problems of doctrinal discipline

        1). Letter to the Galatians............... 103

        2). Letter to the Romans.................. 108

        3). The Second Letter to the Corinthians... 110

    b. Letters from prison........................... 112

      a). The Letter to the Philippians.............. 112

      b). The Letter to the Colossians.............. 118

      c). The Letter to the Ephesians.............. 119

  3. The Pastoral Letters............................ 120

    a. The First Letter to Timothy................... 121

    b. The Second Letter to Timothy................. 125

    c. The Letter to Titus.......................... 127

TABLE OF CONTENTS

Chapter Seven: DISCIPLINE IN THE LETTER TO THE HEBREWS,
                 THE CATHOLIC LETTERS AND THE APOCALYPSE

1. The Letter to the Hebrews
    a. Christians and sin............................ 133
    b. The unforgiveable sin......................... 136
    c. Israel and the pilgrim Church................. 147
2. The Catholic Letters
    a. The Letter of James........................... 153
    b. The First Letter of Peter..................... 156
    c. The Letter of Jude and the Second Letter of
       Peter.. 158
    d. The First Letter of John
        a). Christological heresy.................... 163
        b). Eucharist and heretics.................. 165
        c). Theology of sin......................... 172
    e. The Second Letter of John.................... 176
    f. The Third Letter of John..................... 177
3. The Apocalypse.................................. 179

PART TWO

The Patristic Contribution

Chapter Eight: CHRISTIANITY COMPLETES ITS FIRST CENTURY
1. The Didache.................................... 191
2. Clement of Rome................................ 204
3. Ignatius of Antioch
    a. Heretics and the hierarchy................... 209
    b. The Eucharist and heretics.................. 211
    c. Theology of the Eucharist.................. 213
    d. The treatment of heretics.................. 216
4. Polycarp of Smyrna............................. 219

Chapter Nine: THE CALL TO REPENTANCE

1. The Epistle of Barnabas............................ 222
2. The Second Epistle of Clement to the Corinthians.. 224
3. The Shepherd of Hermas
   a. Paenitentia secunda............................ 227
   b. The classification of sinners................. 230
   c. An ecclesiastical penitential system.......... 234
4. The Epistola Apostolorum.......................... 235

Chapter Ten: ECCLESIA DOCTA DOCENS

1. Preliminary Remarks............................... 238
2. Justin Martyr.................................... 243
3. Irenaeus of Lyons
   a. The Eucharist and heretics.................... 246
   b. Heretics and the bishop....................... 251
   c. Heretics and the Church....................... 255
   d. The Eucharist in the light of the Old
      Testament.................................... 259
4. Excursus: The Easter Controversy
   a. The historical facts.......................... 262
   b. Probable misunderstandings.................... 263
   c. Rome's reaction and reasons.................. 266
5. Clement of Alexandria
   a. The Christian Gnostic and paenitentia secunda.. · 268
   b. Eucharist and ethics.......................... 270
   c. The penitential practice...................... 272
   d. Heretics and sexual conduct................... 274
   e. Religious categories.......................... 275

Chapter Eleven: THE HERESY OF ORTHODOXY

1. Preliminary Remarks............................... 277
2. Tertullian

a. The status of heretics........................ 278

b. The status of Christian discipline............ 284

c. Eucharistic discipline........................ 288

3. Hippolytus of Rome

a. Schism at Rome................................ 294

b. The conditions of the Roman church............ 298

c. Christian discipline and the Eucharist........ 301

Chapter Twelve: THE ZENITH OF ALEXANDRIAN THEOLOGY

1. Origen

a. Biographical background....................... 305

b. Eucharistic doctrine and discipline........... 308

c. Christian discipline and excommunication...... 325

d. The nature and fate of heretics............... 333

2. Dionysius of Alexandria........................ 336

Chapter Thirteen: THE DIDASCALIA APOSTOLORUM

1. The Anti-Judaizing Program..................... 345

2. Christian Ethics and Discipline

a. The treatment of sinners...................... 352

b. The settlement of quarrels.................... 356

c. The theology and purpose of excommunication.... 357

d. Heresy and repentance......................... 361

Chapter Fourteen: CYPRIAN OF CARTHAGE

1. The Calm before the Storm

a. The historical background..................... 365

b. Church and Eucharist.......................... 366

2. Persecution and Apostasy

a. The problem created by the apostates.......... 371

b. The Eucharist and the reconciliation of

apostates, phase one........................... 374

c. The Eucharist and the reconciliation of
   apostates, phase two......................... 383
3. The Schism of the Rigorists
   a. Novatian's rebellion......................... 385
   b. The schismatics' status and the Eucharist...... 387
4. The Question of Rebaptism
   a. Ecclesial unity as the basis for rebaptism..... 390
   b. Baptism and the Eucharist..................... 392
   c. Heretics and their ineffective sacraments...... 395
   d. The theological foundation for refusing
      communicatio in sacris........................ 400
5. In Defense of Heretical Baptism
   a. Rome and Alexandria........................... 405
   b. The treatise, de Rebaptismate................. 407

Chapter Fifteen: SYNTHESIS
1. Preliminary Remarks.............................. 411
2. What Does the Bible Say?
   a. Judaism and early Christian Discipline......... 412
   b. The new Israel and the Eucharist.............. 414
3. The Answer of the Fathers
   a. Baptism and the Eucharist..................... 421
   b. The hierarchy and the Eucharist.............. 423
   c. Communion and penance in the new Israel........ 429
   d. Once again, Baptism and the Eucharist.......... 437
4. Why Eucharistic Excommunication?.................. 439
EPILOGUE.. 445
BIBLIOGRAPHY.. 451
BIBLICAL INDEX...................................... 471
GENERAL INDEX....................................... 484

ABBREVIATIONS

AAS	Acta Apostolicae Sedis, Rome, 1909ff.
ACW	Ancient Christian Writers, ed. by Johannes Quasten and J.C. Plumpe, Westminster, Maryland and London, 1946ff.
Altaner	Berthold Altaner, Patrology.
BL	Bibel-Lexikon, ed. by Herbert Haag, Einsiedeln, 1968 (or 1951 when specified).
BNTC	Black's New Testament Commentaries, ed. by Henry Chadwick.
BKV	Bibliothek der Kirchenväter, ed. by Otto Bardenhewer et alii, 1911ff^2.
CAC	Corpus Apolegetarum Christianorum Saeculi Secundi.
CB	Die griechischen christlichen Schriftsteller der ersten drei Jahrhunderte, [Corpus Berolinense].
CC	Corpus Christianorum.
CSCO	Corpus Scriptorum Christianorum Orientalium, Paris, 1903ff.
CSEL	Corpus Scriptorum Ecclesiasticorum Latinorum.
Dix	Gregory Dix, The Treatise on the Apostolic Tradition of St. Hippolytus of Rome Bishop and Martyr.
DThC	Dictionnaire de Theologie Catholique, ed. by A. Vacant and E. Mangenot, Paris, 1903ff.
Evans	Ernest Evans, Tertullian's Homily on Baptism.
ERE	Encyclopaedia of Religion and Ethics, ed. by James Hastings, Edinburgh, 1925-1940.
Feltoe	Charles Feltoe, ΔΙΟΝΥΣΙΟΥ ΛΕΙΨΑΝΑ: The Letters and other Remains of Dionysius of Alexandria.
Harvey	W.W. Harvey, S. Irenaei...Libri V adversus Haereses.
HB	Herders Bibelkommentar. Die Heilige Schrift für das Leben erklärt, ed. by Edmund Kalt and Willibald Lauck.

HE	Eusebius of Caesarea, Historia Ecclesiastica.
HThG	Handbuch Theologischer Grundbegriffe, ed. by Heinrich Fries, Munich, 1962-1963.
ICC	The International Critical Commentary, ed. by Alfred Plummer.
IDB	Interpreter's Dictionary of the Bible, ed. by George Buttrick et alii, New York and Nashville, 1962.
KEKNT	Kritisch-exegetischer Kommentar über das Neue Testament, founded by H.A. Meyer.
LS	Henry G. Liddel and Robert Scott, A Greek-English Lexicon, Oxford, 1940⁹ (1968).
LThK	Lexikon für Theologie und Kirche, ed. by Josef Höffer and Karl Rahner, Freiburg, 1957².
Mansi	J.D. Mansi, Sacrorum Conciliorum Nova et Amplissima Collectio.
MG	J.P. Migne, Patrologiae cursus completus. Series graeca.
MNTC	The Moffatt New Testament Commentary.
NLCNT	The New London Commentary on the New Testament.
NTS	New Testament Studies, Cambridge and Washington, 1954ff.
PA	Fr. X. Funk, Patres Apostolici.
RAC	Reallexikon für Antike und Christentum, ed. by Theodor Klauser, Stuttgart, 1941 (1950) ff.
RGG	Die Religion in Geschichte und Gegenwart, ed. by Kurt Galling, Tübingen, 1957-1965³.
RNT	Regensburger Neues Testament, ed. by Otto Kuss et alii.
SB	Hermann L. Strack and Paul Billerbeck, Kommentar zum Neuen Testament aus Talmud und Midrasch.
Schwarz	Eduard Schwarz, Eusebius, Kirchengeschichte (Kleine Ausgabe).

ThWB   Theologisches Wörterbuch zum Neuen Testament, ed. by
Gerhard Kittel and Gerhard Friedrich, Stuttgart,
1933ff.

TU   Texte und Untersuchungen zur Geschichte der altchristlichen Literatur, ed. by Oscar von Gebhardt and Adolf
von Harnack, Leipzig, 1883ff.

ZKT   Zeitschrift für katholische Theologie, (Innsbruck)
Vienna, 1877ff.

PART ONE

THE BIBLICAL ROOTS

CHAPTER ONE

CULTIC DISCIPLINE IN JUDAISM

1. Preliminary Remarks

Although the object of this study is to investigate the role
of the Eucharist in early Christian discipline, this can not be
done before the Jewish and Old Testament background of this discipline has been considered. This procedure is made necessary due
to the fact that the main roots of Christianity and its discipline
lie embedded in its own immediate, religious background of Judaism. On the other hand, Christianity not only adopted elements of
Judaism, it also adapted the elements to fit its own developing
religious character, which, in turn, was subjected to many non-
Jewish influences very early in its history. But the first task
in this present study is to see how adequately early Christian eucharistic discipline can be explained in the light of its Jewish
background. After this investigation, Christianity's integration
of this background into its own life in the New Testament must
then be considered. This exposition must be followed by an inquiry into the additional influences and subsequent development of
the initial integration. This process will then be pursued in its
history until one arrives at a time and place in the history of
Christianity where it can be clearly said that the object of the
pursuit--in this case, eucharistic excommunication--has finally
and firmly emerged. The development that follows upon this emergence becomes the topic of a second study, going beyond the
scope of this work. The object of this research, then, is to un-
cover "the motive forces" which stimulated and effected the e-
mergence of eucharistic excommunication. It is hoped that the
facts that are thereby exposed will prove useful and somehow pertinent to today's situation.

2. Forms of Cultic Discipline

a. The curse and the ban.

The forms of cultic discipline in the world of the Old Testament were usually highly inter-related. This was especially true of the curse and the ban. In primitive, pre-scientific cultures, magic word-formulas or actions are used still today to curse or to bless. Traces of this mentality appear in all old oriental cultures. In the Old Testament, however, the force which the curse or blessing needs in order to be effective is ascribed to God.[1] While the effect of a blessing is prosperity, well-being, a long and peaceful life, etc., a curse is followed by some form of the ban--that is, social censure which may range from temporary isolation to capital punishment. The cursed person is "marked," people may point at him, spit on him or throw something at him, especially a stone--therefore, the "appropriateness" of stoning such a person to death.[2] In addition, the cursed person is subject to disease and disgrace. Even the elements rebel against him (Ps 83,13ff).

The reader of Scriptures is confronted with the issue of curse and ban almost at the very beginning of the Bible. In the account of Adam and Eve's expulsion from Paradise (Gn 3,14-19), a number of important elements in the Jewish concept of curse and ban can be distinguished: Some crime of disobedience is committed against

---

1. Cf. P. Van Imschoot, _Fluch_, in: _BL_ 486; Gn 12,3; Herbert Brichto, _The Problem of "Curse" in the Hebrew Bible_, (Journal of Biblical Literature Monograph Series 13), (Philadelphia, 1968[2]) 212, 215.

2. Friedrich Horst, _Segen und Segenshandlungen in der Bibel_, in: _Evangelische Theologie_ 7 (1947/48) 28.

Yahweh or his chosen ones (Gn 12,3; Nm 22). The guilty parties are cursed or given a promise of punishment,[3] which Yahweh himself makes effective. Some form of the ban falls upon those who receive the curse.[4]

When Israel came to regard the covenant (Gn 9,9-17; Ex 6,4f; 19,5f) as the ultimate expression of God's will, then the curse came to bear especially upon those who tried to injure this covenant (Lv 26,14-43). The task of destroying the offenders thus fell upon the tribes of Israel in order to banish evil from their midst (Dt 13,6; 17,1-7). The covenant with Yahweh is itself covered by a curse so that anyone who offends against it becomes, as it were, self-cursed (Dt 29,19f; 30,7; Is 24,5f; Jr 23,10; 2 Chr 34,24). Likewise, anyone who tries to harm Yahweh's chosen people by cursing them becomes a curse himself (Gn 27,29; Nm 24,9). More-

---

3. The peculiarity of Gn 3,14-19 is that even though Adam and Eve are punished for their disobedience, it is the serpent and the earth that are cursed either by way of banishment (the serpent) or by being put under a spell (the earth) so that man's efforts to bring forth produce from the soil are often frustrated. "Hexed" is perhaps the best expression in these two instances. Cf. H. Brichto, op. cit., 86. In modern times still, the snake is called "the accursed one" in Palestine. Cf. Johannes Hempel, Die israelitischen Anschauungen von Segen und Fluchen im Lichte altorientalischer Parallelen, in: Zeitschrift der Deutschen Morgenländischen Gesellschaft 4 (79), (1925) 22, n.2.

4. This is especially true of אָרַר; whereas, קָלַל refers to inner emptiness and hollowness. Cf. F. Horst, art. cit., 30. אָרַר is very probably derived from the Addadian arāru, which means to bind or enchant. The Accadian word seems to be related to the Arabic word ʾarra, which means to chase away or drive out. Cf. Josef Scharbert, "Fluchen" und "Segen" im Alten Testament, in: Biblica 39 (1958) 5; Koehler/Baumgartner, אָרַר, in: Lexicon in Veteris Testamenti Libros, (Leiden, 1953) 89.

over, the total ban was also applied to political enemies and
even the spoils of war (Dt 13,13-19; Jos 6,17-21). This action
was perhaps motivated by the belief that the accursed person was
filled with some sort of curse-inducing matter, so that he, together with his family and possessions, became a dangerous source
of contagion to others.[5]

After the return of the Jews from the Babylonian exile,[6]
excommunication and confiscation of the offender's property were
introduced during Ezra's campaign against mixed marriages (Ezr
10,8). This was a milder form of ban in that it was not accompanied with a curse[7] and the death penalty. However, this case
remained an isolated incident in the tradition,[8] even though the
use of capital punishment became less pronounced in late Judaism.
Nevertheless, the connection between the curse and ban generally
remained, and continued to imply the possibility of death as in
former times (Is 65,15; 1 Mc 5,5). It was upon this basis that

---

5. Cf. W. Speyer, Fluch, in: RAC 7, 1165.
6. Closely connected with this idea is the concept of banishment to the desert. For the Israelite, the wilderness is
   cursed; and this curse is ever ready to spring up even in
   good fields by causing them to bring forth weeds and thistles.
   Cf. Johannes Pedersen, Israel, Its Life and Culture, 1-2
   (London, Copenhagen, 1926) 454f, 457.

7. In the ancient world, the curse was foremost and the excommunication secondary. It is relatively late, e.g., during
   the "golden age" of Greece, that excommunication from either
   religious or civil life is imposed without a curse. Cf. K.
   Mörsdorf, Exkommunikation, in: IDB 2, 184.

8. Cf. Walter Doskocil, Der Bann in der Urkirche, eine rechtsgeschichtliche Untersuchung, (Munich, 1958) 16f, 196. In
   general, only the Israelites so clearly connected the magical view of salvation and non-salvation (in the broad sense)
   with the ethical principle of God's rewarding or punishing
   action. Cf. W. Speyer, art. cit., 1236.

the enemies of Jesus were able to demand his death as a blasphemer (Lv 24,16; Jn 19,7; Acts 7,57). The simple excommunication
from the synagogue which the Forth Gospel mentions (Jn 9,22; 12,
42; 16,2) is very late--perhaps only a few decades before the
birth of Jesus.[9]

b. Pruification rites.

Among primitive religions and peoples, the concept of cultic
purity is closely connected with the curse and ban. This form of
purity or impurity is not identical with the physical or moral
state of a person. Rather, to be "unclean" means to be possessed
of a dangerous power that can harm or infect anyone or anything
that makes contact with the "unclean" person or object. In the
religious realm, this uncleanness prevents intercourse between
the divinity and man.[10] The cultic purification rites--including
the "curse-liturgy" (Dt 27), which is meant to absolve one from
all the enemies of the divinity--supposedly make the community's
cult acceptable to the divinity and protect it against his anger
and curses.[11] Thus, purity and holiness are closely related con-

---

9. At first, this ban was not from the synagogue as such, but
    only from certain of its activities. However, by A.D. 70,
    there was a complete ban from the sysagogue against the "her-
    etics," i.e., the Christians. Cf. K. Mörsdorf, Exkommunika-
    tion, loc. cit.; Der Synagogenbann, in: SB 4/1, 293-333, esp.
    329ff. Eventually this formal excommunication of Christians
    from the synagogue found expression in the form of a curse in
    the 12th of the "Eighteen Prayers" of the old synagogue. Cf.
    ibid., 212f.

10. Cf. P. van Imschoot, Rein, in: BL 1467.

11. Cf. F. Horst, art. cit., 35.

cepts. Both purity and impurity can be transferred through physical contact.

These ideas found wide acceptance in the Old Testament. Holy
persons or their vestments could hallow other persons and objects
through mere contact (Ex 30,29: Ez 44,19), but impurity is more
readily transferred (Hag 2,12f). Any unclean person who partakes
of a sacrifice to Yahweh is to be cast out from the people (Lv 7,
20f), which means the offender's loss of the divine promises made
to Israel and is tantamount to the death sentence. Purification
rites and ordinances ultimately constituted no small part of Israel's religious legislation (Ex 29-37; Lv 11-16).

In late Judaism, the devout Jew had to avoid most contact with
foreigners (Acts 10,28; Jn 18,28). This was especially true when
it was a matter of eating with uncircumcised persons (Acts 11,3).
The earlier legislation in this regard seemed to apply only to
the Passover meal (Ex 12,43-48). However, the laws of purity and
purification were greatly expanded and rigidly regulated during
the time of the Exile and in the diaspora. thereafter.[12] With the
end of the independent Jewish state nearly 600 years before Christ,

---

12. Cf. L.E. Toombs, Clean and Unclean, in: IDB 1, 641-48.
    "It is untrue to say that the concept of ritual uncleaness
    gradually gave way to a higher, moral conception of purity.
    In fact both grew together and in close relationship to each
    other, so that both moral and ritual laws reached their most
    stringent form in the post-exilic Jewish community." Cf.
    ibid., 644. In the earlier days of Israel, aliens could be
    admitted into the community very readily. "But when the alien
    element was utterly hostile, and especially when it clothed
    itself in its own holiness as opposed to that of Israel, then
    a union was impossible, it was ḥerem." Cf. J. Pedersen, op.
    cit., 3-4, 272f. "Post-exilic Israel's convulsive struggle
    to exclude the foreign element involved an increase of the
    impurity of what was alien and the holiness of what was na-
    tive." Cf. ibid., 274.

a new type of bond was required to preserve Israel's religious identity. This new mark of identity was found in the strict and formal laws of purity, which served to set Israel apart from her pagan neighbors and contributed greatly to the preservation of monotheism.[13] Since food and drink were thought to be especially prone to cultic contamination in primitive religions, Israel likewise developed a complex code of dietary laws, which proscribed certain animals as being unclean--either naturally so or due to the manner of the animal's death. In some cases, the proscribed animals were those which the gentiles religiously sacrificed or specially revered. For example, the Greeks sacrificed pigs (1 Mc 1,47 [50]), and many oriental religions worshipped snakes. But perhaps the most basic concept underlying the dietary laws is the desire to develop or maintain holiness (wholeness and wholesomeness) by avoiding creatures which, according to primitive methods of biological classification, have become hybridized with other species and, as a result, are "disordered" and "impure" because they fail to keep to the divinely estab-

---

13. Cf. Rein, in: BL 1469f. For a detailed treatment, cf. Die Stellung der alten Synagoge zur nichtjüdischen Welt, in: SB 4/1, 353-414. According to Otto Böcher, Dämonenfurcht und Dämonenabwehr: Ein Beitrag zur Vorgeschichte der christlichen Taufe, (Beiträge zur Wissenschaft vom alten und neuen Testament 90), (Stuttgart, 1970) 140, pagan lands were unclean because of idolatry, which Israel interpreted as being the result of intercourse with the "sex-demons." The "strange woman" in Wisdom literature (e.g., Prv 2,16; 6,24.29; 7,5.10) perhaps stems from the cultic prostitutes of Canaan. The sexual origin of demons is hinted at in Gn 6,1-4 (ibid., 36) and are especially dangerous in all of man's sexual acts, including menstruation and pollution, which render one ritually unclean (ibid., 136). Cf. also the story of Tobias and his wife, Tb 3,7ff; 6,7f.14ff; 8.

lished categories of creation. Animals, such as bats, hares, os-
triches, scaleless fish and many others, appear to belong to more
than one biological category and for this reason are considered
to be impure.[14]

c. The arcane discipline.

The disciplina arcani can not be considered a later development devised by Christians to protect themselves and their faith
in times of persecution. Rather, its roots reach into pre-Christian antiquity.[15] No one can doubt that since the recent discoveries
at Qumran. But the mainstream of orthodox Judaism also practiced
the arcane discipline in one form or another. The most well-known
case is the ruling against the use of God's name. Secrecy was
likewise practiced in regard to a variety of teachings and in several ways. The basic reason for the practice was always to protect the sacred from profanation both from within and without.
The later Christian practice served much the same purpose. Already Mt 7,6 advises Christians not to give that which is holy to
dogs or to cast pearls before swine. In this context, "these
words of Our Lord are a general injunction not to divulge (much
less give) to infidels what is sacred to Christians."[16] The Didache (9,5) uses this concept in reference to the Eucharist.

3. Qumran and Similar Sects

As a result of the discoveries made near the north-western
shores of the Dead Sea since 1947, the importance of such Jewish

---

14. Cf. Mary Douglas, Purity and Danger, an Analysis of Concepts
    of Pollution and Taboo, (Penguin/Pelican Books, 1970) 67-72.
15. For a thorough treatment of this question, cf. Joachim Jere-
    mias, Die Abendmahlsworte Jesu, (Göttingen, 1960³) 118-31.
16. Cf. J.A. Kleist, Didache, in: ACW 6, 8.

sects as the Essenes[17] for the study of early Christian origins
become especially apparent. Scholars will be at work a long time
yet trying to determine just what effects these esoteric groups
may have had on early Christianity. But since this work is far
from complete, no attempt will be made here to establish any
actual cause-effect relationships between such sects and Christianity. It will be enough just to notice some elements in the
cultic discipline of these religious communities that have similar or even identical parallels in early Christianity.

Exclusion from the community meals was the major form of penance and excommunication at Qumran. The length of time spent in
this disciplinary action could vary from ten days to two years.
Permanent exclusion was also a possibility (1 QS 6,24-9,2).

Upon entering the community, the candidate made a testament
before God, the protector of the purity of the pact. Members who
somehow sinned against this pact fell under a curse and had to be
separated from the others so as to protect the purity of the community and the covenant (1 QS 2,11ff). For fear of cultic contamination, the neophyte was not permitted to touch the community's food during his first year of "novitiate"; nor might he
touch the drink of the community until the completion of his second year of probation, at the end of which time his belongings
became common property (1 QS 6,20-23). If he has deliberately

---

17. It is not necessary here to try to establish whether or not
    the community at Qumran was Essene, a Jewish religious sect
    spoken of already in the writings of Philo, Flavius Josephus,
    Pliny and some of the Church Fathers, but which did not sur-
    vive long after the calamities of A.D. 70. It is, however,
    the contention of most scholars that Qumran was an Essene
    community.

lied concerning his possessions, he must be excluded from the common meal for one year, and one fourth of his food is to be taken away (1 QS 6,23). It is perhaps worthy of note that Ananias and Sapphira received their punishment for lying about their wealth (Acts 5,1-2).

Finally, the importance of baptisms (by immersion), especially for the neophyte, should not be overlooked (1 QS 3). For the Jews, and in particular for the Essenes, only the plunge-bath could render one clean of demonic elements.[18]

---

18. CD (<u>Damascus</u> <u>Rule</u>) 10,10-13; O. Böcher, <u>op</u>. <u>cit</u>., 148.

CHAPTER TWO

RELIGIOUS DISCIPLINE IN THE GOSPELS

1. Adoption and Adaptation
of Jewish Discipline

a. The curse and the ban.

In biblical Greek, ἀνάθεμα and κατάρα (and their derived forms) are the usual words for "curse." Κατάρα has only the meaning of "malediction," while ἀνάθεμα has a deeper religious signification, but is not used in the Gospels except in Lk 21,5, where it is written ἀνάθημα and has the meaning of "Temple gift" or "offering." Mk 14,71 uses the infinitive form in explaining that Peter began to curse and swear (ὁ δὲ ἤρξατο ἀναθεματίζειν καὶ ὀμνύναι) that he did not know Jesus. Since no definite object is given, the meaning is possibly that Peter cursed himself (by lying) as well as the people who recognized him as one of Jesus' disciples.[1] Jesus himself, however, taught his followers by word and deed to forgive adversaries (Lk 23,34) and to repay a curse with a blessing (Lk 6,28; Mt 5,44). Nevertheless, this does not mean that early Christians felt that cultic cursing was devoid of power and meaning and had no place in Christianity.[2]

---

1. Cf. Johannes Behm, ἀναθεματίζω, in: ThWB 1, 357. Peter's threefold denial of Christ followed by bitter sorrow (Mk 14,72 and pars.) which is raised to perfect repentance by his threefold confession of love (Jn 21,15-17) contrasts sharply with Judas' apostasy and despair. Jn 21 thus clearly shows that even Peter's apostasy could be forgiven to the extent of his full restoration as a follower of Christ (v. 19) and head of the Church (vv. 15-17). This chapter of the Fourth Gospel may have been written in order to answer some questions about what to do with repentant apostates in the early Church.

2. The use of the "anathema sit" in even modern ecclesial statements of dogma witnesses to the tenacity of this feeling throughout the history of Christianity.

On the other hand, the New Testament thoroughly reshapes the meaning and function of the curse and ban to fit the true nature of Christianity. But it becomes evident in the process that early Christians did not always take it for granted that such elements of religious discipline had to be reinterpreted in Christian theology. The story of Jesus' cursing of the fruitless fig tree (Mt 21,18-22; Mk 11,12-14.20-26) clearly shows that early Christians ascribed such powers to Jesus. It is also clear, however, that the Gospel writers took pains to reinterpret the story so as to reverse the meaning which was originally given to the account. This is evident from the fact that Matthew and Mark manage to draw the most unlikely conclusions out of the story-- namely, that Jesus wanted to give his disciples a lesson in faith, prayer and forgiveness. A seemingly heartless cursing of a fig tree for its failure to produce figs even out of season[3] can scarcely be construed as an exercise in Christian faith and love. The original function of the story must have been to present in forceful language and imagery the fruitlessness and end of the Old Covenant and the old Israel.[4] This interpretation has several

---

3. The explanation given in <u>SB</u> 1, 856f that fig trees bear two crops a year which ripen unevenly, and that Jesus could therefore rightfully expect figs on a tree in full leaf may be true enough if the story is considered botanically and historically correct. However, Mark's statement that it·was not the season for figs seems to be intended precisely to prevent such a conclusion.

4. Cf. Floyd V. Filson, <u>A Commentary on the Gospel</u> according to St. <u>Matthew</u>, (<u>BNTC</u>), (London, 1960) 225: "Did an earlier form condemn Israel for failing to produce the fruit of faith and obedience?" This question must be answered affirmatively. The story may be etiological in nature, based upon a certain dead fig tree along the way between Jerusalem and Bethany. Cf. Eduard Schwarz, <u>Der verfluchte Feigenbaum</u>, in: <u>ZNW</u> 5 (1904) 80-84.

Old Testament roots, and is further confirmed by Luke's version of the unproductive fig tree (Lk 13,6-9).

Jeremiah (8,13) sees the conditions brought on by a drought as a symbolic description of Israel's barrenness: "There are no grapes on the vines, and there are no figs on the fig trees. Even the leaves have fallen off."[5] In similar manner, Micah (7,1) speaks of Israel as a disappointing vine that has failed to bring forth fruit at the hoped-for time. Luke (13,6-9) takes up the theme, but develops it quite differently from the version of the other two Synoptists.[6] Luke first of all relates the story in the form of a parable rather than under the guise of historical fact. Israel is accordingly described as a well-tended but non-productive fig tree. But when its owner asks that it be destroyed, the caretaker pleads that he be allowed another year to try to induce the tree to bear fruit. If, however, the tree fails to

---

5. The quote is according the LXX since that is the version which early Christian writers knew best.

6. Luke's version keeps the proper relationship between the story and the conclusion to be drawn from it. Matthew and Mark may have intentionally used the "uncharitable version" just as they found it in order to make it unequivocally clear that the story, regardless of its possible historicity, cannot be used to make the claim that Israel is accursed and dead. If this were not the object of the first two Evangelists, then they would have done much better by reshaping the story to correspond with the conclusion. To that end, they could have portrayed Christ as one who brings forth fruit from a barren tree (instead of cursing it in frustration), just as he could wonderously bring forth food for thousands in the wilderness (Mk 6,34-44 and pars.). Moreover, the story of such a miraculous production of fruit on a barren fig tree was not unknown in Jewish Midrash. Cf. SB 2,26.

respond, then it is to be cut down. Luke, therefore, uses the story to show Christ's loving care and patience with Israel. Since the parable does not say that Israel will not respond to further care, the conclusion is that the Christian must likewise patiently wait for Israel's conversion. This leads one to the real Christian understanding of the curse or condemnation--namely, the eschatological aspect.

At the Last Judgment, the condemned receive the order: "Depart from me, you accursed ones, into the eternal fire prepared for the Devil and his angels."[7] Here, the concept of being accursed is applied to explain one's state of relationship to Christ at the eschatological judgment. The command, "depart from me," is found in Ps 6,8 in reference to the psalmist's enemies.[8] Mt 7,23 takes up the expression[9] and applies it to the lot of those who have prophesied, cast out devils and worked miracles in Christ's name, but have failed to do the will of God. These will likewise be condemned on the last day (Mt 7,21: ἐν ἐκείνῃ τῇ ἡμέρᾳ). This eschatological condemnation is imposed by way of the Jewish ban formula, "I know not from where you are."[10]

Although the cultic curse as such found no place in early Christian religious action and discipline, the same cannot be said of the ban, which, through various forms of excommunica-

---

7. Cf. Mt 25,41: πορεύεσθε ἀπ' ἐμοῦ κατηραμένοι εἰς τὸ πῦρ τὸ αἰώνιον κτλ.

8. 'Απόστητε ἀπ' ἐμοῦ πάντες οἱ ἐργαζόμενοι τὴν ἀνομίαν.

9. ἀποχωρεῖτε ἀπ' ἐμοῦ οἱ ἐργαζόμενοι τὴν ἀνομίαν

10. Cf. Lk 13,25: οὐκ οἶδα ὑμᾶς πόθεν ἐστέ. Cf. also Mt 7,23a; SB 1, 469.

tion, was interpreted from the ecclesiological as well as the eschatological point of view. In their awareness of being a real community and ἐκκλησία, the early Christians not only set up various procedures for admission into their number, but they also developed (or adopted) a procedure for expelling relapsed members whenever the need arose. Matthew, whose Gospel account was primarily meant for Jewish readers, mentions a threefold admonition that is to be given to a sinful brother before he is excommunicated if he fails to repent (18,15-18). This was similar to Jewish practice of that time[11] and exactly like that of the community at Qumran (1 QS 5,26-6,1).

A more definite indication that the early Church practiced the ban is found in 3 Jn 10, where the writer remarks that Diotrephes, an otherwise unknown person, has taken it upon himself unjustly to exclude several persons from his church (ἐκ τῆς ἐκκλησίας ἐκβάλλει). It is not known just what the exact nature of this action was, but it is reminiscent of the ἀποσυνάγωγος of the Fourth Gospel, and especially of the case of the expulsion of the formerly blind man from the Jewish synagogue (Jn 9,34). The conclusion, therefore, that the early Christian forms of excommunication depended heavily upon Jewish practices seems reasonably justified.

b. Purification rites.

The various forms of Jewish purification never found any place in Christianity except by way of a completely new interpretation and application in regard to a person's moral state.[12]

---

11. Cf. W. Doskocil, op. cit., 19f.
12. However, Paul's statement in 1 Cor 7,14 that the believing

For example, the foot-washing in Jn 13,4-16 teaches the supreme lesson in Christian humility--a lesson which St. Peter was unfortunately slow to learn and which brought him into embarrassing conflict with St. Paul (Gal 2,11-14). Jesus spared no words in berating the hypocracy which the formalized purity rites encouraged (e.g. Mt 23,23-28; Mk 7,1-13). For him, moral purity was the only thing that mattered (Mk 7,15). With that, Jesus drew a clear line between mere ritual and true morality, between true internal religion and mere external formalism. In the Christian dispensation, nothing is unclean of itself (Act 10,15; 11,9). Christ has freed the Christians from such laws, which are only for the "weak" (Gal 4,9; 5,1).

On the other hand, a system of rites which was so important to Judaism could hardly become totally meaningless in Christianity. A purification rite that could be used to promote real and objective[13] moral conversion was often readily accepted as a Christian practice, or at least as an illustration of what is implied when one decides either for or against Jesus. A clear example of the latter case is found in the account of Christ's sending of his twelve disciples to preach the nearness of the Kingdom (Mt 10,5-15). They are instructed to avoid pagan territory and even Samaria, and to go rather to "the lost sheep of the House of Israel" (v. 6). If the message which they bring is re-

---

(i.e., Christian) marriage partner sanctifies the unbelieving partner with the result that the children of that relationship are also sanctified is an exception to the above assertion. What Paul says here is essentially the same as the Jewish belief and practice in regard to Jewish proselytes and their children. Cf. SB 3, 374. But cf. also note 20 below.

13. That is, objective in that it corresponds to the demands of the New Testament for personal, internal conversion.

jected anywhere, they are to leave that house or town and shake the dust from their feet (v. 14), with the result that such places will fare less well in the Day of Judgment than Sodom and Gomorrah (v. 15).[14] These two towns, known for their sins of social injustice and moral impurity, were the classic example to the Jews of the fate of pagan peoples. Since the Jews considered even the earth of the pagan territory to be impure as a result of the sins committed there (Lv 18,24-30), it was forbidden that any dust or bit of vegetation be brought into the Holy Land of Israel.[15] But now that Jesus commands his disciples to shake the dust from their feet after encountering racially pure Jewish households or towns which have refused his message, it becomes clear that "cleanness" or "uncleanness" no longer have any racial connections. Rather, unclean are those who reject Christ. To do so is to commit a worse sin than all the sins associated with paganism. Had the pagans been awarded the signs that Israel saw, they would have repented in sackcloth and ashes long ago. Therefore, they will fare better in the Last Judgment than the impenitent towns of Israel (Mt 11,20-24; Lk 10,13-16). Again, the strong moral and eschatological aspect is set forth and made the essential element in any Christian concept of purification.

The most important act of Christian Life that can be connected with Jewish purification is Baptism, which has its roots both in

---

14. Lk 10,1-12 is the parallel text to Mt 10,5-15. However, Luke portrays it as the mission of the Church ("the 72") rather than just the immediate disciples of Jesus. Thus, he also says nothing of avoiding pagan territory and Samaria. The non-Jewish readers for whom Luke wrote his Gospel would not have understood the implications of such a statement, and would have probably been offended by such "discrimination."

15. Cf. SB 1, 571.

the baptism of John (and indeed of the ancient world in and out of Judaism) and in the practice of circumcision (Mk 1,1-11; Jn 3,5; Col 2,11-13). But, as a sacrament, Baptism has a truly Christian character, which is expressed beyond mere external compliance with an act of being washed with water.[16] It is not necessary at this time to dwell any longer on the history or theology of Baptism. The important thing for this present study at the moment is that the connection of Baptism with the purification rites be noted, and that a connection is to be made between Baptism and the Eucharist as well. At a certain point, these two sacraments cross each other so as to illustrate and animate Christian life in its most essential form. That is, the point of juncture is the Cross itself.

Christ proclaimed that he came to bring fire to the earth, and that he wished it were already blazing (Lk 12,49). By way of explanation, Jesus repeats the idea with different images by immediately adding: "There is a baptism (with which) I have to be baptized; and how greatly I am oppressed till it is over."[17] Jesus is supposedly speaking here of his death, first of all under the image of fire which will immerse the earth, and then

---

16. Although Baptism with water is as old as the Church and has always been considered necessary for entrance into the Church, it has never been considered the only form of Baptism and therefore absolutely necessary for salvation. That is, "Baptism by desire or blood" have in general been considered sufficient forms as well. In fact, Baptism by blood (martyrdom) has always been considered the "fullest form" of Baptism. Cf. Apc 7,13f; J. Betz, Taufe, in: HThG 2, 629.

17. Cf. Lk 12,50: Βάπτισμα δὲ ἔχω βαπτισθῆναι, καὶ πῶς συνέχομαι ἕως ὅτου τελεσθῇ. Cf. also Mt 3,11 where John the Baptist speaks of the Baptism which Jesus will use as also being a Baptism with fire--that is, the Holy Spirit. Cf. Acts 11,15f.

under the image of something into which he must be immersed just as one is immersed in water at the time of baptism. The death that will swallow him up will at the same time enkindle a fire to "purify" mankind and to separate the slag from the metal. That is, in the light and fire of the Cross, man is forced to make a decision for or against Christ.. Thus, Christian Baptism is not simply baptism into Christ, but also baptism into Christ's death (and by consequence, into his resurrection).[18] Even before his death, Christ is pictured as one already in loving suffering in his desire to bring mankind the lesson and salvation to be found in his Cross. Therefore, on the eve of his death, he announces: "With longing, I desired to eat this Passover with you before I suffer."[19]

Here, then, is the point of juncture between Baptism[20] and the Eucharist. This connection was made possible by the Christian reinterpretation of the religious significance of purification. At first, it may seem a bit difficult to see how the Eucharist can be brought into the framework of "purification" as

---

18. Since Christian Baptism has roots in the pre-Christian practice of baptism, it is only natural to find the practice in the Church before a Christian theology of Baptism was fully developed and promulgated. This soon became one of St. Paul's great tasks and achievements. Cf. Rm 6,3-11; Col 2,12; 1 Cor 1,12-15.

19. Cf. Lk 22,15: ἐπιθυμίᾳ ἐπεθύμησα τοῦτο τὸ πάσχα φαγεῖν μεθ' ὑμῶν πρὸ τοῦ με παθεῖν.

20. I.e., Baptism not only as initiation into Christian life, but also as the "form" and dynamic element of that life in its execution and in its effects on others. Cf. e.g. 1 Cor 7,14 where Paul states that the children of a mixed marriage as well as the non-Christian partner are made holy through the Christian partner. That is, in primitive theological terms, the "purity" that the Christian partner receives in Baptism is more powerful than the "impurity" of paganism.

easily and readily as was the case with Baptism. However, this aspect of the Eucharist becomes readily visible when Christ's death and the Eucharist are considered from the point of view of the New Covenant, which was established in Christ's pouring out of his blood and in the institution of the Eucharist.

According to "Covenant theology," the pouring out of the blood of a sacrificial victim was necessary to conclude the pact.[21] Christ now accomplishes this through his own death, which is "sacramentalized" in the Eucharist in that this sacrament is the sacrifice of the New Covenant (Mk 14,24 and pars.; 1 Cor 11,25). As such, it is the summation, fulfillment and abolition of all the (bloody) sacrifices of the Old Law, which were required for the purification of almost everything, and without which there could be no forgiveness and atonement (Heb 9, 18-22; Lv 16,15-19; Mt 25,28b). However, even though the New Testament clearly states that Christ's blood (death) effects the cleansing (santification) of men,[22] there is another aspect

---

21. Cf. Gn 15,9f; Ex 24,8; Jr 34,18; Ze 9,11. In Ex 24,8, only blood from a sacrificial victim is meant. However, the term, "blood of the Covenant" (בְּרִית דַּם) generally referred to the blood from circumcision in late Judaism. The connection between circumcision and Baptism was probably reenforced by the traditional teaching that there is never a blood-sprinkling that is not accompanied by a bath. Consequently, the Jewish proselyte had to bathe after circumcision. In this way, the Jew entered into the Covenant through circumcision, the bath (of purification), and his gracious acceptance of the blood (of the Covenant). Cf. SB 1, 991f. The purpose of the blood-ritual in the establishment of a covenant is to express a special relationship of unity, duties and rights between the two sides who make the pact. Cf. J. Haspecker, Bund, in: HThG 1, 197, 199.

22. Cf. Mt 26,28 and pars.; 1 Cor 11,24; Heb 9,14; 13,12; 1 Pt 1,2; Apc 7,13-15. Jesus as the "Ebed Yahweh" (Is 42,6f; 49,6; 53) forms the Old Testament background for this theology of

to the Eucharist that does not fit in very well with a covenant theology which only asks that the blood of the covenant
be sprinkled on the people. This is the command to consume
this blood (Jn 6,54-57). And since this feature of the
Eucharist comes to bear so strongly on the "immanence theology"
of the Fourth Gospel (and to a lesser degree in Paul's theology
of the Body of Christ), it also raises the question of the
Christological basis for excommunication from the Church.
Therefore, special consideration of this aspect of the Eucharist
must be given here.

2. Eucharist and Excommunication in the Fourth Gospel

a. Eucharistic immanence.

In the Old Law, the drinking of blood was strictly forbidden; for that meant to feed on the very life of the being. But
life belongs to Yahweh alone.[23] Consequently, cultic blood-
drinking could have no positive place in Judaism, and the concept also springs the framework of New Testament covenant
theology.[24] Its function in the New Testament must therefore be
seen in the light of what the New Testament itself says and in
view of the theological concepts or reasons the Jews had for

---

salvation. Whether or not Jesus consciously presented him-
self as the Suffering Servant of God is beside the point.
The fact remains that the early Church used this theme from
Isaiah in interpreting the life and death of Jesus. Cf.
Acts 8,34; 4,27.30; J. Fischer, Gottesknecht, in: BL (1951)
614-18.

23. Cf. Lv 17,11-14; Gn 4,10; 37,26; Dt 12,15; Ez 24,7; Celas
Spicq, L'Épître aux Hebreux, 2(Études Bibliques 3.60),
(Paris, 1953) 271-85. Perhaps blood-drinking was a form of
forbidden magic. Cf. Lv 19,26.

24. St. Paul and the Synoptists develop the Covenant aspect
of the Eucharist in their Last Supper accounts. Cf. Mk 14,

rejecting the Eucharist as interpreted in Jn 6.

This chapter[25] of the Fourth Gospel is skillfully worked into the context of chapters 5 and 7, which depict Jesus primarily as the great teacher who has replaced the Torah (5,39f; 7,14-19). The theology of these two chapters is a further, but less abstract, development of the Logos theology which introduces the Fourth Gospel.[26] Chapter 6 is fitted into this framework so as to show how the Eucharist "harmonizes" with Logos theology and faith by way of immanence in Christ. The account of the miraculous multiplication of the loaves and fishes introduces the chapter in order to supply the background for a turning point from the Logos theology of chapter five to the eucharistic theology of chapter six by playing on the idea of eating, which serves as a common note between Logos theology

---

24 and pars.; 1 Cor 11,25. The New Covenant is explained in the light of the "chalice" alone. Christ's blood and the cup of wine in the Eucharist are equated with each other. However, the establishment of the New Covenant through and in the Eucharist is not by way of consumption of the contents of the cup, but rather in the pouring out of Christ's blood in death. This aspect introduces an element of inconsistency in eucharistic covenant theology. If the parallel between the Eucharist and the New Covenant were carried completely through, the cup would have to be poured out in libation or sprinkled on those participating in the Eucharist. Cf. 1 Pt 1,2.

25. Whether or not the "eucharistic texts" in Jn 6 are later additions (as the Bultmannian school holds), is not in question here since the whole tradition of the early Church's eucharistic discipline is subject matter for this study.

26. For a more basic treatment of the Jewish background of this theology, cf. SB 2, 352-63; C.H. Dodd, The Interpretation of the Fourth Gospel, (Cambridge, 1953) 66-73, 85f.

and John's theology of the Eucharist. Toward the end of the
chapter, verse 63 serves to furnish another common note between
eucharistic theology and Logos theology, so that chapter seven
can calmly continue with the development of the latter.

In the Fourth Gospel, the story of the multiplication of
the loaves and fishes is to be interpreted eucharistically.
The setting of the scene near the time of the Passover feast
(6,4) is the first indication of this fact.[27] What the actual
historical setting and character of the story was, is not readily established. That there was plenty of grass for a large
crowd to recline upon (v. 10) suggests springtime. Therefore,
the time shortly before the Passover is possible. But the
other elements seem to lack the same sort of "historical credi-
bility." For instance, verse 3 places Jesus on the mountain
with his disciples. Yet verse 15 explains that he withdraws
again and alone onto the mountain. By doing so, Jesus supposedly eludes the crowd, which wants to make him king. But one
must ask what sort of maneuver this really is since the crowd
apparently had little difficulty following him under more complicated conditions (6,1f.22-25). Moreover, no one is even
interested in finding Jesus again until the following day--and

---

27. Ibid., 333. Perhaps the pastoral imagery of Ps 23 with
which John likes to work (ibid., 56f) is likewise present
here. However, that does not vitiate whatever historical
nucleus or other elements the account may have. John displays uncanny ability in using historical elements and
settings in such a way that they become signs and symbols
of deeper theological realities. This, of course, is part
and parcel of a writer who is so obviously influenced by a
world view akin to Philo's. Thus, it is not surprising
that John's acquaintance with the "Logos" would enable him
to see the reflections of "higher realities" in the Old
Testament and historical facts from Jesus' own life.

upon finding him, no one has the least bit of interest in making him king (vv. 22-25). Rather, the crowd still considers Jesus to be simply "Rabbi" (v. 25), and is only interested in seeing if he can supply them with manna from heaven (vv. 30f). In view of what the people supposedly witnessed on the previous day, the demand for manna is indeed surprising if not to say inexplicable[28]--unless, of course, the writer has no intention of reporting historical fact as such. It is clear that this is the case; and the whole complex of "inexplicables" is readily resolved in the light of the events of Jesus' last days of earthly life.

The movement to make Jesus a king was, in all likelihood, an event occuring only near the end of his life (Jn 12,13 and pars.; Jn 18,36f; Mk 15,9.12; Jn 19,19-22 and pars.). The failure of this movement (as an earthly hope) resulted from Jesus' death, which, in the Fourth Gospel, coincides with his glorification (10,17; 13,31f; 17,1.4f). Jesus speaks of his death as his going to the Father (Jn 16,10). This event will remove him from the sight of his followers, but it will also make him visible again-- however, in a fashion other than being visible to physical eyes (Jn 16,10.16.22f). The event of Jesus' death and subsequent return to the Father is quite probably indicated by his lone withdrawal onto the mountain.[29] His reappearance to his disciples

---

28. The request is explicable from a purely theological point of view. Jesus' multiplication of the loaves and fishes showed him to be at least the equal of the Old Testament prophets, especially Elisha. Cf. 2 Kgs 4,42-44. Now the writer shows the people wondering if Jesus is also as great as Moses. The response that follows is intended to show that Jesus is even greater than Moses. Cf. C.H. Dodd, op. cit., 344f.

29. According to Mt 28,16, it was on "the mountain" in Galilee

is under very unusual circumstances--namely, he comes walking to them across a stormy lake (Jn 6,16-21 and pars.). However, Mt 14,23 and Mk 6,47 remark that Jesus, before walking upon the water to his disciples, was alone on the land, but, according to Mk 6,48, he saw his disciples--in spite of the storm and the darkness and the fact that they were in the middle of the lake-- straining at the oars. What Jesus sees, says or does when he is <u>alone</u> cannot be matter for historical documentation.[30] Obviously, then, the story intends to be a literary construc- tion to illustrate truths that lie deeper than in a mere point of time in history. The account is most probably a post-Easter composition meant to show how the struggling, embryonic Church found strength and comfort in their belief in the risen Christ.

This interpretation is further supported by the reaction of the disciples upon seeing Christ. They are frightened (Jn 6,19) and think they see a ghost (Mt 14,26; Mk 6,49). But Jesus re- assures them with his ἐγώ εἰμι (Jn 6,20 and pars.), which, as an expression of faith and comfort, belongs to the post-Easter experiences of the disciples of Jesus.[31] Moreover, the disciples'

---

that Jesus made his first and only appearance to his remain- ing 11 disciples after his death and resurrection. Thus, until the development of the ascension story found in Acts 1, the implication probably was that Jesus "ascended" from this mountain in Galilee to his Father. Cf. Mk 16,7.19.

30. One may argue, of course, that Jesus later confided these facts to someone. But this is a most unlikely and a very unnecessary explanation, especially in view of the scene of Jesus' lone suffering in Gethsemane (Mk 14,32-42 and pars.), where the Evangelist obviously does not hesitate to construct a scene for his own purposes.

31. Cf. Jn 13,19; Lk 24,36.39. Although the ἐγώ εἰμι may be a later insertion in Lk 24,36, it has an impressive manuscript- tradition which supports the contention that the expression was understood very early as part of the post-Easter confes- sion of faith in Jesus' divinity.

first encounter with the risen Christ strikes them with fear and causes them to think they see a spirit (Lk 24,37). In the light of all these considerations, the connection of the accounts of the miraculous multiplication of the loaves and fishes followed by Jesus' walking upon the sea with the post-Easter experiences of the early Church is manifest. However, the connection is made by way of the Eucharist--a fact which must now be briefly considered.

Mark (6,52) ends his account of Jesus' walking upon the water with the remark that the disciples were dumbfounded because they had failed to understand about the loaves, and their heart was blinded. This statement has meaning only in view of the Eucharist as an <u>already</u> instituted sacrament--that is, by Christ at the Last Supper--, and seems to indicate that it took some time for the disciples to realize that Christ's presence among them after his death was to be continued through this sacrament. Mark sums up the eucharistic character of the miracle accounts presently under consideration within a single verse. John, on the other hand, expands this verse into an entire chapter in order to develop his theology of the Eucharist.

Another factor which ties these two miracle accounts to the risen Christ and the Eucharist is that the setting for the events is the Sea of Galilee. John, however, makes a point of adding "Tiberias" to the name of the lake (6,1). This name is found in only one other place in the New Testament--namely, in Jn 21,1 where the name, "Sea of Tiberias," is used without the more usual term, "Galilee." The last chapter of the Fourth Gospel, the so-called "appendix," recounts an appearance of the risen Christ to the disciples after they had labored all night

on the sea in a fruitless effort to catch some fish. The first
14 verses of the chapter recapitulate Jn 6,1-21, but in a sort
of reverse fashion which one may roughly describe as a "mirror-
image." But not only is the order of events reversed. The
action of the characters is to a certain extent likewise reversed, especially as regards Christ and Peter.

Under Peter's instigation, some disciples get into the boat
to go fishing (21,3; but contrast with Mk 6,45 and pars.).
Jesus instructs them to cast the net on the other side of the
boat (v. 6). They do this, and catch a large haul of fish;
with the result that they come to realize that "it is the Lord."
At this news, Peter jumps into the water in order to come first
to Jesus (v. 7; compare with Mt 14,28f, and contrast with Mk 6,48b
and pars.). Once everyone has arrived on shore, Jesus invites
them to partake of a meal of bread and fish (vv. 9-12; contrast
with Mk 6,37 and pars., and compare with Mk 6,39-41 and pars.).
The copiousness of the meal is now represented by the large
number of fish which Peter brings from the boat to shore (v. 11;
compare with Mk 6,43 and pars.). The effect of this extended
chiasmus[32] is to show that the Church under Peter, but still led
by Christ, administers the Eucharist (v. 13; compare with Mk
6,37 and pars.). Now that the eucharistic (and to some extent,
the ecclesiological) character of Jn 6,1-21 has been established,

---

32. This literary construction is also seen in Jn 21,15-19.
    Peter's threefold confession of love contrasts with his
    earlier threefold denial and is analogous to Christ's
    declaration of love for his disciples at his Last Supper.
    Cf. Jn 13,1.34f; 15,9.12. In a sense, Jn 21 is also a
    "last meal." However, this time it concerns Peter's
    death--likewise by crucifixion, and upside down, accord-
    ing to popular ancient tradition.

it is possible to return to a fuller and better treatment of John's eucharistic theology.[33]

After the crowd has found Jesus on the day after the miracle with the bread and fish, he tells the people to seek the food that endures unto everlasting life, which he will give them (Jn 6,27). The people respond by referring to the manna as the "Bread from Heaven" (v. 31). Jesus denies that the manna was bread from heaven (v. 32), but asserts that his Father will give them the true bread from heaven that gives life to the world (v. 32f). When the people ask for this bread, Jesus announces that he is the bread of life (v. 35: ἐγώ εἰμι ὁ ἄρτος τῆς ζωῆς). This statement need not be immediately construed as a direct reference to the Eucharist since the term, "bread of life," simply meant study of the Torah to the Jews.[34] The expression itself is not found in direct connection with the Torah, which is, however, called "the tree of life," "bread," as well as

---

33. Although the exposition on the eucharistic character of Jn 6,1-21 does not directly contribute to the theme of this study, it was felt necessary to treat this section at some length in order to establish a firmer basis for considering the rest of Jn 6 as a eucharistic discourse from beginning to end.

34. Cf. SB 2, 485. Food and drink of life as religious themes were important in Judaism's development of the concept of sacrifice and the eschatological themes of a super-fertile earth and the messianic banquet. The counterpart of the food and drink of life is the food and drink of death--a theme alluded to also in Gn 2-3. Late Judaism "demythologized" the notion by way of a mystical identification of the Torah with the source or sustainer of life. Nevertheless, the more concrete application lived on in the hope that the miracle of manna would be repeated. Cf. Apocalypse of Baruch 29,8. The Fourth Gospel seizes up both of these views as a means of introducing its theology of the Eucharist in chapter 6. Cf. Maurice Goguel, L'Eucharistie des Origines à Justin Martyr, (Paris, 1910) 301-11.

"medicine of life."[35] Therefore, Jesus' designation of himself
as the bread of life must be first of all understood within
this frame of reference--the eucharistic overtones notwithstand-
ing. The expression is an extension of John's Logos theology
in that Christ is made to replace all that the Torah represented;
or rather, he is all that the Torah really had to talk about.
The function of the term, however, is to provide a pivot upon
which the shift from Torah theology to eucharistic theology can
be made.[36]

The Jews[37] begin to murmur after Jesus goes on to declare
that he, the bread of life, has come down from heaven (vv. 38.41).
This statement ascribes pre-existence to Jesus, and is therefore
a point of contention for the Jews since they are well aware of
his earthly parentage (v. 42). On the one hand, this again
places Jesus within the framework of Torah theology, which held
that the Torah existed with God before the creation of the earth[38]
and came down from heaven to Moses (Ex 19-20 and 34). But the
implication drawn from Jn 6,31ff is that Jesus was expected to
perform as the new Moses, that is, the Messiah, whose immediate
origin would be unknown (Jn 7,27). Indeed Bethlehem was known
to be the supposed birth place of the Messiah, but the common

---

35. Cf. SB 1, 481-84. The Torah was sometimes called a fig
    tree, because, just as figs ripen gradually and unevenly,
    so does one's understanding and appreciation of the Torah.
    Cf. SB 2, 16f.

36. The theme of Wisdom is here at work. Cf. Sir 24,21(28).
    Jesus' claim that he, as the bread of life, satisfies all
    hunger and thirst has the effect of saying that he is
    greater than Wisdom.

37. From verse 41 on, "the crowd" is replaced by "the Jews"--
    an indication of the polemic nature the text assumes at
    this point.

38. Cf. SB 2, 353.

belief was that he would remain hidden for a time in some secret place, perhaps even in heaven.[39] Thus, the Jews' knowledge of Jesus' origins prevents them from accepting him in the above indicated roles.[40] Moreover, since the Torah could be identified with Yahweh's covenant with Israel,[41] Jesus' imposition of himself in the place of the Torah implied his becoming the founder, the foundation and the *raison* d'être of the awaited new covenant (Jn 6,45; Jr 31,33f; Is 53,13). But this also means that Jesus takes on (that is, has) a special relationship of identity with God himself, who is to be the teacher in the new covenant-- thereby replacing the Torah. This situation now makes it possible for John to move on to a new phase in the explanation of the Eucharist.

In Jn 6,51, Jesus reaffirms that he is the living bread from heaven, and identifies it with his flesh given for the life of the world. Everlasting life is promised to those who eat this bread (flesh). The introduction of "flesh" is something new, and it stirs the Jews into argument again--this time, over the seeming impossibility of Jesus' claim that he will give his flesh to eat (v. 52). There is sufficient ambivalence about verse 51 so that it need be taken only as a sharper focusing upon John's Logos theology. But at the same time, it causes the

39. Ibid., 488f.
40. Jesus has many "roles" in the New Testament, i.e., the Christ, the great prophet, the son of man, etc. These various roles are all fulfilled in Jesus, who is the fulfillment of all the hopes engendered by the Old Testament and the expectations of Judaism. Cf. Mt 5,17; Rm 10,4.

41. This covenant, according to Jewish Midrash, was made for the sake of the Torah; and as long as Israel has the Torah, God will keep his covenant with his people. Cf. SB 3, 133.

the Jews rightly to suspect that it is more than that. Consequently, this verse is able to serve as another pivot, and allows for the complete "surfacing" of the Eucharist in verses 53-56. This is accomplished by adding the instruction that Jesus' blood is to be drunk. With that, there can no longer be any question of a simple Logos theology or messianic categories.[42]

The notion of blood-drinking (even metaphorically) was an abhorrence to the Jews, and goes beyond any of their acceptable cultic practices. However, the ancient world knew of the practice and applied it sacramentally. Blood-drinking was meant to increase one's strength and power by joining one to other powers. This is the basic concept of a "covenant made in blood." More importantly, it was considered as a means of establishing communion between a divine being and man. Usually, the blood was first mixed with wine and then drunk.[43] The Fourth Gospel develops its eucharistic theology in line with this way of thinking.

The instruction to drink Christ's blood can leave no doubt that John means to say in the hardest manner possible[44]--even though the notion is quickly dropped in favor of bread-eating-- that Jesus' post-resurrection presence in the Eucharist is a

42. Cf. C.H. Dodd, op. cit., 339f.
43. Cf. J.H. Wiszink, Blut, in: RAC 2, 459-72, esp. 464f. Blood-drinking was a common practice among most Semites, and was continued among the Arabs up to Mohammad's time. Cf. W. Robertson Smith, Die Religion der Semiten (Darmstadt, 1967) 240, 281.

44. The statement that Jesus' teaching on the Eucharist is a σκληρὸς λόγος (cf. Jn 6,60) was probably used by those who were scandalized by the claim that the humble, historical Jesus was divine in nature and, above all, that the Eucharist effected his continued presence and power among men. Cf. Oscar Cullmann, Early Christian Worship, (Studies in Biblical Theology 10), (London, 1953) 95-97.

truly living presence. Participation in the Eucharist is participation in Jesus' life, which is the eternal life that he has
from his Father (Jn 5,26; 6,56-58). All the elements of John's
theology of immanence thus come together and climax in the
Eucharist. The Covenant theology of the Eucharist developed by
the Synoptists and Paul is included in John, but subordinated to
the concept of the real sharing of divine life which the recipient obtains from the Father by way of the Son.

<u>b</u>. Immanence and excommunication.

The essential core of the Fourth Gospel's theology of immanence is the mutual indwelling between Jesus and his followers.
In the eucharistic discourse of chapter 6, this indwelling is
most explicitly stated in verse 56: ὁ τρώγων μου τὴν σάρκα καὶ
πίνων μου τὸ αἷμα ἐν ἐμοὶ μένει κἀγὼ ἐν αὐτῷ. The expression,
"abide in me," is found in only one other discourse--namely,
several times in Jn 15,1-17, where Jesus describes himself as
"the true vine."[45] The process of indwelling is by way of love
(vv. 9f), but this means keeping the commandments of Jesus
(v. 10), especially the commandment that his followers love one
another as he loves them (v. 12). The result of this process
is that the branches remain on the vine and bear fruit (vv.4f).[46]
The Father will prune such branches so that they may bear still

---

45. Perhaps it would be better to translate ἡ ἄμπελος ἡ ἀληθινή
    as "the real vine," i.e., that Christ is the reality which
    Israel only foreshadowed in applying the vine-image to it-
    self. Cf. C.H. Dodd, <u>op</u>. <u>cit</u>., 139.

46. The exact meaning of bearing fruit is not clear, but is
    probably best described as "<u>tätige</u> <u>Liebe</u> <u>zu</u> <u>den</u> <u>Brüdern</u>."
    Cf. Rainer Borig, <u>Der</u> <u>wahre</u> <u>Weinstock</u>, <u>Untersuchungen</u> <u>zu</u>
    <u>Jo</u> <u>15,1-10</u>, (<u>Studien</u> <u>zum</u> <u>Alten</u> <u>und</u> <u>Neuen</u> <u>Testament</u> 16),
    (Munich, 1967) 245.

more fruit (v. 2b). This operation is presented under the image
of "cleansing."

In Lv 19,23, a tree must be "cleansed of its uncleanness"
(περικαθαριεῖτε τὴν ἀκαθαρσίαν αὐτοῦ). Its fruit for the first
three years is likewise considered "unclean" (ἀπερικάθαρτος).
The use of עָרֵל (i.e., circumcise) in the Hebrew text and the
designation of the first years of fruit as עָרְלָה (i.e., fore-
skin) indicate the religious context of the process of pruning so
as to make the tree acceptable.[47] This is the effect that the
Father's "cleansing" has upon those who abide in Christ and in
love.

But besides taking care of the fruitful branches so that they
may bear even more fruit, the vine-dresser (the Father) also performs another task. He removes the fruitless branches entirely
(v. 2a). His action is to be understood within an eschatological context (v. 6). Moreover, since it is the Father himself who
removes the fruitless branches, the text cannot be considered as
a basis for a juridical understanding of the Church's right to
expel unworthy members.[48] On the other hand, the eschatological
aspect is not to be understood as something that takes effect
only at the end of time or with the individual's death. To begin with, this would be contrary to John's presentation of eschatology, which generally views eschatological elements as already
present. Just as the Father's action of cleansing the fruitful

---

47. Cf. also Is 5,6. Circumcision in its metaphorical sense
    means "to be properly ordered": circumcised lips (Ex 6,12.30),
    ears (Jr 6,10), heart (Lv 26,41; Ez 41,9; Jr 9,25). Cf. also
    Acts 7,51; Col 2,13.

48. Against K. Mörsdorf, Kirchengewalt, in: LThK 6, 220. Cf. R.
    Borig, op. cit., 40, n. 94.

branches takes place in the present, so does his action of removing the non-bearing branches.[49] When one truly abides in
Christ, then one abides in love and bears fruit. As such, this
passage cannot be taken as a theology of excommunication.[50]

Besides the question of what relationship Jn 15,1-17 has with
a theology of ban or excommunication, there is also the question
of its possible eucharistic nature. This is a more difficult
question to decide, because there is very little material that
supports one view or the other. C.H. Dodd[51] points to the Synoptic use of "vine" as a synonym for "wine" in their accounts of
the Last Supper. As a result, he asserts that the passage has
"eucharistic associations." However, this is a cautious and harmless expression which can scarcely be denied since the text's
"eucharistic associations" are precisely what move modern readers
to ask if it is truly a eucharistic text. There are no conclusive arguments which might compel one to make such a conclusion.
This is so simply because the whole of the text in question is
developed upon Old Testament themes and depends in no way on the
Synoptists.[52]

---

49. Jn 15,1-10 probably served to explain to the early Church why
there were apostates in her ranks. Cf. R. Borig, op. cit.,
41.

50. W. Doskocil (op. cit., 42) considers this passage to be the
ultimate basis upon which a theology of excommunication must
build. Certainly no one will contest the statement that
love is to be the ultimate element for consideration in any
ecclesial act of excommunication. However, one must take
great care not to attribute to Jn 15,1-17 an ecclesial juris-
prudence, which simply is not contained in these verses.

51. Op. cit., 411f.
52. Cf. R. Borig, op. cit., 94, 113.

Another question closely related to the above one is the
question of the possible allusion to Judas' apostasy[53] in
verse 2. Again, there seems to be nothing to compel one to see
the verse as such. It is simply a description of the fate of
apostates in general. Verse 3, however, might imply something
about Judas. Here, Christ says that his disciples are already
clean because of the word he has spoken to them. This is very
close to the idea already expressed in Jn 13,10, where Jesus declares all of his disciples, except one, to be clean. However,
the problem of Judas' apostasy is very complicated, especially
since there may also be a question of eucharistic excommunication in his case (Jn 13,26-30). The next chapter attempts to
illuminate the problem and to give some answers.

53. Cf. R.H. Lightfoot, St. John's Gospel, a Commentary, (Oxford,
1956) 282.

CHAPTER THREE

EXCURSUS: JUDAS ISCARIOT AND THE LAST SUPPER

1. Judas in the New Testament

The question of Judas Iscariot's possible presence at or absence from the institution of the Eucharist in the Synoptic accounts of the Last Supper has not yet been satisfactorily answered.
The Synoptists themselves seem to imply that Judas was present.
But John's version of the Last Supper shows Judas being sent forth
during (or possibly after) the meal (Jn 13,26-30). What relationship this action might have in regard to the institution of the
Eucharist is not clear since John says nothing about the Eucharist
at this point. Likewise, all attempts at explaining the ψωμιον
which Judas received (Jn 13,26) have remained equally inconclusive
as to whether or not it was the Eucharist.[1] If it can be shown
that Judas did not partake of the Eucharist, then the underlying
reasons and the possible motivations for his non-participation
must be investigated.[2] The results of such an inquiry might enable
one to determine if it is permissible to speak of eucharistic excommunication in Judas' case, or if his case can contribute in
any way to a theology of excommunication.

---

1. Originally, ψωμίον, the diminuative of ψωμός, meant "tidbit."
    The verb, ψωμίζω, means to "feed by putting little bits into
    the mouth." Cf. LS 2029. Thus, the word did not at first
    specify the substance of what was eaten, but the manner in
    which it was eaten. However, the Papyri use the word to mean
    "bread." Therefore, it is not likely that Jn 13,26f.30 refers
    to the bitter herbs of the Passover meal. Cf. E. Ruckstuhl,
    Judaskommunion, in: BL (1951) 869.

2. The problem of determining the historical nature of the Last
    Supper and the institution of the Eucharist is, for the mo-
    ment, of secondary importance. More important is the consider-
    ation of the theology that is involved in the Last Supper ac-
    counts provided by the Evangelists.

The Synoptists mention Judas Iscariot for the first time in their list of the Apostles (Mt 10,2-4 and pars.). On this occasion, he is identified as the one who betrayed Jesus. From then on, he receives no more attention until just prior to the Last Supper when he conspires with the Chief Priests and Elders against Jesus (Mt 26,14-16 and pars.). The Fourth Gospel, on the other hand, maintains a "running interest" in the character of the betrayer, and attempts to interpret the role Judas played in the life of Jesus.[3] But in spite of his more detailed interest in Judas, John curiously omits the account of the betrayer's actual collaboration with the conspirators prior to the Last Supper (Mt 26,14-16 and pars.). Even more curious, however, is the Synoptic ommission of Judas' dismissal from the Last Supper. In their present form, the Synoptic accounts of this meal fail to explain how Judas managed to separate himself from the rest of the Apostles in order to alert the conspirators and lead them to the proper

---

3. Cf. Jn 6,64.70f; 12,4-6; 13,2-30. Jesus' reference to his future betrayer as a devil (Jn 6,70f) provides the key to the Fourth Gospel's interpretation of Judas. Such statements are a special character of Johannine writing. Cf. W. Foerster, σατανᾶς, in: ThWB 7, 163. Jesus' use of the term does not specify a real being. Rather, it refers to anybody opposed to the will of God and the work of Christ. For this reason, Peter is referred to as "Satan" for preferring man's ways to God's. Cf. Mt 16,23. In Jn 8,44, Jesus accuses his Jewish opposers of being the children of the devil, who is a murderer and the father of lies. By describing Judas as a devil, Jesus meant that here is a person who has nothing to do with him-- he is the foe that Christ has come to cast out. Cf. Mk 1,34. Jesus' statement is probably meant as an anticipation of Judas' disenchantment when he at last realized that Jesus would not set himself up as a worldly messiah of an earthly kingdom, but proposed spiritual values instead. Cf. Judas, in: BL (1951) 866f.

place for the arrest of Jesus. The betrayer is present at least
before the institution of the Eucharist according to Mt 26,20-25
and Mk 14,17-21. Luke's version (22,14-23) implies that Judas is
present for the Eucharist. But in all three Synoptists, he just
simply and inexplicably fades out of the picture after being mentioned at the Last Supper, and then just as inexplicably reappears
in Gethsemane (Mt 26,47-50 and pars.). At any rate, the Synoptists offer nothing either by way of statement of historical fact
or by theological construction that would directly support a theology of excommunication (eucharistic or otherwise) built on
Judas' dismissal from the supper as recorded by John.

Early Christianity and the Middle Ages were undecided about
the nature of Judas' dismissal and its relation to the Eucharist.
All Church writers and theologians in both the East and the West
up to the 13th century who deny that Judas took part in the
Eucharist are dependent on Tatian's Diatessaron,[4] which places
Judas' dismissal just before the institution of the Eucharist.
Most other commentators of those centuries prefer Luke's account,
and therefore hold that Judas was present for the Eucharist.
They support their claim from John's account, and reason that the
dismissal of Judas is closely associated in time with the foot-
washing, which normally came at the beginning of the meal.[5]
Nevertheless, this is still an unsatisfactory explanation.

In the first place, it is obvious that John uses the supper
only as a setting for the long discourses that follow. Therefore,
the actual order and chronological spacing of events at the meal
are not his real interest. But a more serious objection appears

---

4.   Cf. E. Ruckstuhl, Judaskommunion, in: BL (1951) 866f.
5.   Ibid.

when one asks why Judas was even present at the Last Supper if
he had already informed on Jesus. Would it not have been all too
risky for him to join the group for supper immediately preceding
Jesus' arrest? He had no need to be present in order to learn
where Jesus would go after the meal. He knew quite well that
Jesus could be found at his accumstomed place on the Mount of
Olives after an evening repast.[6] Finally, one is forced to ask:
"What sort of plot would depend on the mere chance that the key
figure in the conspiracy will be able to slip away from the disciples of Jesus in order to alert the other conspirators that an
opportune moment for the arrest was about to present itself?"
Judas had no way of knowing beforehand that Jesus would dismiss
him from the meal. And yet, if he had already informed on Jesus,
he certainly would have included in his plans the necessary provisions for eluding the other Apostles once he had rejoined them
after entering the conspiracy. Under these seemingly contrived
circumstances, it is easier to believe that Judas himself has yet
to enter into the plot rather than to concede that he is already
a part of the conspiracy and nevertheless present at the Last
Supper. Consequently, the entire problem-complex would enjoy a
much better solution if it could be shown that Judas' presence at
the meal and subsequent dismissal actually belong to a different
meal other than the Last Supper itself--that is, that there was
a "supper of betrayal" just prior to Judas' entrance into the conspiracy, and that this supper cannot be identified with the Last

---

6. Cf. Jn 18,2; Lk 22,39. Since Jesus went to his accustomed
    place on the Mount of Olives after his last meal with his
    disciples, it may be an indication that the meal was like-
    wise of an accustomed sort. That is, it was probably not a
    real Jewish Passover supper.

Supper.[7] Perhaps the supper in Jn 13 (at least the footwashing and Judas' dismissal) and the allusions to Judas as the betrayer in the Synoptic accounts of the Last Supper are really reporting on a supper which preceded the Last Supper and the institution of the Eucharist by at least 24 hours.[8] If that is the case, then Judas' "fade out" at the Last Supper in the Synoptics and his unexplained reappearance at Gethsemane are easily explained-- along with most of the other disharmonies between John's and the Synoptists' account of Jesus' final days.

The above suggested solution to the historical problem concerning Judas' participation or nonparticipation in the Eucharist still does not directly answer the theological question whether or not Judas' dismissal in any way implies an excommunication from the Eucharist. In other words, does John in any way ignore the historical facts in order to develop a theology of eucharistic excommunication, that is, of the Church's right to exclude certain persons from the reception of the Eucharist? However, since the Fourth Gospel omits any reference to the Eucharist at this point, it seems that this question must be answered in the negative. As a result, a case for eucharistic excommunication cannot be developed either historically or theologically from

---

7. For a more complete defense of this thesis, cf. the present writer's article, Judas Iscariot: Key to the Last Supper Narratives?, in NTS 17 (1970/71) 227-32.

8. In Jn 13,2.11.21, Judas' act of betrayal is referred to in such a way, that the present and future aspect of the act are accented. However, at the moment of Jesus' arrest--the climax of Judas' treachery--, John emphasizes the past aspect of the betrayal. Cf. Jn 18,2.5. Perhaps John considers Judas' initial decision to betray Jesus and his informing on the Master as the real act of betrayal. If that is so, then the supper in Jn 13 must refer to a meal previous to the evening of Jesus' Last Supper and arrest.

Judas' dismissal from supper even though it seems historically probable that he did not participate in the Eucharist. However, this does not mean that the New Testament in no way uses Judas' apostasy in order to develop a concept of excommunication in general. The accounts of the betrayer's death (Mt 27,3-10; Acts 1,15-20) seem to include a theology of excommunication to some extent.[9]

The two New Testament versions of Judas' violent end vary greatly in that Matthew says that Judas committed suicide by hanging, while Acts maintains that he died of injuries suffered in an apparently accidental fall in the field which he bought with the money for betraying Christ.[10] Both narratives are dependent on a common tradition that the field[11] was bought with

---

9. Unless otherwise stated, the following exegesis concerning Judas' death is based on an article by Otto Betz, The Dichotomized Servant and the End of Judas Iscariot, in: Revue de Quram 5 (1954) 43-58, esp. 49f, 58.

10. The various manuscript-readings of Acts 1,18 show evidence of early attempts to harmonize several traditions concerning the nature of Judas' death. The Vulgate reads "suspensus," and therefore falls back upon Mt 27,5. The conjecture that πρηνής was a medical term for "swollen," or should be read as πεπρησμένος in view of Nm 5,21-27, could possibly be of very early origin since Papias of Hierapolis records about A.D. 130 in Fragment 3 that Judas was taken down before he died from hanging, and that he lived for several more years. However, he became so bloated that even his head could not pass where a wagon could. His body became covered with worms, and he began to rot. But his actual death finally resulted from suffocation due to the bloating.

11. The tradition or popular story that Judas bought a field probably had its source in an early Christian interpretation of the area outside Jerusalem known as "Gehenna," where the potters had their factories, and where the poor and outcasts were buried. Acts 1,25 refers to it as Judas' τόπος ἴδιος. Cf. Pierre Benoit, Exégèse et Théologie, 1 (Paris, 1961) 348, 357.

blood-money. Beyond that, each account goes its own way. It
seems that Matthew's version wants to give the historical cause
of Judas' death; whereas, the version in Acts attempts a theological interpretation of that death.

The idea that Judas "burst in the middle" (Acts 1,18) is
based on a dramatic interpretation of the Old Testament formula
of excommunication, "to be cut (נכרת) from the midst" (1 Sm
20,15), which is to be associated with the banishment of evil
from Israel's midst (Dt 13,6). In the New Testament and Qumran,
the idea is used as a formula of cursing and punishment, but with
a strong eschatological orientation (1 Cor 5,5.13; 1 QS 2,16f).
Likewise, the Greek expression in Mt 24,51 (διχοτομήσει αὐτόν) is
derived from this notion. In the case of Judas, the expression,
"cut from the midst," is reformulated to "cut (i.e., split) in
the middle (i.e., belly)" in order to show that Judas' tragic
death was seen as an act of God and made parallel to the fate of
the wicked servant in Mt 24,51. However, unlike the case of the
wicked servant, where the eschatological dimension (the Last
Judgment) is in the foreground,[12] Acts 1,18 emphasizes Judas
Iscariot's violent death over the eschatological aspect--that is,
Judas' departure to "his own place" (v. 25). Nevertheless, what
is common to both cases is that the Last Judgment and the ensu-
ing reward or punishment are not reserved for the "Last Day," but
follow upon the individual's death. The eschatological orientation of earliest Christianity is herewith altered and diminished,

---

12. Originally, the servant's punishment was understood as one
    eschatological act. But in Mt 24,51, the act is divided in
    two: the moment of sudden, cruel death, and the later giving
    over of the person to lasting torture. Cf. O. Betz, op.,
    cit., 58.

but by no means given up. Exclusion from the Church is still seen principally as an act effected by God in his own way of doing things.

2. Judas in Early Christian Tradition

Even though the New Testament treatment of Judas Iscariot offers no basis for a theology of eucharistic excommunication, this does not mean that early Christians failed to make a connection between Judas' dismissal from the supper and the institution of the Eucharist. A tradition that he was dismissed just before and out of respect for the Eucharist arose toward the end of the second century as a result of Tatian's ordering of events in his Diatessaron.[13] According to this arrangement, the disciples come to Jesus on the first day of the Unleavened Bread and ask where they should prepare the Passover supper. But before Jesus answers, a "flashback" composed of Jn 13,1-20 and Lk 22,27-30 apparently takes the reader back in time to another supper before the Passover feast. The devil has already put it into the heart of Judas to betray Jesus; and after the washing of the disciples' feet, Jesus remarks that someone who is eating bread with him will raise his heel against him. No further allusion is made to Judas' treachery at this point. Tatian then returns to the events of the

---

13. Tatian, a pupil of St. Justin Martyr, was probably born in Syria (date unknown), travelled extensively, became a Christian in Rome and returned to his native land sometime after 172. Here he founded his own Gnostic-Encratite sect and wrote the Diatessaron. This "patch-work" harmony of the four Gospels, written most probably in Syriac and later translated into Greek (of which only fragments remain), quickly became the exclusive rendition of the Gospel in the East until it was finally replaced by the four-Gospel text several centuries later. Cf. Altaner 128; J. de Fraine, Diatessaron, in: BL 333.

first day of the feast, when the Paschal Lamb is slaughtered.
Peter and John are sent to prepare the meal; and that evening at
table, the Fourth Gospel's account of the Last Supper is completed. Judas is more fully unveiled as the traitor; and after he
has eaten the morsel which Jesus gives him, he is sent forth.
Christ then refers to this as the moment of his glorification,
and proceeds to establish the Eucharist.

The so-called Apostolic Constitutions, composed about 380 and
heavily dependent on the Didascalia,[14] follows very closely--and
with much elaboration--the order of events of Jesus' final days
as presented in the Diatessaron. Again, Judas is dismissed just
before the institution of the Eucharist. However, this action is
given no special theological interpretation as regards the Eucharist or excommunication.

St. Ephraem's Commentary on the Diatessaron is approximately
contemporary with the Apostolic Constitutions, and attempts a
theological interpretation of Judas' presence at the Last Supper
and subsequent dismissal. At this point, however, St. Ephraem
departs from the Diatessaron and prefers another tradition. Accordingly, Judas is present for the institution of the Eucharist,
but he is not permitted to receive anything more than the bread
of the Eucharist dunked in water. St. Ephraem interprets this
action as follows:

> If it is indeed certain that the Lord gave His disciples
> the mystery of His body when He gave them the bread, then
> one must also believe that He gave His murderer the bread as

---

14. The Didascalia was probably written by a Jewish Christian
for a North Syrian, Greek-speaking community of the 3rd century. The first six books of the Apostolic Constitutions
are a modified version of the Didascalia.

the mystery of His body lying in death. Thus, He dunked
His body into the water before it was dunked into His blood
in order to indicate Judas' total involvement in His death.
Or else He dunked it in order to keep from concluding the
testament with him. The bread was moistened and then pre-
sented--moistened, first of all, due to the events which were
to follow. Judas' avarice had indicted and separated him
from the perfect members of the Lord, just as He, who gave us
His life, had shown in His gentle teaching. Judas was not a
member of the body of Jesus' Church. Rather, he was only the
dust which gathered on the disciples' feet. That is why, during the night in which Jesus exposed him and separated him
from the others, He washed the filth from their feet so as to
teach them that, with the water, He had removed Judas (who
was likened to the feet of the body in that he was the last of
the Twelve) from the feet of the disciples like refuse ready
to be burned. Likewise, by means of the water, the Lord separated Judas from the Apostles, when He dipped the bread into
the water and gave it to him; for Judas was not worthy of the
bread which was given with the wine to the Twelve. He was
permitted to receive only the bread which saves from death
the one who was going to deliver It unto death.[15]

It is clear, then, that St. Ephraem considers Judas to be excommunicated. The strange twist, however, that he gives to his
interpretation is that Judas is not excommunicated _from_ the Eucharist, but rather _by means of_ the Eucharist. And at the same time,
it must be added that Judas was excommunicated from at least a
"portion" of the Eucharist.

It is difficult to say just what the source of the tradition
concerning the water-soaked eucharistic bread is. But Cyrillonas,
a Syrian poet writing in Edessa about the year 400, takes up the

---

15. Translated from the French and Latin renditions of the Syriac.
Cf. Éphrem de Nisibe, Commentaire de l'Évangile Concordant ou
Diatessaron, translated and annotated by Louis Leloir, in:
Sources Chrétiennes 121 (Paris, 1966) 332f; Saint Éphrem:
Commentaire de l'Évangile Concordant (version Arménienne), ed.
by L. Leloir, in: CSCO 137/Arm. 2 (Louvain, 1953) 269f.

idea and develops it differently so as to indicate unequivocally that Judas was totally excommunicated from the Eucharist.
He writes:

> "Tell us, who is it that dares this monstrous deed, who
> has your assassination in his heart and his hand in your
> bowl...?" "Fear not, my lambs. For the goat will be driven
> out. The snake that has made its den here will now be chased
> away..."
> At that point, our Lord dunked the bread into the water,
> gave it to Judas and sent him forth...But why did he dip the
> bread into the water and give it to him thus? He did this
> in order to remove its strength and the taste of its sweet-
> ness. For the bread was blessed and hallowed...Now he dunked
> that bread and took its blessing away; he stripped it of its
> strength and emptied it of his words. From the bread he took
> away the blessing; from Judas, the throne. The breath of
> Omniscience blew, and the chaff was borne away; Justice aimed
> its gaze at him, and Judas went out the door.
> At eventide, Judas left the dining hall...Now the wheat
> was free from weeds, and the berries of the vine were free
> from sour grapes...Christ, the eagle, cast him out of the
> nest; and at once, the accursed Snake snatched him up. The
> disciples were left in great joy...
> Then our Lord arose like a hero and stood like a warrior.
> Like a husbandman, he picked the fruit, prayed as the heir to
> his Father...He stood and bore himself out of love and held
> his own body high in his hands...His living body gazed out
> from his bread; and from his wine, his holy blood.[16]

Cyrillonas musters all the images of excommunication that he
can think of to express Judas' expulsion from the Church--that is,
Jesus' disciples. He is given only a bit of water-soaked bread
which is not only not the Eucharist, but is even deprived of the
blessing which Christ originally gave it. However, the tradition
that Judas was excommunicated from the Eucharist is minor--though
at times elaborate--when compared to the tradition of the opposite

---

16. Translated from the German rendition of the Syriac First
    Homily on the Pasch of Christ. Cf. P.S. Landersorfer, BKV
    6, 34-37.

view. Even later Gospel-harmonies patterned on the Diatessaron
do not always follow the view initiated by Tatian.[17]

In general, it may be said that Judas served as a type for
eucharistic excommunication only for a few writers, and only to a
very limited extent. Judas' dismissal is never used as an argument that certain people are to be refused the Eucharist. Rather,
he is more often viewed as an example of Christians who receive
the Eucharist unworthily,[18] or as an example of those who somehow
betray the Church.[19] His role as someone who has been expelled
from the group of Christ's disciples is less pronounced, and generally not interpreted as the prototype of the excommunicated
Christian.[20] That is, the early Church did not use the case of
Judas' defection to develop a theology of excommunication as such.

---

17. This is true of e.g. the Persian Diatessaron and the Diates-
    saron of Liège, both of which place the institution of the
    Eucharist before Judas' dismissal.

18. Cf. e.g. Origen, Com in Jn 32,2-16. E. Ruckstuhl points out
    that Jn 13,18 renders the LXX-quote from Ps 41,10 with τρώγων,
    which may indicate that Judas received at least the eucharis-
    tic bread (Jn 6,54.58). Cf. Judaskommunion, in: BL (1968)
    896. The same idea is presented by Lionel S. Thornton, The
    Common Life in the Body of Christ, (London, 1942) 351f.

19. In the pseudo-Cyprianic work, ad Novatianum, Novatian, the
    schismatic, is compared to Judas: "Iudas ille inter apostolos
    electus qui semper in domo Dei unanimis et fidelis ipse post-
    modum Deum prodidit." Cf. CSEL 3/3, 64. According to Euse-
    bius (HE 5,16,13), Montanus and Maximilla may have ended their
    lives by hanging themselves. In this, they are just like
    Judas, the Traitor. Finally, those who betrayed St. Polycarp
    are likened to Judas in the Martyrdom of St. Polycarp, Bishop
    of Smyrna 1,2 and 6,2.

20. St. Irenaeus (adv Haer, 2,20,2) argues against a Gnostic claim
    that Judas, though excommunicated, was nevertheless eventually
    received back into the number of the disciples and thereby
    became the representative of the suffering of the 12th Eon.

Irenaeus argues that this cannot be since Matthias was elected to replace Judas, who thus was never restored to his
place with the other disciples. In this explanation, Irenaeus
comes closer than any other early Christian writer in interpreting Judas' dismissal followed by Matthias' election as a
case of real, juridical excommunication from the first Christian community.

THE EUCHARISTIC CHARACTER OF THE CHURCH

1. Preliminary Remarks

At this point, it is necessary to investigate the theoretical ecclesiological basis of excommunication. In the context of
the present study, this requires a brief consideration of several
of the Church's essential aspects as they are related to the
Eucharist. But first, the nature of the Church's existence must
be mentioned in so far as it makes excommunication from the Church
a real and legitimate possibility. The word "excommunication"
already suggests what the nature of this ecclesial existence is--
namely, existence as a visible community. In its widest meaning,
"community" describes a form of lasting bond among certain persons who strive as a unit to achieve values which they hold in
common esteem.[1] Since the values which the members of the Church
hold in common esteem were instilled into her by Christ himself,
the Church, unlike other communities, is not free to alter these
values. United to the will of Christ, the union of men that
constitutes the Church is theologically known as the "(Mystical)
Body of Christ." Therefore, the Church is first and foremost a
community in Christ--a Christological community. However, because Christ has ascended to the Father, his presence in his
Church is by way of the Spirit which he sent to guide and sustain
her (Jn 16,5-15). This means that Christ is active in his Church
in a way that renders his presence known but "invisible." That
is, his presence is sacramental--a presence that is made known
only by various signs.[2] Consequently, the Church has a sacra-

---

1. Cf. J. Höffner, Gemeinschaft, in: HThG 1, 462.
2. Here, "sacramental" refers to all the signs of Christ's presence in his Church, and not just his presence in and through
   the sacraments narrowly defined and limited to a definite
   number.

mental character. However, it is not an end in itself, but only a sign of some other reality--a reality that constitutes the future of the Church, but not simply as some future form of the Church developed from within herself. This aspect is therefore "eschatological," and constitutes the "ultimate reality" for the Church. Nevertheless, the eschatological aspect is not so "exhaustive" that the present existence of the Church is dissolved into some sort of hazy structure without a real program of action for the here and now. The establishment of the Church upon the Apostles constitutes her as a visible and historical society which must therefore operate in the light of certain principles of action governing human relationships. These principles of action were likewise instilled into the Church by her founder--namely, the principles of love and brotherhood (e.g., Jn 15, 12-17; 1 Thes 4,9-12; 5,12-15). These four aspects of the Church--the Christological, sacramental, eschatological and fraternal[3] aspects--must now be considered in the light of the Eucharist in order to determine their relationship to this sacrament and the principles of ecclesial discipline.

2. The Church in Eucharistic Perspective

a. The Christological aspect.

Christ's founding of the Church by means of the Eucharist as the memorial of his death established the Church as God's new People and his partner in the New Covenant. But since Christ also founded the Eucharist through his total self-emptying sacrifice on

---

3. For lack of a better word, "fraternal" is here used to indicate that aspect of the Church's life in immediate, concrete situations which are characterized by διακονία and ἀγάπη.

the cross, his role as the highpriest and victim of the New
Covenant is manifested and imparts a sacrificial aspect to the
Eucharist.[4] And whatever the head is, so are the members in their
own way. Therefore, in regard to the Eucharist, the common priesthood of all Christians becomes especially apparent. That is, the
continual renewal of the Eucharist is the action of the Church in
Christ, whereby she offers herself with Christ to the Father. It
is in this light that the most nearly systematic treatment of the
Eucharist in the New Testament is given (1 Cor 10,14-22).

As far as Paul is concerned, Christians may eat the meats of
pagan sacrifices when there is no danger of scandal (1 Cor 10,27-
29). But the case is entirely different when there is a question
about participation in pagan sacrificial cult. This is forbidden
under all circumstances; for that would be to set up cup against
cup, table against table, sacrifice against sacrifice, whose purpose is to effect a communion between the divinity and man (vv.
20f). Hence, Paul demands fidelity to the Eucharist due to its
character as the only sacrifice of Christianity and because he
felt pagan sacrifice united the participants with demons. Unfaithfulness towards the Eucharist is likewise unfaithfulness to
God, Christ and the New Covenant. It was only logical that the
early Church considered participation in pagan sacrifice to be
tantamount to ipso facto excommunication.

---

4. It is not the purpose of this study to define the often contested sacrificial character of the Eucharist. But for an
   excellent treatment of this aspect from the viewpoint of a
   Reformed Christian, one can cf. Max Thurian, L'Eucharistie,
   Mémorial du Seigneur, Sacrifice d'action de grâce et d'intercession (Neuchâtel, Paris, 1959). For an Anglican's comments
   concerning the necessity of a proper recognition and understanding of the "sacrifice of the Mass," cf. Arthur M. Allchin, The Eucharistic Offering, in: Studia Liturgica 1
   (1962) 101-14.

b. The sacramental aspect

Although Christianity is not a "temple-religion," but embraces the entire universe (Jn 4,21-24), the early Church's separation from the Temple and synagogue did not come at once or
easily. In the beginning, Christian life naturally lacked a fully
independent structure of its own. However, this also meant a
lack of formalism, and left the way open for the youthful Church
to see her own developing worship and discipline in the light of
real moral concern and not merely as a matter of juridical functions or customary actions which one performs simply because "it's
the thing to do." As a result, there was a strong bond between
the early Church's "interior life" and her visible "active life"
in preaching the Gospel, initiating new members through Baptism,
and in preserving the life of the community through prayer and the
breaking of the bread (Acts 2,38-41). From the very beginning,
the life of the Church was sacramental in nature.[5] But, as already explained, this places the life of the Church in the category of "signs"; that is, things which signify a reality beyond
themselves. In regard to the Eucharist, the signification is
that of the New Covenant enriched by Jesus' life. However, the
Eucharist, as a symbol and anticipation of the future Kingdom,
also signifies the present state of incomplete fulfillment of the
New Covenant. Therefore, excommunication, particularly excommunication from the Eucharist, is likewise a sign--namely, a sign of
the loss of the realities symbolized and anticipated in the
Church's life.

---

5. Cf. Joseph A. Jungmann, <u>Der Gottesdienst der Kirche</u>, (Inns-
    bruck, 1955) 11.

c. The eschatological aspect

Since sacraments are, among other things, signs of anticipated
realities, the Church cannot be properly viewed except in an eschatological perspective. This aspect was especially characteristic of the early Church, when there was overwhelming hope and con-
fidence that Christ would not delay his second coming. Under the
influence of this expectation, Baptism naturally received the
greatest emphasis as the sacrament which prepared the individual
for this event by incorporating him into the number of the "saved"
(Acts 2,47). The delay of the second coming, however, brought
with it a shift of emphasis from Baptism to the Eucharist as the
action through which one sustained his baptismal innocence. The
Eucharist then became a daily or nearly daily event which was
meant to "rejuvenate" the effects of Baptism so that one might be
ever ready for the Lord.[6] Therefore, a proper understanding of
the Eucharist in its eschatological perspective demands a proper
understanding of Baptism in its relationship to eschatology.

Christian Baptism is essentially the sacramental rite of dying
and, as a consequence, rising with Christ (Rm 6,3f; Col 2,12). In
biblical thinking, dying came to man as punishment for his disobedience to God (Gn 3,1ff; Rm 5,12). But death, according to the
Bible, is normally not mere punishment. Rather, it is expiation
for the wrong done (Dt 19,11-13; 32,43), and may even be to the
ultimate benefit of the offender (1 Cor 5,5). It supposedly re-
establishes the right relation between God and man. This is the
basic concept of sacrifice, especially bloody sacrifice. The
death may be one that is offered as atonement for the sins of

---

6. Cf. Paul Neuenzeit, Das Herrenmahl, Studien zur paulinischen
   Eucharistieauffassung, (Studien zum Alten und Neuen Testament
   16), (Munich, 1960) 230.

others, just as Moses' death was interpreted as expiation for the
sins of Israel (Dt 3,23ff; 4,21f). The violent death of the
"Suffering Servant of Yahweh" is likewise seen as atonement for
others; and yet, his death is paradoxically viewed as the means
whereby the Suffering Servant achieves long life (Is 53,4ff).

With Jesus' death as the Messiah, however, the ultimate in
expiation has been reached.[7] Consequently, the death of other
persons has meaning and purpose only when united to Christ's
death. Baptism is thus a participation in his death, which, in
turn, gives one a share in the benefits of this death--namely,
resurrection to life. With that, Baptism becomes anticipation of
the eschatological event of the resurrection of the dead.

The Eucharist likewise concerns itself with Christ's death
and resurrection, since it celebrates and anticipates the state
of existence that is the result of the resurrection, which, in
turn, is made possible through union with Christ's death.

This union with Christ in his death and renewed life is summed
up in the term, "the New Covenant." The "new" is to be understood first of all in terms of what the Old Covenant attempted to
do but could not achieve--namely, the freeing of men from moral
impurity (sin and guilt) so that they could hold communion with
God. Jesus alone was able to do this. Therefore, communion with
God is possible only by way of union with Jesus (Lk 10,22; Jn 14,6).
But the καινὴ διαθήκη became fully meaningful only in view of the
βασιλεία τοῦ θεοῦ. That is, the historical form of the New

_____

7. It is necessary to avoid a masochistic interpretation of
    Christ's suffering and death. Jesus did not preach asceti-
    cism as the way to eternal life (cf. Mt 11,18f and par.), not
    to speak of masochism. He did not love suffering, but suf-
    fered out of love for mankind. Cf. Jn 13,1; Mk 14,34-36 and
    pars.

Covenant as made present in the Eucharist is not an end in itself. It functions in the present form only "until the Lord
comes" (1 Cor 11,26) and establishes his Kingdom in its fullness.[8] Since the Eucharist is the main means through which the
Church anticipates participation in this Kingdom, it is likewise
the sacrament through which the Church especially expresses and
experiences her eschatological character which gives her direction and transcendence beyond her present existence. This is
the "vertical aspect" of the Church and the Eucharist. From this
point of view, excommunication is not only a sign of the loss of
future realities. Rather, it _is_ loss of the future realities as
they are anticipated in the present. It is the loss of proper
"orientation." In so far as excommunication is a juridical act
on the part of the Church, it is the Church's recognition and
confirmation of this loss.

d. The fraternal aspect.

If the above "vertical aspect" of the Eucharist were left
standing alone, there would be great danger of turning Christianity into an atomized state, where the community of Christians
would be totally subordinated to a radical individualism which
would leave the Church without divine purpose or theological
foundation. But such is not the case. For it is precisely
through the Eucharist that the Church is given a "horizontal
aspect" which makes the relationships between man and man an
essential part of the New Covenant and its complete realization
in the coming of the Kingdom.

---

8. Cf. Constitutio Dogmatica de Ecclesia, "Lumen Gentium",
   48, from the documents of Vatican II.

In <u>Acts</u> <u>of</u> <u>the</u> <u>Apostles</u>, the first Christian community is described as a κοινωνία in the "breaking of the bread" while living together and sharing all things in common (2,42.44-46). This is the first time the term κοινωνία occurs as an absolute, and it indicates the awareness of the writer of <u>Acts</u> that the group of faithful at Jerusalem had formed itself into a unique community distinct from all other types of communities in that it took root in the teaching of the Apostles, expressed itself liturgically in the Eucharist and in prayer, and realized itself in charity.[9]

St. Paul's <u>First</u> <u>Letter</u> <u>to</u> <u>the</u> <u>Corinthians</u> gives further witness to the fact that the Eucharist in its "fraternal aspect" formed an essential part of the reason for the gathering of the early Christians (11,17-34). For Paul, fraternal charity is a <u>sine</u> <u>qua</u> <u>non</u> of the Eucharist.[10] It is so important in Paul's mind, that, in the case of the Corinthians who have overlooked it in regard to the poor in the community, he bluntly and scornfully says they are not really holding the Lord's supper at all in such gatherings (v. 20). Therefore, Paul does not view the Eucharist in the narrow cultic categories of later thought, wherein Eucharist and community suffer a division from each other that goes well beyond a legitimate formal distinction. Rather, the Eucharist is here seen as the "element" which both motivates and effects the inner relationship of love within the community. It is not a merely cultic function that can be fruitfully undertaken without regard for the life and welfare of the entire community.

---

9. Cf. Giuseppe D'Ercole, <u>Communio</u>, <u>Collegialità</u>, <u>Primato</u> <u>e</u> <u>Sollicitudo</u> <u>omnium</u> <u>Ecclesiarum</u> <u>dai</u> <u>Vangeli</u> <u>a</u> <u>Costantino</u>, (<u>Communio</u> 5), (Rome, 1964) 97.

10. Cf. P. Neuenzeit, <u>op</u>. <u>cit</u>., 234; ----, <u>Eucharistie</u> <u>und</u> <u>Gemeinde</u>, in: <u>Una</u> <u>Sancta</u> 2 (1970) 116-30.

A <u>fortiori</u> is this the case when the Eucharist is made an occasion of not only neglecting positive acts of charity, but of even promoting divisions within the community and of bringing sharp embarrassment to its poorer members (vv. 18f.22).

Even in 1 Cor 10,14-33, where the Eucharist is considered in its more specifically religious and sacramental aspects, Paul does not overlook the role of brotherly love--and indeed, brotherly love that extends beyond the boundaries of the Christian community. It is for the sake of one's neighbors and associates that the Christian should refuse on occasion to eat meats sacrificed to idols--not because the sacrificial foods mean anything in themselves that makes them unfit for Christians, but because less-understanding consciences would be offended to realize that a Christian would <u>knowingly</u> eat such food. Out of love, the Christian should be willing to forego his freedom, because that will be beneficial toward the salvation of those who would otherwise be offended (vv. 24.28-33).

The eucharistic meal, as Paul implies, is not merely a moment of union with "my Jesus." Rather it is union with Christ, the head of the Church and the Lord of the world and of history.[11] Union with Christ means union with the entire Church. This union is not possible without love. Love and the Eucharist thus become

---

11. Cf. J. Auer, <u>Einheit</u> <u>und</u> <u>Frieden</u> <u>als</u> <u>Frucht</u> <u>der</u> <u>eucharistischen</u> <u>Mahlgemeinschaft</u>, (<u>Aktuelle</u> <u>Fragen</u> <u>zur</u> <u>Eucharistie</u>), (Munich, 1960) 135. In view of this aspect, it should be pointed out here that this most important of all elements in regard to the unity of the Church in the Body of Christ immediately implies the "creative activity of the Spirit," who makes love possible and thereby overcomes the egoism among Christians and sustains the unity of the Body. Cf. L.S. Thornton, <u>op</u>. <u>cit</u>., 94f.

inseparable in the life of the Church and the individual Christian.

The community at Corinth, like most early Christian communities, had taken it upon itself to express and practice love in the
Eucharist by keeping it in the meal-setting in which it had been
instituted. The meal must have presented itself quite naturally
to the early Church as a very suitable way to express charity in a
manner immediately connected with the Eucharist. Yet, this sacrament has its own specific form of independence in the life of the
Church. It did not depend on the meal for its "right to exist."
With or without the meal, the eucharistic theology of 1 Cor 11,17-
33 can only be rightly understood when approached from the "fraternal character" of the Eucharist.

Paul certainly does not mean to condemn or frown on the custom of uniting the Eucharist with the agape-feast.[12] What he con-
demns is the fact that, <u>even</u> <u>with</u> <u>a</u> <u>meal</u>, the Corinthians are
overlooking an essential aspect of the Eucharist. Although the
Eucharist is not a question of the type of eating and drinking
that can be done at home (v. 22a), it is meant to promote love
and responsible brotherhood which are expressed in <u>service</u> (διακονία). It implies a relationship of host to guests, where the
host is likewise the humble servant of the guests (Lk 22,24-26)
and administers to their needs. That is, the saving act which
Christ has presented to his Church through the sacrament of the
Eucharist demands an answer that can only take the form of love

---

12. St. Paul could scarcely have any real objection to the immediate joining of the Eucharist with the agape and still give
the command that the Corinthians should wait for one another
before beginning the agape (v. 33). Moreover, the lovefeast
was most likely the only opportunity that many of Corinth's
poor had of getting an occasionally good meal. Cf. <u>RGG</u> 1
(1957) 169.

and service to one's neighbor.[13] But the Corinthians have not
only failed to administer to the needs of their poorer members,
they have even made them embarrassed of their poverty. How can
anyone guilty of such conduct dare to take part in the κυριακὸν
δεῖπνον, the sacramentalized form of Christ's love for his Church?
That is utter hypocrisy--a breaking of faith with Christ and his
Church.[14] To the Christian, the Eucharist is analogous to
Christ's death in that this death brought all those concerned
with it into a critical situation which forced them to share in
that death either worthily or unworthily, depending on their decision. Those who chose to participate unworthily in the Lord's
death did so by calling down his blood upon themselves in self-
condemnation (Mt 27,25). Likewise, one who participates in the
Eucharist unworthily (i.e., without charity) is guilty of the
Lord's body and blood (1 Cor 11,27). Such disregard for the poor
members of Christ's Body, the Church, is equivalent to renouncing
one's Baptism by way of unworthy participation in the Eucharist.[15]

St. Paul commands that each and everyone scrutinize his own
conscience in regard to charity before approaching the Eucharist.[16]
In this way, those who have failed in brotherly love will not be

---

13. Cf. P. Neuenzeit, op. cit., 234. Mention should also be made
    here of the collection for the poor of Jerusalem that Paul
    commanded the churches to take up at their Sunday Eucharist.
    Cf. 1 Cor 16,1-3.

14. Paul presupposes that whatever one does to the least of
    Christ's brethern, he does to Christ. Cf. Mt 25,40.45;
    cf. also Acts 9,4f and pars.

15. Cf. C.D.F. Moule, The Judgment Theme in the Sacraments, (The
    Background of the New Testament and its Eschatology; Studies
    in Honour of C.H. Dodd), (Cambridge, 1964) 471.

16. The examination of conscience in connection with the Eucha-
    rist appears in the Didache (14,1) as a confession of sins
    before the celebration of the Eucharist.

inclined to participate in the Eucharist and thereby eat and
drink to their own condemnation. Behind these thoughts of Paul
lies a certain logic which is not fully stated, but which can be
easily discerned if the fraternal aspect of the Eucharist is
kept firmly in sight.

Verse 27 states that unworthy communion is an offense against
the body and blood of the Lord. That is, it is an offense
against the Lord personally and aside from the Church. Verse 29
informs the reader that unworthy communion[17] invites condemnation upon oneself. In the same verse, unworthy communion is defined as failure to "discern the body" (μὴ διακρίνων τὸ σῶμα).
The key to the interpretation of the text is to be found in the
correct meaning of "body" in this verse. Does it refer exclusively, or even primarily, to Christ's presence in the Eucharist?[18]

---

17. Actually, this verse speaks of "eating and drinking unworthily," and so seems to refer to the agape as well as the
Eucharist. The interpretation of "body" in this verse to
mean "Church" gives greater probability to this conclusion.
Cf. note 19 below.

18. W. Doskocil (op. cit., 71) interprets "body" to mean the
eucharistic elements, and then draws the conclusion that Paul
is advising the Corinthians to examine their conscience and,
if need be, to refrain voluntarily "lediglich von der Eucharistie." This interpretation of "body" and the resulting conclusion concerning self-excommunication from the Eucharist
miss the point of the examination of conscience, which is to
be made in the light of one's practice of charity at the agape.
If there is a question of self-excommunication here, it applies to the agape as well since it would be no solution to
the problem of the uncharitable agape if the offender only
needed to avoid the Eucharist proper in order to escape God's
unfavorable judgment. That is, Paul expects positive results
from the self-examination--namely the restoration of charity
to the agape. When this is done, the problem of unworthy
communion is likewise corrected. In so far as the Eucharist
joins Christians together into the body of the Church, it

If that were the case, then verse 29 would only be a repeti-
tion of verse 27, and the entire point that Paul is so clearly
making would be missed--namely, that participation in the Eucharist without charity offends the Lord precisely because it stems
from an offense to his Body, the Church. Therefore, it seems
necessary to interpret "body" in verse 29 to mean primarily
"Church."[19] But from the entire context, it is clear that Paul
is here speaking of a particular aspect of the Church which is
to be defined as "the Church as reflected in her needy members."
An unworthy communion is one in which the participant communicates while despising and neglecting the needs of his brothers
in Christ.

As a practical consequence, St. Paul does not permit the
Corinthians to separate worship to God and charity toward neighbor. He therefore commands them to keep the meal together with
the Eucharist[20] as a means of expressing the fraternal aspect

---

does so especially by joining them together in responsible
love for each other. Paul's understanding of this sacrament
does not, as in later times, revolve around the "question of
the elements," but rather the "indissoluble inner connection
of sacrament and Church." Cf. Günther Bornkamm, Herrenmahl
und Kirche bei Paulus, in: NTS 2 (1955/56) 206.

19. This interpretation is supported by 1 Cor 10,17, where Paul
plays on the word "body" in order to draw a parallel between
the Eucharist and the Church. Thus, the Eucharist and
Christ's body are not excluded. Cf. L.S. Thornton, op. cit.,
345. It is obvious, then, that St. Paul speaks of "discern-
ing" the Body in such a way that it is not a question of abstraction and analysis whereby "body" is reduced to a single
meaning. In other words, it is a matter of "synthetic"
rather than "analytic" judgment.

20. In this verse (33), τὸ φαγεῖν clearly indicates that Paul
means the agape as well as the Eucharist. If only the Eucharist were meant, it would imply that each faction that had

of this sacrament. It is the practical expression of Paul's
statement: "If anyone does not love the Lord, a curse on him.
'Marana tha.'"[21]

3. The Nature of Eucharistic Unity

The problem that must now be confronted concerns the relationship between unity in faith and unity in cult. That the
Eucharist presupposes unity as well as produces it is clear

formed at Corinth not only ate its own meal without regard
for the poor, but also celebrated its own Eucharist. In that
case, there would be no real explanation of why they ever
came together ἐν ἐκκλησία (v. 18) to begin with if not at
least for a common Eucharist.

21. Cf. 1 Cor 16,22: εἴ τις οὐ φιλεῖ τὸν κύριον, ἤτω ἀνάθεμα.
μαράνα θά. O. Cullmann, Early Christian Worship, 19f, considers 1 Cor 16,20ff to be fragments of a eucharistic liturgy.
Cf. also H. Lietzmann, Mass and the Lord's Supper, (Leiden,
1953ff) 186. E. Käsemann ascribes "Rechtscharakter" to this
statement in which the curse anticipates the eschatological
condemnation of one who does not love the Lord. These "Sätze"
are the Christianized, "eschatologicalized" version of the
jus talionis as shown in e.g. 1 Cor 3,17; 14,38. Cf. Ernst
Käsemann, Sätze heiligen Rechtes im Neuen Testament, in: NTS
1 (1954/55) 249-51; Günther Bornkamm, Das Anathema in der
urchristlichen Abendmahlsliturgie, in: Theologische Literaturzeitung 75 (1950) 228. The fact that Paul uses the Aramaic term "Maranatha" without explaining to his Greek-speaking readers what it means, indicates that it was a "standard"
part of a liturgical formula, expressing faith in Jesus as
the Lord. Moreover, the use of the term in 1 Cor 16,22 and
again in the Didache (10,6) shows that it was used as a formula of threat and judgment. Cf. Karl G. Kuhn, μαραναθά,
in ThWB 4, 473ff. However, the statement is not a directive
for some human religious institution (e.g., the community or
a particular group within the community) to exercise the
"power of the keys" toward this or that offender. Cf. Werner
Elert, Abendmahl und Kirchengemeinschaft in der alten Kirche
hauptsächlich des Ostens, Berlin, 1954) 94.

enough. But just how these two poles relate to each other in view of the Christian faith itself is not immediately clear. It is, however, evident that "faith" cannot be here understood as an impersonal, abstract body of defined doctrine. According to Acts 2,42, Apostolic instruction in the faith was integrated into the Christian community's Eucharist and prayers.[22] Obviously, the newly baptized Christians partook of the Eucharist before they were really well instructed in Christian doctrine. When the Church broke fully with Judaism and had to seek her members almost exclusively from pagan society, the catechumenate was introduced to instruct the future Christian in the faith before he was baptized. Nevertheless, there were many converts from paganism during Apostolic times whose instruction in the faith followed upon Baptism (Acts 10-11). Moreover, the catechumenate was introduced later not only for the sake of instruction, but also as a period of probation during which the candidate's conduct of life was carefully observed to make sure that he could live up to the moral demands of the faith. This form of catechumenate became prevalent during the third century, but disappeared with the mass "conversions" of entire pagan societies whose invasions brought down the Roman Empire and introduced the "Dark Ages."

In general, it can be said that the faith which the early Church demanded of its members was one of personal commitment to Christ as experienced in his Body, the Church. Doctrine was not unimportant, but, as a body of abstract teaching to which one gave

---

22. Here is a witness to the basic word-sacrament structure of Christian life and worship from the beginning. Cf. Bernard Cooke, Eucharist: Source or Expression of Community?, in: Worship 40 (166) 341.

intellectual assent, it was not what early Christians meant when
they spoke of "the faith." For them, unity in faith meant unity
in personal commitment. This included doctrine, but was primarily directed to the special "system" of human relationships
prescribed by Christ and the Apostles.[23] Consequently, "faith"
becomes immediately associated with love; for without love, there
can be no personal commitment to the Body of Christ.

Unity in love is the presupposed condition when Christians
come together to worship. This lesson is clearly taught in Mt 5,
23f, where the order is given that one leave his gift before the
altar and go to be reconciled with his brother before returning
to offer the gift at the altar. However, it would be wrong to
conclude that the unity of the Church is simply the unity born
out of the mutual love of the members. The Body of Christ is not
quantitatively identical with the sum of the members of the
Church.[24] The members do not "corporate" to form the Church.
Rather, they are incorporated into the Body of Christ by Baptism,
the sacramental profession of one's personal commitment to the
faith. Therefore, one can distinguish three aspects in the nature
of the unity presupposed in eucharistic worship: 1. Unity through
baptismal incorporation into Christ. 2. Unity of the members with
each other through charity. 3. A sincere, personal commitment to
follow and be guided by Apostolic catechesis, which includes moral
exhortation as well as doctrinal instruction. It now remains to
be seen in what way or ways the Eucharist is effective of unity.

---

23. The designation of the early Church in Acts as "the Way" adds
    support to this interpretation. Cf. Wilhelm Michaelis, ὁδός,
    in: ThWB 5, 93-95.

24. Cf. Ernst Käsemann, Anliegen und Eigenart der paulinischen
    Abendmahlslehre, in: Evangelische Theologie 7 (1947/48) 211.

The unity that is produced by the Eucharist is, first of all,
a further step in the process of incorporation begun in Baptism.
Baptism is the first step; and whatever is first is non-repeat-
able. Yet, all which is implied in the first step can be "reju-
venated" and brought to development. This is the objective of
the Eucharist. However, eucharistic incorporation goes beyond
the "individual incorporation" of Baptism.[25] The unity effected
by the Eucharist is one of continued "growing into" the Body of
Christ through the corporate action and love of the Church in
her performance of the Eucharist. In so far as this sacrament is
the continued fulfillment of the command, "do this in memory of
me,"[26] it effects unity because it is the objective of the community's existence in the pilgrim Church.[27]

In this explanation of the unity effected by the Eucharist,
it is necessary to note a certain "ascending hierarchy" of dis-
tinctions to be made in the Church--namely, the community or
local church, the pilgrim Church (formerly called "the Church
militant"), and the Body of Christ. The whole process of unifi-
cation into the Body of Christ can now be outlined as follows:
1. Through Baptism, one is incorporated into the entire Body of
Christ as such, irrespective of the local Christian community and,
in a certain sense, irrespective of the pilgrim Church since even
a non-Christian can administer Baptism to a person wishing to

---

25. Cf. J. Auer, art. cit., 146f.
26. Cf. Lk 22,19; 1 Cor 11,24f. Alan Richardson, *An Introduc-
    tion to the Theology of the New Testament*, (London, 1958)
    368, points out that the Eucharist as an anamnesis means,
    among other things, that "God is being sought to 'remember
    his Messiah'."

27. Cf. B. Cooke (art. cit., 346) who lists several ways in which
    the Eucharist effects unity. But they are all just further
    refinements of the first way which is stated above.

become a Christian, or a non-Christian can achieve the same grace alone through "baptism of desire or blood." 2. Through the Eucharist, one is concretely and historically incorporated into the local community celebrating the Eucharist. 3. But since the local community, though fully a church, does not exhaust the Church as a whole, the Eucharist of the local church joins that church to the eucharistic action of all other Christian communities and effects the incorporation of the local church into the entire pilgrim Church. 4. The pilgrim Church, on the other hand, does not exhaust the Body of Christ, but tends toward fulfilled incorporation[28] in that Body.

---

28. Here, "fulfilled incorporation" is preferred to "full incorporation" since it can be argued that full incorporation is already the effect of Baptism.

CHAPTER FIVE

THE HISTORICAL BASIS OF ECCLESIAL EXCOMMUNICATION

1. The Theological Basis according to the Gospels

When it is a question of the Church's right to exercise the
power of excommunication, then only three short Gospel-texts come
directly into consideration. The first passage, Mt 16,13-20, concerns Peter's confession of faith that Jesus is "the Christ, the
Son of the living God," and the subsequent delegation of the power
of binding and loosing to Peter. The second text, Mt 18,15-18,
concerns fraternal correction, and indicates that the power of
loosing and binding belongs to the whole Church and not only to
Peter. The third passage is Jn 20,22f, which likewise indicates
that all of the Church participates in the "power of the keys."
The investigation of this power to bind and to loose will begin
with Mt 18,15-18 since its meaning is clearer and can thus contribute toward a better understanding of the more controversial
text, Mt 16,13-20.

While there is no reason to doubt that Jesus taught forgiveness of sinners and offenders as often as they repented, Mt 18,
15-18 certainly cannot be considered the _ipsissima verba Jesu_.
The use of εκκλησία in verse 17 can only refer to an already fully
established Christian community such as the one formed in Jerusalem[1] after Christ's death and resurrection. Even though such
a Christian community would still be fully attached to Jewish worship, the εκκλησία spoken of here can only refer to the Christian
community as distant from the Jewish synagogue. The passage is

---

1. The reference to pagans and tax-collectors in verse 18 betrays the Palestinian origin of the passage. Cf. Rudolf
Bultmann, _Die Geschichte der synoptischen Tradition_, (Göttingen, 1921) 121.

a clear example of the early Christian adoption of Jewish disciplinary practices. However, even though it was no compliment in Judaism to be called a pagan or a tax-collector, the ban from the synagogue was never imposed with the formula: "Let him be treated as a pagan or a tax-collector."[2] Jewish Christians, on the other hand, could very readily employ such an expression in order to indicate their full detachment from an expelled person until he repents. That is, if the synagogue were to impose the ban with such a formula, it would have to mean the permanent expulsion of someone from the Jewish community since the pagan and tax-collector were always excluded from Jewish worship and life. But such was not the case in the Christian community.

The emphasis in Mt 18,15-18 is on leading the offender to repentance.[3] Therefore, the images of the pagan and tax-collector only serve to express the state of one who has become hardened in his sins and has _de facto_ formed himself into a class apart from the Christian, who, although a sinner himself, never fully gives up the struggle against his own failings. Excommunication in this case is not so much an active exclusion of the offender from the Church as it is a declaration of what has already come to pass in

---

2. Pagans and tax-collectors were not admitted at all. Cf. W. Doskocil, _op_. _cit_., 33. After Jerusalem fell to Pompey in 63 B.C., the Jews developed many far-reaching customs restricting their association with non-Jews. The publican (i.e., tax-collector) was generally of native birth, but under contract with the Roman authorities. Since he not only collected taxes for a pagan, foreign power, but also fleeced his own pockets in the process by over-taxing, he was considered to be no better than a pagan. Cf. SB 1, 377-80; 4/1, 353ff.

3. This is to be seen especially in the light of the moral-ethical character of Christian discipline, which is specifically directed to repentance and forgiveness of sins. Cf. Jn 20,23.

the offender's relationship with the Church. The fuller meaning
of the power to bind and to loose will be discussed below in connection with the power of the keys given to Peter in Mt 16,19.

Those who argue for an historical placement of the substance
of Mt 16,13-20 within Jesus' own lifetime generally feel that
such words concerning a delegation of authority from Jesus to his
followers would have come near the end of his life when it became
apparent that most of Judaism would reject Christ's message.[4]
Oscar Cullmann[5] thinks that the passage in question might very
probably belong to the Last Supper accounts. However, there are
several good reasons for not associating this text with the last
days of Jesus' life, and especially not with the Last Supper.
First of all, the movement to give Jesus public recognition as
the Messiah and the King of Israel apparently reached its climax
toward the close of his life.[6] By this time, Jesus' command to
Peter and the others not to make the confession of faith public
would be completely meaningless (Mt 16,20 and pars.). Thus,
Peter's confession was probably originally a declaration that he
saw the long-awaited Messiah in Jesus.[7] But since Jesus commanded
silence on this matter, the declaration would have had to precede

---

4. Cf. J. Schmid, Petrus, in: HThG 2, 310.
5. Cf. Πέτρος, in: ThWB 6, 103-09, esp. 106f.
6. Jesus' enthusiastic following must have eventually represented
   a very serious threat to the established Jewish and Roman authorities. Cf. Mk 14,2 and pars.; Jn 11,48-50. The movement
   to make Jesus king is the most likely element which led the
   Roman authorities to sentence Jesus to death. Cf. Jn 19,12-16.

7. If Peter used the expression, "Son of (the living) God," in
   his confession, it did not necessarily mean that he was confessing Jesus to be of divine nature or origin, but only to be
   one especially favored by God. However, Matthew's use of the
   expression indicates that the title implied Jesus' divinity.
   Cf. Mt 26,63-66.

the open movement to make him king.[8] Nevertheless, this does not necessarily mean that the verses concerning Peter's name, the foundation of the Church, and the power of the keys must be within the same historical context as Peter's confession of faith.

First, one must ask, "What were the historical circumstances surrounding the bestowal of the name 'Peter' on Simon son of Jonah?" If Jesus did confer the name, then one would not only expect an explanation of the name from Jesus, but also that the name would be explained when it was given. Peter's confession of faith in Jesus' messianic character would have been a likely occasion for this event.[9] In that case, one would expect quite rightly that the pun which Jesus makes in Mt 16,18 to explain the establishment of his Church would also be historically associated with

---

8. The title, "King of the Jews" (e.g., Mt 2,2; Mk 15,2), very readily becomes the messianic title, "King of Israel" (Mt 27, 42; Mk 15,32; Jn 1,49; 12,13), although not very often. At any rate, there is every reason to believe that the texts which refer to Jesus as a king have a real historical basis within Jesus' own lifetime. Cf. Karl L. Schmidt, βασιλεύς, in: ThWB 1, 577-79.

9. The statement that Simon was given the name of "Peter" is found already in the accounts of the appointment of the Twelve. Cf. Mk 3,16 and pars. However, only Jn 1,42 seems to say that Jesus gave Simon his unique surname upon their first meeting. But closer inspection of the text betrays its obvious theological construction of typical Johannine character in keeping with Jesus' pre-existence and full grasp of the situation, knowledge of men's hearts, and clear vision of the past, present and future that make up John's portrait of Jesus from the very beginning of his Gospel. Therefore, when Jesus looks upon Simon, his gaze penetrates to the "inner essence" of the disciple to reveal that he is "rock," the characteristic that makes Simon Peter what he is in Christianity. Cf. also the use of ἐμβλέπειν in Jn 1,36.42; Mt 19,26 and par.; Mk 10,21; Lk 22,61.

the conferral of the name and Peter's confession of faith.[10]
Whatever the historical basis within Jesus' life may have been
for Peter's name, there are several indications that verses 17-19
of the text in question must be substantially ascribed to the
time after Jesus' death and resurrection.

The first indication of this fact is that "flesh and blood"
did not reveal Jesus' nature to Peter. In Matthew's Gospel, this
means that there was nothing in Jesus' human character and activity, or in Peter himself, or in the relationship of others to
Jesus which revealed his divine nature to others. Rather, Peter's

---

10. Christ's statement that he has prayed for Peter so that his
faith may not fail him and that he may strengthen the other
disciples (Lk 22,32) could be considered an occasion when
the name might have been given at the Last Supper. But there
are several objections to be made to that possibility. The
passage occurs only in Luke and seems to be a post-resurrection comment on Peter's experiences after Christ's death.
Moreover, Peter is addressed here only and emphatically as
"Simon" (v. 31). Also, the text would place Peter's name
in a different light--that is, "rock of support and refuge"
(e.g., Pss 31,3; 62,8)--but say nothing about the Church.
Finally, Peter is praised as "happy" in Mt 16,17 for his confession in faith. According to Mt 11,6 and par., those who
are not scandalized in Christ are happy. But on the eve of
his arrest, Jesus tells his disciples that they will be
scandalized in him. Peter objects that even if the others
are scandalized, he will not succumb. Cf. Mt 26,31-33. Yet,
during Jesus' trial, Peter is the most scandalized and the
most unhappy of all the disciples. Cf. Mt 26,69ff and pars.
Only his belief in the risen Christ could make him truly
"happy." Most probably, the early Aramaic speaking Christian
community placed this praise of Peter and promise of the
power of the keys (Mt 16,17-19) in the mouth of the risen
Lord, as Jn 20,22f; 21,15-19 indicate. Cf. R. Bultmann,
Geschichte der synoptischen Tradition, 147-50, 277f; Ernst
Lichtenstein, Die älteste christliche Glaubensformel, in:
Zeitschrift für Kirchengeschichte 63 (1950/51) 58f.

confession was due to the Father alone, and was therefore a pure act of faith such as cannot be made without God's grace. However, if the Evangelists really intended to describe the historical facts of Jesus' life and Peter's confession of faith, then they would have been forced to say that indeed it was "flesh and blood" that revealed Jesus' divine nature to Peter after he had witnessed such signs and miracles as the Evangelists ascribe to Jesus.[11] But Matthew is praising Peter's faith in the <u>divine sonship</u> of Jesus, which, from all other indications, is the nature of Peter's faith only <u>after</u> Jesus' death and resurrection. For this faith, Peter is praised as μακάριος (v. 17). The tenor of Mt 16,17 reminds one of the risen Lord's words to Thomas in Jn 20,29: "Because you have seen me, you have believed. Happy are those who believe even though they do not see."[12] That is, those who receive the grace of faith to believe that Jesus is divine and therefore living are praised as "happy" in spite of never having seen Jesus after his death.[13] Consequently, Mt 16,17 praises Peter's

---

11. It is not a question of metaphysical proof of Christ's divinity; for no miracle can prove that, and only the "miracle of faith" can overcome this situation. But metaphysics was not a <u>forte</u> in the world of Jesus and the Evangelists. Thus, the miracle accounts, if fully historical, would have been more than enough to supply Peter and the others with personal, subjective proof of Jesus' divinity. The miracle accounts are not primarily <u>demonstrations</u>, but rather <u>illustrations</u> of Christ's true nature.

12. Ὅτι ἑώρακάς με, πεπίστευκας; μακάριοι οἱ μὴ ἰδόντες καὶ πιστεύσαντες.

13. Faith which reveals Christ's true nature is that which makes one μακάριος. Therefore, the poor (in spirit) are called "happy" (Mt 5,3 and par.), because they are "rich in faith." Cf. Jm 2,5. Even the eyes and ears are called "happy" which perceive in Jesus what others longed to see and hear. Cf. Mt 13,16f and par.

post-resurrection faith, which enabled Jesus' followers to organize themselves as Christ's Church built upon Apostolic faith and
teaching.[14] Because of Peter's faith which enabled the Church to
become a concrete reality, the Church has access to the power of
binding and loosing. The implications of this power must now be
investigated.

In Is 22,22, the image of the transferral of the keys from
the master to the servant represents <u>delegated</u> dominion which cannot be taken away except by the master himself (Is 22,19). The
symbolism of the keys and the terminology of binding and loosing
are technical rabbinical terms which refer primarily to the right
to take disciplinary measures. To be bound or loosed means respec-

---

14. It is most probable that πέτρα means Peter himself in Mt 16,
    18, and that it is not simply a cover-word for the content of
    Peter's confession of faith. Cf. O. Cullman, Πέτρος, in: <u>ThWB</u>
    6, 105f. However, the real question is not the meaning of
    πέτρα, but rather: "What is <u>Peter's name</u> all about?" In the
    light of all that has been said here on the text in question,
    only one answer is possible--namely, "Peter's faith." Or more
    precisely, it is Peter's primacy of faith (1 Cor 15,5-9) in
    the real nature of Jesus and the resurrection. It does vio-
    lence to the text to try to separate Peter from his confession
    of faith in such a way that only the content of that faith is
    implied in πέτρα. On the other hand, it is equally destruc-
    tive to the text to try to identify πέτρα with Peter without
    any regard for the fact that the name "Peter" means something
    other than simply the <u>person</u> of Simon son of Jonah. The
    latter is only the "pre-history" of the former. Mistakes in
    interpretation of the text arise all too easily when it is
    viewed as something that Matthew inserted after the Apostle's
    death in order to defend successorship to the Petrine office.
    The passage was indeed written after Peter's death. But the
    use of μακάριος in verse 17 makes it especially clear that
    the text is a <u>eulogy</u> and not an <u>apology</u>. This is the first
    factor that must be considered in any apologetic application
    of Matthew's account of the Church's being founded upon Peter.

tively to be put unter the ban or to be absolved from it. However, the terms were also used to define authority in matters of
doctrine. A forbidden teaching or opinion is one that was "bound";
whereas, a permitted doctrine is one that was "loosed."[15] From
Mt 18,18 in context, it is clear that disciplinary authority is intended. However, the authority of the Church is primarily a teaching and pastoral authority with missionary responsibility (Mt 28,
18-20; Mk 16,16) which finds its ultimate theological foundation
in the principle that whoever hears the Church, hears Christ (Lk
10,16; Mt 10,40 and pars.). This broader aspect of authority is
intended in Mt 16,19. Moreover, Jesus' complaint that the Scribes
and the Pharisees close rather than open heaven to men (Mt 23,13)
is a clear indication that he wants his Church to use this authority positively and not negatively.

Perhaps Matthew took it upon himself to develop a theology of
ecclesial authority in concrete terms because the Church of his
times felt the need for it. More than any other Evangelist,
Matthew warns against false prophets and wolves disguised as sheep
(7,15-20), false Christs who lead the faithful astray by working
great marvels (24,24; 7,21); many will be deceived, and so the
faithful are to be on their guard (24,4f.11). The effect of these
foes is the destruction of love in most people (24,11).

In the Fourth Gospel, the power of the keys is somewhat rephrased and, most importantly, granted to the disciples by the
risen Christ. Thus, Jn 20,22f, the latest of the biblical witnesses to this power, shows that John placed special value on it
for the Church. The outstanding and conspicuous place and ecclesiological context of these verses emphasize the fact the for-

---

15. Cf. SB 1, 736-41, 792f; J. Hollweck, op. cit., xv-xvii.

giveness is not just a matter for certain individual sinners--as might appear to be the case in Matthew--, but that all Christians stand in need of forgiveness. Moreover, the most probable reading of Jn 20,23 states that the sins have been forgiven or retained; whereas, Matthew says that the sins will be forgiven or retained in heaven. Matthew emphasizes the future, eschatological aspect of forgiveness and retention, while John emphasizes the "hic et nunc" aspect of this action on the part of the Church. The power of the keys, therefore, is seen by John as the basic, original administrative power granted to the Church.[16]

2. The Practice of Excommunication

in Acts of the Apostles

a. Discipline toward individuals.

The first "history of the Church" to be written may very well incorporate many bits of historically reliable information. But Luke still intended Acts to be an interpretative account of the first generation of Christians. In contrast to the Synoptic Gospels, Acts no longer breathes the air of eschatological anxiety and hurry brought on by the expectation of Christ's second coming.[17] The very fact that the author presents a history of the Christian community shows that the Church's interest had shifted from that of immediate preparation for the end of the

---

16. Cf. Hans von Campenhausen, Amt und geistliche Vollmacht in den ersten drei Jahrhunderten, (Beiträge zur historischen Theologie 14), (Tübingen, 1953) 152f.

17. Cf. Acts 1,6-8. Already in the Third Gospel, Christ's second coming and the end of the world are put off indefinitely. Cf. Lk 21,24.

world to that of establishing herself within the world for a long future.[18]   It is from this point of view, which did not become prominent until the end of the first century, that Acts must be understood.

After the reorganization of Christ's followers in Jerusalem, the first item on the Church's business agenda was the election of a witness of Jesus' resurrection (Acts 1,21f) to replace Judas Iscariot.   In doing so, Jesus' followers officially recognized and ratified the loss of Judas to their number.   By way of commentary to the traitor's dishonorable end (1,18f; Wis 4,19), the author chooses Ps 69,25(26): "Let his camp be reduced to ruin with no one left living in it."   This verse is taken from the last half of the psalm, which is characterized as its "cursing half."   Likewise, the statement, "Let another take his office," is taken from a cursing psalm (Ps 109,8).   However, the use of such psalms and statements by Luke is not meant to pronounce judgment on Judas' eschatological fate as such, but rather to lead up to Peter's statement that someone should be elected to fill the position abandoned by Judas.   Therefore, this case cannot be considered an example of ecclesial discipline in the strict sense.   Nevertheless, it supplies a certain literary-theological basis or form for the first case of discipline described in Acts--namely, the death of Ananias and Sapphira (5,1-11).

Like Judas, Ananias and Sapphira seek to betray the Lord and his Church, and are cut off by sudden death.   Moreover, their crime involves money and business dealings over a field.   The new feature is that Peter's (i.e., the Church's) recognition of the

18. Cf. Rudolf Bultmann, Theologie des Neuen Testaments, (Tübin-
     gen, 1968[6]) 467-470.

deceiver's guilt is simultaneously ratified by God's punishing visitation. The episode should most likely be seen as part of a literary scheme illustrating the establishment of the Church in parallel to the founding of the Israelite nation (Jos 7). It is not meant as an ideal example for the Church to follow.[19] Accordingly, Achan and his family are destroyed at the hands of the Israelites because he had defied the ban which Joshua had placed on the spoils taken at Jericho (Jos 7,19ff). In like manner, Luke illustrates that the new assembly[20] of God cannot be defrauded even in material matters. But, in the case of the Church, God acts directly within the community.[21] The story of Ananias and Sapphira is obviously so thoroughly reconstructed and manipulated for Luke's interpretative purposes, that it is only possible to guess what the actual historical core (if any) of the account is.

Perhaps the first actual historical example of excommunication is to be found in Peter's reaction to Simon the Magician's attempt to buy spiritual powers (Acts 8,18-24). Peter's words to Simon take the form of a curse, but are not meant to have any effect other than the repentance of the recent Samaritan convert (vv. 20-24). Although it is not entirely clear, it seems that

---

19. Cf. D.S. Schaff, Discipline (Christian), in: ERE 4, 716. H. von Campenhausen (op. cit., 143f) correctly points out that such stories in Acts do not illustrate ecclesial discipline as such, but rather the holiness of the Church and the "Wunderkraft" of the Apostles.

20. Cf. Acts 5,11. This is Luke's first use of ἐκκλησία to refer to the Christian community. After this point, the term is relatively frequent in Acts.

21. This is part of Luke's overall-plan, which shows that the time of Israel was followed by the time of Christ Jesus, which is followed by the time of the Church. Cf. Hans Conzelmann, Die Mitte der Zeit, Studien zur Theologie des Lukas, (Tübingen, 1954).

Peter's harsh statement effected the hoped-for change of heart in Simon.[22] Bernhard Poschmann[23] considers this passage to be an example of a real act of excommunication. This may be so. However, Luke's purpose in telling the story is to demonstrate graphically that the wonders ascribed to those who worked them in the name of Christ were not to be viewed as some sort of magic.[24]

Another example of the early Church's encounter with a magician (Acts 13,6-12) shows that the Lord acts through his Church not only upon those within the Church, but also upon those outside of her. Paul is attempting to convert the proconsul, Sergius

---

22. The Western Text concludes the episode by adding that Simon wept bitterly and unceasingly. On the other hand, the Fathers of the early Church generally speak of Simon Magus as the founder of Gnosticism. However, it was normal for the Fathers to see the Apostolic times as formative for everything in the Church, including the rise of heresies. Cf. Johannes Munck, The Acts of the Apostles, (Anchor Bible 31), (New York, 1967) 74. As a matter of fact, Gnostic thought had a strong Jewish element; but it pre-dates Christianity and Simon Magus. Cf. R. McL. Wilson, Gnosis and the New Testament, (Oxford, 1968) 11,31. English speaking theologians generally distinguish between Gnosis and Gnosticism, and confine the latter to the elaborate systems of the 2nd century. Ibid., 7-10. German theologians tend to be less explicit about the difference of meaning between the two terms. But when they do distinguish, the terms are generally applied oppositely from the English usage. "Die gnostischen Phänomene pflegt man an Hand einzelner Anschauungen, die jeder Gnosis gemeinsam sind, unter dem Sammelnamen 'Gnostizismus' zusammenaufassen." Cf. K. Rahner/H. Vorgrimler, Gnosis, in: Kleines Theologisches Wörterbuch, (Basel, Vienna, 1967[6]) 143.

23. Cf. Paenitentia Secunda, die kirchliche Busse im ältesten Christentum bis Cyprian und Origines, (Bonn, 1940) 16.

24. In the New Testament, "magic" generally refers to astrology. Cf. Gerhard Delling, μάγος, in: ThWB 4, 362.

Paulus, but is opposed by the Jewish court advisor, Bar-Jesus (called "Elymas Magos" in Greek). For his opposition to the work of God, this magician[25] is termed a "false prophet" and "son of the devil" (vv. 6.10). Paul announces that the Lord will strike the opponent with blindness for a time, and Bar-Jesus is instantly struck blind so that he must grope about for someone to lead him by the hand (v. 11). With that, the proconsul is converted (v. 12).

Historically, very little can be made out of the story, which is structured very much like the accounts of Paul's own conversion (Acts 9,8f and pars.). Once again, Luke shows how God is active in and through his Church, the new Israel. The struggle between Paul and Bar-Jesus is that of a struggle between two religions, with Christianity clearly and dramatically triumphing. The magician's ill fate followed by the proconsul's conversion has the role of showing how God brings good out of evil situations.

b. Discipline toward the Jews and gentiles.

With the arrival of Paul on the missionary scene, Luke gives much of his attention to the cause and growth of the rift that gradually separated Judaism and Christianity as was already observed in the missionary's encounter with Bar-Jesus. After the Jews of Antioch had expelled Paul and Barnabas from the city, Luke comments that "they shook the dust from their feet in protest against them and went to Iconium" (Acts 13,50f). It is only in a very broad sense that one can speak of excommunication here. However, the use of the expression again emphasizes the early

25. Jewish magicians (i.e., astrologers) were spread throughout the Greek-Roman world of the New Testament. Cf. P. van Imschoot, Magic, in: BL 1075.

Church's awareness of herself as the new or true Israel. Thus, when the Jews of the old Israel willfully reject the Christian message, they expel themselves from the People of God and become "unclean."

The climax of the break with Judaism came in Corinth after Paul had preached Christ Jesus to the Jews of that city, who, in turn, contradicted Paul and blasphemed (Acts 18,5f). At that point, Paul takes off his cloak and shakes it in front of them declaring: "Your blood be upon your own head; I am rid (lit., clean) of you now and will go to the gentiles."[26] By shaking out his coat, Paul symbolizes his innocence of the Jews' refusal to accept the message offered them.[27] That is, they must accept full responsibility for the consequences of their action. The "blood" not only indicates their guilt, but also marks them out for God's punishment (Lv 20,9-16; 2 Sm 1,16; Mt 27,25).

This incident with the Jews of Corinth did not mean that Paul no longer sought to bring the message of Christ to Jews elsewhere. Consequently, Luke ends his history of the Church by placing Old Testament quotes in Paul's mouth concerning the Jews' blindness of heart (Acts 28,26f). Paul's last statement in the book explains what it means for him to go to the gentiles; namely, the salvation that once belonged to the Jews will now become the possession of the gentiles (v. 28).

Besides the problems caused by the nonbelieving Jews, the Church of Luke's time and earlier was confronted with the diffi-

---

26. τὸ αἷμα ὑμῶν ἐπὶ τὴν κεφαλὴν ὑμῶν. καθαρὸς ἐγὼ ἀπὸ τοῦ νῦν εἰς τὰ ἔθνη πορεύσομαι. It would be difficult to speak of an historical climax in the struggle between Judaism and Christianity. The scene Luke presents here is simply a dramatic climax.

27. Cf. SB 2, 747.

culties raised by many converted Jews who still insisted on whole or partial observance of the Mosaic Law. The problem became especially acute with the conversion of the gentiles to Christianity. According to Acts 15,1, the Judaizing party insisted that even gentile Christians had to be circumcised in order to be saved. The dispute which grew out of this claim eventually led to the Council of Jerusalem[28] for the purpose of reaching a common agreement over the binding-force of the Mosaic Law on the gentiles. There are three versions of the results of this meeting.

According to Paul's letter to the Galatians (2,10), it was decided that they (i.e., Paul, Barnabas and the gentile Christians) would not have to observe the cultic regulations of the Law, but that they should only remember to help the poor.[29] However, Luke draws a different conclusion in Acts 15,20.29; 21, 25. The Eastern Text of Acts, which is generally considered to be the "official" version, says that gentile Christians should refrain from food sacrificed to idols, from (consuming) blood,

---

28. It is difficult to say what the real nature of this meeting was which probably took place about A.D. 50.

29. The discrepancies between Paul's version and Luke's account of the Council of Jerusalem have raised a number of questions which have not yet been definitively answered by New Testament scholars: Is the meeting which Paul describes earlier than the council, even though Paul indicates that it was only his second meeting with the other Apostles in Jerusalem, and Luke describes the council as Paul's second meeting in Jerusalem? Was Paul even present for the council? Does the decree of the council as described by Luke have good historical roots that go back to the time of the meeting? The easiest solution is to say that the decree is largely the product of Luke's pen. It is also the most feasible explanation, but conclusive proof is lacking.

from the meat of strangled animals and from marriage within the forbidden degrees of relationship (πορνεία: 1 Cor 5,1; Mt 19,9). The Western Text,[30] however, reshapes the cultic regulations into moral stipulations--idolatry, murder and fornication--and re-enforces the ethical value of the prescriptions by adding the golden rule. No doubt these were the great sins of the pagans in Jewish eyes; and for a long time, the early Church was not always and everywhere sure that Christians who committed such sins could be readmitted to communion.[31] The ceremonial precepts of the Eastern Text require closer examination.

James concludes his speech[32] at the council with the recommendation that gentile Christians abstain from the above-mentioned ceremonial offenses, because there were Jewish preachers in every town for many generations already, and the Law is read aloud in the synagogues every Sabbath (15,20f). The implied solution to the problem treated at the council is that Jewish Christians should observe the Law of Moses in full, while gentile Christians should observe the Law of Moses in the way the Law itself prescribes for the "stranger within the gate" in Lv 17-18. In this way, Moses still remained the universal Law-giver.[33] Although

---

30. This text-form is found already early in the 2nd century. It deserves careful attention due to its antiquity and is to be preferred in several instances to the Eastern Text. Cf. Alfred Wikenhauser, Einleitung in das Neue Testament, (Basel, Freiburg, Vienna, 1961⁴) 244.

31. Cf. F.J. Foakes-Jackson, The Acts of the Apostles, (MNTC 5), (London, 1931) 140f.

32. Since the speech uses the LXX-version and the argument is built on a Hellenistic understanding and interpretation of the passage, it can scarcely stem from James. Cf. Ernst Haenchen, Die Apostelgeschichte, (KEKNT), (Göttingen, 1956) 410f.

33. Cf. J.C. O'Neill, The Theology of Acts in its Historical

these regulations were apparently not applied universally to
gentile Christians during Paul's lifetime,[34] there is no reason
to doubt that gentile Christians observed them at the time Acts
was written. Second century Christianity offers a number of
witnesses to the fact that upright Christians preferred to die
rather than eat blood or strangled meat.[35]

The meeting of the Apostles and the presbyters that is described in Acts 15 established a mile-stone in the Church's understanding of herself and of how she should conduct affairs. Most
important in a study on ecclesial discipline is the authority that
Luke claims for the council's decisions. This authority is none
other than the Holy Spirit himself (v. 28). In making this statement, Luke uses a formula (ἔδοξε τῷ πνεύματι τῷ ἁγίῳ καὶ ἡμῖν)
that is structured along the lines which the ancient πόλις used
in formulating its resolutions and decrees (ἔδοξε τῇ βουλῇ καὶ τῷ
δήμῳ). Just as the πόλις claimed "divine right" to legislate, so
now the ἐκκλησία (originally, a secular institution of the πόλις)
of Christians applies this right to itself in order to give "divine legitimacy" to its conciliar legislation.[36] Luke thereby

---

Setting, (London, 1961) 101f. Exegetes extract this Jewish
law for the gentiles from Lv 17,8.10-14; 18,6ff.

34. Cf. e.g. 1 Cor 10,25-27. However, in 1 Cor 5,1f, Paul applies
the ruling from Lv 18,8. But this ruling, even though it
would not be considered an incestuous marriage in most modern
societies--on the assumption that the wife of the man's
father is his stepmother and his father is dead--, is applied
by Paul simply because he felt such a marriage was immoral.
From this, it is clear that the socio-moral consciousness of
a certain culture can rightfully make claims upon the moral
conduct of Christians within that culture. Cf. e.g. 1 Cor 10,
27f.

35. Cf. E. Haenchen, op. cit., 413f.
36. Cf. Erik Peterson, Die Kirche, (München, 1929) 12-15.

defines the Church as a concrete, visible reality and institution that, on the one hand, can rightfully claim the hearing of men and, on the other, exclude from its ranks those who refuse to acknowledge that it is the Holy Spirit that speaks through the legislation that is enacted by the Church's ultimate apostolic governing body. This divine guidance, a theme that Luke already establishes in the story of Pentecost (Acts 2,1-4) is the ultimate deduction that can be drawn from the concept of a Church built upon the principle that only those who accept Jesus as the Christ are eligible for the benefits accruing to the new Israel. Already in Peter's second public discourse (Acts 3,12-26), Luke develops the "exclusiveness" of the Church by interpreting the prophet promised in Dt 18,15.18 to be none other than Jesus, whom the Israelites have rejected and delivered to execution. Those who now refuse to listen to and obey this prophet "will be destroyed from the people."[37] With that, the author of Acts indicates that the Church, as the new people of God, has the right and duty to exclude from her numbers all those who refuse to accept Jesus as the Christ.[38]

---

37. Cf. Acts 3,23 (Lv 23,29): ἔσται δὲ πᾶσα ψυχὴ ἥτις ἐὰν μὴ ἀκούσῃ τοῦ προφήτου ἐκείνου ἐξολεθρευθήσεται ἐκ τοῦ λαοῦ.

38. For a fuller treatment of the passage in question, cf. Carlo M. Martini, L'esclusione dalla comunità del popolo di Dio e il nuovo Israele secondo Atti 3,23, in: Biblica 50 (1969) 1-14.

DISCIPLINE IN THE PAULINE AND PASTORAL LETTERS

1. Preliminary Remarks

The special value of the collection of epistles found in the New Testament is that they furnish the reader with a direct insight into the actual life of the Church at the time of their writing. This evaluation, of course, is applicable only to those epistles which are truly letters, and not just literary works written in the form of a letter. When the time, place, circumstances, author, etc., of a letter are known, then the "special value" of the epistle is greatly increased. St. Paul's letters, the oldest complete compositions found in the New Testament, are of this nature, even though "internal evidence" is usually all that the theologian has to work with in determining the time, etc., of the letters that are generally ascribed to Paul. The so-called Pastoral Letters are much less readily attributed to Paul than in previous times. But some literary connections and influences do exist between Paul and the Pastorals which make it feasible to treat them in one and the same chapter.

The divisions made in the treatment of Paul's letters are meant to present the material chronologically and, to a lesser degree, systematically. The major systematic division made in this chapter between problems of moral discipline and problems of doctrinal discipline can only be given along very general lines since Paul himself did not make a sharp distinction between the two. One reason for this is that, in practice, very little distinction could be made or seen. Heretics were at first considered moral perverts because their version of Christianity very seldom left the moral character of contemporary Christianity intact. The "immoral Christian" was simply one who did not meet the moral standards demanded of him because he found them too difficult or disagreeable; whereas, the "unorthodox Christian" was one who supported his mode of conduct in moral issues by means of a philosophy or system of doctrine that permitted what was offensive to other Christians of that time. This, of course, raises the question: "What is orthodoxy, and by what norm did early Christians judge orthodoxy?" Only a brief and incomplete answer can be attempted here.

From a doctrinal point of view, the first converts to Christianity had only to confess that Jesus was the Christ. But this immediately implied repentance[1] followed by Baptism and the reception of the Holy Spirit (Acts 2,38). At this level, there is a complete unity of _fides quae creditur_ and _fides qua creditur_. Faith in Jesus as the Christ meant the acceptance of a way of life that is identified with truth itself (Gal 2,14-16; Jn 6,69). Orthodoxy thus had a strong ethical character and could not be separated from correct conduct of life (1 Jn 2,3f). But be it a question of doctrine or morals, the problem cannot be separated from that of living authority; for no written word, spoken tradition or formerly living authority can, of itself, enforce itself as normative for the present. As has already been seen, Luke offered the solution to the question of authority by appeal to the Council of Jerusalem and the Holy Spirit (Acts 15,28). St.

---

1. Since the repentance spoken of the Gospels includes the pious as well as the sinner, it does not mean so much a turning away from the past, but rather a turning toward the future by opening up oneself unreservedly to the kingdom of God. Cf. P. Hoffman, _Umkehr_, in: _HThG_ 2, 721ff. In Acts 2,38, it means to have a change of mind about having originally rejected Jesus and, positively stated, to confess him to be the Christ.

Paul was very much aware of the principle of authority also. He does not threaten excommunication (either ecclesial or eschatological) to those who do not follow the regulations that he lays down "by right of his authority." But it is a different story when his right to that authority is challenged.[2] With that, full "orthodoxy" includes adherence to right authority as well as right doctrine and morals.

Once the claim to the right of authority has been recognized and accepted by those concerned, the danger of being unseated by a rival is greatly reduced. But the death of the one in authority

---

2. Cf. 2 Cor 10-13; 1 Cor 14,37f; H. von Campenhausen, op. cit., 48f. In 1 Cor 14,37f. Paul's statement, εἰ δὲ τις ἀγνοεῖ, ἀγνοεῖται, sounds very much like a command to the Corinthians to expel or at least avoid anyone who contests his right to establish ecclesial regulations as κυρίου ἐντολή. However, the expression might have only eschatological implications if it is to be taken as the equivalent of "not know" in Mt 7,23. Cf. R. Bultmann, ἀγνοέω, in: ThWB 1, 117. To return to the question of Paul's authority, it may be that he purposely mentions that he shook hands in partnership with "James, Cephas and John" (in lieu of an imposition of hands from the Apostles) to show that his calling from God before the gates of Damascus put him on a par with the other Apostles. Cf. Johannes Neumann, Der Spender der Firmung in der Kirche des Abendlandes bis zum Ende des kirchlichen Altertums, (Meitingen, 1963) 31-33. On the other hand, it must not be overlooked that Paul, in spite of his insistence that he is a fully legitimate apostle of Christ, never claims to be exactly the same "type" of apostle as is characterized by the group of the "Twelve Apostles" and all that the number twelve implies for the legitimate connection between the Kingdom which Christ preached and the Church which came in its stead. Neither Paul nor later tradition points to a "Pauline succession" that belongs to the foundational structure of the Church in the same way as does "apostolic succession" from the Twelve Apostles. For this reason, it is by no means improper to say that the essence of the Church is tied to "the Twelve" as such rather than to Paul. Cf. E. Peterson, op. cit., 10f.

very often triggers a crisis of authority as regards successor-
ship to the position of authority and the nature of that authority
thereafter. The story of this transition is to be read between
the lines in the Pastoral Letters and in many other writings of
early Christianity. And sometimes, as in 3 Jn 9-12, it develops
into a struggle that is placed right on the line for all to see.
This era is generally referred to as the "period of episcopalism."
The question of authority and its many ramifications cannot be
pursued any further here. It is sufficient for the moment to note
what has been stated above and to see it as the "canvas" upon
which the picture of ecclesial discipline, including eucharistic
excommunication, must be painted.

2. The Pauline Epistles

a. Letters before Paul's first imprisonment.

a). Problems of moral-ethical discipline.

1). Letters to the Thessalonians.

Paul's two letters to the Thessalonians are the earliest complete compositions to be found in the New Testament.[3] The second
letter followed the first by perhaps just a few months, and contains a note of concern about certain parties who were causing
disorder in the community by their overly enthusiastic teaching
about the proximity of Christ's second coming. As a result, the
Thessalonian community was in danger of breaking into factions because some of its members, believing that the end was very near,
refused to work and provide for their own welfare. They thereby

---

3. That is, about A.D. 51 or 52. Unless otherwise stated, the
   dates and data for the New Testament writings are those proposed by A. Wikenhauser, op. cit.

became a burden to the rest of the community (2 Thes 3,6-12).
Paul's statement that the second coming must be preceded by certain signs and events and therefore no one should become overly
expectant or think that the second coming has already arrived, is
meant to bring the enthusiasts to the sober realization that it
is still necessary that everyone provide for his own future sus-
tinence (2,1-4).

Those who fail to heed Paul's admonitions are to be noted;
that is, their names are to be announced to the entire community so
that corrective steps can be taken. They are to be avoided and
shamed (3,6.14), and, if necessary, to be deprived of the community's food (3,10). But they are to be admonished as brothers
rather than enemies (3,16). These are the prescriptions which the
synagogue used in imposing the ban.[4] However, the prescription
that those who refuse to work are to get nothing to eat (3,10) indicates the sharing of common wealth and follows more closely the
regulations found in Qumran (1 QS 7,2ff). But at Qumran, the refusal to allow an offender to share in the "pure meal of the congregation" is cultic in that it is for "the sake of his soul"
(1 QS 7,3). In the case of the Thessalonians, the discipline is
not of a truly religious nature since it does not deprive the offender of anything proper to Christian life as such.[5] Nevertheless,
the character of the discipline is formal and seems to follow the
same course layed down in Mt 18,15-18; for already in 1 Thes 5,14,
Paul asks that the disorderly persons (ἄτακτοι) be given a warning.

---

4. Cf. <u>SB</u> 3, 642.
5. Cf. Guiseppe D'Ercole, <u>Penitenza Canonico-Sacramentale, dalle
   Origini alla Pace Costantiniana</u>, (<u>Communio</u> 3), (Rome, 1963)
   39.

Except for the irregularities caused by the expectation of the second coming, Paul sees no further problems at Thessalonica; and the problem itself is not really of a doctrinal nature as such, even though it is caused by a false understanding of the future. However, it is important to notice that Paul asks that the ban be imposed in view of the "teaching" he has given.[6] Therefore, he means that his teaching, even when primarily of a practical nature as in this case (2 Thes 3,7-9), is to be recognized as normative.

2). The First Letter to the Corinthians, spring, A.D. 57.

This community of Christians, situated in a large commercial city, was affected by all the vices and difficulties that go with life in a populous port city (actually, two ports) full of detached people. Perhaps as high as two-thirds of the population belonged to the slave class or was otherwise very poor. It is not surprising then that the Church at Corinth seemed to have more than its share of moral problems and that factions were common in the community.

In 1 Cor 5,2, we are confronted for the first time with an explicit, unequivocal statement concerning the fact of real (i.e., full) excommunication. Appalled that the Corinthians are even proud of their tolerance toward the incestuous man, Paul says they should be mournful instead, "so that the one doing this might be put away from your midst."[7] The practice of such an excommunica-

---

6. Cf. 2 Thes 3,6: Παραγγέλλομεν δὲ ὑμῖν, ἀδελφοί, ἐν ὀνόματι τοῦ κυρίου Ἰησοῦ Χριστοῦ, στέλλεσθαι ὑμᾶς ἀπὸ παντὸς ἀδελφοῦ ἀτάκτως περιπατοῦντος καὶ μὴ κατὰ τὴν παράδοσιν ἣν παρελάβετε παρ' ἡμῶν. This is comparable to the ban that was imposed in Judaism when someone chose to disregard a ruling imposed by a doctor of the Law. Cf. SB 3, 642.

7. Cf. 1 Cor 5,2: ἵνα ἀρθῇ ἐκ μέσου ὑμῶν ὁ τὸ ἔργον τοῦτο πράξας.

tion was apparently already known to the Corinthians since Paul is
surprised that the step has not yet been taken to expel the offender. This is the obligation of the entire community. Therefore,
Paul charges them to assemble in the name of the Lord (v. 5) and
"hand the fellow over to Satan unto the destruction of the flesh,
so that the spirit may be saved in the day of the Lord."[8]

Cf. also 1 Cor 5,13. This excommunication is to be considered
as the counterpart to Baptism in that it is equivalent to being estranged from Christ (Gal 5,4) and being handed back to
the powers of darkness and the consequences of one's sins
(Col 1,13). However, it is not the annulment of one's Baptism,
but rather the giving over of someone to God's "wrath," which
is primarily for the sake of the sinner's salvation and not
his damnation. Cf. E. Käsemann, Sätze, 251f. In this article,
Käsemann seeks to show that the eschatological administration
of divine judgment preached by the prophets and charismatics
of the early Church deeply affected and formed the first Christian community, so that this preaching formed the basis for
all later legislation in the ordering of the community and
even of ecclesial (canon) law (258). In the New Testament
Church, this legislation is not a mere function of the Spirit,
but rather the Spirit (that is, the Lord's presence in the
Church: 1 Cor 5,4) "ist Garant und sanktionierende Instanz
des Rechtes" (256). This position in regard to the early
Church's "divine legislation" has been challenged by Klaus
Berger, Zu den sogenannten Sätzen Heiligen Rechts, in: NTS 17
(1970) 10-40, who mainly takes issue with Käsemann over the
literary origin of such "Sätze." K. Berger ascribes them
chiefly to Wisdom literature, and thus holds that they are
to be interpreted as exhortation (Paränese) rather than as
statements of early Christian legislation placed under divine
sanction. However, apart from the literary origin of such
statements in the New Testament, it is clear enough that the
early Christians, including Paul, saw in them more than mere
exhortation and advice.

8. παραδοῦναι τὸν τοιοῦτον τῷ σατανᾷ εἰς ὄλεθρον τῆς σαρκός,
    ἵνα τὸ πνεῦμα σωθῇ ἐν τῇ ἡμέρᾳ τοῦ κυρίου. This does not only
    mean the flesh "as a source of moral evil (e.g., Rm 7,5), but
    the physical flesh itself." Cf. C.K. Barrett, A Commentary on
    the First Epistle to the Corinthians, (BNTC), (London, 1968)
    126.

Although the notion of handing someone over to Satan cannot be
traced back further than the third century A.D. in the literature
of rabbinic Judaism, it was most likely a common expression in antiquity.[9] The curses employed at Qumran (1 QS 2,5-9.11ff) are important in this regard. They do not actually speak of handing anyone
over to Satan, but rather to the lot of the Children of Darkness,
which means, however, to hand someone over to the realm of Satan.
The peculiarity about Paul's employment of the expression is that
it makes Satan a partner in the sinner's ultimate salvation rather
than loss.[10] This aspect, however, is not entirely foreign to the
Old Testament; for Satan also torments Job physically, but can in
no way effect a separation between God and him. Paul ascribed some
of his own torments to Satan (2 Cor 12,7). Consequently, the term
does not mean to be possessed by Satan, but only to be afflicted by
him (Lk 13,16). But in so far as it implies excommunication, it
means "to be excluded from the sphere in which Christ's work was
operative" and "to be thrust back into that in which Satan still
exercised authority."[11] This authority is not absolute, however,
because Satan, as a punishing angel, becomes a tool to save the
offender while his flesh is destroyed with physical suffering. Although this means both sickness and death, it does not follow that
Paul necessarily intends his order to be taken as a principle of
ecclesiastical law and discipline stating that such a sinner is to
be permanently excommunicated from the Church. This is not the object of the course of action which Paul recommends at this point.

---

9. Cf. Friedrich Büchsel, παραδίδωμι, in: ThWB 2, 1972.
10. Cf. Werner Foerster, σατανᾶς, in ThWB 7, 162.
11. Cf. C.K. Barrett, op., cit., 126.

Rather, the expulsion of the incestuous man is to be interpreted in the light of Paul's theology of sin and death as explained in his Epistle to the Romans.[12]

Accordingly, Paul makes a mystical identification or connection between death, sin, the Law, Christ's death, Christian Baptism and the Christian's own physical death in Christ (Rm 5,12-8, 13). The Christian, because he has been baptized into Christ's death, should now be dead to sin just as Christ is dead to sin (6,1-6.10f). At the same time, however, death to sin is also a process in the life of the Christian (6,12-19); and it is one's physical death itself that puts an end to one's sinning (6,7). However, Christ's death and the Christian's Baptism into that death has freed the Christian from slavery to sin (6,3.16-18). The individual's salvation now depends on his continued union with Christ through the imitation of his death (6,5). Consequently, when Paul commands the Corinthians to hand the sinner over to Satan for the destruction of his flesh so that his spirit may be saved on the day of the Lord (1 Cor 5,5), he implies the hope that the affliction and possible death which Satan may bring upon the sinner will cause him to stop sinning, with the result that there will still be, so to speak, quantitatively enough Christian (who is already qualitatively saved) left in the man so that his spirit (that is, the Christian as a converted person who is no longer subject to sin) may ultimately be saved. The present condemnation of the incestous man is meant to prevent his ultimate eschatolo-

---

12. The present writer is most grateful to Prof. Dr. Otto Betz for the information that follows in the next paragraph. However, the actual exegesis is that of the present writer's, who is therefore responsible for any errors or inaccuracies in the interpretation.

gical condemnation. From the <u>ecclesial</u> point of view (in contrast to the soteriological aspect), the purpose of the excommunication is to preserve the purity of the community, as implied in the concept of putting sinners away from the midst of God's people (1 Cor 5,2.6f.13; Dt 13,6; Lv 18,24-30). This process is similar to the graphic portrayal of the Holy Spirit's cleansing of the first Christian community through the deaths of Ananias and Sapphira (Acts 5,1-11).

The process of excommunication that Paul orders to be undertaken is both formal and cultic. The action taken is first and foremost effected by the Spirit--that is, Christ as he is present in the Church. Therefore, Paul need not be present.[13] However, his reference to his spiritual presence (v. 4) gives the added touch of authority to the process to be undertaken.

By way of comment to the orders which he has just given the Corinthians, Paul reminds them that he had written to them at an earlier date[14] to say that immoral persons, usurers, idolators, slanderers, drunkards, and dishonest persons are to be deprived to the intimate associations of the community, including the common table.[15] There may be more than just an accidental or indirect

---

13. Cf. E. Käsemann, <u>Sätze</u>, 251f.
14. On the problem of the lost epistles to the Corinthians cf. A. Wikenhauser, <u>op</u>. <u>cit</u>.,, 276, 283f.
15. Cf. 1 Cor 5,11. There are three possible ways of understanding the statement, τῷ τοιούτῳ μηδὲ συνεσθίειν: 1. neutrally, "and not to eat with such a one"; 2. consequently, "and not even to eat with such a one"; 3. primarily, "and especially not to eat with such a one." The third possibility is the least probable grammatically, but the most probable logically since Paul's command not to associate intimately (μὴ συναναμίγνυσθαι) with the offender would exclude table companion-

reference to the Eucharist here. From 1 Cor 11,17ff, it is known
with certainty that the Corinthian Christians held the agape and
Eucharist together. Thus, anyone excluded from the meal was <u>a
fortiori</u> excluded from the Eucharist. The eucharistic character
of the command that those placed under ban for the above-mentioned
offenses be excluded from the meals of the community may be implied when Paul speaks of throwing out the old leaven in order to
feast on unleavened bread.[16] In spite of Paul's metaphorical uses
of leavened and unleavened bread at this point, it is still quite
possible that he has the Eucharist in mind just as he has Baptism
in mind in 6,9-11 when he tells the Corinthians that immoral persons, idolators, thieves, etc., will not possess the kingdom of
God.

In chapter 10 of this same letter, Paul speaks very openly of
the Eucharist in its role of defining and limiting Christian life
in regard to paganism. Because the Christians have the Eucharist,
so Paul argues, they cannot share the table of demons in pagan sacrifices and still be partakers of the Lord's table (v. 21). The
theological basis for this statement is that the Eucharist gives
the Christian κοινωνία in Christ's body and blood (v. 16). Just
as the Jews become partakers (κοινωνοί) of the altar[17] through

----

ship from the very beginning. Moreover, Paul's Jewish background and propensity to employ Jewish discipline would make
it a self-understood fact that expulsion from the common table
would be, as at Qumran, a first rather than a last step in the
excommunication of a sinner. It should be further noted that
Paul's catalogue of serious sins is the same for the sins that
exclude one from the kingdom of God and those which excommunicate one (by avoidance) from the community. Cf. Gal 5,19-21;
Eph 5,5; 1 Cor 6,9f; Col 3,5-8.

16. Cf. M. Goguel, <u>op</u>. <u>cit</u>., 161-63; W. Elert, <u>op</u>. <u>cit</u>., 71f.
17. Cf. 1 Cor 10,18: οὐχ οἱ ἐσθίοντες τὰς θυσίας κοινωνοὶ τοῦ

their sacrifices and the pagans become associates (κοινωνοί) of demons through their sacrifices, so the Christian finds union with Christ through the Eucharist (vv. 16.18.20). It is this concept of sacrifice that lies behind Paul's insistence that there can be no middle ground between belonging to Christ and participating in pagan sacrifice.[18] The nature of the κοινωνία which Christians

---

θυσιαστηρίου εἰσίν; Paul certainly does not mean that Jewish sacrifice only achieved communion with the altar but not with God. If that were the case, then he could not make the sort of objection he does make concerning Christian participation in pagan sacrifice. However, the expression, "associates of the altar," prevents the example of Jewish sacrifice from overshadowing or obtaining equal rank with the Eucharist. Furthermore, Paul seems to have a more positive reason for using the expression, because he must use such an image in order to make a comparison and a contrast between the Eucharist and Jewish sacrifice. The role of the altar is to pinpoint the "mechanism of unity." That is, if one has union with the altar, he also is somehow included in all the sacrifices performed on the altar; and, above all, he has union with the divinity honored in the sacrifices. But the basis of this union with the divinity depends on the altar's dedication and not on the sacrifice itself, since the sacrifice is in turn dedicated to the divinity by the altar. Cf. Mt 23,19. Since Judaism offers sacrifice only to Yahweh, there is only one altar of sacrifice for them. That is, qualitatively there was only one altar even before Judaism had concentrated all its sacrificial cult in the one temple upon the quantitatively one altar of holocaust in Jerusalem. By referring to the (qualitatively) one loaf of the Eucharist, Paul is able to transfer this entire corpus of ideas to the Eucharist.

18. Again, Paul's Jewish background makes this especially clear. A Jew could eat meat acquired in a pagan shop only if a Jew had slaughtered the animal, if the meat has not yet come into contact with meat from a pagan sacrifice, and if the shopkeeper could affirm that forbidden meats, such as pork, were not sold there. Above all, a Jew's participation in a pagan sacrifice was immediately construed as a sign of his apostasy

have by way of the Eucharist has a twofold character, uniting
Christians as one body with Christ and uniting Christ to all communicants so as to form them into one body.[19]

When the concepts are seen from the point of view of discipline and excommunication, it is clear that Paul means that idolatry separates one entirely from Christ and his Body, the Church.
This does not mean, however, that Paul rules out the possibility
of repentance and readmission into the community. Eucharistic excommunication, for as long as it lasts in any given case, is meant
to be an empirical expression of the separation from Christ (and
the Church) that the sinner experiences through serious sin.[20] In
the case of those Corinthians who thought the Eucharist gave them

---

from Judaism. Cf. SB 3, 419 f. Paul is unbending only in the
case of participation in pagan sacrifice. The Christian view
of foods in general is found in 1 Tm 4,4, where it is explained that every creature of God is good and nothing need be rejected provided only that grace (thanksgiving) is said.

19. Johannes Weiss, Der Erste Korintherbrief, (KEKNT), (Göttingen,
1910) 260, is quite correct in saying that κοινωνία is the
presupposition for partaking in a sacrifice. However, this
does not exclude the κοινωνία that is achieved through participation in a sacrifice. It is this aspect of the Eucharist
that Paul is obviously talking about here. This is made possible by the fact that the covenant theology of the Christians
forms a common bond between Baptism and the Eucharist, so that
the Eucharist is seen as a continuous renewal of Baptism itself. Baptism is the individual's entrance into the New Covenant. With that, the individual becomes an "associate"
(κοινωνός) of the Eucharist. But the ultimate goal of becoming a member of the "association" is the achievement of the
κοινωνία acquired only by actual participation in the Eucharist. This is what Paul means and explains when he speaks of
the κοινωνία in Christ's body and blood which is had through
participation ἐκ τοῦ ἑνὸς ἄρτου. Cf. 1 Cor 10,16f.

20. Cf. W. Doskocil, op. cit., 76.

physical immortality,[21] the realization that this sacrament does not produce union with Christ apart from a life of obedience to his commands[22] must have been very sobering. At least this is the effect Paul hopes to achieve when he asks the Corinthians if they are provoking the Lord to jealousy with their idolatry, and if they are stronger than he is (v. 22). This is a reference to what Paul had just previously told his readers--namely, that, even though the Israelites in the desert ate spiritual food (manna) and drank water from the spiritual rock (which Paul identifies with Christ) after having been baptized with Moses in the cloud and in the sea, God did not spare their lives when they fell into various sins (vv. 1-10). These things all happened as a type and were meant to serve as a lesson for Christians (v. 11). Therefore, Christians who fall into serious sins cannot expect to escape the "jealousy" of God simply because they have been baptized and eat "spiritual food" (the Eucharist).[23]

The relationship between the Eucharist and discipline is explicitly treated in 1 Cor 11,27-34. It may be that the problems which ultimately prompted Paul to speak of this aspect of the Eucharist were founded in a Gnostic movement at Corinth.[24] The factions (αἱρέσεις) spoken of in 11,19 perhaps refer to actual schools of thought that were forming in Corinth in opposition to the "public and lawful" gatherings of the Corinthian Christians.[25]

---

21. Cf. M. Goguel, op. cit., 66f.
22. Cf. E. Käsemann, Anliegen, 271.
23. Cf. M. Goguel, op. cit., 165.
24. Cf. Karl H. Schelkle, Das Neue Testament, seine literarische und theologische Geschichte, (Kevelaer, 1966) 147.
25. Cf. P. Neuenzeit, op. cit., 27f. The relationship of the four party-divisions found in 1 Cor 1,12 with the factions mentioned in 11,18f is uncertain.

However, since the problem which Paul is trying to correct at this point is of an ethical rather than doctrinal nature, the passage in question will be treated here.

Seizing up the "judgment character" of the sacraments, Paul notes that the unworthy recipient of the Eucharist calls down Christ's blood upon himself for failing to realize that the Lord's death forces one to decide either for or against Christ--either to use his death as a means to salvation and life, or else to side with those who condemned him to death and, as a result, called down a curse upon themselves. Therefore, "the Eucharist is an occasion of judgment."[26] First of all, the recipient must judge himself in regard to his attitude toward his neighbor. This is a voluntary anticipation of the more severe judgment he would otherwise receive directly from the Lord, which is, nevertheless, hopefully for the ultimate good of the person concerned (vv. 31f). Although the disciplinary aspect of the Eucharist is still seen in an eschatological perspective, the effects of the Lord's judgment are not reserved for the "Last Day," but are experienced in sickness and death in the present age (v. 30).

The punishment that Paul speaks of supposedly results from unworthy participation in the Eucharist. This implies that if the unworthy party did not receive the Eucharist, he would be spared the punishment even though it is the Lord himself who metes out the chastisement. Paul avoids pointing the finger of guilt at anyone personally since he does not say that all cases of illness and death at Corinth are to be attributed to unworthy communions. But in "many" instances, this is the reason (v. 30). For these persons, the Eucharist was more like consuming poison than "the medicine of life."

---

26. Cf. C.D.F. Moule, op. cit., 472.

The notion that a food or drink could have toxic effects for those who are not properly morally disposed is basic to the practice of "trial by ordeal" found in the Old Testament (Nm 5,11-31; Ex 22,20) and still practiced during Paul's time.[27] Judaism had originally borrowed the custom from its neighbors, but it was adapted to the Jewish religious system so that Yahweh, and not the potion itself, was regarded as effecting the punishment of the guilty party.[28] Such a trial by ordeal could not be called "magic" in so far as the Jews saw no disproportion between the effect and the cause. Consumption of the harmless potion was not the <u>cause</u> of the ill effect, but only an <u>occasion</u> of Yahweh's judgment. In like manner, Paul sees the Eucharist as an occasion of the Lord's judgment.

Nevertheless, one must not overlook the fact that Paul says that unworthy communion in the Eucharist makes the recipient who is already guilty of abusing his brother also "guilty of the Lord's body and blood";[29] that is, he becomes guilty of sharing in the murder of Christ. Therefore, Paul does not consider the Eucharist itself to be a mere "potion" that Christians take in order

---

27. Various forms of trial by ordeal were sanctioned by the Church and state in the Middle Ages and exist even today in primitive societies. It was suspended in Judaism between A.D. 60-70 "because adulterers became too numerous and it hence lost its ordeal character," and "it was efficacious only when the husband was innocent." Cf. <u>The Jewish Encyclopedia</u>, 9 (New York, 1901) 427f.

28. Since Paul sees no contradiction in showing that Satan is sometimes God's tool (1 Cor 5,5), C.K. Barrett (<u>op</u>. <u>cit</u>., 275) is probably correct when he says in reference to 1 Cor 11,30: "Those who abused the Lord's table were exposing themselves to the power of demons, who were taken to be the cause of physical disease."

29. Cf. 1 Cor 11,27: ἔνοχος ἔσται τοῦ σώματος καὶ τοῦ αἵματος τοῦ κυρίου.

to separate the guilty from the nonguilty. He means to imply real moral guilt for partaking unworthily of the Eucharist. In the ordinary trial by ordeal, it was not a question of acquiring <u>further</u> guilt in drinking the potion, but only of assuring punishment for the offender's crime. The additional guilt that the Christian acquires for unworthy communion, as Paul sees it, must force one to say that Paul attributed magical effects to the Eucharist unless he himself believed in Christ's real presence in this sacrament.

   b). <u>Problems of doctrinal discipline</u>.

     1). <u>Letter to the Galatians, about A.D. 55 or 56</u>.

In this epistle, Paul is found in the midst of his struggles against a party of Jewish Christians who wanted to turn the Church into a Jewish sect by forcing all Christians to observe the Law.[30] The Apostle to the gentiles immediately sees the real theological danger of this movement because of its nullifying effects on faith and Christ's death. In no other letter is Paul so harsh and even sarcastic. The brief introduction offers no praise for the Galatians. Rather, it goes at once to the heart of the matter by stating the theses which the letter is to defend: Paul's authentic apostleship, and Jesus as the real and only saviour (1,1-4). Paul is astounded that the Galatians have so quickly forgotten the Good News which he brought to them and have allowed themselves to be led astray by some troublemakers preaching another version of the Gospel (1,6f). The agitators apparently claimed that Paul preached a Gospel that, by abandoning the Law and its severity,

---

30. These agitators may have been infected with Gnostic elements. Cf. K.H. Schelkle, <u>op. cit.</u>, 140.

was only geared to bring him popularity rather than to please God (v. 10). Paul retorts that, if he or even an angel from heaven[31] were to preach a Gospel other than the one preached earlier by him, he or that angel would be ἀνάθεμα (vv. 8f).

No definition of anathema is ever undertaken by Paul, and the four cases where he uses the expression (Rm 9,3; 1 Cor 12,3; 16,22; Gal 1,8f) do not suffice to give a complete theology of the concept in its New Testament setting.[32] In the case under consideration and in 1 Cor 16,22, Paul has concrete instances in mind. The anathemas he pronounces on these occasions have real implications, which, however, are not at all clear as regards their practical

---

31. The notion of an angel coming from heaven to earth to preach the Gospel seems to embrace a number of popular Jewish ideas: e.g., that angels gave Moses the Law (Gal 3,19; Acts 7,38), that Moses, Elias or some prophet would return to preach the Law anew (Mal 3,1; Is 40,3), or that an angel would teach the Law to the gentiles. Cf. SB 3, 554-56.

32. Cf. W. Doskocil, op. cit., 57f. John Bligh, Galatians, a Discussion of St. Paul's Epistle, (Householder Commentaries 1), (London, 1969) 91, points out that the anathema of 1 Cor 16,22 (cf. also Didache 10,6) is part of the liturgy and thus the "nonliturgical" anathema of Gal 1,8f "probably means that the Galatians must not allow Judaizing teachers to partake of their Eucharist." He finds this to be parallel with Apc 22,15, which lists a number of types of sinners which will be excluded from the New Jerusalem and which supposedly "warns the congregation that a Christian who commits certain grave sins must not approach the Eucharist and is excluding himself from the kingdom of God." However, the present writer considers it highly unlikely that Paul or the writer of the Apocalypse has the Eucharist so directly in mind in these two passages even though Apc 22,15 may very well have its "Sitz im Leben" in the early Christian celebration of the Eucharist. To this extent, J. Bligh's statement is correct, but it should not be construed to mean that the writer of the Apocalypse intended that meaning in Apc 22,15.

execution. Perhaps some hint as to what Paul means by the term
in these cases is to be found in his own life.

As a zealous Jew and Pharisee, he was a fanatic "inquisitor"
of the "Nazarene sect." After his conversion, he himself suffered many things from his Jewish compatriots, who placed him
under the ban and swore to kill him for preaching a message other
than the Mosaic Law.[33] Certainly, the implications of such a ban
pronounced under oath (i.e., an anathema) were well known to Paul
and his churches. It was not necessary for him to state in words
that the preacher of heresy is to be fully excommunicaed and abandoned to the Lord for punishment. In Jewish thought, one who
fell under the anathema became unclean and had to be destroyed
from the midst of the people. Moreover, anyone associating with
the banned person fell under the same ban. In its Christian context, then, Paul uses the term in cases concerning offenses of
such a serious nature that the person must be avoided by all and
fully excommunicated from Christian life at least until the wrongdoer repents.

Once the fact has been stated that those who preach another
Gospel are to be cursed (1,9), Paul proceeds to demonstrate how
those who insist on keeping the Law are indeed under a curse (3,
10-14). To this end, he employs the most devastating of all forms
of argument; that is, by accepting the zeal of the Judaizing party
for the Law, he uses their own sources to prove that the Law is
not binding on Christians. As the Law itself says, one must

---

33. Cf. Acts 21,28; 23,12-15. This event supposedly took place
    shortly after Paul had written the Letter to the Galatians,
    but it still witnesses to the character of the Jewish ban
    during Paul's life.

observe everything in the Law to avoid being cursed (v. 10; Dt 27, 26). Among the prescriptions is that a man must live by faith in order to be justified.[34] Yet, the Law itself does not rest on faith, because it claims that he who does the works of the Law shall live by them (v. 12; Lv 18,5). Therefore, those who rely on the works of the Law rather than faith in Christ are cursed (v. 10); for no one can free himself from the curse of the Law[35]

---

34. Strictly speaking, the prescription is not taken from the Book of the Law, but from the prophet Habakkuk (2,4). But Paul uses the term in its broad sense so as to include the entire Old Testament. Cf. Martin Noth, "Die mit des Gesetzes Werken umgehen, die sind unter dem Fluch", (Theologische Bücherei, Neudrucke und Berichte aus dem 20. Jahrhundert 6: Martin Noth, Gesammelte Studien zum Alten Testament), (Munich, 1957) 156. Paul's exegesis at this point rests upon the LXX-rendering of Hb 2,4, which reads ἐκ πίστεώς μου (Paul deletes μοῦ in Gal 3, 11) in place of the Hebrew "from his faithfulness" (באמונתו).

35. Cf. Gal 3,13: κατάρα τοῦ νόμου. This expression is simply a compact way of saying that those under the Law are likewise included in the Old Covenant, which was concluded under an oath (Ex 24,3-8; Dt 28,15-29,1.9-30,20). But an oath always implies a sanction which calls down a curse upon the one who is unfaithful to his sworn word. Cf. H. Brichto, op. cit., 27-38. This is what Paul has in mind when he speaks of "the curse of the Law." However, it is not clear if this should be taken as a subjective or objective genitive. M. Noth (op. cit., 171) explains how the Law is a curse to those who are under it (Dt 27,26; Gal 3,10) since, in reality, the Law does not claim that one can earn the blessing by performing the prescribed works of the Law. It is by right of the Covenant itself-- therefore, through God's free choice in making his promises-- that the Jew receives the blessing. However, a transgression against the Law brings with it a curse even though fulfillment of the Law as such does not produce the blessing as if the Law-abiding Jew had thereby earned it. If this is also Paul's understanding of the curse of the Law--and from all indications, that is the case--, then κατάρα τοῦ νόμου is to be understood as an objective genitive. That is, the Law itself is not a curse, but can only produce a curse upon those who transgress

except through Christ, who is able to free Christians from the
Law because he himself became a curse and thus died outside of
the Law.[36] In this way, even the gentiles can have access to the
blessing of Abraham (v. 14). But since no one is really a keeper
of the Law unless he observes the whole Law, the implication is
that even the Judaizers should know that the circumcision of the
gentile Christians is religiously useless. Moreover, since they
themselves do not keep the whole Law (6,13), there is utterly no
logic in their insisting upon circumcision for the gentiles.

This Christian freedom from the Law that Paul insists upon explains his boldness in withstanding Peter to his face for preaching in practice a different Gospel than the Gospel of truth
preached by Paul (2,11-14). Peter's improper ethical practice
of refusing to eat with gentiles when Jewish Christians were present threatened to foster the heresy so opposed to Paul's work and
to split the Church so as to make it impossible for all Christians
to sit together at one table. This means that Peter probably also
withdrew from the eucharistic meal of the gentile Christians.[37]

---

against it; whereas, fulfillment of the Law is not that which
produces the blessing. In view of this, it becomes clear why
Paul can praise the Law and yet describe its function as something merely negative. Cf. esp. Rm 7,7-12. Thus, Paul's analogy between the Law and Faith is perfect; for anything done
without faith is sin. Cf. Rm 14,23. And yet, Paul does not
mean that faith is the good work which earns salvation for
the believer. Rather, salvation still remains the free gift
of God even for the man of faith.

36. Cf. Gal 3,14; Dt 21,23. Paul's argument, of course, assumes
that one has already accepted Christ in spite of the curse.
The phrase ἀνάθεμα 'Ιησοῦς in 1 Cor 12,3 probably alludes to
a real curse that Jews had pronounced on Jesus (cf. SB 1,84f),
but refers to a completely different situation from the one
found in Gal 3,13, where Paul affirms that the curse of the
Law came upon Jesus.

37. Cf. Heinrich Schlier, *Der Brief an die Galater*, (KEKNT),

For Paul, there can be no true compromise between the Law and Christ. One cannot be half Jew and half Christian either in theory or in practice. This is to be half slave and half free by trying to claim to be the son of Hagar as well as of Sarah (4,21-31)--an obvious impossibility. Anyone who causes further trouble in this matter "shall bear the judgment (βαστάσει τὸ κρίμα), no matter who he may be" (5,10). Obviously, Paul means that such a person is to be cast out of the community (or kept from entering) to face the punishment God may wish to visit upon him. There is only one law that Christians must obey, and that is "love your neighbor as yourself" (5,14). Here, Paul sees even the doctrinal problems mainly in the light of the practice of love and not as an abstract body of dogmatic formulae. Therefore, the correction of misbehavior in the community must be done in great humility and charitableness (6,1). But, as one can see in Paul's own action, this does not rule out sternness, especially when the offense threatens to destroy Christian love itself.

2). Letter to the Romans, probably early in A.D. 58.

Since this epistle takes up the themes from Galatians and develops them in a deeply theological and peaceful manner, it seems best to treat it here even though 2 Cor was probably written a few months earlier. In 2,17ff, Paul addresses a certain Jewish Christian who is apparently trying to impose the law of circumcision on the community at Rome. It is quite probably the same person that

(Göttingen, 1965⁴) 48f. From Gal 2,11-14, it is clear that the freedom which the Gospel brings has a definite connection with the Eucharist that is expressed in the full communion of all Christians with each other at the Lord's Supper. Cf. Josef Blank, Eucharistie und Kirchengemeinschaft nach Paulus, in: Una Sancta 23 (1968) 181.

Paul has in mind already in 2,1, where he warns that "in judging others you condemn yourself since you behave no differently from those you judge."[38] Paul does not instruct the Romans to take any direct action against this man, but he warns the offender of God's judgment to come "on a day of wrath."[39]

Toward the end of the letter, Paul interrupts his long exchange of greetings in order to give a last warning concerning the troublemakers. The Roman community should be on its guard for such persons and avoid them (16,17). The reference is perhaps to Judaizers. However, the teaching (διδαχή) of these wrongdoers (v. 17) is immediately described as some sort of ethical offense (v. 18). Therefore, the warning most likely concerns another category of troublemakers. These persons could very well be infected with some strain of Gnosis since they are trying to win followers through smooth words and flattery.[40]

---

38. ἐν ᾧ γὰρ κρίνεις τὸν ἕτερον, σεαυτὸν κατακρίνεις· τὰ γὰρ αὐτὰ πράσσεις ὁ κρίνων.

39. Cf. Rm 2,5: ἐν ἡμέρᾳ ὀργῆς. Perhaps it would be better to translate the expression as "on the day of wrath" even though there is no article in the Greek. There are numerous references to the "day of judgment" in the New Testament where no article is used in the Greek, but is clearly implied. Cf. e.g., Mt. 10,15; 11,22.24; 2 Pt 2,9. In Apc 6,17, it is referred to as ἡ ἡμέρα ἡ μεγάλη τῆς ὀργῆς. However, from the point of view of Paul's theology, it is also possible to say "on a day of wrath" since Paul frequently indicates that God's wrath is already actively punishing the offender. Cf. e.g., Rm 1,18; 2,8. Since the apocalyptic image of the Last Day and Final Judgment do not play any specific role in Paul's theology, "a day of wrath" and "the day of wrath" can coincide to mean the day of the sinner's death and the immediate consequences.

40. Cf. Jacques Dupont, "Gnosis". La connaissance religieuse dans les épîtres de saint Paul, (Universitas Catholica Lovaniensis; Dissertationes ad gradum magistri in Facultate Theologica con-

3). The Second Letter to the Corinthians.

About fall of A.D. 57, Paul wrote this letter while possibly staying at Ephesus, where he may have heard that false missionaries had penetrated the Corinthian community in order to lead it away from his teaching and influence.[41] He names these opponents ψευδαπόστολοι, ἐργάται δόλιοι, and accuses them of being Satan's servants disguised as the servants of righteousness whose end, however, will be according to their works (11,13-15). They are Jewish Christians (vv. 22f), and very probably under Gnostic influence since Paul defends his own γνῶσις against theirs even though he admits that his words may be rude.[42] They are described as Ἑβραῖοι (11,22), and attempt to discredit Paul for not having personally known Jesus (5,16). Therefore, they are very likely Palestinians claiming to be from the "party of Christ" mentioned in 1 Cor 1,12 and perhaps alluded to in 2 Cor 10,7; 11,23. Besides trying to enforce certain elements of Judaism upon the Corinthians, they may have also promoted a libertinistic life as a result of their Gnostic views; or perhaps Paul has both a Judaizing party and a Gnostic party to contend with at Corinth.[43] But in either case, the ethical problems they may be causing are the result of their erroneous teaching.

Paul leaves the door of repentance open (12,21), but he warns that he will be unsparing on his next visit if all is not in order by then (13,2). By this, he seems to mean to say he will conduct some sort of process of excommunication, for this is al-

---

sequendum conscriptae. Series II, tomus 40), (Louvain-Paris, 1949) 27f.

41. Cf. 2 Cor 10,1-13; K.H. Schelkle, op. cit., 152.
42. Cf. 2 Cor 11,6; K.H. Schelkle, op. cit., 157.
43. Cf. A. Wikenhauser, op. cit., 282.

ready the second warning (v. 2); and now that he will be visiting
them for the third time, final judgment will be made on the word
of two or three witnesses (v. 1). But he hopes that when he comes,
he will be able to act according to the authority invested in him
by the Lord for building up rather than destroying.[44] It is
therefore clear that Paul claims the right to bind and to loose
even though he does not explicitly use the expression.

A more positive example of Paul's use of his authority and of
ecclesial discipline is found in 2,5-10 where the community is
asked to reaccept someone who had previously offended Paul. It
is not likely that this offender is the one referred to in 1 Cor
5,1 since both the offense and the punishment appear to be of a
different nature. The incident probably occurred after Paul had
written 1 Cor and seems to have been treated in a letter referred
to in 2 Cor 2,4.9; 7,8.12, but which became lost before the New
Testament canon was concluded.

The offense remains unclear, but it must have been a rather
personal affront to Paul's character or authority. Yet, it cannot be of the same nature as the problems Paul is opposing elsewhere in 2 Cor; for it is clear that the Corinthian community
has excommunicated or somehow punished this offender, but still
has to take steps against the new opponents.[45] At any rate,
Paul is ready to pardon the offender, and asks the Corinthians
to do the same. In doing so, he attests to the community's right

---

44. Cf. 2 Cor 13,10: εἰς οἰκοδομὴν καὶ οὐκ εἰς καθαίρεσιν.
45. W. Doskocil (op. cit., 76, 80-82) does not see this as an
    example of real excommunication since he (unlike B. Poschmann,
    op. cit., 34) does not interpret this as an example of re-
    acceptance into the Church, but only as a matter of fraternal
    correction that had been followed by an indefinite period of
    penance other than excommunication.

to grant pardon to anyone, and he will also pardon the person
(2,10). To remain hard and unforgiving would only play into
Satan's hands to the harm of the one who refuses to be forgiving
(v. 11). Paul can be stern when the situation calls for it, but
his readiness to forgive extends to most if not all categories
of wrongdoing provided only that the sinner will repent (12,20f).

b. Letters from prison.

In about A.D. 58, the Jews fell upon Paul as he was visiting
the Temple in Jerusalem. He was rescued by the Roman guard, but
was to remain the captive charge of the Romans until early 63.
The first portion of the imprisonment (58-60) was at Caesarea,
Palestine's main seaport. Paul finally decided to appeal his
case to Caesar; and so came the long, hazardous journey to Rome,
followed by another two years of imprisonment. During this time,
Paul kept in contact with his churches by means of his pen. The
dates and unity of the letters from this period are very much debated. But whatever the case may be, these letters give the modern reader many valuable insights into the situation and problems
faced by the Church of Paul's times. According to ancient tradition, Paul was imprisoned again several years later in Rome and
died a Martyr's death in A.D. 67. However, unless the Pastoral
Letters are attributed to Paul, there are no existent epistles
from him after his first imprisonment.

All of the disciplinary problems treated in the Pastorals are
generally of a doctrinal nature. Therefore, no attempt will be
made to divide the issues as in the previously treated letters.

a). The Letter to the Philippians.

It was traditionally believed that this letter was written
during Paul's first imprisonment at Rome. However, there is some

reason to date it about as early as 1 Cor since the two letters
share many similarities. According to a number of scholars, the
Epistle to the Philippians is actually a redacted work consisting
of two or even three Pauline letters to the Philippians. The
three-letter theory has not gained much of a following, while the
two-letter theory is gaining in popularity. One of the more recent commentators on this epistle, Joachim Gnilka, divides it into
letters A and B. Letter A was supposedly written about A.D. 55-56
when Paul was in some sort of prison--most likely at Ephesus.
Letter B, composed especially to combat heretics at Philippi and
later inserted into letter A as Phil 3,1b-4,1.8f, was then written about A.D. 56-57 from Corinth.[46]

The first indication that the Church at Philippi is having
difficulties with troublemakers is found in 1,28, where Paul encourages his readers to remain firm and united in their resistance to the adversaries (ἀντικείμενοι), who are most probably
pagans or Jews.

In 3,2, the Philippians are told to beware of the dogs, the
evildoers and the mutilation (κατατομή)--that is, circumcision.
At this point, Judaizing Christians are being called to task for
their behavior. Most likely, they are the same as the "enemies
of the cross of Christ" spoken of in 3,18. They glory in what
should be their shame (i.e., circumcised member), their god is

---

46. Cf. J. Gnilka, Der Philipperbrief, (Herders Theologischer
Kommentar zum Neuen Testament 10/3, ed. by A. Wikenhauser
et alii), (Freiburg, Basel, Wien, 1968) 10-13, 20-25. The
heretical troublemakers at Philippi, according to Gnilka
(ibid., 211-18), tried to de-emphasize the importance of the
Cross in Christ's life and in the Christian faith by preaching Christ as a θεῖος ἀνήρ much like Jewish midrash interpreted Moses.

their belly (i.e., dietary laws), and they are destined to be lost (3,19). Perhaps they are also Gnostics to some extent; for Paul may have intentionally mentioned the "excellence" of Christ's knowledge in 3,8 in order to combat their false Gnosis.

The uncertainty and disagreement among scholars concerning the unity of the epistle in question and the nature of the trouble-makers at Philippi is relatively slight in comparison to the dis-agreement over the interpretation of 3,15f, which reads: "Let all of us, therefore, who are perfect, be of this spirit; and if you are minded otherwise in anything, this also will God reveal to you. Howbeit, walk in that unto which we have already pro-gressed."[47]

---

47. Ὅσοι οὖν τέλειοι, τοῦτο φρονῶμεν· καὶ εἴ τι ἑτέρως φρονεῖτε, καὶ τοῦτο ὁ θεὸς ὑμῖν ἀποκαλύψει: πλὴν εἰς ὃ ἐφθάσαμεν, τῷ αὐτῷ στοιχεῖν. The very last word here, "to walk," is an "imperative infinitive." It is frequent in Homer and again in classical forensic language where it emphasized the legal or moral obligation implied in the command. Paul's oscilla-tion between the first and second person plural in this pas-sage makes it difficult to determine if he means "let us walk" or "you (should) walk!" The manuscript tradition of this com-pact statement indicates that attempts were eventually made to "correct" or clarify the text in the light of Gal 6,16. But in reality, this neither respects the meaning of Gal 6, 16 in its context, nor does it render the real meaning of Phil 3,15f more clearly. Gal 6,15f reads: "For neither is circumcision nor uncircumcision of any account, but a new creation. And as many as walk by this rule, upon them and upon the Israel of God (be) peace and mercy." (οὔτε γὰρ περι-τομή τί ἐστιν οὔτε ἀκροβυστία, ἀλλὰ καινὴ κτίσις. καὶ ὅσοι τῷ κανόνι τούτῳ στοιχήσουσιν, εἰρήνη ἐπ᾽ αὐτοὺς καὶ ἔλεος, καὶ ἐπὶ τὸν Ἰσραὴλ τοῦ θεοῦ). The alterations that manuscript copyists made in Phil 3,16 contorted the text to make it read: "Howbeit, as regards what we have attained, let us think the same thing and let us also abide in the same rule." (Verumtamen ad quod pervenimus ut idem sapiamus, et in eadem permaneamus regula.) The Vulgate rendition of this verse is

Even though Paul had just admitted that he is not perfect (3,12), he still wants the Philippians to imitate him (3,17). Now he includes himself with "those who are perfect." Is he

---

given here because it has undoubtedly had the greatest and longest influence in western theology. The many Greek variations are best seen in <u>Nestle-Aland's</u> critical apparatus. The reworked language of Phil 3,16 is no longer capable of supporting the range of thought and practice in regard to Christian doctrine which Paul originally tolerated or even insisted upon in principle. An interesting study, which unfortunately cannot be undertaken here, would be to see if less liberal attitudes of later copyists influenced their alterations of this text, or if the altered text eventually led to less liberal attitudes in later Christianity. At any rate, a full investigation of what Paul himself meant in asking Christians to be of one mind would seem to indicate that he gave a rather liberal interpretation to this principle, but in such a way that ecclesial divisions could be overcome rather than fostered. Thus, for instance, Paul says in 1 Cor 1,10: "I beseech you, brothers, in the name of our Lord Jesus Christ, that all of you say the same thing, and let there be no divisions among you, but rather that you be restored in the same mind and same opinion." (Παρακαλῶ δὲ ὑμᾶς, ἀδελφοί, διὰ τοῦ ὀνόματος τοῦ κυρίου ἡμῶν Ἰησοῦ Χριστοῦ, ἵνα τὸ αὐτὸ λέγητε πάντες, καὶ μὴ ᾖ ἐν ὑμῖν σχίσματα, ἦτε δὲ κατηρτισμένοι ἐν τῷ αὐτῷ νοΐ καὶ ἐν τῇ αὐτῇ γνώμῃ.) Isolated from its context, the passage would seem to advocate absolute uniformity of thought. However, the unity that Paul asks for here is specifically that of union in the belief that Christian Baptism is not to be considered as Baptism into the name of the minister, but into Christ himself (vv. 12-15). There is only one Baptism among Christians, and so there can be no reason to build divisions upon that basis. This is so because the unity of the Church through Baptism into Christ goes far deeper than the relationship of individuals to each other. It is the unity that precedes the baptismal incorporation of members (1 Cor 12,13) and raises the Church above the status of a mere social structure which exists only in so far as its members constitute it by initiating and sustaining its existence through their own efforts. Cf. E. Käsemann, <u>Anliegen</u>, 271. The restrictive, uniform measures that some parties tried to impose on the Church--especially among the

contradicting himself? No. Not if v. 15a is taken as a bit of irony. Yet it seems clear that the irony is not primarily intended; otherwise, Paul could scarcely have used the first person plural, which fairly dampens any irony in the statement and weakens its effect on any troublemakers claiming perfection. Paul affirms perfection at least as the ideal goal of all Christians striving for spiritual maturity (1 Cor 2,6; 14,20; Eph 4,11-13; Col 1,28; 4,12). At most, then, one can only say that Paul's use of the term contains no more than a touch of irony that functions to stimulate the thoughts which follow; for he could not possibly want to belittle any Christian's desire for perfection even if it is misdirected. So, by taking up the notion and applying it even to himself, Paul says in effect: "Since we claim to strive for perfection, and in doing so actually achieve it to some degree [for a close look at the cited passages on Christian perfection show that Paul sees it as a process and not only as an absolute state], then it behooves us to be of the spirit which I have just described--namely, that we aim at full perfection by relying on Christ and not on the Law."

Likewise, v. 15b contains no more than a touch of irony when reference is made to the fact that God will reveal if anyone thinks otherwise in anything. Moreover, it is the <u>content</u> of this "thinking otherwise in anything" that God will reveal.[47a]

---

gentiles--are precisely what moved Paul to insist upon unity in certain principles that were ultimately liberating rather than restrictive for the Church.

47a. J. Gnilka (<u>op</u>., <u>cit</u>., 201f) overemphasizes the irony in this verse and even begs the question in affirming it in regard to Paul's reference to revelation in 15b: "<u>Offenbarungen</u>, <u>deren</u> <u>sich</u> <u>die</u> <u>Gegner</u> <u>gerühmt</u> <u>haben</u> <u>mögen</u>, <u>spielten</u> <u>offenkundig</u> <u>in</u> <u>ihrer</u> Verkündigung <u>eine</u> <u>Rolle</u>, <u>wie</u> <u>der</u> Satz ‚Auch

This way of looking at 15b is in complete conformity with Paul's own view that anyone in a Christian community can receive a special revelation for all from God (1 Cor 14,6.26; 14,30; Eph 1,17; 3,5). But he is also convinced that no such revelation could contradict what he has already taught; for what he knows is also a matter of revelation from the one and same divine source (Gal 1, 11f; 2,2; Eph 3,3; 1 Cor 2,6-13; 2 Cor 12,1.7). Paul now concludes that there can be no legitimate reason for the Philippians to abandon his teachings in favor of other contradictory teachings which likewise, although falsely, lay claim to derive from divine revelation. Ultimately, Paul does not demand uniformity of thought, but rather conformity in thought. This interpretation is supported by 2,2-8, where it is originally explained to the Philippians what it means for them to be of one and the same mind--namely, that they assent and conform to some basic principles

---

dies wird euch Gott offenbaren' zu verstehen gibt." This unfortunate lapse of logic then leads J. Gnilka into a couple of other non sequiturs concerning the nature of the grammatical antecedents of the relative and indefinite pronouns in this verse. In his opinion, τι and τοῦτο must refer to the information about the spiritual experiences and attitudes which Paul has just described in the preceding verses. The indefinite pronoun in 15b is without an antecedent (as indefinite pronouns are wont to be by nature) and initiates a new thought. As a consequence, τοῦτο in 15b, while referring back to τι, cannot also refer back to τοῦτο in 15a. Finally, Gnilka's reasoning leads him to conclude: "Wenn verschiedene Handschriften κανόνι als Norm des στοιχεῖν ergänzen [in v. 16], so liegt das durchaus in der Intention des allzu knapp Gesagten [in v. 15]." While Gnilka is right in wanting to avoid making Paul the "Fürsprecher eines die Auflösung fördernden Individualismus," it is one thing to defend Paul against religious individualism and quite another to approve a textual alteration that appears to make him the advocate of rigorous religious uniformity.

governing Christian faith and conduct. These principles are
viewed dialectically as they move back and forth between the positive and negative poles of expression: Be likeminded; that is,
do not act out of strife and vainglory, but rather with humble
concern for one another, not looking to your own advantage, but
rather to the good of all (2,2-4). Christ himself, in his humble
submission to the Father, is the example par excellence for the
Christian (2,5-8). Most likely, it is in this context, especially
if Gnilka's divisions of this epistle into letters A and B is
essentially correct, that the disagreement between two women at
Philippi is to be viewed and brought to a happy resolution (4,2).

b). The Letter to the Colossians, about A.D. 61-62.

A syncretistic movement of Jewish Gnostic character seemed to
be winning followers in Colossae. Finally, the Christian community was moved to seek Paul's advice on certain theological mat-
ters--especially Christological questions. The Gnostics very
likely wanted to place Christ within their category of demiurges
along with the Thrones, Dominations, Sovereignties and Powers
(1,16; 2,10.15), who were worshipped as half-gods for their own
glory.

Paul sees the Colossian inquiry about Christ as a sincere
search for truth in Christianity's confrontation with various
Weltanschauungen. So, rather than scolding, he takes up the
ideas and images of the universe used by the opposition in order
to explain that Christ is not one of the demiurges, but rather
the answer and fulfillment of all questioning, whether prompted by
Gnosticism or by Judaism. Paul strongly warns against the false
Gnosis (2,4.8.18.23), but he does not give specific commands or
threaten to punish anyone. His main concern is only to show that,

whatever truth there may be in such philosophies, they are at
most only pale reflections of the reality that is found in Christ
(2,17). To fail to recognize this is to become severed from
Christ and the body of his followers (2,19).

   c). The Letter to the Ephesians.

The date of composition, destination and occasion of this
epistle are very much debated. Of all the letters attributed to
Paul outside of the Pastorals, the Pauline authorship of the
Letter to the Ephesians is the most highly contested. However,
its thoughts and themes are remarkably similar to those found in
Colossians, which accents Christ as the unity of creation, while
Ephesians emphasizes Christ as the unity of the Church (1,22ff;
4,15).

   In 2,2, Paul speaks of the "Sons of Disobedience" (cf. also
5,6). This may be an allusion to the heterodox agitators, but it
is not very specifically directed. Whatever the religious character of these false teachers may be, they seem to be trying to lead
Paul's readers astray with libertine doctrine (5,5). The Christian should not allow himself to be deceived by their arguments,
and he should take precautions not to be included in their numbers (5,6f).

   God's wrath will come upon these evil persons (5,6), who are
apparently not members of the Church since Paul leaves their fate
entirely in the hands of God (1 Cor 5,12f). Nevertheless, he
makes it amply clear that such people have no place in the Church
in that they have no inheritance (κληρονομία) in the "kingdom of
Christ and of God" (5,5). The important thing to notice is that
Christ's followers receive an inheritance in the kingdom. A
transcendental presence of this kingdom is alluded to here;

however, one can still lose his inheritance to it. This is what belonging to the Church means. By contrasting the "Sons of Disobedience" with the "Children of Light" (τέκνα φωτός) in 5,8, Paul takes up a messianic theme which was very pronounced in similar terms at Qumran and turns it into an eschatological theme. Likewise, the reference to the "kingdom of Christ and of God" does not indicate two separate kingdoms or the Church plus the kingdom, but rather it indicates that God's eschatological rule has been already established in Christ.[48]

Although the Christians have no specific liturgical steps to take against the offenders in this letter, they must at least be on their guard against them and stand ready with the "shield of faith" to meet their attacks (6,16).

3. The Pastoral Letters

The problem of dating these letters must be solved in the light of their authorship, which is very uncertain. If they stem from Paul, then the letters were probably written about A.D. 63-65. If Paul is not the author--a view generally accepted by present-day exegetes--, then these literary works are to be dated around the end of the first century.[49] They are addressed to specific persons, who, however, are not monarchical bishops since, for one thing, the author looks upon Timothy as the temporary representative of Paul, who is supposedly pre-occupied in Macedonia (1 Tm 1,3) and who eventually asks Timothy to come to

---

48. Cf. Rudolf Schnackenburg, Gottes Herrschaft und Reich, (Freiburg, Basel, Vienna, 1959) 200f.

49. Cf. Norbert Brox, Die Pastoralbriefe, (RNT 7/2), Regensburg, 1969) 58.

him in prison (2 Tm 4,9). Titus is expected to come to Paul at Nicopolis (Ti 3,12), and is last reported to be in Dalmatia (2 Tm 4,10).

Although internal evidence indicates that these epistles were most probably not written by Paul, they are not without genuine Pauline elements. These, along with Paul's name as the writer, are used to perpetuate and extend the Pauline tradition and to give a needed aspect of "apostolic authority" to the directives of these pseudepigrapha,[50] which treat of specific cases or problems connected with false Gnosis, especially of a Jewish nature (1 Tm 1,7; Ti 1,10.14f; 3,9).

a. The First Letter to Timothy.

Immediately after the short two-verse introduction, the writer refers to an earlier date when he asked Timothy to remain at Ephesus to put a check on certain false teachers (1,3f). These are people who have wandered from the truth into empty speculation of a Jewish Gnostic character typified by the study of Gnostic mythology and long genealogies (1,4). Their twisted thinking has finally led them to a false asceticism which forbade marriage and the consumption of certain foods (4,1-3). Consequently, some Christians have disregarded their consciences and have wrecked their faith--such men like Hymenaeus and Alexander, who have been "handed over to Satan so that they might learn not to blaspheme."[51]

These two offenders are apparently false teachers and not just immoral as in the case of the incestuous man at Corinth who was likewise given over to Satan (1 Cor 5,5). But not only

50. Ibid. 53, 61f, 120.
51. Cf. 1 Tm 1,19f: οὓς παρέδωκα τῷ σατανᾷ, ἵνα παιδευθῶσιν μὴ βλασφημεῖν.

is the nature of the offense different; the nature of the punishment is also different even though both cases are given over to Satan. Therefore, it is necessary to determine what the writer means by blasphemy, since Hymenaeus and Alexander should be so treated by Satan that they learn not to blaspheme.

In 1,13, the writer, who identifies himself as Paul, the Apostle of Jesus Christ (1,1), accuses himself of being a βλάσφημος during the time when he opposed (persecuted) the faith. Blasphemy, then, is not simply a matter of irreligious words. Rather, it describes the act of resisting the salvation found in Christ.[52] Therefore, the two men in question should be excommunicated for as long as it takes them to repent and to discontinue their false doctrine. Unlike the incestuous person in 1 Cor 5,1-5, Hymenaeus and Alexander are not to be abandoned by the Church unto the destruction of their flesh (i.e., until death[53]). Consequently, there is explicit hope for their return to a proper Christian life after they have been sufficiently chastized[54] so as to give up their opposition to the true faith.[55]

---

52. Cf. Hermann W. Beyer, βλασφημέω, in: ThWB 1, 623.
53. Perhaps Paul thought in 1 Cor 5,5 that the curse spoken against the offender would even hasten his death. Cf. Johannes Schneider, ὄλεθρος, in: ThWB 5, 170.

54. The verb, παιδεύω, can be used to express all the phases or "intensities" of ecclesial discipline. As already seen, in 1 Cor 11,32 it can even refer to the death of an unworthy communicant. In 2 Cor 6,9, it indicates some sort of ecclesial censure, but obviously not death. 1 Tm 1,20 is perhaps a bit more severe due to the curse character, but still similar to 2 Cor 6,9. In 2 Tm 2,25, it means to correct by way of admonishment and instruction so as to rescue those already caught in the snare of the devil. Finally, in Ti 2,12, it refers to edification through grace and is similar to Heb 12,6, which, however, includes the trials and ills that the Lord may choose to send upon even those whom he loves.

55. Cf. W. Doskocil, op. cit., 86.

One of the more controversial passages in this letter to
Timothy is 5,22, where the writer warns the letter's recipient:
"Do not lay hands (too) quickly upon anyone, and do not be a
partner in the sins of others; keep yourself pure."[56] Does the
laying on of hands here refer to ordination to some ecclesial
office as it often does elsewhere in the New Testament? Or
does it mean the reconciliation of the sinner to the Church?
If the latter is meant, then this is the earliest existing witness to the practice of granting the pax by way of a formal laying on of hands.[57] There are several good indications that this
is the case even though the text would then be a very isolated
historical example of such a method of reaccepting a repentant
person into the Church.

In 5,17, the writer mentions that the πρεσβύτεροι should receive proper honor. Verse 19 says that Timothy should not accept a complaint made against one of the elders unless there are
two or three persons to testify to the elder's misconduct.
Those (elders?) who have sinned should be reprimanded in the
presence of all so that the others will come to fear to commit
an offense (v. 20). This procedure is to be followed without
prejudice or respect of persons (v. 21). Thus, the immediate
context of verse 22 concerns the process of ecclesial discipline.
Moreover, the expression, μὴ κοινώνει (v. 22), was a common ex-

---

56. χεῖρας ταχέως μηδενὶ ἐπιτίθει, μηδὲ κοινώνει ἁμαρτίαις
    ἀλλοτρίαις· σεαυτὸν ἁγνὸν τήρει.

57. The earliest unambiguous statement to this effect is found
    in Cyprian's complaint (probably early in A.D. 250), con-
    cerning the ecclesial reconciliation of apostates "ante ac-
    tam paenitentiam, ante exomologesim grauissimi adque extremi
    delicti factam, ante manum ab episcopo et clero in paeniten-
    tiam inpositam." Cf. CSEL 3/2, ep. 15,1, 514.

pression in the early Church, indicating a rupture of communion with a transgressor.[58] This interpretation is further supported by the writer's remark that Timothy should keep himself pure (v. 22). It seems best to understand ἁγνός to mean "uncontaminated" or "blameless" rather than "chaste." If ἁγνός means "chaste" here in the literal sense, then it would have no direct relationship to the context and it would imply at least a suspicion on the part of the writer that Timothy had need of such a reminder. But this is most unlikely. Instead, it is more reasonable to take the expression in this case as a summarization and explanation of what has just been said--that is, that as long as a sinner is not fully repentant, Timothy should refuse to reconcile him to the community lest he himself become guilty of sin. As already seen, unnecessary and unauthorized association with a person under the ban was forbidden in Judaism lest one contract the transgressor's "impurity." The procedure for fraternal correction described in 1 Tm 5,19 shows that the writer was influenced, directly or indirectly, by Jewish practice.

The historical isolation of this passage as a reference to a penitential rite, if it is that, may be explained by the fact that early ecclesial writers simply did not consider it necessary to speak of a formal rite for granting the pax until the third century, when there was reason to be concerned about the practice of some priests and bishops in the laying on of their hands all too readily upon former apostates from the faith in order to grant them the pax before a real test had been made of the sincerity of their repentance. This could well be the basic situation in 1 Tm 5,22.

---

58. Cf. G. D'Ercole, Penitenza, 101f; ----, Communio, 220f.

b. The Second Letter to Timothy.

As in 1 Tm, the writer again identifies himself as Paul, but now writing from prison (1,1.8). This would then mean Paul's second and final imprisonment in Rome before his death under Nero. The letter is devoted mostly to personal advice and exhortation for Timothy, the bishop of Ephesus according to tradition (1 Tm 1,3). Among other things, he is told how to deal with the immediate danger presented by the false teachers, Hymenaeus (probably the same person as in 1 Tm 1,20) and Philetus, who claim that the resurrection had already taken place.[59] These two should serve as examples of what comes of those who get caught up in pointless philosophical discussion which leads away from the truth. Timothy himself is to avoid initiating such speculations (2,14.16.23). But any person who wants to dispute what he says should be gently corrected with the hope that he will be granted a change of mind (2,25f; 4,2).

The difficulties, at least in part, do not seem to have arisen from within the community at Ephesus since the writer must tell Timothy to be on his guard against the coppersmith, Alexander, (1 Tm 1,20), who strongly contests everything which the writer has taught (4,14f). But "the Lord will repay him according to his works."[60] With this Old Testament curse (Pss 28,4; 62,12; Prv 24,12), it is not certain if the writer means to intensify the excommunication (1 Tm 1,20) or not—that is, to a life-long excommunication of Alexander. However, the statement does not seem to

---

59. Cf. 2 Tm 2,18f. As the names of the troublemakers indicate, they were probably very sympathetic to Greek philosophy, which found the notion of bodily resurrection quite abhorrent.

60. Cf. 2 Tm 4,14: ἀποδώσει αὐτῷ κύριος κατὰ τὰ ἔργα αὐτοῦ.

imply anything beyond the original formula of excommunication, since being handed over to Satan is not essentially different from being repaid by the Lord.

The writer warns of a more specific type of Gnostic danger in 3,6f. In this case, certain persons claimed to have possession of special knowledge or other graces which they proposed to pass on to unwary women by way of sexual intercourse. They are compared to Jamnes and Jambres, two Egyptian magicians according to Jewish legend, who pretended to convert to Judaism at the time of the Exodus. However, they only wanted to be in a position to provoke Moses and to lead the Israelites into various sins, especially the sin of idolatry in the adoration of the golden calf.[61] This comparison clearly implies that there were such men within the Church. They are most likely to be identified with the seducers and imposters (πονηροὶ καὶ γόητες) in 3,13. Since, however, the writer apparently does not declare any of these Christian evildoers to be permanently or fully extra ecclesiam, one is forced to ask: "What then is the relationship of such persons to the Church according to the writer?" The answer to this question seems to be given in 2,20f. Here, the author speaks of a great house (μεγάλη οἰκία) where there are vessels of gold, silver, wood and clay. Some of these vessels are for dignified purposes (εἰς τιμήν), while others are used for undignified purposes (εἰς ἀτιμίαν). Then the writer says: "If anyone, therefore, has cleansed himself from these (i.e., the vessels for undignified use), he will be a vessel

---

61. Cf. SB 3, 660-64.

for dignified purposes, sanctified and useful to the master,
ready for every good work."[62]

Obviously, the μεγάλη οἰκία is the Church (1 Tm 3,15), and
the vessels are the various types of members who are in the Church.
Yet, some of these vessels have a dishonorable character, and
those members who want to serve honorable ends must keep themselves ready for the Lord by disassociating themselves from the
dishonorable vessels. It is easy enough to identify these latter
vessels with sinful Christians, but there is no clear indication
that one may go so far as to say that men like Hymeneus, Philetus
and Alexander belong even to this group in the mind of the author.
However, it is the writer's mentioning of Hymeneus and Philetus
in 2,17f which induced him to give such a description of the
Church. Consequently, it seems logical to conclude that he considered such men to have some sort of real relationship to and
membership in the Church even when under censure. In spite of
the fact that the author of the letters to Timothy sees the presence of such men as a sign of the last days (1 Tm 4,1; 2 Tm 3,1),
nowhere does he abandon the false teachers so completely that he
leaves their ultimate salvation to be determined solely from an
eschatological point of view without any further reference to the
Church (2,25f).

c. The Letter to Titus.

Once more, the writer identifies himself as Paul (1,1), but
not yet in final imprisonment since he is planning on spending
the coming winter in Nicopolis (3,12), a city probably located in

---

62. Cf. 2 Tm 2,21: ἐὰν οὖν τις ἐκκαθάρῃ ἑαυτὸν ἀπὸ τούτων, ἔσται
σκεῦος εἰς τιμήν, ἡγιασμένον, εὔχρηστον τῷ δεσπότῃ, εἰς πᾶν
ἔργον ἀγαθὸν ἡτοιμασμένον·

Epirus, a country in the north-western part of ancient Greece.
According to the letter, Titus himself is in charge of the Church
in Crete (1,5).

In 1,10-16, the author speaks of those who are teaching false
doctrine for money. They are mostly, though not exclusively, of
the Judaizing party, and have reached the point of not caring
about the truth anymore. Corrupted in mind and conscience, their
infirm faith stems from their claim of having knowledge of God
while actually denying him. They are abominable, disobedient and
incapable of doing any good work.[63] This is reminiscent of 2 Tm
2,21, where the "dignified vessel" is described as being ready
for every good work. But the tone in the letters to Timothy is
not as sharp as in this letter. Yet, hope is expressed that these
wrongdoers will repair their faith after they have been sharply
rebuked (1,13).

Titus is to be uncompromising in teaching all the instructions
given in the letter (3,8), and any factious person[64] who disputes

---

63. Cf. Ti 1,16: Βδελυκτοὶ ὄντες καὶ ἀπειθεῖς καὶ πρὸς πᾶν ἔργον
ἀγαθὸν ἀδόκιμοι·

64. Cf. Ti 3,10. This is the only place where the term, αἱρετικός
appears in the Bible, and it is the first time that any deri-
vative of αἱρέω is used in connection with a clear case or
definition of excommunication in reference to an (unnamed) individual. Here it has special relevance to the Christian
(i.e., baptized) state of the person--an aspect which now belongs to the formal definition of "heretic." In the religious
terminology of the New Testament, such words are used first of
all to distinguish the parties or sects within Judaism. Cf.
Acts 5,17; 15,5; 26,5. In this sense, it is employed to describe the first Christian community. Cf. Acts 24,5.14; 28,
22. Paul applies the term to the undesirable divisions in
the Corinthian community. Cf. 1 Cor 11,19. But here it has
nothing to do with formal excommunication. However, this

him is to be avoided as a self-condemned sinner (ἁμαρτάνει ὢν
αὐτοκατάκριτος) after one or two warnings (3,11). Does this mean
permanent excommunication? The exact disciplinary effect of being
designated as "self-condemned" cannot be fully determined from the
text or from the Fathers who used the expression. But by examin-
ing the opposite meanings of κατακρίνειν, some light can be cast
upon the meaning of αὐτοκατάκριτος. These are such concepts as
"eternal life," "salvation," "redemption," "justification," and
the like.[65] Thus, to be "damned" or "condemned" has strong eschatological overtones rooted in the early Church's self-awareness of
being the new Israel--that is, οἱ σῳζόμενοι (Acts 2,47). To be
condemned, therefore, means to be given over to the number of
those going to perdition (ἀπώλεια, Phil 1,28; 3,18f; Rm 9,22), a
term that is generally associated with death and hell in the Sep-
tauginta and the New Testament.[66] To be "self-condemned" must be
understood as an intensification of the basic concept in "condemnation" with all its eschatological coloring.

The verse in question contains the only use of αὐτοκατακρίνειν
in the entire Bible. Apparently, the only other known example of

---

tendency is present in Gal 5,20 where αἱρέσεις is listed among
the "works of the flesh" which prevent one from entering the
"kingdom of God." Ti 3,10 refers to an individual rather than
a sect. But the process of development is completed in 2 Pt
2,1, where the Christian Church can now speak of fully heretical sects--that is, baptized groups of Christians following a
"confession of faith" other than that which the main body of
the Church represents. At this point, Christianity is in a
relationship to its sects in a way that is analogous to Judaism's relationship to Christianity in its expulsion from the
synagogue. Cf. Jn 9,22; 12,42 and esp. 6,12.

65. Cf. H. Köster, Verdamnis, in RGG 6 (1962) 1260.
66. Cf. Albrecht Oepke, ἀπώλεια, in: ThWB 1, 395f.

the word is to be found in a fragment from Philo concerning a
person who commits the same sin which he has condemned in another.[67]
Philo's choice of word (if he himself did not also coin it) is for
obvious reasons. What does the use of "self-condemned" in Ti 3,11
have in common with the Alexandrian philosopher's use of the expression? This question would seem to admit of only one answer--
namely, that in both cases the sinners are fully aware of the
seriousness of the sin. For, in the one case, the person knows
that the offense is serious, because he has already condemned it
in another person. In the other case, the wrongdoer has been already twice admonished and thus knows quite well that he is doing
serious wrong. The writer of the epistle therefore looks upon
the factious man's stubborn refusal to reform himself as a hardened state of sinfulness and nonrepentance.

Concepts from the Old Testament seem to be at work here too.
Although the word "self-condemned" is used just this one time in
the Bible, the notion of self-condemnation is by no means alien
to the Old Testament. This is especially true when it is a question of one's breaking the Covenant, which means to go back on
the oath of the Covenant and, in this way, to fall under the curse
(sanction) of the oath and thereby to become self-condemned.[68] If
the author of Titus is influenced (consciously or unconsciously)
by these ideas, then he must consider the opposition of the factious person to be tantamount to a repudiation of a Christian's
covenant with Christ.

---

67. The fragment was found in the Sacra Parallela, a "florilegium"
    generally ascribed to St. Johannes Damascenus (d. c. 750), and
    is quoted here as supplied by Friedrich Büchsel, αὐτοκατάκριτος
    (κρίνω), in: ThWB 3, 954: μηδενὶ συμφορὰν ὀνειδίσῃς...μήποτε
    τοῖς αὐτοῖς ἁλοὺς αὐτοκατάκριτος ἐν τῷ συνειδότι εὑρεθῇς.

68. Cf. H. Brichto, op. cit., 26-38.

In addition, the full meaning and force of αὐτοκατάκριτος
in Ti 3,11 can only be extracted in view of the Jewish and New
Testament theology of judgment, condemnation, and forgiveness.
Accordingly, the world is to be judged, and salvation will depend
on one's having an influential advocate to plead his cause before
God's throne.[69] Jesus promised to perform this task for his
faithful followers (Mt 10,32 and pars.; 2 Tm 2,12f; Apc 3,5).
The Christian who rejects Christ has no one to "put in a good
word for him," and is, for all practical purposes, self-condemned.
However, Ti 3,11 obviously means that such a person is likewise
excommunicated from the Church since it is a contradiction for
him to claim to be a member of the Church which is considered to
comprise only the "saved." The self-condemned offender is not
handed over to Satan for the destruction of his flesh so that the
spirit may be saved. Rather, his excommunication accents the possibility of final loss of salvation; for αὐτοκατάκριτος clearly
implies that there is no real reason to hope that the person will
undergo a change of mind and heart or that there is any "qualitative" Christian left in the person so that he can still be saved
even if death were to intervene to stop his sinning. In Ti 3,11,
the real sin of the αἱρετικός does not precede his self-condemnation, but is simultaneous with it. Such a state of existence in
separation from the "saved" is a real anticipation of the final
state of nonsalvation. The αὐτοκατάκριτος is relatively permanently excommunicated in that the Church does not seriously anticipate

---

69. Cf. F. Büchsel, art. cit., 935-55; Otto Betz, Der Paraklet,
    Fürsprecher im häretischen Spätjudentum, im Johannes-Evange-
    lium und in neu gefundenen gnostischen Schriften, (Arbeiten
    zur Geschichte des Spätjudentums und Urchristentums 2),
    (Leiden, Köln, 1963) 192ff.

his conversion. But if he should happen to repent, there is no reason to believe that the writer would refuse to reaccept him into the Church.

DISCIPLINE IN THE LETTER TO THE HEBREWS,
THE CATHOLIC LETTERS AND THE APOCALYPSE

1. The Letter to the Hebrews

a. Christians and sin.

Although this epistle was traditionally ascribed to Paul, it
is more likely that it was written about A.D. 80-90, but not much
later, since Clement of Rome cites it already in his letter to
the Corinthians written about A.D. 95-96. The element that char-
acterizes the discipline advocated in this letter is the fact
that the early enthusiasm of the Church which Paul had witnessed
is long gone (Heb 10,24f.29; 5,11). Yet, the expectation of the
Parousia is still very much alive (10,25.37). Along with this
cooling of religious enthusiasm comes a colder and harder attitude toward sinners.[1] However, it is not clear as to just how
rigidly this attitude was actually applied. A careful examination of the texts reveals that the charge of "rigorism" is not
really justified.[2] Whatever rigid elements the epistle may con-

---

1. The seemingly hard line which Hebrews takes toward sinners
   gave the Montanists and the Novatianists of the 3rd century
   the basis for their heretical rigorism. Cf. W. Doskocil, op.
   cit., 102.

2. Hebrews is not rigoristic; for it does not say sinners can
   not be admitted to Penance (the topic is not discussed in
   the epistle), but that, once a person has fully turned his
   back on the Church, his situation is dispairing. Furthermore, the letter seeks to offer its intended readers encouragement and support in the faith rather than to develop an
   ecclesiastical disciplinary system. Hebrews only becomes
   rigoristic when it is anachronistically treated in a Montanistic context, where the Church's right to grant repentance
   for serious sins committed after Baptism is already denied.
   Cf. H. von Campenhausen, op. cit., 244-46, n. 4.

tain, are best defined as a reaction to the increased moral and doctrinal problems accompanying the loss of the Church's initial fervor.

The theology of sin and punishment in this epistle is developed in the light of the author's Christological soteriology. In 2,1, he asks that Christians be more attentive to the teachings of their faith lest they drift away in ignorance and apathy. Since the Mosaic Law, which was promulgated by angels, was sanctioned with severe penalties for every infringement and act of disobedience (v. 2), then Christians could only expect worse punishment for disobedience to the Gospel of salvation first announced by the Lord (v. 3).

To illustrate the effect of disobedience to the Old Law, the writer refers to the punishment meted out to the Israelites in the desert during the Exodus. For their hardheartedness, they were condemned to spend 40 years wandering aimlessly about the wilderness until the rebellious persons had died. Only then were they permitted to enter the promised land (3,7-11; Ps 95,5-11). Thereupon, the author admonishes his readers to take care that none of them will be found with an evil heart of unbelief in the apostasy from the living God.[3]

This verse is very difficult to translate because it is not immediately clear just what the author has in mind in speaking of ἐν τῷ ἀποστῆναι ἀπὸ Θεοῦ ζῶντος. Generally, the phrase is trans-

---

3. Cf. Heb 3,12: Βλέπετε, ἀδελφοί, μήποτε ἔσται ἔν τινι ὑμῶν καπδία πονηρὰ ἀπιστίας ἐν τῷ ἀποστῆναι ἀπὸ Θεοῦ ζῶντος   The apostasy referred to here becomes a reality in the lives of Christians when they harden their hearts against the "new revelation" in Christ as the fulfillment of the "old revelation." Cf. Otto Kuss, Der Brief an die Hebräer, (RNT 8/1), (Regensburg, 1966) 52.

lated so as to indicate that it is the type of action that results from an unbelieving heart. This is also the course taken
by the Vulgate: "cor malum incredulitatis discendendi a Deo vivo."
However, the context indicates that a more literal translation
from the Greek would be much more satisfactory. In this way, the
meaning of the infinitive construction under consideration remains
concrete and objective. Moreover, the temporal aspect that is
generally characteristic of the Greek infinitive construction with
ἐν is preserved (Heb 3,15; Lk 1,21; 2,43; 9,34; 18,35). This is
very important for a correct understanding of the text since the
author is obviously trying to draw a parallel between the time of
the Israelites in their pilgrimage through the desert (when their
repeated murmurings led many of them to rebel against God) and
the contemporary situation of his Christian readers. Consequently,
the expression, ἐν τῷ ἀποστῆναι ἀπὸ Θεοῦ ζῶντος, refers to both
the past apostasy of the Israelites in the desert and the present
hardening of hearts and possible final apostasy of contemporary
Christians. This is augmented by the use of the future tense
(ἔσται) after the conjunction μήποτε. Such a construction is
most closely defined as a "future most vivid condition." Therefore, ἐν τῷ ἀποστῆναι must also contain a future aspect. In
other words, the author is telling his readers to take care now
lest any of them develop an evil (i.e., hardened) heart as the
result of sin's deceit (v. 13) and thus be found in rebellion
against God in the future when the climactic moment of decision
comes.

The entire expression must be understood in the light of Ex
32,26, where Moses commands that the Israelites decide whether or
not they want to take God's side or follow those apostates who
worshipped the golden calf. The author concludes that Christians,

if they wish to enter into the Rest of the final Sabbath (4,1-11), should persevere in the faith (3,14) and confidently draw near the throne of grace to obtain mercy and grace for the time of need (4,16). Consequently, chapters 3 and 4 warn against the sin of nonrepentance that results from hardness of heart and leads to ultimate rebellion against the living God at the end of the present "Today" (3,13; 4,7). One must now ask: "What is the effect of the hardened heart and consequent disbelief when viewed ecclesiologically rather than eschatologically?" The answer to the question must be sought in several passages of the epistle.

b. The unforgiveable sin.

In chapter 6, the writer asserts that he wishes to discontinue the elementary teaching about Christ in order to make room for other matters of importance (v. 1). Therefore, he will not repeat the issue concerning repentance and faith, nor talk about baptisms and the laying on of hands,[4] nor about the resurrection and eternal judgment (v. 2). In other words, he wants to treat something other than the "initiation" of Christians on the one side, and eschatological events on the other. Instead, Christ's priestly relationship to the New Covenant will be considered along with some aspects of Christian life and conduct. By way of introduction, the author explains why it is that apostates will be deprived of the salvation promised to the faithful (vv. 4-9).

---

4. It is not clear if this action refers to "ordination," "penance," blessings, exorcisms or to all of these possibilities. Most likely, it is to be understood as a part of Baptism-- that is, Christian initiation--since Heb 6,1-3 seems to be directed toward two categories of theological reflection-- namely, the first and the last things of Christian life.

It is the writer's conviction that "it is impossible to renew again unto repentance those who, being once enlightened, have gotten a taste of the heavenly gift--thereby becoming partakers of the Holy Spirit--and having savored God's excellent word as well as the powers of a coming age, but who, falling away, recrucify the Son of God for themselves and make sport of him."[5] Clearly, the writer is very skeptical about the readmission of apostates into the Church. This may be for one of two reasons: he may feel that a person who has once reached a mature knowledge of the faith-- but still turns so completely against Christ--cannot be expected to repent; or, he may be of the opinion that the apostate cannot be renewed by Baptism since it is ἅπαξ. In other words, even the repentant apostate is still fully _extra_ _ecclesiam_ and cannot be readmitted, because this would theoretically require a second Baptism--which is impossible since it is unrepeatable. In the first case, the impossibility is on the part of the apostate; in the second case, on the part of the Church. But even in the second case, the impossibility need not be necessarily of a theological nature. That is, the author may be of the opinion that it

---

5. Cf. Heb 6,4-6: Ἀδύνατον γὰρ τοὺς ἅπαξ φωτισθέντας γευσαμέ-
    νους τε τῆς δωρεᾶς τῆς ἐπουρανίου καὶ μετόχους γενηθέντας
    πνεύματος ἁγίου καὶ καλὸν γευσαμένους θεοῦ ῥῆμα δυνάμεις τε
    μέλλοντος αἰῶνος, καὶ παραπεσόντας, πάλιν ἀνακαινίζειν εἰς
    μετάνοιαν, ἀνασταυροῦντας ἑαυτοῖς τὸν υἱὸν τοῦ θεοῦ καὶ παρα-
    δειγματίζοντας. If "being once enlightened" suggests Baptism,
    then "having tasted the heavenly gift" suggests the Eucharist.
    Cf. Acts 20,11. "But the 'heavenly gift' need not be restric-
    ted to the Eucharist; it may indicate the whole sum of spiri-
    tual blessings which are sacramentally sealed and signified
    in the Eucharist." Cf. F.F. Bruce, Commentary on the Epistle
    to the Hebrews, (NLCNT), (London, Edinburgh, 1964) 120f. The
    reference to recrucifying Christ could possibly imply unworthy
    reception of the Eucharist. Cf. 1 Cor 11,27.

cannot be expected that the Church will be able to convince a hardened sinner and apostate of his errors so that he will be moved to repent.[6] But whatever the nature of this impossibility, it is not meant in an absolute, eschatological sense. This seems to be the conclusion that must be drawn from the analogy which the author makes between Christians and earth that is often watered by rain and tilled by the caretakers (v. 7). If the earth brings forth suitable produce, it receives God's blessing (v. 7); but if it brings forth thorns and thistles, "it is rejected and well-nigh a curse whose ultimate destiny leads to burning."[7]

This short, two-verse comparison contrasts the faithful with the unfaithful Christians. The rain[8] of God's graces comes upon both (Mt 5,45). But in the one case, useful fruits[9] are produced; whereas, in the other case, thistles and thorns--indications of cursed earth (Gn 3,17)--come forth. The end of the latter is in burning (Mt 13,30; 2 Pt 3,7.10.12), but the former receive God's blessing. However, this blessing cannot be directly construed as eschatological salvation as such since it is bestowed already in the present. Nevertheless, it includes final salvation as its future consummation, just as loss of final salvation (burning) is the certain and future lot of those who are now unproductive and

---

6. The opinion that certain circumstances led to the moral impossibility of repentance was common in the old synagogue. Cf. <u>SB</u> 3, 689f.
7. Cf. Heb 6,8: ἀδόκιμος καὶ κατάρας ἐγγύς, ἧς τὸ τέλος εἰς καῦσιν.
8. In rabbinical theology, rain is viewed as the male principle of fertility. The earth and its moisture is considered to be the female principle; and together, they cooperate to bring forth fruit. Cf. <u>SB</u> 3, 690.
9. The "usefulness" of the fruits is similar to the image of Christians as "honorable vessels, suitable unto the master for every good work." Cf. 2 Tm 2,21.

are therefore rejected and considered "near a curse." Their present state includes damnation as the future consummation of their present fruitlessness (Jn 15,6) unless it is somehow remedied in the meantime. But this aspect is present only by way of implication since the author leaves room for it by describing the apostate's present situation as "well-nigh a curse." The implication is that once the curse is actually there, then the sinner is truly lost.[10] This is most probably to be interpreted as the sinner's state only after death. In the meantime, however, the apostate is, for all practical purposes, already lost in so far as his sin leads him into a state of subjective inability to repent. In Scholastic language, he has willfully destroyed his "potentia oboedientialis" so that God's grace cannot but remain ineffective in him.[11] The author wants to emphasize this fact above all else.

The next passage which can contribute any further information to the questions under consideration is 10,26-39. At this point, the author continues to develop the idea concerning the impossibility of the apostate's renewal to metanoia (6,4-6). After exhorting his readers to continue steady in the faith and to be regular in attendance at the assembly (10,23-25), he says: "For, if we willfully sin after having received the full knowledge of the truth, there no longer remains a sacrifice for sins."[12] Two ques-

---

10. It is primarily God himself who can remove a curse through a blessing. Cf. Dt 23,6; Neh 13,2; Ps 109,28. But if the curse is from God himself, then a fortiori can he alone remove it. Cf. B. Poschmann, op. cit., 42.

11. Cf. Peter Ketter, Hebräerbrief, (HB 16/1), (Freiburg im Breisgau, 1950) 46.

12. Cf. Heb 10,26: Ἐκουσίως γὰρ ἁμαρτανόντων ἡμῶν μετὰ τὸ λαβεῖν τὴν ἐπίγνωσιν τῆς ἀληθείας, οὐκέτι περὶ ἁμαρτιῶν ἀπολείπεται θυσία.

tions must now be considered: 1. "What constitutes 'willful sin-ning'?" 2. "Why is there no sacrifice for sins after the commis-sion of such a sin?"

The concept of "willful sin" is found already in Nm 15,30, following the explanation that "unwillful or inadvertent sins" can be expiated by way of various sin sacrifices (Nm 15,22-29). But the man who commits a deliberate sin outrages Yahweh himself and must be exterminated (v. 30). He has nullified the word of God and must be destroyed because his sin is upon him--that is, it cannot be removed from him by means of the sin sacrifices (v. 31). An illustration of such a sin is at once given in the ac-count of a man whom Yahweh commands to be stoned to death for gathering wood on the Sabbath (vv. 32-36).[13] The gravity of this

---

13. The Interpreter's Bible 2, 218 says of this passage: "This little narrative was probably meant to illustrate the fate of those who sin 'with a high hand.'" Such a sinner had just previously been defined as anyone who "solemnly sets himself to disobey Yahweh" and thus "reviles his God and therefore cannot offer himself for reconciliation." W.H. Gipsen, Het Book Numeri, 1, (Commentaar op het Oude Testament), (Kampen, 1929) 250, comments on the willful sin in Nm 15,30 as follows: "Het is het opheffen van de hand in openlijke opstand tegen Jahwe" ("It is the lifting up of the hand in open opposition toward Yahweh"). To take such a position against God, in Jew-ish thought, does not necessarily or primarily imply psycolo-gical willfulness that results from a fully reflected course of action. However, Heb 10,26 emphasizes the true willfulness of the sin by stating that it follows "after receiving the knowledge of truth." This is analogous to the knowledge of the Law presupposed in the Law-conscious Jew. The death pen-alty imposed on the Sabbath-breaker is not a matter of vindica-tion and vengence, but of self-protection for the rest of the community. That is, "to break the sabbath is a breach of holiness and hence exposes all life to unexpected dangers." Cf. J. Pedersen, op. cit., 291.

crime is not to be seen in its "internal content," but in its
cultic significance for the Jewish religion. Breaking the Sabbath day is tantamount to breaking Israel's covenant with Yahweh
(Ex 20,8-11; 31,13.17; Ez 20,12). Thereafter, the offender no
longer has access to the expiation obtainable from the sin sacrifices and, being cursed by his sin of apostasy, he must be excluded (by death) from Israel. However, this still does not explain
the "willful" or "deliberate" aspect of such a sin.

The Hebrew text of Nm 15,30 says literally that the one who
"acts with his hand raised aloft"[14] must be destroyed. The image
is probably of one who deceitfully places himself under an oath,
since it was characteristic to swear with the hand raised (Gn 14,
22; Dt 32,40; Ex 6,8; Pss 106,26; 144,8.11). Such false swearing
was strictly forbidden by the Law (Ex 20,7; Lv 19,12; Dt 5,11);
and the one who places himself under an oath also places himself
under a curse in order to attest to his confirmed intention to
fulfill the conditions of the oath (1 Sm 14,44; 20,12f; Acts 23,
12-21). The one who fails to keep his oath becomes "self-condemned." The Jew who does anything against the covenant must therefore be treated as one who has failed to keep his promise of
faithfulness to Yahweh; for the covenant was concluded under an
oath and curse.[15] A "willful sin" is thus always some form of
apostasy from God himself. That is, the sinner radically rejects

---

14. וְהַנֶּפֶשׁ אֲשֶׁר־תַּעֲשֶׂה בְּיָד רָמָה . The LXX reads: Καὶ ψυχὴ
ἥτις ποιήσῃ ἐν χειρὶ ὑπερηφανίας.

15. Cf. N. Lohfink, Bund, in: BL 267. For an excellent treatment
of the oldest biblical text concerning God's בְּרִית with
man (Gn 15,18) as being basically an oath cf. Norbert Lohfink,
Die Landverheissung als Eid, (Stuttgarter Bibelstudien 28),
(Stuttgart, 1967). Cf. also Gn 21,23f; 26,28-31; Dt 29,11;
Jos 9,15; 1 Sm 20,42; P. van Imschoot, Eid, in: BL 367f.

God's mercy and grace which form the essence of the covenant with him (Ps 89,4; 1 Kgs 3,6; Is 55,3). But now it is necessary to see how all this applies to Heb 10,26.

When it is said that the author of the <u>Letter</u> <u>to</u> <u>the</u> <u>Hebrews</u> is speaking of apostasy, this must be understood in the broad sense as defined above in the explanation of Nm 15,30. Consequently, his warnings are not directed exclusively against the danger of a Christian's falling (back) into Judaism.[16] Rather, they are concerned with the fundamental moral-religious decisions which a Christian must make and practice with sincere faith.[17] The writer is, as a result, able to introduce the topic of "willful sinning" by taking up the example of those lax and lapsed Christians who customarily (καθὼς ἔθος) stay away from the assembly (v. 25) since their conduct is radically opposed to the purpose of the covenant in Christ's blood. They resist the grace of the Spirit by regarding the blood of the covenant as something profane (κοινόν) rather than sanctifying (v. 29). With the very foundation of their previous Christian commitment now annihilated, they can in no way fruitfully participate in the covenent (i.e., Christian life in all its aspects) and must simply be left to the Lord's judgment (vv. 27.30f). This conclusion leads into the second question asked above concerning what the author means by saying there is no sacrifice for sins "if we sin willfully after receiving full knowledge of the truth" (v. 26).

---

16. Whether or not the letter's intended readers were Jewish Christians is a very much debated question since the 19th century. It is also possible that both gentile and Jewish Christians are meant. Cf. A. Wikenhauser, <u>op</u>. <u>cit</u>., 332.

17. <u>Ibid</u>.

A comparison between 10,18 and 10,26 shows that the author distinguishes between "an offering for sins" (v. 18: προσφερὰ περὶ ἁμαρτίας) and "a sacrifice for sins" (v. 26: θυσία περὶ ἁμαρτιῶν). The "offering" is the historical act, which, in the case of Christ's death and offering of his body, is made efficacious through his sinlessness and obedience (9,14; 10,10). But because it is efficacious, it need not be repeated (10,18) and is therefore "once and for all" (10,10: ἐφάπαξ).

However, this does not mean that Christians cannot obtain forgiveness of the sins they commit after Baptism. This is clear in 12,1, where the writer exhorts his readers to put aside all their sins. Thus, as the θυσία for sins in 10,26 implies, forgiveness of sins that are not a radical break with Christ is possible.[18] This can only mean that Christ himself in his func-

---

18. Besides apostasy in the strict sense, the author of Hebrews probably also includes in the category of "willful" sins those vices which Judaism found especially repugnant and "typical" of pagan life--namely, idolatry, sexual immorality and murder. In 12,15, the writer warns his readers against "any root of bitterness" (τις ῥίζα πικρίας), which means idolatry according to Dt 29,18(17) and 1 QH 4,14 of the Qumran texts. In addition, he warns against anyone's becoming a "profane person like Esau" (v. 16: βέβηλος ὡς 'Ησαῦ), who cared so little about his birthright to his father's special blessing that he gave it up for a bit of meat and could not obtain the blessing even though he cried bitterly for it when the time came. But "he was rejected, for he found no place of repentance" (v. 17: ἀπεδοκιμάσθη, μετανοίας γὰρ τόπον οὐκ εὗρεν)--that is, it lies fully in the capacity of a Christian to "gamble away" his salvation thoughtlessly. Cf. O. Kuss, op. cit., 201. Tradition pictured Esau as an uncouth, totally irreligious person guilty of all the sins that are particularly hateful to God, especially idolatry, murder, thievery, fornication and hypocrisy in religious and practical life. His relinquishment of his birthright

tion as victim and eternal highpriest is the θυσία[19] for the expiation of those sins which are not "willful." However, those
who do sin "willfully" no longer have access to the θυσία since
that is precisely what they reject in their sin.[20] Therefore,

was interpreted as disregard for the resurrection from the
dead and thus meant that he gave up his right to participate
in a future life. Cf. SB 3, 748f. In 13,4, it is stated
that "God will judge fornicators and adulterers" (πόρνους
γὰρ καὶ μοίχους κρινεῖ ὁ θεός). As already seen, such language implies permanent excommunication from the Church in
so far as it is not expected that anyone who makes these
sins a "way of life" can be urged to repentance before his
death or Christ's second coming.

19. Cf. the conclusion of this treatment on Hebrews for the possible eucharistic implications of this term. If 10,19-22 is
an encouragement for Christians to receive the Eucharist,
then the θυσία spoken of in 10,26 must indeed have eucharistic implications. Cf. also the next note.

20. Cf. C. Spicq, op. cit., 322. In Judaism, those who had
apostasized (e.g., through idolatry or even for attempting
to offer wine--that being a pagan practice) were specifically excluded from making an offering and were thereby excluded from the sin sacrifices. Cf. SB 3, 743f. The nature
of the crime committed by those who sin "willfully" is further illucidated in Heb 10,29. Here, the writer says that
such a sinner "has trampled on the Son of God and deemed the
blood of the covenant as something profane" (ὁ τὸν υἱὸν τοῦ
θεοῦ καταπατήσας καὶ τὸ αἷμα τῆς διαθήκης κοινὸν ἡγησάμενος)--
an act which is an insult to "the spirit of grace" (τὸ πνεῦμα
τῆς χάριτος). The expression concerning the trampling on the
Son of God is reminiscent of the Illiad 4,157 where the expression for breaking an oath reads: "they trampled on the
treaty" (κατὰ δ' ὅρκια πιστὰ πάτησαν; cf. ὁρκιατομέω, in: LS
1251). The use of a personal object with this verb "denotes
contempt of the most flagrant kind." Cf. James Moffatt, A
Critical and Exegetical Commentary on the Epistle to the
Hebrews, (Edinburgh, 1924) 151. Again, this may have some
reference to the Eucharist, especially in view of the reference to the sin of considering "the blood of the covenant"

they no longer have Christ as their intercessor and saviour (7, 25), and their eschatological fate is most uncertain and left directly and solely in the hands of God (10,30f). This action is the Christian analogue to the capital punishment practiced by the Israelites (10,27-29).

There is still one other aspect to be discussed concerning the "willful" sinner's relation to the Church and Christ. Such a one is apparently considered to be permanently lost to the Church due to the nature of the sin itself and the historical

---

to be worthless. Cf. Johannes Betz, Die Eucharistie in der Zeit der griechischen Väter, 2/1, (Freiburg im Breisgau, 1955) 154-57. In Christian circles, the eucharistic over-tones of such an expression would have been immediately noted. Cf. Mt 26,28 and pars. On the other hand, however, Jewish Christians, or Christians well-versed in Jewish thought, could just as easily have understood the expression in terms of their Baptism in that this is analogous to circumcision, and "blood of the Covenant" came to mean the blood of circumcision in later Judaism. Cf. SB 1, 991f. If this latter explanation is to be applied to Heb 10,29, then it would mean that the apostates simply took the view that their Baptism was no more than a common washing and therefore obliged them in no way to be faithful to the baptismal promises. Whether or not the passage is to be given eucharistic nuances depends on determining the Jewish or gentile mentality of the writer and his intended readers. However, the connection of the Eucharist with Baptism in Heb 6,4-6 may indicate that the Eucharist formed part of the entire baptismal rite in Hebrews and that the betrayal of one's Baptism was likewise a disregard for the Lord's Supper. Cf. J. Betz, op. cit., 1/1,29. Heb 10,28f could very well be a phase in the early Church's struggle to get Judaizing Christians to accept the eucharistic chalice. The sin in Heb 10,26 is un-forgiveable, not because those who absented themselves from the Christian gatherings did so for the sake of their own convenience and comfort, but because it was principally a manifestation of their rejection of the Eucharist as indicated in Heb 10,29. Cf. ibid., 1/1, 26-35; 2/1, 156.

ἅπαξ-character of Christ's self-offering. The author arrives at
such a view and interpretation of Christ's sacrificial death by
way of his eschatology.

Christ's first coming was timed to coincide with the end of
the ages (9,26: ἐπί συντελεία τῶν αἰώνων). This is the factor
which makes Christ's self-sacrifice for the annulment of sin
ἅπαξ from without. That is, this does not destroy the ἅπαξ-
character of Christ's self-sacrifice that arises from within--
from its efficaciousness (10,18); but it does make it unnecessary as far as the author is concerned for him to speculate on
the relationship of future generations with Christ's sacrifice,
which, however, is fully retroactive in its effects.[21] Salvation
for those Christians living at the "end of the ages" depends on
their remaining attached to Christ as their sin sacrifice (10,26)
so that they may be found sinless when Christ appears the second
time (9,28). The author does not speculate about the possibility
of salvation for his contemporary non-Christians. However, it
would be incorrect to think that he simply considered non-Christians to be outside of the order of salvation since they are not
members of the New Covenant in Christ. Rather, he only comments
about the grave possibility[22] of loss of salvation for those who
apostasize, which is only possible if they are first baptized into the faith. Moreover, the author stresses that it is the attempt to return to their pre-Christian status after they have full

---

21. Cf. J. Moffatt, op. cit., 132f.
22. In Heb 10,31, the writer remarks that "it is a terrible thing
    to fall into the hands of the living God." Although this
    would not impress the sinner as being very comforting, it can
    also be understood as being entrusted to God's punishing and
    yet merciful treatment. Cf. 2 Sm 24,14.

knowledge of the truth that places the apostates against, but not
absolutely beyond, the order of salvation.[23] It is only in this
sense that the Letter to the Hebrews would affirm the conviction
of later Christianity that "extra ecclesiam nulla salus est."
But this raises the issue concerning the "limits" of the Church,
especially in her relationship to the old Israel. The author
only touches upon this question. Nevertheless, he makes some
very significant statements in this regard, and they must now be
considered.

c. Israel and the pilgrim Church.

Verse 10 of chapter 13 states that "we have an altar from
which those who serve the tabernacle have no authority to eat."[24]
There can be no doubt that "those who serve the tabernacle" are
those who belong to the old Israel. This is clear from the preceding verse where the author states that the heart should be
confirmed by grace rather than by foods which do not profit those
who ate them. The Israelites in the exodus through the desert
are the ones that are meant here since they are described as
those who are "walking" (οἱ περιπατοῦντες), and are spoken of in
the past tense when the writer says "they were not profited"
(οὐκ ὠφελήθησαν) by those foods (βρώματα). In verse 11, the
image of Israel in the desert is continued by means of reference
to the fact that the blood of sin sacrifices was brought into the
sanctuary (τὰ ἅγια), but the bodies of the animals were burned

---

23. Cf. Otto Michel, Der Brief an die Hebräer, (KEKNT 13),
    (Göttingen, 1936) 350f.

24. ἔχομεν θυσιαστήριον ἐξ οὗ φαγεῖν οὐκ ἔχουσιν ἐξουσίαν οἱ τῇ
    σκηνῇ λατρεύοντες.

outside of the camp (ἔξω τῆς παρεμβολῆς). This is then compared with Jesus' death outside of the gate (v. 12: ἔξω τῆς πύλης). The conclusion is that Jesus' followers must go forth from the camp of Israel to Jesus (v. 13) since they have no permanent city here (v. 14). These six verses (i.e. vv. 9-14) form a very complex and compact image of the Church.

As elsewhere all through his letter, the author chooses here also to develop his theology in the light of the Israelites in the desert. His reason may have been historically prompted by the destruction of Jerusalem and the Temple in A.D. 70. But the basic theological reason is to make a comparison between the Israelites journeying through the wilderness toward the Promised Land and the Church in pilgrimage to the Heavenly City. It is now necessary to examine these verses more closely in order to see how the author develops the image of the Church.

The first task is to find the "missing link" between verses 9 and 10. In effect, the author says that those Israelites walking in the wilderness had food that was wonderously supplied to them, but which did not really give them holiness and life; whereas, Christians have an altar from which the Israelites may not eat. Consequently, there seems to be only one logical answer--in spite of its unpopularity with many New Testament scholars--, and that is the Eucharist. The "foods" spoken of in verse 9 are not metaphorical; therefore, it is not likely that "altar" in verse 10 is to be understood as a metaphor for faith in Christ or for Christ's "mystical" presence in his followers. The first instance is ruled out because it would make no sense to say that the Israelites have no right to believe in Christ. The second instance is likewise ruled out since it is by way of faith that

Christ is present in his followers at all times. Thus, the altar (θυσιαστήριον) means just that, and it refers to Christ's presence in an equally concrete manner so that it is to be quite literally understood that those who <u>do</u> <u>not</u> <u>yet</u> <u>believe</u> in Christ have no <u>right</u> (ἐξουσία) to partake of the Eucharist.

As in 1 Cor 10,18, "altar" is here used to pinpoint the "mechanism" of Christian unity. The text is a statement which sets a "eucharistic limit" to the Church and excommunicates from the Eucharist those who have not accepted Christ. Moreover, the author leaves no doubt that following Christ also means leaving Judaism behind (v. 13). He arrives at this conclusion by way of a sort of "word-association" process, which may be very roughly outlined as follows: In verse 9, "grace" is to be associated with manna, which was God's special grace or favor to the Israelites in the desert. This, in turn, is associated with "foods." But before anything new is associated with the foods, the implicit image of the manna suggests the Eucharist (1 Cor 10,3; Jn 6,27-33), but likewise only implicitly. However, a new association now explicitly arises from the preceding images--namely, "altar." This leads to the implicit association with "sacrifice," which gives rise to the explicit mention of victims (v. 11). The implicit association is now made with Christ, but the explicit association is with the high priest who offers the blood of the victims in the sanctuary; however, their carcasses are burned beyond the camp's perimeter. The implication is that salvation is to be found where the high priest makes the offering. But Jesus offered his entire self "outside of the gate."[25] Therefore,

---

25. Cf. Heb 13,12. The author obviously says "gate" in order to

his followers must leave Israel's camp and go to him (v. 13).
Finally, the image of the camp and Jesus' death beyond the gates
suggests Jerusalem, which is not named, but leads to the comment
that Christians have no permanent city here. This is associated[26]
with the city (i.e., the "heavenly Jerusalem") to come (v. 14).
This plan can be sketched to help clarify the author's thought-
progression. But one has to realize that such an outline must,
of necessity, be very schematic and overly simplified.

---

keep the image as close as possible to the camp of Israel.
That is, the picture of Israel encamped in the wilderness is
more suitable for the concept which the writer is seeking to
explain since the camp supposedly enclosed the whole of
Israel. Consequently, when he says that Christ died outside
of the gate, he means that the Saviour, like the scapegoat
(Lv 16,20-22), took the people's sins upon himself and died
beyond the confines of Israel. But in doing so, salvation
is no longer present in Israel's camp. F.F. Bruce (op. cit.,
402-404) points out that salvation outside of the camp of
Israel is indicated in the account following the story of
the Israelite worship of the golden calf. Because of this
great crime of unfaithfulness to Yahweh, Moses took the "Tent
of Meeting" or "Testimony" and pitched it outside of the camp;
and Yahweh thus revealed himself outside of the camp during
this time. Cf. Ex 33,7-11. The theological parallel and
point of interest that the author of Hebrews is trying to
make here does not concentrate on the comparison of the high-
priestly sacrificial offering and Christ's self-offering on
the cross so much as on the theological content in the notion
of "outside"--the region of shame and estrangement where the
Church now finds itself. But since Christ himself also belongs to this "outside," it is likewise the region of salvation and triumph. Cf. O. Kuss, op. cit., 220.

26. Obviously, this term is being used here to describe a well-
planned literary form rather than the "free association of
thoughts" employed in psychoanalysis.

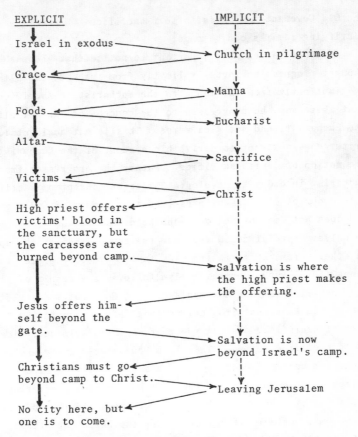

EXPLICIT

Israel in exodus

Grace

Foods

Altar

Victims

High priest offers victims' blood in the sanctuary, but the carcasses are burned beyond camp.

Jesus offers himself beyond the gate.

Christians must go beyond camp to Christ.

No city here, but one is to come.

IMPLICIT

Church in pilgrimage

Manna

Eucharist

Sacrifice

Christ

Salvation is where the high priest makes the offering.

Salvation is now beyond Israel's camp.

Leaving Jerusalem

In view of the above explanation, one problem still remains to be solved--namely, the association of the Eucharist with sacrifice. This connection requires some explanation since the Epistle to the Hebrews would seem to contradict itself if it sees the Eucharist as a sacrafice. It is not possible here to give an adequate treatment of the letter's description of sacrifice in the Old Covenant and Christ's self-sacrifice. However, a few clarifying remarks can be made.

It is, first of all, important to notice that the author's thought-progression moves explicitly from grace to the altar, and implicitly from the manna to the Eucharist to sacrifice. That is to say, he progresses to the concept of sacrifice from the Eucharist, and not vice versa. This is not accidental. The writer does not want to derive his concept of the Eucharist from the notion of Jewish sacrifice. Rather, he progresses from the Eucharist in order to develop a <u>Christian</u> concept of sacrifice. This order of development preserves the freedom of God's grace and does not destroy the ἅπαξ-character of what had taken place on Calvary several decades before the composition of the epistle. In other words, by giving primacy to the order of grace, the manna (foods) and everything else follows as a <u>result</u> of grace. The Eucharist is thus not man's gift to God, but God's gift to man.[27] In an almost ironical reversal of the conventional concept of sacrifice, one can say that Christ's self-sacrifice was God's sacrifice to man. This is a "one-time-only-event." The Eucharist must be understood in this perspective. Since the writer is able to say that there is no longer any offering (προσφορά) for sin wherever there is forgiveness (10,18) and still speak of a θυσία for forgiveness of sins which Christians commit (10,26; 12,1), there is no contradiction between Christ's self-sacrifice and the sacrificial aspect of the Eucharist that is

---

27. This statement is in no way meant to prejudice the concept of "human instrumentality" in regard to the Eucharist as Christ's offering of himself to the Father as illustrated in Heb 13,12f.

expressed in the reference to the altar (13,10: θυσιαστήριον).
This does not mean that the Eucharist as such--that is, as an
historical act--is the "sacrifice for sins." But in so far as
the Eucharist means Christ's special presence as the θυσία περὶ
ἁμαρτιῶν in the Church, a connection can be justifiably made.

2. The Catholic Letters[28]

a. The Letter to James.

This letter, whose date of composition is placed anywhere
from A.D. 40 to 150, reveals a very early and simple form of
Christian life much like that which is found in the Gospel accord-
to Matthew. Although there can be little doubt that the letter
was intended for Jewish Christians, it also gives indications of
Greek influence, especially when the source of temptation to sin
is placed in one's desires (1,14) rather than in some external
power--that is, Satan.[29]

Giving in to one's desires, or the attempt to fulfill them by
devious means rather than in reliance upon God, ties one to the
world and makes him an enemy of God (4,1-4; 1,2-6). Temptation,
if endured, works toward the sanctification of the person (1,12);
but giving in to one's desires leads to sin, which ultimately
matures and brings forth death (1,15).

---

28. Since the dates of these letters are so uncertain and controversial, no attempt will be made here to present them
chronologically. Rather, the content of these letters along
with the apparent interdependence of some of them will be
used as the criteria for the order of treatment.

29. Cf. James H. Ropes, A Critical and Exegetical Commentary on
the Epistle of St. James, (ICC), (Edinburgh, 1916) 155f.
However, it should be pointed out that James does not entirely give up the idea of the devil as a tempter. Cf. Jm 4,7.

The writer takes it for granted that his readers know what
this means, and much of the letter is given over to practical advice, mostly in the form of Jewish wisdom literature, intended to
guide Christians along the path of proper conduct of life. Emphasis is placed on doing, and not only hearing, the word (1,22).
From this point of view, the writer is able to dwell on the sins
of omission as well as those of commission (4,17). Especially the
wealthy come under attack for their neglect of charity while relying on "faith" to save them as if it were the good work that guaranteed their salvation (2,14ff; 5,1-6). The respect of persons
that the wealthy usually command even in the Christian assembly
(2,2-4) is particularly singled out as a sin committed against
the poorer members of the community, and it is to be looked upon
as a transgression against the entire Law (2,9f; Mt 5,19).

This is reminiscent of Paul's statement about the curse of
the Law (Gal 3,10; 5,3; Dt 27,26). But, whereas Paul develops
his doctrine in this regard from the Old Testament itself, James
gives a different reason; namely, the author of the Law in all
its points of legislation is one and the same (2,11). However,
in spite of his respect for the Law, James is aware of the fact
that Christians will be judged according to the "law of liberty"
(νόμος ἐλευθερίας) and should speak and act with this fact in
mind (2,12). By this, the writer seems to mean that Christians
should act with mercy and forgiveness towards others, because
they themselves have been granted great mercy--probably in that
they are no longer bound by the strictness of the Law which could
unmercifully demand the death of its transgressors (Heb 10,28).
But if a Christian acts without mercy, then he will be judged
without mercy (2,13). Thus, Christians should not give vent to
querulous feelings towards one another lest they be condemned by
the judge who is already standing before the door (5,9).

The last few verses of the letter are very important in the history of the development of Christian penitential discipline. In verse 14 of chapter 5, the writer gives the instruction that if anyone in the community is ill, the elders should be called in to pray over him and anoint him with oil in the name of the Lord. The result is that "the prayer of faith" (ἡ εὐχὴ τῆς πίστεως) will save the sick person in body and soul, so to speak, since "the Lord will raise him up" (i.e., cure him) and forgive whatever sins the sick person has committed (v. 15). Several elements from Jesus' life as depicted in the Gospels are alluded to in these verses, which also describe Jewish practices in regard to religious concern for the ill.

Although the writer does not define "the prayer of faith," it very probably does not only refer to the prayer of the presbyters over the sick person, but also the prayer of the sick person himself. This corresponds to the confession of faith in himself which Jesus generally elicited from those who came to him to be cured (e.g., Mt 8,10; 9,22.28). It is likewise implied in the instructions that the anointing is to be done in the Lord's name since this expression refers to the source of the action's healing effects rather than to a commission from the Lord himself that his Church should perform such an act.[30] However, such anointing of the sick with oil, like baptism, was common practice in Judaism during Jesus' lifetime, and its religious use in the early Church (and thereafter) should not cause surprise (Mk 6,13).

The significant thing to note for this present study is that the action of anointing and healing along with the forgiveness of sins is placed under the charge of the presbyters of the commun-

---

30. Cf. F. Mussner, Krankensalbung, in: LThK 6 (1961) 585.

ity, who are not the charismatic healers reported elsewhere in the Bible. Their duties appear to be parallel to Christ's own actions and experiences when he was summoned to visit a sick person (Mt 8,5f; 9,18; Jn 11,3) and healed both body and soul in one act (Mt 9,1-8; Jn 5,8.14). The summoning of some prominent religious personage to visit a sick person and to pray for him was also a common practice in Judaism.[31]

Having dealt with the care that is to be shown someone who is ill, James turns to consider the spiritual welfare of the community as a whole. To this end, Christians should confess their sins to each other and pray for one another (5,16). Those who have wandered from the truth should be sought out and converted in order that they may be saved (vv. 19f). Although no details are given as to how the process of the confession of sins was to be carried out, there is no reason to limit it to a procedure that took place exclusively or even chiefly between the community and its presbyters or leaders. The process is most probably to be derived from the practice of the synagogue, which made provisions for fraternal correction;[32] and even though the confession of one's own sins did not have a fully institutionalized character in Judaism, it was not an unknown practice (1 Kgs 8,33-35; Neh 9,3-5; Dn 9,4-20).

b. The First Letter of Peter.

If this letter, addressed to the Christians of Asia Minor (1,1), is to be ascribed to Peter, then it must be dated before his death under Nero in or shortly after A.D. 64. The refined

---

31. Cf. SB 1, 475; ibid., 4/1, 573-78.
32. Ibid., 1, 787-92.

Greek of the epistle speaks against its being an immediate composition by Peter. But whether or not it was written by him before
his death or by someone else at a later date, the theology is
primitive in flavor and Palestinian rather than Hellenistic in
influence.[33] The letter is a valuable witness to the Church's
attitude toward herself and the world as she entered a trying
period of suffering and persecution.[34] Charity is recommended
toward everyone of the brethren (1,22). Obedience is to be given
to the emperor (2,13). Christians should act decently among pagans so that, even though they are now called wrongdoers by the
pagans, the pagans may note their good actions and give glory to
God on the "day of visitation" (2,11f) which is swiftly approaching (4,7). Christians who were formerly pagans themselves can
only expect that their abandoning of a life of immorality and
idolatry should bewilder the pagan and bring him to speak evil
of them (4,3f). God, however, is the judge of the pagan.[35]

Other than these few and very general remarks concerning
Christian behavior, this letter offers little to the present study.
However, it should be noted that the writer instructs his readers
to enact a discipline of subordination within the community as well

---

33. Cf. J.N.D. Kelly, A Commentary on the Epistles of Peter and of
Jude, (BNTC), (London, 1969) 27, 30.

34. K.H. Schelkle (op. cit., 214) believes that the writer may have
the persecution under Emperor Domitian (A.D. 81-96) in mind.

35. Cf. 1 Pt 4,5. This verse is to be interpreted as a sign of
real hope for the salvation of pagans as already seen above in
the text. That is, there is hope that they will give glory to
God ἐν ἡμέρᾳ ἐπισκοπῆς. Although the "day of visitation" can
indicate punishment (Is 10,3; Jr 6,15), it can also mean a special time when God offers salvation. Cf. Lk 19,44. This is
most probably meant in 1 Pt 2,12, where the expression is used
eschatologically. Cf. J. Kelly, op. cit., 106.

as to the emperor. Christians should be "obedient children," not given in to their former lusts (1,14). Civic obedience should be given to all such authorities (2,13-17). Servants are to be subject to their masters, even if they are harsh lords (2,18f). The Christian is indeed free (2,16), but it is better if he subject himself in imitation of Christ's obedience (2,21). Wives are to be subject to their husbands as Sarah was to Abraham (3,1.5f). The younger ones should submit themselves to the older ones;[36] and finally all are to be subject to one another (5,5). Although the writer does not compare this subordination with any sort of heavenly hierarchy as found in some of the early Fathers, the tendency in this direction seems to be present, especially when he mentions that Christ is in heaven at the right hand of God, with the angels, authorities and powers being made subject to him (3, 22). Likewise, Christians who humble themselves now will be exalted by God in due time (5,6).

c. The Letter of Jude and the Second Letter of Peter.

Although the two letters are most probably of very different dates (Jude about 70-80, 2 Pt anywhere from 80-180), the literary dependence of 2 Pt on Jude and the similarity of the two letters make it desirable to treat them together. Both letters combat false doctrine that apparently encourages moral laxity. It is difficult to make a clear distinction between doctrinal and moral issues. Some incipient form of Gnosticism is probably the cause of the difficulties, but it still is far from the mature forms and systems that are found in the second century.[37]

---

36. Since the writer indirectly addresses the πρεσβύτεροι and identifies himself as a συμπρεσβύτερος in 1 Pt 5,1, verse 5 is probably to be understood ecclesially, with the "elders" in a position of authority over the others regardless of age.

37. Cf. J. Kelly, op. cit., 230f.

In verse 4 of <u>Jude</u>, certain persons are said to have insinu-
ated themselves into the Christian communities in order to erode
the faith. According to 2 Pt 2,1-22, they are ψευδοδιδάσκαλοι
who scoff at the notion of the Parousia, which 2 Pt reaffirms in
forceful apocalyptic images. This doubt in Christ's second coming, which was especially awaited after the destruction of Jerusalem in A.D. 70,[38] is something antithetic in the New Testament.[39]
The troublemakers are apparently itinerant preachers and teachers
who, rather than form their own sect, prefer to infiltrate the
various churches and infest them with libertine doctrine.[40] They
partake of the community meals, but are treacherous guests full
of greed and adultery and ready to seduce souls.[41]

---

38. Since the Gospel had reached the main parts of the Empire
    before A.D. 70 (1 Thes 1,8; Rm 1,5.8; Col 1,6.23), the escha-
    tological discourse in Mt 24 seems to be clear evidence of
    this hope.

39. This doubt is clearly expressed again in the letter of Clement
    of Rome to the Corinthians (23,3-5).

40. Cf. J. Kelly, <u>op</u>. <u>cit</u>., 248f. However, these troublemakers do
    in fact create sects within the community. Cf. Jude 17.

41. Cf. Jude 12; 2 Pt 2,13f. These two passages have an extremely
    confused manuscript traditon. Jude 12 speaks of the presence
    of these evil guests at the agape-meals of the sincere Christ-
    ians (ἐν ταῖς ἀγάπαις ὑμῶν). But 2 Pt 2,13 reads: "in their
    deceits" (ἐν ταῖς ἀπάταις αὐτῶν). Perhaps the author or some
    early transcriber of 2 Pt intended a pun by calling the agape-
    feasts of heretics "deceivings." Cf. Jakob Jonsson, <u>Humor</u> <u>and</u>
    <u>Irony</u> <u>in</u> <u>the</u> <u>New</u> <u>Testament,</u> <u>illuminated</u> <u>by</u> <u>parallels</u> <u>in</u> <u>Talmud</u>
    <u>and</u> <u>Midrash,</u> (Reykjavik, 1965) 249f. Or, the difficulty may
    have begun when some copyists were offended by the idea of such
    sinful persons partaking of an agape, and so they altered the
    expression in Jude 12 to read "in their deceits." Such a manu-
    script would then have been used as the basis for 2 Pt. How-
    ever, it seems that later copyists may have tried to "correct"
    2 Pt 2,13 by way of manuscripts containing the original read-

The character of these false teachers and immoral persons is further illuminated through a series of comparisons with various persons of the Old Testament and with other suitable images. They are the followers of Cain (Jude 11) and cursed children (2 Pt 2, 14), impious men who are the fulfillment of old predictions of such condemnations (Jude 4) and whose judgment and damnation from of old is now at hand (2 Pt 2,3). In contemporary Judaism, Cain was considered "a child of the evil one" (1 Jn 3,12), an egoist and rebel against God, one who relies only on himself and leads to godlessness and sensuality. Such persons are destined to eternal loss.[42] The curse of Cain that is upon them will not only have eschatological effects, but probably also indicates their present excommunication from the Church.[43] They are guilty of Balaam's error (Jude 11; 2 Pt 2,15), who, according to a later and unfavorable tradition,[44] led the Israelites into idolatry and accepted Balak's bribes.[45] "He thus became the prototype of unprincipled people who will not shrink from any enormity for monetary gain and, like him, are doomed to hell."[46] These heretics

---

ing of Jude 12 since, by that time, the agape had fallen into disuse, and thus the idea of sinful Christians at an agape no longer appeared so offensive. Whether or not the agape spoken of in Jude 12 was still connected with the Eucharist is another question which cannot be answered on the basis of presently available evidence. However, there can be no doubt that _Jude_ considered such a meal to have a special religious character. One may therefore conclude that the complaint is essentially the same as the one Paul makes in 1 Cor 11,20-22. Cf. J. Kelly, op. cit., 269-71, 341.

42. _Ibid._, 266f.
43. Cf. W. Doskocil, op. cit., 109f.
44. For the earlier, more favorable tradition cf. Nm 22-24; Jos 24,9f; Mi 6,5
45. Cf. _SB_ 3, 771, 793.
46. Cf. J. Kelly, op. cit., 267f.

are further compared with Korah (Jude 11), who led the rebellion
against Moses and Aaron (Nm 16). This comparison seems to indicate that the agitators were bold enough to challenge the authority of the various overseers of the churches while creating unrest and divisions within the communities. The writer says that
such men "have perished" (ἀπώλοντο), which is but an emphatic
way of saying that, as far as he can determine, their eventual
destruction is already a settled matter.[47]

Now the authors of Jude and 2 Pt turn to nonpersonal images
in their description of the false teachers. At the love feast,
they are like rocky reefs wrecking the ship of faith,[48] like
autumn trees bearing no fruit, twice dead and uprooted, waterless
clouds carried about by the winds, and wandering stars whose ultimate destiny is eternal darkness (Jude 12f; 2 Pt 2,13.17). They
are fruitless because they are sterile and lifeless--that is, destined for the "second death" at the end of the world as well as
physical death in the present. Therefore, they are "twice dead."[49]
Their uprooted condition implies that they no longer belong to the
community in any true sense.[50] As "straying stars," they exemplify
disobedience to God and disorder in the universe since the ancients
thought that the planets[51] violated God's established order and

---

47. Ibid., 268.
48. This seems to be the meaning of Jude 12, which simply says
    that such persons are σπιλάδες at the agape; whereas, 2 Pt 2,
    13 speaks of them as "spots" (σπίλοι) at a meal. Perhaps 2
    Pt means that these unwelcome persons are as difficult to get
    rid of as the stains that careless guests make on fine table
    linen.
49. Cf. SB 3 830f.
50. Cf. J. Kelly, op. cit., 274.
51. Note the play on words in Jude 11.13: v. 11, πλάνη, i.e., de-
    ception; v. 13: πλανῆται, i.e., wandering stars.

stability of the heavens because they had come under the influence of disobedient angels, who were being punished forever in a fiery abyss for their sin. "The false teachers resemble them because they too, as a result of rebellion and sin, have gone off course, and while pretending to give light in fact lead people astray."[52] They are like dogs returning to their vomit, or the sow which returns to wallow in the mud after being washed (2 Pt 2,22). It would have been better had they never learned of Christianity and the way to sanctity; for their return to a wicked life only makes them that much worse and more responsible (2 Pt 2,20f). But now that such men have appeared, one can be sure that the end is near since they are a sign of the immanent end of time (Jude 17f; 2 Pt 3,2f).

Finally, a three-class distinction[53] is made according to the way one should treat with those who are unsteady in the faith or moral commandments (Jude 22f): There are those who have doubts, but they are to be reassured of the truth; then there are those who need to be rescued "from the fire"; and there are those who are to be pitied with fear and even whose clothing is to be avoided. The fire is equivalent to the lasting destruction that was visited upon Sodom and Gomorrah (Jude 7) and which will destroy sinners on the Last Day (2 Pt 3,7). Being already condemned per-

---

52. Cf. J. Kelly, op. cit., 274.
53. The three classes are found in Codex Sinaiticus and Alexandrinus and other manuscripts. According to Codex Vaticanus and Clement of Alexandria, there are only two classes: the doubters to be saved from the fire, and those to be avoided. The longer version may be an expansion of the shorter text, which is abrupt and unclear. Cf. J. Kelly, op. cit., 288. But even if that is the case, the longer version must be very early and therefore a valuable witness to the beginnings of a systematic classification of sinners into three categories.

sons, they are under a curse. Therefore, their clothing is contaminated and must be avoided. However, this idea must not be
taken literally. The χιτών was generally considered an under-
garment, or was at least worn next to the skin. In view of this,
the contact spoken of here is most probably meant to be understood
as the direct influence that flows from personal acquaintance with
someone rather than literal contact with his tunic. The comparison is somewhat similar to the Pauline concept of σάρξ, which
often means the unconverted man who is still ensnared in his sins,
especially sins of the flesh (Rm 6,19; 7,5f; Gal 6,18; 1 Cor 5,5).
Consequently, contact with a sinner's tunic means to be in danger
of being influenced by his unconverted ways or teaching. However,
even though such persons are left to the judgment of God, fraternal admonishment and intercessory prayers for them probably are
part of the community's procedure in regard to such persons.[54]

d. The First Letter of John.

  a). Christological heresy.

This letter, along with the other two letters ascribed to
John, was written very probably toward the end of the first century, and displays some rather radically changed conditions in
the Church as over against earlier times. Not only are zealous
false teachers creating internal strife, but the unholy ambition
of other Christians--although still orthodox--is complicating the
situation. The role of the itinerant prophet is especially threatened by these persons, and his status is in transition. No names

----

54. Cf 2 Thes 3,15; Didache 2,7; Ignatius of Antioch, ad Smyrn
    4,1; J. Kelly, op. cit., 289.

can be definitely placed on the false teachers and their doctrine, but Cerinthianism and Docetism are often named as possibilities.[55]

In 1 Jn, the false teachers are called ἀντίχριστοι (2,18.22; 4,3; 2 Jn 7). Although this is the first use of the term in the Bible, Jewish apocalyptic thought is undoubtedly the source of the concept.[56] The work of these anti-Christs is to deny that Jesus is the Messiah and the Christ. This means to deny that Jesus is the Son of God, and, indeed, it is a denial of God himself.[57] The core of the heresy is found in the claim that the Christ did not come in the flesh; that is, the heretics do not deny the humanity of Jesus, but only that the Christ is incarnate in Jesus (2,22; 4,2f; 2 Jn 7). The writer thus proposes a simple test in order to distinguish the false prophets and their disciples from the true ones: Whoever confesses that Jesus Christ[58] has come in

---

55. Docetism did not deny that Jesus was the Christ, but only that he did not have a real human nature. Cerinthianism admitted Jesus' real human nature, but held that he was the Christ only after his baptism until--but not including--his death. One or the other of these heresies is generally cited as a possibility by the various commentaries. However, as will become clear in the text above, the present writer is inclined to believe that the Letters of John have another Christological error in mind, which denied that Jesus ever was the Christ in any real way. Cf. Franz Mussner, Christologische Homologese und evangelische Vita Jesu, (Zur Frühgeschichte der Christologie, in: Quaestiones Disputatae 51), (Freiburg, Basel, Vienna, 1970) 64.

56. Cf. A.E. Brooke, A Critical and Exegetical Commentary on the Johannine Epistles, (ICC), (Edinburgh, 1912) 52.

57. Cf. 1 Jn 2,22f. "Die Leugnung, dass Jesus der Christus ist, ist also geradezu Gottesleugnung." Cf. Rudolf Bultmann, Die drei Johannesbriefe, (KEKNT 14), (Göttingen, 1967) 43.

58. In 1 Jn, "Jesus Christ" is used as a single title consistently except in 2,22, where it is made clear that the heresy concerns the Christ's incarnation in Jesus.

the flesh has the Spirit of God. Whoever denies this confession of faith has the spirit of anti-Christ (4,1-3). Those who listen to the teaching of the writer are of God; while those who refuse to listen possess the spirit of falsehood (4,6).

Perhaps it was the fundamental Gnostic dualism which radically opposes God and matter as the principles of Good and Evil that led the false teachers to advocate a Christology that must ultimately deny the soteriological significance of Jesus and his death. However, they did not organize themselves to form their own sect, but claimed to be orthodox believers and undertook to belittle the rest of the community for its "inferior faith."[59] Rather than make any statements threatening or pronouncing excommunication, the writer simply declares that such persons have already left the Church of their own accord and, in fact, never did really belong to her; otherwise, they would have never left (2,19).

b). Eucharist and heretics.

One of the more controversial passages of this letter is found early in chapter 5. Besides the debate over the authenticity of the so-called comma johanneum[60] in verses 7f, the discussion concerning the possible eucharistic character of verses 6-8 has developed into a serious game of seesaw, with the greater number of exegetes sitting on the side which opposes such an interpretation. Verse 5 affirms that Jesus is the Son of God, and verses 6-8 (less

---

59. Cf. R. Bultmann, Johannesbriefe, 41, 44f.
60. The comma, which stands here between parentheses, appeared first in the Vulgate, probably during the course of the 8th century: "Quoniam tres sunt, qui dant testimonium (in caelo: Pater, Verbum, et Spiritus sanctus: et hi tres unum sunt. Et tres sunt, qui testimonium dant in terra:") etc. This text does not appear in any of the Greek manuscripts preceding the 15th century.

the comma johanneum) continue: "This is he who came through water and blood--namely, Jesus Christ; not in the water only, but in the water and in the blood; and the Spirit is the one who bears witness, in that the Spirit is the truth. For there are three that bear witness: the Spirit and the water and the blood, and the three are in accord."[61]

The proponents of the eucharistic interpretation generally see a connection between this passage and the piercing of Christ's side as recounted in Jn 19,34f, which they also interpret eucharistically. The opponents, however, usually respond by pointing out that the term "blood" alone does not suffice to label this passage "eucharistic." Moreover, the reference to Christ as ὁ ἐλθών rather than ὁ ἐρχόμενος in verse 6 supposedly rules out any real allusion to the Eucharist, which, as a continuous act in the Church, would require that the participle be in the present rather than the aorist tense. Such arguments are indeed weighty; however, they are not conclusive, and so still open to rebuttal.

First of all, it must be remembered that the Johannine "burden of proof" for the Eucharist falls entirely upon the word "blood" (Jn 6,53-56). It may very well be that the mention of "blood" alone in Johannine literature suffices on occasion to indicate the Eucharist. Indeed, this may be the key to understanding John's otherwise unexpected and inexplicable remark that "the flesh profits nothing" (Jn 6,53), for the quickening spirit is ascribed to the blood.

---

61. Οὗτός ἐστιν ὁ ἐλθὼν δι' ὕδατος καὶ αἵματος, Ἰησοῦς Χριστός· οὐκ ἐν τῷ ὕδατι μόνον, ἀλλ' ἐν τῷ ὕδατι καὶ ἐν τῷ αἵματι· καὶ τὸ πνεῦμά ἐστιν τὸ μαρτυροῦν, ὅτι τὸ πνεῦμά ἐστιν ἡ ἀλήθεια. ὅτι τρεῖς εἰσιν οἱ μαρτυροῦντες, τὸ πνεῦμα καὶ τὸ ὕδωρ καὶ τὸ αἷμα, καὶ οἱ τρεῖς εἰς τὸ ἕν εἰσιν.

The second argument against a eucharistic interpretation of
1 Jn 5,6-8 is not really as forceful as it might first appear to
be. A glance into any good Greek grammar of the New Testament
will produce several feasible explanations for the use of the
aorist participle even when the passage is given a eucharistic
interpretation.[62] Of itself, the aorist says nothing about the
tense of the action, but only indicates the type of action. The
argument of the opponents actually requires a pluperfect, or at
least a present perfect, participle in order to be conclusive.
Consequently, the relative tense-aspect of the participle in question must be sought in the main verb, which is the present tense
(ἐστίν). In English, it is still quite possible to respect the
type of action which an aorist form with present aspect requires
by means of the simple present rather than the progressive present
form. Thus, ὁ ἐλθών can be legitimately translated as "the one
who comes" instead of "the one who came." But "the one who is
coming" is not permissible. Further evidence that the writer of
1 Jn does not hesitate to use such a present tense and aorist with
present aspect is found in verse 1 of chapter 2. This verse will
be treated later. But now it is necessary to approach 1 Jn 5,6-8
more positively to see what the passage implies if it is indeed
eucharistic.

---

62. The ingressive aorist denotes the beginning of an act that has
    continuing effects, such as ἐσίγησεν ("it became quiet") in
    Acts 15,12. Cf. also 2 Cor 8,9; Rm 14,9. The complexive
    aorist stands for a lasting act which is presented as a com-
    pleted whole or even repeated for a certain number of times.
    Cf. Acts 28,30; 2 Cor 11,25. The gnomic aorist represents an
    act that was, is or will be "once and for all times." It is
    used mostly in narratives. Cf. Mk 4,3-9; Lk 10,30-35. The
    future aorist is used after a future condition. Cf. Jn 15,8.

Most frequently, the verses in question are seen as an attack on those heretics who held that Jesus became the Christ at the time of his baptism in the Jordan, but that the Christ "deserted" him at the time of his passion and death. This was the supposed teaching of Cerinth, John's great antagonist at Ephesus according to tradition. While such false teaching may very well be implied in 1 Jn 5,6-8, to stop at this point, however, would seem to distort the writer's real intention. The notion that Jesus became the Christ through water (i.e., baptism) is not affirmed anywhere in Johannine literature. Rather, the Christ is pre-existent as the Son of God and is incarnated in Jesus' birth.[63] It is likewise clear that 1 Jn confesses Jesus in his entire existence to be the Christ and the Son of God (4,2f). From this, it appears most probable that the heresy which this letter attacks held that Jesus never was the Christ even for a moment. It is scarcely possible, in view of the above mentioned facts, that the reference to water in 1 Jn 5,6-8 has anything to do with the Synoptic version of Jesus' baptism by John the Baptist. That this passage should refer exclusively or even primarily to Jesus' baptism in the Jordan is made even more improbable by the statement at the end of verse 6 that "the Spirit is the one who bears witness" (τὸ πνεῦμά ἐστιν τὸ μαρτυροῦν). This is obviously in parallel to οὗτός ἐστιν ὁ ἐλθών at the beginning of the verse. However, if the aorist participle, ἐλθών, only refers to the past events of Jesus' baptism and death, then it must be assumed that the witness

---

63. Cf. Heinrich Schlier, Die Anfänge des christologischen Credo, (Zur Frühgeschichte der Christologie, in: Quaestiones Disputatae 51) 19, 38, 42f, 54f; R. Bultmann, Theologie des Neuen Testaments, 385-94; Rudolf Schnackenburg, Christologie des Neuen Testamentes, in: Mysterium Salutis 3/1, 337-41.

of the Spirit that is spoken of here likewise refers to a particular event of the past--namely, Jesus' baptism in the Jordan when
the Holy Spirit descended on him. But this explanation is impossible since the present participle, μαρτυροῦν, rules out any past
reference. But, as already seen, the aorist participle, ἐλθών, is
quite capable of present or even future reference provided that
the action is not a continuous state. Nor does this necessarily
rule out an act that can be or is repeated. It only means that
the act is "isolated" with the result that the aorist stresses
the fact of the act as such. It is not necessary to dwell on
these points any longer. We may now turn to deal with some other
questions concerning the passage.

Since it is most improbable that the water spoken of is an
indication of Jesus' baptism in the Jordan, one is forced to ask
if the blood spoken of refers primarily to Christ's death on the
cross. Once more, it seems necessary to give a negative answer.
The reasons for this reply are already contained to a large extent in the above treatment concerning the water, and their ela-
boration is not necessary here. However, a few points can be
added.

In a Christology that uses Jesus' baptism by John as an explanation of how Jesus became the Christ--or at least how he
was manifested as the Christ--, the concept that the Christ came
through or in the water has meaning. But what should it mean to
say that the Christ came through or in blood when blood simply
means Jesus' death on the cross? The question defies satisfactory answering. Moreover, outside of the reference to blood in
its treatment of the Eucharist in chapter 6, the Fourth Gospel
mentions Christ's blood in only one other place. This is in the

account of the piercing of Jesus' side with a lance (19,34)--
an event that comes <u>after</u> Jesus has already died.[63a]   But if
neither the grammar of 1 Jn 5,6-8 nor Johannine Christology
lends itself to an interpretation which would restrict the meaning of water and blood in 1 Jn 5,6-8 to Jesus' historical baptism and death, then it is necessary to turn to the sacraments
in order to find the correct and full meaning of this passage.
The major question that now remains is: "Do these verses refer
to both Christian Baptism and the Eucharist, or only to the Eucharist?"

At first glance, it would seem more feasible to interpret the
passage with reference to both Baptism and the Eucharist. Nevertheless, an exclusively Eucharistic interpretation cannot be rejected <u>a priori</u>.[64]   Whichever of these two possibilities is the

---

63a. J. Betz (<u>op</u>. <u>cit</u>., 2/1, 193) explains that the water and blood
from Christ's side show that even after his death Christ continues to give out these elements sacramentally (i.e., Baptism and Eucharist). 1 Jn 6,6 is John's way of saying that
Jesus is the Son of God both in these sacraments just as he
was when he came through water and blood--that is, in his
death and the open side.

64. M. Goguel (<u>op</u>. <u>cit</u>., 210f) theorizes that there was a group
of Christians in Asia Minor who, similar to some followers of
Christ at Ephesus (Acts 19,1-6), knew only of Baptism, but
still had to learn of the necessity of the Eucharist. Or,
M. Goguel continues, another possibility might be that 1 Jn
is trying to correct an improper eucharistic practice--namely,
the omission of wine in the Eucharist. However, J. Betz (<u>op</u>.
<u>cit</u>., 2/1, 197f), who sees in 1 Jn 5,6-8 an attack against
the "Qumran-Christians" for whom Baptism alone was all-important, rejects this interpretation since the "<u>Wasserkelch</u>" of
the Ebionites appears to be a later compromise and John's
theology would have rejected a "<u>Wassereucharistie</u>" as a real
and effective Eucharist; and yet 1 Jn 5,6 says Christ comes
(not only) through water.

correct one is a matter that seems to depend largely for its solution upon the meaning of εἰς τὸ ἕν in 1 Jn 5,8.

One of the major themes in John's Last Supper account concerns Jesus' wish to unite his disciples with himself and the Father (Jn 17,11.21-23). Earlier, John had said that Jesus' death was meant to gather into one (συναγάγη εἰς ἕν) all of God's scattered children (11,52). It seems possible, then, to interpret 1 Jn 5,8 ecclesiologically rather than sacramentally in an exclusive and narrow sense. If that is the case, the verse in question would imply that individuals are united as one with Christ and the Father in the Church through the action of the Holy Spirit in Baptism and the Eucharist. But if τὸ ἕν refers only to the Eucharist, the verse would be saying that the one act of the Eucharist involves the working of the Holy Spirit in the water and wine of the Eucharist. However, there is no reason to believe that bread was omitted in the Eucharist of the "Johannine Church," and one may rightly ask why this element is not mentioned if the text is exclusively eucharistic. On the other hand, if τὸ ἕν does mean the act of the Eucharist considered as a unified whole, then the aorist participle, ἐλθών, in verse 6 is made even more explicable than before. But whatever the case may be, it is probably that the passage is somehow directed against the false teachers opposed by the letter; and it is the consequence of their doctrine that is of real concern to the letter's author.

The effect of the heretics has been the endangerment and destruction of the community-life and love of the churches they have infected. The real objection of the author is not to be found at the level of abstract doctrine. Rather, his message is primarily ethical, and concerns the Christian's proper union with God and

with one another. The truth must be _lived_ and not only claimed
(1,6f). This is to walk in the light and to have fellowship with
one another and to be cleansed of sin by Christ's blood (1,7).
But this forgiveness of sins means that the Christian must confess them (1,9). Perhaps this confession of sins is to be likened to the one that is to be made before the celebration of the
Eucharist[65] as prescribed in the _Didache_ (14,1) and, to some extent, implied in 1 Cor 11,28.

   _c_). Theology _of_ _sin_.

A deeper probe into the epistle's theology of sin is now
necessary for a fuller understanding of the ecclesial discipline
that the letter advocates. The author states in 2,1f that he is
writing in order to prevent his readers from sinning (ἵνα μὴ ἁμάρ-
τητε). At first, this seems to be incompatible with 3,6, which
says that one who lives in God does not sin (οὐχ ἁμαρτάνει).
However, the use of the aorist in the former phrase quoted from
2,1 "suggests definite acts of sin rather than the habitual state,
which is incompatible with the position of Christians who are in
truth what their name implies."[66] The use of the present tense
in 3,6, on the other hand, clearly indicates a habitual and willful state of sin that prevents union with God and others. Such a
sinful life means to belong to the devil (3,8). These sins are
not those of the flesh--which are not mentioned in the letter--,
but rather the major and willful relapses in Christian charity
that result from the work of the false teachers. But no one who
fails to love his brother belongs to God (3,10). The prime example

---

65. Cf. _Ibid._, 208-10.
66. Cf. A.E. Brooke, _op. cit._, 23.

of such a sinner was Cain, who belonged to "the Evil One" and slew his brother (3,12). And a murderer is anyone who hates his brother (3,15). This lack of love for one's neighbor is precisely that which prevents union with God, because God is love (4,8).

As the author continues to explain the nature and effects of sin, he finally reaches a climax in 5,16, where one first encounters the expression "sin unto death" (ἁμαρτία πρὸς θάνατιν). The Christian should pray for a brother who sins in a lesser way. But he need not pray for someone who "sins unto death."[67]

The meaning of the expression is most likely the same as that of the "willful sin" in Heb 10,26. If the writer of 1 Jn has the whole letter in view when he makes this statement,[68] then it refers to apostasy from the true faith. This is very probably what is

---

67. In so far as this is truly a lasting sin of rejection of Christ (i.e., made lasting by refusal to repent), it can be identified with the "unforgivable sin against the Holy Spirit" found in the Synoptists (Mt 12,24.30; 23,13; Mk 3,22.30; Lk 12,9), who generally consider sin in its final stages and effects rather than in its origins. Cf. Piet Schoonenberg, Man and Sin, (De Macht der Zonde, 1962), (London, Melbourne, 1965) 14. But it should be pointed out that the "sin unto death" is not fully identical with the "sin against the Holy Spirit." Nor does 1 Jn forbid prayer for someone who "sins unto death." Rather, the writer's object is to inform his readers that they can and should pray for a brother who commits a sin not unto death, but there is no obligation towards someone who "sins unto death." The reason is that such a sin places the sinner beyond the normal sphere of Christian intercession of brother for brother since the sinner has renounced the fatherhood of God by rejecting the brotherhood of Christ and his followers. Cf. A.E. Brooke, op. cit., 147. Cf. also note 69 below.

68. R. Bultmann (Johannesbriefe, 11, 89) maintains that 1 Jn 5, 14-21 is an "Anhang" from a later redactor.

intended in 5,21, where the letter's readers are told to guard
themselves against the idols (φυλάξατε ἑαυτὰ ἀπὸ τῶν εἰδώλων).
Since there is no question of literal idolatry in the letter,
the expression just quoted must refer to the type of false doctrine that leads to the apostasy from the faith that the writer
or redactor has in mind for the entire letter.[69]

---

69. This is not to say that apostasy was not often actually effected through literal idolatry. But it seems clear that
the writer (or redactor) means willful transgressions as in
Heb 10,26, or perhaps even definite sins such as the triad
of "unforgivable sins" (according to some early Fathers) of
apostasy, adultery and murder as listed in the Western version of Acts 15,20.29. But the "unforgivable sin against
the Holy Spirit" is not meant. Cf. R. Bultmann, Johannesbriefe, 90, n. 2. B. Poschmann (op. cit., 76) attempts to
identify the two with each other. However, it is nowhere
stated that the "sin unto death" is unforgivable in the same
way that the "sin against the Holy Spirit" is declared unforgivable in this age and the one to come. Cf. Mt 12,32.
According to rabbinic thought (cf. SB 1, 636-38), the Holy
Spirit meant the Torah, the Spirit of prophecy and inspira-
tion. To speak against the Torah was to commit a sin unto
death--a sin which implied capital punishment in former times.
Eventually, rabbinic theology made some restricted allowances
for the forgiveness of such sins, especially if the sinner
repented and did penance. Some teachers of the Law would
have applied this concept even to those who denied God's
Lordship, disregarded the Torah and did not observe the rite
of circumcision. But repentance and penance were prerequisite requirements. The death of a person was considered especially efficacious in effecting atonement for such sins
provided that repentance and penance have preceded. But now,
the Synoptists (esp. Mt 12,32) affirm that there is definitely a sin that even death will not atone. It is itself a
state of permanent nonrepentance and nonreconciliation which
is rooted in this life due to the sinner's constant and unrepented resistance to grace. Mt 12,32 and pars. may seem
harsh, but one must keep in mind that the Synoptists are not
discussing penitance at this point, but rather the fact of

Orthodox faith is described in 5,20 as knowledge and life in the true God. That is, orthodoxy of faith is necessary if one is to have access to and union with the true God. Although the author is not thinking of idolatry in the true pagan sense, he views adherence to the new Israel as absolutely necessary for true worship since, as in the old Israel, all worship in foreign lands by the non-Israelites is considered idolatry.

Although early Christianity had removed the legalistic, ritualistic and geographical aspects from the concept of impurity, the idea that the world outside of the new Israel was in the power of the devil was quite vivid in the early Church. True worship to the true God is possible only within Christianity (2,15f; 5,19); and when 1 Jn 5,21 equates the false teaching with idolatry, it is the same as designating the heretics as pagans who are ἐκ τοῦ κόσμου (4,5). Consequently, it is fully logical for 1 Jn to speak

---

the real possibility of eternal loss. The "sin against the Holy Spirit" is thus a theological-soteriological fact; whereas, the "sin unto death" (like the "willful sin" of Heb 10,26) must be considered from an ecclesial-disciplinary point of view. That is, one who "sins unto death" does so by disclaiming somehow the fatherhood of God and the brotherhood of man in Christ. The Church is not able to say anything about the soteriological effects of such an act in any particular case precisely because she has no way of knowing that the sinner has allowed his state of separation to persist right on into and through his death. But as long as the sinner is separated from the Church through a "sin unto death," he can make no claim to the fraternal prayers of other Christians. Further clarification is given in 1 Jn 3,14, where it is said that anyone who refuses to love his brother remains in death. Consequently, "sin unto death" is sin which returns one to a state of hatred; but this can be reversed if the sinner can truly return to love. The "sin against the Holy Spirit" is a qualitative increase in the state of hatred; that is, a state of absolute permanence.

of faith as victory over the world (5,4) since true faith overcomes the sin of "idolatry."[70] But not every sin is such a sin
against faith, and therefore not unto death (5,16).

e. The Second Letter of John.

The main objective of this brief letter is to warn against
the false teachers who deny that Jesus Christ came[71] in the
flesh (vv. 7-11). Since the author uses the title of Christ with
the name of Jesus so that it appears as a single proper name, it
is not clear if he means that the heretics denied Jesus' humanity,
or if they denied that Jesus was the Christ. However, the writer
is not really concerned about explaining the nature of the false
teaching. Rather, he proposes a test for detecting such persons;
namely, those who do not remain in the teaching of Christ, but go
beyond it, are false teachers (v. 9). The content of Christ's
teaching is not defined here, but such a test as the writer proposes in this letter presupposes a "body of doctrine" ascribed to
Christ and considered normative for the faith. Anyone who brings
in novel doctrines is to be rejected and refused the normal marks
of hospitality such as lodging and even a greeting; for that would
only encourage the false teachers and, in fact, give one a share
in their evil (v. 11).

The evil works of these wandering false prophets may be of a
moral as well as doctrinal nature. The letter does not make this
clear. But it has been seen often enough already that false doc-

---

70. This seems to be Paul's idea as well when he says acts performed without faith are sin. Cf. Rm 3,23-26; 5,8-11; 14,
22f.

71. The author actually says "is coming" (ἐρχόμενος). Perhaps
he is using a standard term of his times (Mt 3,11; 11,3; Jn
1,9; 6,14; 11,27); thus, he keeps the Parousia in view as well
as the past.

trine was very often typified by disregard for the Christian
principle of love if not also by undisciplined, libertine conduct.
It is especially characteristic of Johannine literature that love
is defined as keeping Jesus' commandments, the most significant of
which is to love one another. These sentiments are also expressed
in this letter (vv. 5f).

f. The Third Letter of John.

As in 2 Jn, the writer immediately identifies himself as "the
Elder" (ὁ πρεσβύτερος). However, he addresses his letter to a
certain Gaius on this occasion rather than to a church or church
leader. The reason for this becomes clear in verse 9, where it
is explained that a certain Diotrephes, who, by hook or crook,
holds the leading position in the community, refuses to accept
any writing or person sent to him by the Elder. Moreover, he does
not even hesitate to excommunicate[72] anyone who would otherwise
receive such persons (v. 10).

A proper assessment of the situation requires a more extensive
knowledge of the ecclesial rank or position of Diotrephes and
Gaius as well as of the Elder and his disciples. However, the
modern reader can do no more than make "educated guesses" in this
regard. The Elder is most probably the leader, or at least the
spokesman, of a group of itinerant prophets who are organized
among themselves in order to preach the Gospel and tend to spiritual needs in several local churches. Whether or not the Elder is
in some way identical with the Apostle John and the author of the
Fourth Gospel is another question. Most commentators are reluctant

---

72. The use of the present tense in ἐκ τῆς ἐκκλησίας ἐκβάλλει in-
    dicates a policy of action, and not a single act as in Jn 9,
    34f.

to make such an identification for a number of reasons--not the least of which is the problem of authorship and redactorship of the Fourth Gospel itself. Nevertheless, most commentators are equally reluctant to say that there is no meaningful connection between John's Gospel and the Johannine letters.

Gaius seems to be a very special and reliable friend of the Elder, and has given lodging and hospitality to these prophets in past times (vv. 3.5f). In this way, Gaius is likewise a co-worker in the task of spreading the truth of the Gospel (v. 8); but he himself does not seem to have any special ecclesial rank or power.

The ambitious and quarrelsome Diotrephes is even more diffi-cult to define. However, since he seems to have authority in his local church and the support of the majority--otherwise, he could not assume the right to reject the prophets and to excommunicate those who would give them hospitality--, he is very probably a legitimate, even though unpleasant, leader of the community.[73] Perhaps it is for this reason that the Elder makes no threat of excommunication against Diotrephes. Nor does the writer declare that this disagreeable person, in spite of his malicious words and deeds, is a false teacher of any sort and therefore ipso facto excommunicated as are the false teachers mentioned in 1 Jn 2,19.

The beginnings of monarchical episcopacy may very well be im-plicated in this struggle between some wandering prophets and the

---

73. Walter Bauer, Rechtgläubigkeit und Ketzerei im ältesten Christ-entum, (Beiträge zur historischen Theologie 10), (Tübingen, 1964[2]) 97f, thinks Diotrephes is a heretical power-figure in the community and that he is comparable to the opponents in Clement of Rome's letter to the Corinthians. However, Dio-trephes' action indicates that he is more concerned about his personal image and importance than about defending a heretical or schismatic position.

"established authority" of a local church.[74] However, this remains only a matter of speculation that awaits concrete proof or
evidence. And even if this is the case in 3 Jn, the problem still
remains of determining the actual origin of the monarchical bishop.
That is: Is he the "creation" of the local community as seems to
be the case in the Didache (15,1f)? Or is he an "outsider" who has
been "apostolically" appointed to his office as appears to be the
case with Timothy and Titus (1 Tm 1,3; Ti 1,5)? Perhaps the best
answer is "both-and." But whatever the answer may be, the eventual emergence of the "monarchical" bishop as typified in Ignatius
of Antioch had far-reaching effects on ecclesial discipline and
the Church's understanding of herself.

3. The Apocalypse

Of special interest for the present study is the writer's
letter to the seven churches of Asia Minor, which gives the modern
reader a special insight into these churches and their problems at
that time--about A.D. 95. The persecutions from the days of Nero
are behind them now; but the hostility of the state has not sub-
sided, and the new persecutions can be expected. The messages to
the seven churches should therefore be seen as pastoral admonitions
to Christians facing a discouraging future.

The Church at Ephesus is the first to be addressed (2,1-7).
This city was the most important sea port in Asia Minor at that
time, and its zealous pagan culture and superstition were prover-
bial throughout the Empire. The author, who identifies himself as
John, the servant of Jesus Christ (1,1), commends the Christians at

---

74. Cf. Adolf von Harnack, Über den dritten Johannesbrief, in: TU
    15 (1897) 3.

Ephesus for their keen ability in applying the test to those who claim to be apostles (2,2; cf. also Mt 24,11f; 1 Thes 5,20f; 2 Cor 3,1; 1 Jn 4,1-3). But not all is in order within the community. There is namely a lack of love (v. 4)--perhaps as a result of "an inquisitorial spirit" in the confrontation with the false teachers.[75] Whatever the cause, the effects are extensive enough for John to assert that the Ephesian Christians are in danger of losing their status as a church. This would seem to be the conclusion that must be drawn from the statement that Ephesus will have its lamp removed unless the Christians there have a change of of heart (v. 5). This means that the Church at Ephesus either will cease to exist as an earthly promoter of the work of Christ, or, what is perhaps more directly implied, the Ephesians will no longer be recognized as Christ's own, and hence, without his protection, they will perish in the general cataclysm of the "last days" that are quickly approaching.[76]

The seven gold lamps mentioned in 1,12, probably represent the seven churches as earthly institutions, while the seven stars are their celestial complements gathered into the hand of Christ. This picture is, in all probability, a reworking of the image of the seven-branched candelabra described in the Book of Zechariah (4). This symbol of Israel's election and of God's presence in the midst of his people[77] is now "redistributed" by the author of the Apocalypse to affirm the Church as the new Israel and each

---

75. Cf. G.B. Caird, A Commentary on the Revelation of St. John the Divine, (BNTC), (London, 1966) 31.

76. Cf. Martin Kiddle, The Revelation of St. John, (MNTC), (London, 1940) 24.

77. Cf. SB 3, 716f.

individual church as having both universal fullness and yet participation in the one universal Church.[78] If one keeps this
image before his eyes, it becomes clear that the removal of the
lamp means that Ephesus will lose its union with Christ and the
other six communities.[79] The fact to be specially noted here is
that, since John's warning is directed to the whole community, an
entire local church is threatened with excommunication from the
universal Church; and the author gives no indication that Ephesus
will be able to call itself a church of Christ if that should
happen. However, since there is also no indication that the removal of the lamp is accompanied by a rejection of the Ephesian
star in Christ's hand, the author may wish to indicate that such
an excommunication is not necessarily final and permanent, but
only a matter that is left entirely in Christ's hand for judgment.

Rather than end his communication to the Ephesians on a
threatening note, the writer prefers to encourage these Christians
by commending them for their hatred of the deeds of the Nicolaites
(v. 6). Although Irenaeus of Lyons (adv Haer 1,26,3; 3,11,1)
sought to identify the Nicolaites as a Gnostic sect of libertines
supposedly founded by Nicolas, the proselyte from Antioch mentioned in Acts 6,5, it is far more likely that John is only giving
a Greek translation of an etymology for the name "Balaam" taken
from Jewish folklore. As already seen in connection with 2 Pt 2,15
and Jude 11, later tradition held that Balaam led the Israelites
into idolatry. Accordingly, his name--originally Bileam--was interpreted to mean Balaʿ ʿam; that is, "he swallowed up the people."

---

78. Cf. G.B. Caird, op. cit., 24.
79. Cf. W. Doskocil, op. cit., 112.

The Greek translation, νικᾷ λαόν, which John provides is obviously choosen for the sake of the word play made on the name in verse 7 where food from the tree of life in Paradise is promised "to the one who conquers" (τῷ νικῶντι). It is probably with this Hebrew folk-etymology in mind that the writer also chooses to speak of eating (balaʿ) from the tree of life (φαγεῖν ἐκ τοῦ ξύλου τῆς ζωῆς) rather than to speak directly of the tree's fruit. In view of the fervid and fanatic paganism of Ephesus, the crimes of the Nicolaites may very well have been connected with pagan worship and sacrificial foods.

Further evidence of the probability of this interpretation of the name and the sin of the Nicolaites is given in the message addressed to Pergamon (2,12-17), a splendid city of ancient Greece and famous for its sophistication and excellent libraries. If Ephesus presented paganism with a carnival atmosphere, Pergamon must have made its pagan worship very attractive for the "intelligentsia." Their religious fervor led them to be the first city to build a temple to the "Divine Augustus" (Σεβαστὸς Αὔγουστος), thereby acquiring a leading role in the emperor-worship that often proved so treacherous for Christians. A huge altar to Zeus stood atop a high terrace and commanded a view over the entire city. Undoubtedly this is the "Throne of Satan" that is mentioned in verse 13. Two verses later (v. 15), the Nicolaites are mentioned again, right after the author has complained that the Church at Pergamon has some people in her midst who hold the teaching of Balaam (v. 14). Once more, John displays his fondness for word play by declaring that Balaam taught Balak to cast a stumbling-block (Βαλαάμ, ὃς ἐδίδασκεν τῷ Βαλὰκ βαλεῖν σκάνδαλον) before Israel so as to lead the Hebrews to eat the sacrifices of idols (φαγεῖν εἰδωλόθυτα) and to commit fornication. The latter term (πορνεῦσαι) need not necessarily mean literal sexual laxity, but may be only another expression for idolatry in general.

Although it is not entirely clear from the text that the author lays these charges directly against the Nicolaites, his complaint against them seems to be that they are too ready to condone pagan conduct which could not be acceptable to real Christians. The specific charge against the Christians of Pergamon would then be that they were too tolerant toward the offenders by allowing them to remain in the community while somehow contributing to pagan worship.

The community is ordered to repent (v. 16), which can only mean to rid itself of these syncretistic elements and tendencies. This call to repentance is made with the threat of Christ's coming to fight the offenders with the sword of his mouth. The implications of this statement are not clear, but it indicates that, if the community fails to correct its own members, then Christ himself will intervene directly to do it--perhaps through physical illness or death.[80] But "to the one who conquers" (τῷ νικῶντι), he will give "the hidden manna" (δώσω τοῦ μάννα τοῦ κεκρυμμένου) and a white stone (ψῆφον λευκήν) with a new name written on it that is known only to the recipient (v. 17).

These are indeed obscure and ambiguous images. The manna, as the proper substitute for the food of pagan sacrifices, suggests the Eucharist. However, it is something that <u>will</u> be given, but is now hidden. Thus, the illusion can scarcely be <u>directly</u> to the Eucharist. Here, the manna is clearly the parallel of the

---

80. Cf. G.B. Caird, <u>op</u>. <u>cit</u>., 41.

tree of life in verse 7. It is the promise that "the one who conquers will not be hurt in the least by the second death."[81]

The white stone is even more difficult to interpret, mainly because such a stone could indicate one of several things at the time the Apocalypse was written. Usually, a ψῆφος λευκή was a small stone that was cast to indicate someone's affirmative vote. It was also a pebble used to indicate one's acquittal of charges in a lawsuit, or to give one admission to some event or feast. Sometimes a number or symbol was written on the stone, which was then used in divination or carried as an amulet. It could also be a sort of stone monument upon which a public decree was written.[82] Finally, and what is most probably the case in view of the victory theme of the passage under consideration, the white stone could be a trophy stone with the victor's name engraved upon it.[83] The "new name" on the stone is probably further indication of the victory. One may recall at this point such names as "Alexander the Great" or "William the Conqueror." To be given a new name by God means to be granted his blessings and to have an intimate, personal relation with him (Is 43,1; 62,2; 65,15). But since only the recipient of the stone given by Christ knows the name written on it, it seems that John wants to indicate that victory over sin and evil is possible in the present, even though it remains a matter known only to the individual. Or it might also indicate that knowledge of the name means salvation itself; which is something that only the recipient knows of

81. Cf. Apc 2,11: Ὁ νικῶν οὐ μὴ ἀδικηθῇ ἐκ τοῦ θανάτου τοῦ δευτέρου.
82. Cf. ψῆφος, in: LS 2022f.
83. Cf. Peter Ketter, Die Apokalypse, (HB 16/2), (Freiburg im Breisgau, 1942) 64.

upon his death. The latter possibility is more probable in view
of the promise of the hidden manna. However, the two ideas are
not necessarily mutually exclusive.

The author picks up the theme of the struggle against pagan
influences again in his next message, which is addressed to the
Church at Thyatira (2,18-29). This city, located between Pergamon and Sardis in western Asia Minor, was an active commercial
and industrial center. Various ancient inscriptions found there
show that the city's workers were organized much like the guilds
of medieval Europe. This must have proved especially difficult
for the Christians of Thyatira since most of them very probably
came from the working classes and were therefore expected to belong to some such guild, which, like the guilds of Europe, kept
its own calendar of special feasts to various divinities. Moreover, the Sibyl, Sambethe, had her sanctuary here. There can be
little question that she is the one that John means when he scolds
the Christians of Thyatira for yielding to "the woman Jezabel,"
who claims to be a prophetess, and leads Christ's followers "to
commit fornication and to eat idol sacrifices" (v. 20: πορνεῦσαι
καὶ φαγεῖν εἰδωλόθυτα).

According to 1 Kgs 16,31f, Jezabel attempted to syncretize
the cult to Baal with the religion of the Israelites. However,
tradition nowhere specifically charges her with sexual immorality
or the crime of leading others into such sins. Perhaps John is
only describing the Sibyl's sins of idolatry metaphorically as
fornication due to the fact that Jezabel's unfaithfulness to Israel's God brought her the charge of harlotry (2 Kgs 9,22).
Nevertheless, the possibility cannot be excluded that the writer
of the Book of Revelations intended these words literally. Those

concerned at Thyatira certainly knew what was meant; and that sufficed for the writer and his original readers.

Since this sorceress refused to repent in a given amount of time (this implies that she had been somehow warned earlier to stop enticing Christians), she will be cast into bed, and all her lovers will experience great suffering and eventually death unless they repent (vv. 22f). As has already been seen, it was not out of the ordinary for Christians of the early Church to look upon God to send affliction upon religious offenders. Therefore, temporal suffering followed by death can very well be literally intended here. The door of repentance, however, is still open for those who have sinned under Sambethe's influence.

After a brief note warning the Christians of Sardis to be on the alert for Christ's coming (3,1-6), and a complimentary message to the Church at Philadelphia (3,7-13), the writer turns his attention to the Church at Laodicea (3,14-22). Like Thyatira, Laodicea was an important industrial and commercial city. Workers' guilds were especially numerous, and the city's great wealth and many banks made it the "Wall Street" of Asia Minor if not of the entire Empire. Obviously, much of this money found its way into the coffers of the city's Christians (v. 17). As a result, the Church at Laodicea had grown lukewarm in faith and religion. Christ therefore warns that he is about to spue these Christians out of his mouth (v. 16).

According to rabbinical theology, there are three tablets of names kept for the final judgment. The first tablet contains the names of the just, the second of the damned, and the third of those whose fate has not yet been completely decided since they are mediocre. They are to be given a period of "ten days" (i.e., ample time) to repent and to do penance. Failing that, they are to be added to the list of the damned.[84] This is apparently the tradition behind the charge of lukewarmness and the threat made to the complacent Laodiceans.

The writer tells them that life cannot be all roses, for Christ rebukes and chastises even those whom he loves. So they should take heart and repent (v. 19). At this point (v. 20), the writer makes one of the most encouraging and beautiful statements found anywhere in Holy Scriptures. He presents Christ as saying: "Behold, I stand at the door and knock; if anyone hears my voice and opens the door, I will enter unto him, and I will sup with him and he with me."

Although this verse could possibly be interpreted in an entirely eschatological sense, its language is unquestionably eucharistic, and the early Christians would have been even more sensitive to it than most modern readers. It seems to indicate a hope for a special coming of Christ before the actual Parousia. This would be in the Eucharist, which brings a more intimate and personal association with Christ than can be had simply through membership in the Church or her "corporate worship."[85] The passage, if actually eucharistic, is important in that it points out the conditions necessary for fruitful participation in the Eucharist--namely, hearing the call to repentance and opening one's heart to Christ.

---

84. This bit of rabbinic speculation was first recorded in about
    A.D. 300; but it applies well to the case in question, and
    the late date is no conclusive argument against earlier exis-
    tence of this concept. This is especially true in a religion
    so conscious of the history of its theological speculation as
    Judaism. Cf. SB 2, 170.

85. Cf. G.B. Caird, op. cit., 58; R.H. Charles, A Critical and
    Exegetical Commentary on the Revelation of St. John, 1, (ICC),
    (Edinburgh, 1920) 100f.

PART TWO

THE PATRISTIC CONTRIBUTION

CHAPTER EIGHT

CHRISTIANITY COMPLETES ITS FIRST CENTURY

1. The Didache

The date or dates, the unity of composition, the place of
composition, the intended readers--in short, just about everything concerning this work except its actual existence are still
very much debated.[1] But whatever may be said, the ideas and theology of the Didache belong essentially to the first century after
Christ; although, later redactions are possible. Most commentators agree that the text in its final form and arrangement was
completed before the second half of the second century and that
it is a modest attempt to present the Church's moral teaching and
discipline systematically. In this respect, the Didache is the
forerunner of several other ancient documents which attempt to
formulate a primitive "code" of Church law. It therefore offers

---

1. The Teaching of the Twelve Apostles, or Διδαχὴ κυρίου διὰ τῶν
    δώδεκα ἀποστόλων τοῖς ἔθνεσιν, seems to have been written in
    Syria (Antioch?) or Palestine (Jerusalem?). It is built upon
    the Jewish moral teaching of the Two Ways. According to a
    very interesting and well-developed theory proposed by Jean-
    Paul Audet, La Didachè: Instructions des Apotres, in: Etudes
    Bibliques 49 (1958) 110-15, the Didache was written in two
    major phases, to which a later redactor added a few interpo-
    lations. Or, the interpolations may even be from the same
    author or a contemporary. The first version, about A.D. 50-
    70, supposedly ended with 11,2. This version was then re-
    worked and expanded by the same writer before the end of the
    first century. Ibid., 199, 212f, 219, 433-35. The critical
    Greek text given by J-P Audet (ibid., 226-42) is the one cited
    in the present study. At the other extreme concerning the
    date and nature of the Didache, special note must be made of
    Dom Hugh Connolly, who considers this work to be a Montanist
    writing of the latter part of the 2nd century. Cf. The
    Didache and Montanism, in: Downside Review 55 (1937) 339-49.
    This theory, however, has not won many followers.

some valuable, although not always clear, insights into the discipline and the eucharistic liturgy of the early Church.

The Christian convert is told that he must give up his former companionship "with the high and mighty" (3,9: μετὰ ὑψηλῶν)
and to seek out the just and the humble and the company of the
saints for daily instruction (4,9). Since 4,5-8 speaks of the
mutual sharing of goods, it may be that the writer has in mind a
time or conditions in which Christians could lead a life with a
community of goods (Acts 2,44f; 4,32.34f). But the situation is
not entirely the same as the idealized picture of the Church giv-
en in the first few chapters of Acts. For one thing, the author
feels it is necessary to inform the convert that he should not
cause schism within the ranks, but should be ready to mediate
peace wherever there is strife.[2] If this instruction is to be
taken as anything more than as a general regulation or statement
of edifying Christian conduct, then the writer is possibly thinking of factions similar to those mentioned in 1 Cor 11,18f. Further indication that this may be actually the case is given a few
lines later in 4,14, where the injunction is given that the Christian should confess his faults in the gathering and not to enter
in to pray with a bad conscience.[3] This action would then be

---

2. Cf. Di 4,3: Οὐ ποιήσεις σχίσμα, εἰρηνεύσεις δὲ μαχομένους
   κρινεῖς δικαίως, οὐ λήψῃ πρόσωπον ἐλέγξαι ἐπὶ παραπτώμασιν.

3. Ἐν ἐκκλησίᾳ ἐξομολογήσῃ τὰ παραπτώματά σου, καὶ οὐ προσε-
   λεύσῃ ἐπὶ προσευχήν σου ἐν συνειδήσει πονηρᾷ. J-P. Audet
   (op. cit., 345) sees in this a continuation of the Jewish
   practice of confession before a sin offering is made. Cf.
   Lv 5,1-5; Jb 33,27f; Ps 32,1-6. B. Poschmann (op. cit., 90)
   believes this was only a confession of one's sinfulness as
   in the Confiteor of the Mass. However, since the writer's
   instructions are directly addressed to "my child" (4,1),
   and the Christians of the Didache led a close community life

homologous to the self-examination which St. Paul requires of anyone who intends to participate in the Eucharist (1 Cor 11,28).
In chapter 14,1f the Didache explicitly states that the confession of sins, along with the reconciliation of quarreling parties,
is the prerequisite for this action.

> Having gathered together on the Lord's day, break bread
> and give thanks after having confessed your faults, so that
> your sacrifice may be pure. But anyone having a quarrel with
> an associate of his is not to join you until they are recon-
> ciled, so that your sacrifice may not be profaned.[4]

This sacrifice is then immediately identified with the universal,
pure sacrifice foretold in the Old Testament (14,3; Mal 1,11.14).

Of importance for this study is the fact that the Didache, in
viewing the Eucharist as a sacrifice, requires a corresponding
"purity" between the Eucharist itself and the recipient. The confession of sins and reconciliation with one's neighbor lead to a
pure conscience,[5] which insures the acceptableness or effectiveness of the sacrifice (Ps 51). No indication is given as to just
how the Eucharist itself is desecrated when there are unworthy

---

with a mutual sharing of goods, this confession of faults was
very likely more specific than the Confiteor. Perhaps the
"chapter of faults" practiced in many orders and societies of
religious, and which is somewhat similar to Lv 5,1-5, is a
better comparison.

4. Καθ᾽ ἡμέραν δὲ κυρίου συναχθέντες κλάσατε ἄρτον καὶ εὐχαρισ-
τήσατε, προεξομολογησάμενοι τὰ παραπτώματα ὑμῶν, ὅπως καθαρὰ
ἡ θυσία ὑμῶν ᾖ. Πᾶς δὲ ἔχων τὴν ἀμφιβολίαν μετὰ τοῦ ἑταίρου
αὐτοῦ μὴ συνελθέτω ὑμῖν, ἕως οὗ διαλλαγῶσιν, ἵνα μὴ κοινωθῇ
ἡ θυσία ὑμῶν.

5. The Didache obviously means the moral state of a person when
it speaks of "conscience." Nowadays, we would say "pure
heart" or "pure soul." Cf. Heb 9,9.14; 10,22; 1 Pt 3,21;
Johannes Stelzenberger, Syneidesis im Neuen Testament, (Abhandlungen zur Moraltheologie 1), (Paderborn, 1961) 59.

participants present.[6] The fact that the Christian concept of
purity was always spiritual and ethical does not mean that early
Christians did not maintain a certain notion of "purity in cult"[7]
which, in some instances, led them to believe that unworthy communion "reduced" the Eucharist to something not holy for the unworthy recipient and lessened or nullified its effectiveness for
the other participants.[8] Consequently, the moral state of the
recipient could never be a purely "private matter." It is not
surprising, then, that the Didache not only demands the confession of faults and the reconciliation of differing parties, but
also provides for active fraternal correction and, if need be,
even limited excommunication: "Correct one another not in anger
but in peace, as you have it in the gospel; and let no one speak
with anyone who has transgressed against his neighbor, nor let
him hear anything from you until he repents."[9]

---

6. J-P. Audet (op. cit., 462), in reference to Di 14,1-3 and this
   question, remarks that the Eucharist as a "sacrifice" is not
   meant "en soi." Rather, the eucharistic act of the offering
   community is meant. This is all true enough. But, as an
   answer, it evades the question of how the eucharistic sacrifice (or the community's act of offering) is desecrated.

7. Cf. Hans Achelis, Das Christentum in den ersten drei Jahrhunderten, (Leipzig, 1925) 110f.

8. 1 Cor 11,20.27-30.34 sets the "tone" for this concept. Likewise, as already seen in this study's treatment of Judas Iscariot, some Fathers of the Church felt that the traitor received an "inferior" Eucharist and/or was sent forth so that
   the Eucharist of the others would not be somehow "devaluated"
   by his presence. It will also be seen in this study how St.
   Cyprian of Carthage has several stories to relate concerning
   unworthy communicants who find that the Eucharist becomes
   fire, ashes or poison for them.

9. Cf. Di 15,3: Ἐλέγχετε δὲ ἀλλήλους μὴ ἐν ὀργῇ, ἀλλ' ἐν εἰρήνῃ,
   ὡς ἔχετε ἐν τῷ εὐαγγελίῳ· καὶ παντὶ ἀστοχοῦντι κατὰ τοῦ ἑτέρου

Another important passage concerning eucharistic discipline
is found at the end of chapter 9 of the Didache: "Let no one who
has not been baptized into the Lord's name eat or drink of your
Eucharist; for, in regard to this the Lord has also said: 'Do not
give to dogs that which is holy'" (Mt 7,6).[10] Assuming that the

---

μηδεὶς λαλείτω μηδὲ παρ' ὑμῶν ἀκουέτω, ἕως οὗ μετανοήσῃ.
The reference to the gospel (cf. also 8,2; 11,3; 15,4) suggests some sort of written Gospel or "canon" of scriptures
for the Church. Cf. James A. Kleist, ACW 6 (1948) 165, n.
97. J-P. Audet (op. cit., 112) agrees with this as far as
the second version of the Didache is concerned.

10. Cf. Di 9,5: Μηδεὶς δὲ φαγέτω μηδὲ πιέτω ἀπὸ τῆς εὐχαριστίας
ὑμῶν, ἀλλ' οἱ βαπτισθέντες εἰς ὄνομα κυρίου· καὶ γὰρ περὶ
τούτου εἴρηκεν ὁ κύριος· Μὴ δῶτε τὸ ἅγιον τοῖς κυσί. Adolf
Struckmann, Die Gegenwart Christi in der Hl. Eucharistie nach
den schriftlichen Quellen der vornizänischen Zeit, eine dogmengeschichtliche Untersuchung, (Theologische Studien der Leo-
Gesellschaft 12), (Vienna, 1905) 8f, uses this passage and the
previously discussed text from Di 14 as an argument that such
discipline supports the doctrine of Christ's real presence in
the Eucharist. This approach is used throughout Struckmann's
entire work wherever possible against the liberal Protestant
theologians of the 19th century. The argument is certainly
not without some value; although, Struckmann often overevalu-
ates it, and sees in the doctrine of the real presence itself
the basic motive for the prescribed eucharistic discipline.
Ibid., esp. 50f, 60. However, belief in the real presence
alone does not suffice to explain the Christian concern for
certain disciplinary measures in regard to the Eucharist.
That is, the "deeper motives" must still be found. For example, when the husband's boss comes to dinner, the wife
tidies up the house and serves the most exquisite meal that
she can muster from her culinary arts. It would not be false
to say that she is motivated to do all this because her husband's boss is coming to dinner. However, this statement is
simply a cover-up for the real motives: to make a good impression, to enjoy an evening with an important person, and--
above all--to get a raise for her husband. It is these "deeper motives" that are the concern of the present writer's study
of the early Church's eucharistic discipline.

actual Eucharist--and not just an agape less the Eucharist--is
meant,[11] then this is the first explicit statement in Christian
antiquity concerning eucharistic excommunication or exclusiveness, if the passage is to be dated before Heb 13,10. It is, at
any rate, the first unambiguous statement of its kind. As such,
it clearly indicates a eucharistic centered ecclesial consciousness among the early Christians. The designation of the nonbaptized as "dogs" is not to be taken as a derogatory remark (Mt 15,
26f and par.). This is evident already in view of the fact that
the statement implies that nonbaptized persons were present for
at least part of the agape meal and liturgy.[12]

---

11. The real difficulty found in the Didache concerns 9-10, where
    there is question about the nature of the meal and prayers
    recorded here. Some see only an agape in these chapters, but
    no Eucharist. Cf. e.g., Dom Hugh Connolly, Agape and Euchar-
    ist in the Didache, in: Downside Review 55 (1937) 476-89.
    Others see here a liturgy for the "daily Eucharist" as oppos-
    ed to the more solemn "Sunday Eucharist" mentioned in Di 14.
    Cf. P. Drews, Untersuchungen zur Didache, in: Zeitschrift für
    neutestamentliche Wissenschaft 5 (1904) 74ff. Most scholars
    treat the chapters in question as a Eucharist joined to or
    inserted into an agape. Cf. J.H. Srawley, Eucharist (to end
    of Middle Ages), in: ERE 5 (1954) 546. The peculiarity of
    these chapters, if they are eucharistic, is that they make no
    reference to the Last Supper. Rather, everything is directed
    toward Christ's second coming. Cf. also the next note.

12. J. Kleist (op. cit., 7-9) feels that the nonbaptized were pre-
    sent for all of the agape, but for none of the Eucharist. He
    explains this by maintaining that Di 9 is an agape for every-
    one present at the meal; but for the Christians, it was also
    a preparation for the Eucharist. Di 10 is supposedly only a
    thanksgiving for the completed agape and Eucharist. Thus,
    after Di 9, the nonbaptized had to withdraw--or else the bap-
    tized withdrew--so that the Christians could be alone for the
    Eucharist. After that, the baptized and the nonbaptized came
    together again. Nothing is said of the actual Eucharist, how-
    ever, because the writer was applying the arcane discipline.

This situation leads to the problem of determining the intent of 10,6b, where, at the end of the prayer to the Father and
the Son, the exhortation is given: "If anyone is holy, let him
come; if anyone is not, let him repent: Maranatha!"[13] It is not
clear what is meant by either "holy" or "let him come." Likewise, it is uncertain what "let him repent" implies. Jean-Paul
Audet[14] interprets "holy" to mean "baptized" and the instruction,
"let him repent," as an exhortation to anyone who is not holy
(i.e., unbaptized) to become baptized. Ἐρχέσθω, however, does
not mean "come forward to receive the Eucharist," but rather
"let him come to the major Eucharist." The Christians apparently
withdraw into another part of the house for the actual Eucharist.
Audet sees the text "comme un rituel de 'passage' entre la 'frac-
tion due pain' et l' 'eucharistie' majeure."[15]

However, it seems necessary to concede that this solution remains solely in the realm of conjecture. Hans Lietzmann[16] offers
a more feasible explanation, which can readily fall back on other
elements of the Didache for support. Accordingly, "holy" means

---

With this theory, J. Kleist is able to explain why there is
no reference to the "words of institution" or the Last Supper. However, it seems extremely awkward to break up the
meal in this way, with one or the other group leaving the
room for awhile and then returning for a last bit of bread
and wine and prayers of thanksgiving. The only feasible
place for the Eucharist is at the end of Di 10 so that the
great hope for the Parousia and Christ's coming in the Eucharist are both expressed by "maranatha." Cf. W. Doskocil,
op. cit., 120f; J-P. Audet, op. cit., 411f.

13. Εἴ τις ἅγιός ἐστιν, ἐρχέσθω· εἴ τις οὐκ ἔστι, μετανοείτω·
μαραναθά.

14. Op. cit., 415.
15. Ibid.
16. Op. cit., 391-93.

not simply a baptized person, but also a Christian who is fully eligible to receive the Eucharist in so far as he has confessed his sins and has no existing quarrels with his neighbor. The instruction, "if anyone is holy, let him come," is therefore not a direct command for the "holy" to come forward to receive--for the verb would then be προσερχέσθω--, but rather an exhortation that whoever is "eligible" to receive the Eucharist should now do so.[17]

Many commentators hesitate to treat chapters 9 and 10 of the Didache as the actual Eucharist or eucharistic prayer, because there is no apparent "formula of consecration" said over the bread and wine. This position assumes that such a "formula" is and always was absolutely necessary for the celebration of the Eucharist and that the formula was, from the beginning of Christ-

---

17. A possible objection to this argument would be that the Didache would have excluded a priori those who did not confess their sins and/or reconcile themselves with their neighbors, and therefore were "ineligible" to receive the Eucharist. However, since "eligibility" could be something that only the individual would be able to determine for himself at times, the exhortation either to come or to repent can be readily understood as a "last-minute" counsel just in case there is still someone in the group who really should reconsider his "eligibility" to receive the Eucharist. In effect, the author says: "If anyone is (still) not holy, let him repent." and vice versa: "If anyone is (still) holy, let him come." The emphasis is obviously on the possible need for repentance. The sentence may be rephrased as follows: "If you can honestly say to yourself that you have maintained or retained the proper moral disposition for the reception of the Eucharist, you are eligible; but if you cannot honestly say that you have such a disposition, then do whatever is necessary to obtain it first before receiving the Eucharist." This interpretation not only fits well with the Didache's concept of the need for a "pure conscience" (cf. above, note 5), but it also makes the exhortation equally applicable to the nonbaptized to become baptized.

ianity, built on the "words of institution" (Mt 26,26-28 and
pars.). However, this point of view must be reconsidered in
the light of known historical facts.[18]

The earliest record of such words is found in 1 Cor 11,24f.
But, even though St. Paul explains that he has received knowledge
of the Eucharist from the Lord and has passed this practice on to
the Corinthians (1 Cor 11,23), it does not necessarily follow
that the "words of institution" were already known and used by
the Corinthians in their Eucharist. If that were the case, then
Paul would probably not have repeated these words in such detail.
Rather, it is quite likely that Paul felt that the conditions at
Corinth warranted an institutionalized form of the Eucharist which
the Corinthians already had.[19] The purpose for this would be to

---

18. One of the most recent and most original of the many historical studies on the Didache has been made by Johannes Betz,
Die Eucharistie in der Didache, in: Archiv für Liturgiewissenschaft 11 (1969) 10-39. Betz believes that the prayers found
in Di 9,2-10,5 were originally eucharistic prayers, which,
however, have been reshaped and "demoted" to simple agape
prayers (without a Eucharist) in the Didache (16). The writer
of the Didache did not exclude the "words of institution"
since they were not originally included in the prayers; but
rather these words were given over to the prophets to pronounce (19). However, this entire theory seems to be assuming too much for which there is no real historical evidence.
On the other hand, Betz' article quite correctly points out
that the eucharistic liturgy which Di 9,2-10,5 implies (be
it before the composition of the Didache or in the Didache itself), places the emphasis on the "Messiasereignis," whereby
Jesus' death is only lightly hinted at in the concept of the
Servant of God (31). The Eucharist is thus in an especially
eschatological light as the renewed Tree of Life from Paradise (26f). Cf. also Apc 2,7; 22,2.14.

19. Cf. H. Lietzmann, op. cit., 204-08: Paul Creates a Rite from
the Passion Story.

insure that the Corinthians could have no doubt concerning the nature of the Eucharist. Just as it is clear that Christians practiced Baptism from the beginning before a full or unified theology of Baptism had been developed in the light of various baptismal practices,[20] so does it likewise appear evident that the same process of theological development is to be applied to the Eucharist.

About 112-113, Gaius Plinius, the governor of Bithynia, wrote his famous letter (ep 96) to Emperor Trajan with the explanation that nothing had been learned from the informants, apostates and tortured Christians concerning the religious practices of the Christian "superstition" except that:

> They had been accustomed to meet on a fixed day before dawn, pronounce a chant among themselves to Christ as to a god, and bind themselves by an oath, not for the sake of performing some criminal act, but to refrain from thievery, robbery and adultery, and neither to break their word nor to refuse (to make) a deposit when asked; to which was added that upon the conclusion of this, it had been their custom to depart and then meet again to take some food--however, only the ordinary and harmless kind; but that they had discontinued even this after my edict (was made) in accordance with your regulation that sacred societies are to be banned.[21]

---

20. Cf. Hans Hubert, Kirchenbild, Sakramentsverständnis und Kindertaufe, in: Münchener Theologische Zeitschrift 20/4 (1969) 315-29; Oscar Cullmann, La Signification de la Sainte-Cène dans le Christianisme Primitif, in: Revue d'Histoire et de Philosophie Religieuses 16 (1936) 16.

21. "Adfirmabant autem hanc fuisse summam vel culpae suae vel erroris, quod essent soliti stato die ante lucem convenire carmenque Christo quasi deo dicere secum invicem, seque sacramento non in scelus aliquod obstringere, sed ne furta, ne latrocina, ne adulteria committerent, ne fidem fallerent, ne depositum appellati abnegarent: quibus peractis morem sibi discendi fuisse, rursusque coeundi ad capiendum cibum, promiscuum tamen et innoxium; quod ipsum facere desisse post

Plinius' words indicate that he has some inkling that the
Christians supposedly do not eat "ordinary and harmless food" at
their gatherings. But his investigation has led him to conclude
that this is not the case. Therefore, he emphasizes this fact
along with the fact that Christians do not seem to be guilty of
any other crime that might normally be ascribed to a secret society of those times. However, if the Christians of Bithynia
used the "words of institution" at their Eucharist itself, then
it seems that these words would have eventually become known to
the pagan populace and their governor, with the effect that Plinius could no longer calmly speak of the "ordinary and harmless
food" of Christians. The use of such words spoken in connection
with bread and wine would have left Plinius suspecting that Christians were guilty not only of cannibalism, but also of orgiastic

---

editum meum, quo secundum mandata tua hetaerias esse vertueram."
Cf. Heinricus Keil, C. Plini Caecili Secundi Epistularum,
Libri Novem Epistularum ad Traianum Liber Panegyricus, (Leipzig, 1896) 213f. W. Bauer (op. cit., 94f) is of the opinion
that the Christianity which Plinius confronted was very probably of a heretical nature and origin since, about 40 years
later, Dionysius of Corinth gives instructions that these
"heretics" from Pontus (perhaps Marcionites) should be received into the Church. Cf. HE 6,23,4-6. If Bauer's thesis is
true, and if it is also true that these Christians celebrated
a Eucharist without the use of the words of institution (as is
suggested here), then perhaps one may go a step further and
say that such a Eucharist was more characteristic of heretical
groups than of orthodox Christianity. But whether or not such
a Eucharist itself was considered "unorthodox" is another
question for which no definite answer can yet be given. Gregory Dix, The Shape of the Liturgy, (Westminster, 1954) 230ff,
proposes an early Eucharist without the words of institution.
However, he seeks to take his evidence from various liturgies
of later date than the material in Di 9-10, which he considers only as an agape. Ibid., 96.

celebrations and criminal or even treasonable conspiracies.
Wherever the Christian teaching on the Eucharist did come into
the possession of misunderstanding and hostile pagans, such
charges were frequently made against the Christians.[22] This is
easy enough to see in view of the fact that orgies and conspiracies often involved the drinking of blood mixed with wine.[23]
Words such as "this is my blood" spoken over a cup of wine would
have sufficed to confirm all of the pagan's worst suspicions concerning the Christians of Bithynia once such a eucharistic practice had become known to any nonsympathizing non-Christian of
that area. It is therefore quite possible that the disciplina
arcani, if actually practiced at this time and place, extended not

22. Cf. Tacitus, Annals 15,44; Minucius Felix, Octavius 9; Justin
    Martyr, Dialogue 10,1f; Tertullian, Apologeticum 7,1; 39; ad
    Nationes 1,5; Ausgewählte Martyr-Akten, Sammlung Ausgewählter
    kirchen- und dogmen-geschichtlicher Quellenschriften, neue
    Folge 3, ed. by R. Knopf and G. Krüger, (Tübingen, 1929) 20f,
    25 for further examples. F. Fourrier, La Lettre de Pline à
    Trajan sur les Chrétiens (X 97), in: Recherches de Théologie
    ancienne et médiévale 31 (1964) 161-74, attempts to show that
    the "carmen" which Plinius says the Christians sing to Christ
    implies a "formule consécratoire" (162) which Plinius may have
    connected with the "conjuration" of the Bacchanalia (167f).
    He concludes that Plinius was trying to enforce the law pro-
    hibiting these drunken orgies which a senatusconsultum of 186
    applied to Rome and Italy. An earlier researcher, Franz J.
    Dölger, Sol Salutis; Gebet und Gesang im christlichen Alter-
    tum, (Liturgie-geschichtliche Forschungen 16/17), (Münster,
    1925²) 110-15, sees in the "carmen" a hint that Plinius looked
    upon this action of the Christians as an incantation. Thus,
    they were suspected of practicing black magic and possibly of
    calling down divine curses upon the Empire or its rulers.

23. Cf. W.E. Mühlmann, Blut, in: RGG 1 (1957) 1327f; Herodotus,
    Historiae 3,11. Sallustius (about 86-34 B.C.) mentions that
    blood was drunk as part of the rite for the conjuratico Cati-
    linae. Cf. Sall Cat 22,1: "...Catilinam...humani corporis
    sanguinem vino permixtum in pateris circumtulisse."

only into Christian writing, but also into the Christian liturgy itself. The omission (or noninclusion) of the "words of institution" in the Eucharist at Bithynia would only be possible if early Christians--or at least some of them--did not feel they were absolutely necessary for the proper (nowadays, we would be inclined to say "valid") celebration of the Eucharist.

Besides the fact that the circle of Christians for whom the Didache was intended may not have celebrated the Eucharist with the "words of institution" or some specific "formula of consecration," another unusual feature of their Eucharist seems to be that the prophet had a leading role in the eucharistic celebration even though he is in the process of being replaced by a "local clergy." His exact role--if he had an exact role[24]--in the Eucharist is not clear, but he is to be allowed to offer thanks (εὐχαριστεῖν) for as long as he wishes (10,7).

On the other hand, chapter 11 mentions several tests for the purpose of detecting false prophets.[25] A false prophet is one who

24. The question is often raised, especially by Catholics, if the prophets in the Didache could preside (i.e., act as "priest") at the Eucharist since there is no indication that the prophets of the early Church were "ordained" ministers. Most probably, such prophets were not (sacramentally) ordained, but the Didache still refers to them as "apostles" (11,3-6) and "high priests" (13,3). Moreover, after the directions concerning the Sunday Eucharist (14), the Didache's readers are instructed to elect bishops and deacons to fulfill the office of the prophets and the doctors (15,1f), who are apparently becoming less numerous in relation to the expanding Church. Therefore, it seems that presidency over the Eucharist was one of the duties or rights of the prophets. In a sense, they were also ordained since they were an ecclesially recognized office and were not considered simply as "laymen."

25. Whereas Paul's testing of the spirits meant seeing if the prophet confessed Jesus as Christ, the Didache presents a prac-

seeks to stay more than three days in one place (5), demands money for himself (6), does not practice what he preaches (10), and, above all, he fails to preach the same teaching as in the Didache (1f). One who has been exposed as a false prophet is presumably excommunicated from the community since the order is given that no one should listen to him (v. 2: μὴ αὐτοῦ ἀκούσητε).

In general, one may say that the Didache is a phase in the expansion of the hierarchy in the process of engulfing and replacing the prophet and the greater liberty of earlier times.[26] However, the transition, as depicted in the Didache, is one of "parallel substitution" rather than simple exclusion. That is, the birth of a regular Sunday-liturgy required the establishment of a "local clergy" to insure the availability of someone to perform the same λειτουργια as the prophets do whenever they happen to come along.[27]

2. Clement of Rome

The so-called First Epistle of Clement, written to the Church at Corinth about A.D. 96, is the only one of the many works now formerly ascribed to St. Clement which is now recognized as authen-

---

tical-ethical test, which places the prophet beyond further criticism once he has passed the test. With that, the Didache is in danger of delivering itself up to a "superstitious awe" of "spiritual men," and Church-membership becomes more a matter of cult and ethics than of living in the Spirit. Cf. H. von Campenhausen, op. cit., 78f. The importance of "moralizing" of the Gospel in the development of the practice of excommunication is obvious. Cf. W. Elert, op. cit., 60.

26. M. Goguel (op. cit., 239) speaks of this process as "la lutte" between the developing hierarchy and the prophets. However, this is misleading. Real conflicts between the local ecclesial authorities and the traveling prophets were, as far as can be determined, the exception rather than the rule.

27. Cf. Di 15,1; J-P. Audet, op. cit., 195.

tic. The occasion which prompted the letter was a fresh occurrence of an old problem in the Corinthian community--namely, schism. Writing in the name of the Church at Rome, Clement denounces the split at Corinth as most unbecoming the elect of God (1,1). Although the problem is not one of doctrine or ethics-- but a question of legitimate authority at Corinth--, Clement sees the troublemakers as sinners (44,4) motivated by jealousy (3-6) and a lack of love (49 and 54), who are tearing the body of Christ assunder (46,7; 37,5). Their action is not only harmful to the internal order of the Church, but it is also blasphemous because of the scandal it occasions among those outside of the Church, pagans and Jews alike (47,7).

The leaders of the schism are viewed in the light of the Old Testament concept of the curse since their frowardness and attitude is characteristic of those cursed by God. Their ultimate lot was death for their disobedience (30,8; 53,3-5; 41,3). However, there is no thought of actually excommunicating the agitators if they are willing to become obedient again to the presbyters, thereby saving themselves from the penalty of sin and eternal death (57,1; 9,1). Rather than resort to threats, Clement appeals to the dissenters to put aside their haughty ambitions; for it is better to be small but honorable in the flock of Christ instead of having a pre-eminent reputation at the cost of being cast out from the hope of Christ (57,2). Love is the necessary element and solution, because it admits of no schism (49,5). For the sake of peace, love should even motivate one who finds himself the cause of strife and division to leave the community and go elsewhere (54,1f). This does not mean that the one concerned excommunicates himself from the Church. Rather, the apparent intention is that he go to another community where his ambitions or

mere presence will not become the occasion of division. Nevertheless, such action can be considered as a limited form of excommunication in that the dissenter is exhorted to leave the present
community. As will be seen later on, such "local excommunications"
often became matters of contention between bishops or between a
bishop and his clergy, because one party or the other refused to
recognize the excommunication. But Clement is certainly not thinking of such a fully developed form of local excommunication. His
purpose in the letter is to re-establish peace in the Church at
Corinth, and not to develop forms of ecclesial ban. Peace in the
Church, however, is dependent upon the order and authority established by the Apostles (42-44). Clement supports his arguments
for the need of established order by pointing to the order which
God has put into his creation (20). Human experience itself speaks
for such a need, and sees its realization in some sort of hierarchy of authority (37; 40; 43;). This, of course, implies that
authority must be invested with an institutionalized character.

Apparently, a few members[28] of the Church at Corinth assumed
to depose the community's lawfully established authority. Clement
points out that the Apostles had made provisions for "approved
men" (δεδοκιμασμένοι ἄνδρες) to succeed them in office (44,1f).
However, it is not a question of a strictly monarchical episcopacy since the writer does not hold that it is theologically impossible to remove a person from a position of legitimate authority when there are justifying reasons for doing so.[29] But if

---

28. Perhaps the allusion to the fact that the troublemakers could
    go elsewhere (54,1f) is an indication that they were wander-
    ing prophets.

29. Cf. Johannes Neumann, Der theologische Grund für das kirch-

such reasons are lacking, then it is thoroughly reprehensible:

> Therefore, we maintain that those who have been appoint-
> ed by them (i.e., the Apostles) or successively by other es-
> teemed men (and appointed) with the consent of the entire
> Church, and who have blamelessly, tranquilly and becomingly
> led the flock of Christ with humility, and who have been
> long attested by everyone, are not worthily devested of of-
> fice. For our sin is not slight if we depose from the epis-
> copacy those who have sacrally and faultlessly offered the
> gifts.[30]

There are two elements to be especially noted at this point.
First of all, Clement makes a real but undefined connection between an authoritative ecclesial office and the personal moral
state of the one holding the office. There is, however, no hint
of the later concept that the _effectiveness_ of one's ordination
to such an office and the _effectiveness_ of one's actions within
the office depend on the worthiness of the office-holder. Nevertheless, it is easy to see how Clement's position on the matter
leaves the way open to this later concept found in Donatism and,
to some extent, already in Cyprian.

The second thing to notice is the eucharistic aspect or tendency of the above quote. Not only is it likely that "the gifts"
mean the Eucharist,[31] but the combination of the adverbs, ἀμέμπτως

---

liche Vorsteheramt nach dem Zeugnis der Apostolischen Väter,
in: Münchener theologische Zeitschrift 14 (1963) 256f.

30. Cf. 1 Clem 44,3f; PA 1 (1901) 156: τοὺς οὖν κατασταθέντας ὑπ'
ἐκείνων ἢ μεταξὺ ὑφ' ἑτέρων ἐλλογίμων ἀνδρῶν συνευδοκησάσης
τῆς ἐκκλησίας πάσης, καὶ λειτουργήσαντας ἀμέμπτως τῷ ποιμνίῳ
τοῦ Χριστοῦ μετὰ ταπεινοφροσύνης, ἡσύχως καὶ ἀβαναύσως, μεμαρ-
τυρημένους τε πολλοῖς χρόνοις ὑπὸ πάντων, τούτους οὐ δικαίως
νομίζομεν ἀποβάλλεσθαι τῆς λειτουργίας. ἁμαρτία γὰρ οὐ μικρὰ
ἡμῖν ἔσται, ἐὰν τοὺς ἀμέμπτως καὶ ὁσίως προσενεγκόντας τὰ δῶρα
τῆς ἐπισκοπῆς ἀποβάλωμεν.

31. Cf. Rudolf Knopf, Die Lehre der Zwölf Apostel/Die zwei Clemens-
briefe, (Handbuch zum Neuen Testament, Ergänzungsband: Die

καὶ ὁσίως, with the verb, προσφέρειν, is unmistakably sacerdotal language indicating the prerequisite necessity of the offering priest's own purity and sanctity.[32] With that, it becomes clear that Clement ultimately sees the unity of the Church in euchar-istic perspective since the apostolic successors have a relation-ship of dependence on the Eucharist, and unity and order in the Church require obedience to lawful authority.

Clement's desire to bring peace and order to the Corinthians leads him to explain the Old Testament distinction between the priests and the laity (40,4). Out of this, he concludes:

> Brothers, let each of us reverently give thanks to God
> with a good conscience, (each) in his own rank without go-
> ing beyond the prescribed regulation of his office. Per-
> petual sacrifices of prayer or for sins and faults are not
> offered in all places, brothers, but only in Jerusalem; nor
> is an offering made in any place other than upon the altar
> in the atrium of the temple, after the offering has been
> carefully inspected by the high priest and the prescribed
> ministers.[33]

This passage does more than just point out the need for hier-archical order within the community. It also seeks to explain this order within a practical context applicable to the Christian community assembled for the Eucharist. Thus, the schism at Co-

---

Apostolischen Väter 1), (Tübingen, 1920) 119f; Joseph A. Fischer, Die Apostolischen Väter, (Munich, 1956) 81, n. 258; Johannes Neumann, Vorsteheramt, 258.

32. Cf. Heb 7,26; ὁσία and ὁσίωσις, in: LS 1260f.
33. Cf. 1 Clem 41,1f; PA 1, 150-52. "Ἕκαστος ἡμῶν, ἀδελφοί, ἐν τῷ ἰδίῳ τάγματι εὐχαρεστείτω τῷ θεῷ ἐν ἀγαθῇ συνειδήσει ὑπάρχων, μὴ παρεκβαίνων τὸν ὡρισμένον τῆς λειτουργίας αὐτοῦ κανόνα, ἐν σεμνότητι. οὐ πανταχοῦ, ἀδελφοί, προσφέρονται θυσίαι ἐνδελε-χισμοῦ ἢ εὐχῶν ἢ περὶ ἁμαρτίας καὶ πλημμελείας, ἀλλ' ἢ ἐν Ἱερουσαλὴμ μόνῃ· κἀκεῖ δὲ οὐκ ἐν παντὶ τόπῳ προσφέρεται, ἀλλ' ἔμπροσθεν τοῦ ναοῦ πρὸς τὸ θυσιαστήριον, μωμοσκοπηθὲν τὸ προσ-φερόμενον διὰ τοῦ ἀρχιερέως καὶ τῶν προειρημένων λειτουργῶν.

rinth seems to concern the question of who has the right to conduct the community in the celebration of the Eucharist. Perhaps
there were some in the community who had the custom of celebrating this sacrament without the consent and against the will of
the bishop and presbyters.[34] To end the schism, the Corinthians
are to adhere to those whose concern for peace is born of genuine
piety and not from hypocrisy (15,1). These are God's elected
ones, innocent and just (46,4).

3. Ignatius of Antioch

a. Heretics and the hierarchy.

During the reign of Trajan (98-117), Ignatius, Bishop of Antioch, was taken prisoner and transported to Rome, where he was
given to the lions in the arena about 110. Enroute to his martyrdom, he wrote seven letters to various churches in Asia Minor,
to the Church in Rome, and to Polycarp, Bishop of Smyrna. These
letters[35] take up where Clement of Rome left off in many instances. The hierarchical structure of the Church is more fully illucidated. In the process, the role of the Eucharist is often
clearly stated. The discipline accompanying the Eucharist and
most other aspects of ecclesial life for Ignatius can only be
understood in view of his concept of the Church's hierarchical
structure.

Whereas Clement only took the hierarchy back to the Apostles,
Ignatius derives it directly from Christ, and makes the three-fold
distinction of bishops, presbyters and deacons even more clearly

---

34. Cf. M. Goguel, op. cit., 227.
35. Many works have been falsely ascribed to Ignatius, but these
    letters are now generally accepted as genuine. An expanded
    version, however, was made about 380.

than Clement (ad Trall 2,1-3). These three orders of the hierarchy are made analogous to the Father (i.e., the bishops), to
Christ (i.e., the deacons) and the Apostles (i.e., the presbyters);
and without these, no ecclesial assembly may be convoked (ad Trall
3,1). Ultimately, all ecclesial functions must receive the approval of the bishop. His presidency is "totale...mais nullement
totalitaire."[36] Whether or not this is to be termed a "monarchical episcopate" will depend very much on how one defines "monarchical" in such an analogous usage.

The historical-existential conditions which stimulated the
growth of the hierarchy as just described are not entirely clear.
However, as has already been seen, the inability of the system of
"wandering ministers" effectively to control orthodoxy and order
within the Church and even within their own ranks certainly encouraged the local churches to seek a more stable system which
could cope with the problems of doctrine and discipline they faced.
Likewise, Ignatius' letters to the churches of Asia Minor reveal
the threat of Judaizers[37] and Christological errors similar to
those mentioned in the Johannine epistles (e.g., ad Trall 9-10).
However, the Bishop of Antioch very probably has real and fully
matured Doceticism in mind in his attacks on the Christological
heresies. But rather than attempt to combat these problems through

---

36. Cf. Maurice Jourjon, La Présidence de l'Eucharistie chez
    Ignace d'Antioche, in: Lumière et Vie 16 (1967) 26.

37. Cf. e.g., ad Philad 6,1. According to Einar Molland, The
    Heretics Combatted by Ignatius of Antioch, in: The Journal of
    Ecclesiastical History 5 (1954) 1-6, the troublemakers were
    Docetists who claimed to be able to prove their Christologi-
    cal doctrine from the Old Testament. It is thus their use
    of the Old Testament that Ignatius stamps as "Judaism."

speculative theology, Ignatius seeks to enforce a system of ecclesial discipline centered on the Eucharist and mediated by the
bishop in order to present the Church with a concrete, empirical
principle of self-identification. To this end, he presents the
Church as harmoniously organized around and directed toward the
Eucharist under the presidency of the local bishop assisted by
the presbyterium and deacons. Any ecclesial function outside of
this structure is considered invalid since no part of the Church
can be found outside of this composite but organized unit (ad
Trall 3,1; ad Magn 7; ad Smyrn 8,1). This ecclesial structure
insured that the Church could take an uncompromising stand against
false teaching--the "foreign herb" from which Christians must abstain (ad Trall 6,1).

b. The Eucharist and heretics.

Ignatius' mystical language--Johannine in tone--and unfixed
eucharistic terminology[38] offer many difficulties in an analysis
of his works. Nevertheless, he is the first Christian writer to
express some direct and reasonably clear opinions in regard to
the Church's attitude toward heretics and their relation to the
Eucharist. Certainly, he repeats much of what has already been
said in Part One of this study. But "the eucharistic function
of the episkopos" brings a new dimension to the material.[39] A
closer examination of some individual texts readily illucidates
this aspect.

---

38. Ad Smyrn 1,1, for example, speaks of faith as body and spirit
in Christ's blood, which gives Christians stability in love.
The passage is probably an allusion to the Eucharist since Ignatius considers faith and love to be integral to this sacrament, which gives one a real union with Christ. Cf. J.H.
Strawley, loc. cit., in note 11.

39. Cf. B. Cooke, art. cit., 343.

The "validating" nature of the bishop's presidency over the Eucharist and Baptism is unequivocally stated in the letter to the Smyrneans (8,1f):

> Without the bishop, let no one do anything which pertains to the church. That Eucharist is valid which is held by a bishop or by one whom he himself has delegated...Without the bishop, it is not permitted either to baptize or to celebrate the agape.[40]

As regards the Eucharist, the object and ideal is that the community be fully united around one Eucharist:

> Take care, therefore, to hold one Eucharist; for there is (but) one flesh of our Lord Jesus Christ and one cup for the unity of his blood, one altar just as there is (but) one bishop together with my fellow servants, the deacons and the presbyterium.[41]

Such strict and precise legislation must indeed be considered a further step in the suppression of the "private Eucharist."[42] However, it was not meant to restrain the initiative of the local churches, but rather to enable Christians to distinguish orthodox ecclesial functions from those especially of the Docetics, who held their own "private" gatherings and Eucharist while refraining

---

40. μηδεὶς χωρὶς τοῦ ἐπισκόπου τι πρασσέτω τῶν ἀνηκόντων εἰς τὴν ἐκκλησίαν. ἐκείνη βεβαία εὐχαριστία ἡγείσθω, ἡ ὑπὸ ἐπίσκοπον οὖσα ἢ ᾧ ἂν αὐτὸς ἐπιτρέψῃ...οὐκ ἐξόν ἐστιν χωρὶς τοῦ ἐπισκόπου οὔτε βαπτίζειν οὔτε ἀγάπην ποιεῖν. Cf. PA 1, 282. Since the Eucharist and the agape were still joined during Ignatius' time, the order concerning the agape is essentially the same as that concerning the Eucharist. Cf. Odo Casel, Die Eucharistielehre des hl. Justinus Martyr, in: Katholik 3/6 (1914) 257.

41. Cf. ad Philad 4; PA 1, 266: Σπουδάσατε οὖν μιᾷ εὐχαριστίᾳ χρῆσθαι. μία γὰρ σὰρξ τοῦ κυρίου ἡμῶν Ἰησοῦ Χριστοῦ καὶ ἓν ποτήριον εἰς ἕνωσιν τοῦ αἵματος αὐτοῦ, ἓν θυσιαστήριον, ὡς εἷς ἐπίσκοπος ἅμα τῷ πρεσβυτερίῳ καὶ διακόνοις, τοῖς συνδούλοις μου·

42. Cf. M. Goguel, op. cit., 249.

from the bishop's eucharistic assembly. The reason, of course,
was that their Christological errors could not be harmonized
with the Christology taught and implied in the <u>ecclesiastical</u>
Eucharist under the bishop.[43] It is obvious that Ignatius had
no doubt that the heretics' Eucharist was invalid when he says:
"Let no one make a mistake (about it). If one is not within
(the circle of) the altar, he is deprived of the bread of God."[44]
From all that has been said so far, it is clear that Ignatius did
not think that the validity of the sacraments depended on one's
valid reception of Orders. Rather, it seems that unity with the
bishop was the only requirement; for no where does Ignatius say
that the bishop can only delegate those who are already presbyters or deacons to baptize or lead the community in the eucharistic celebration. On the other hand, the bishop's delegation itself must be seen as sort of real ordination.[45] If the celebration of the Eucharist or any other ecclesial function lacks the
bishop's consent, however, then it is the devil that is served
by it (<u>ad</u> <u>Smyr</u> 9,1).

<u>c</u>. <u>Theology</u> <u>of</u> <u>the</u> <u>Eucharist</u>.

Looking at the Eucharist positively, St. Ignatius sees two
major purposes or effects of it. First of all, it is a means of

---

43. F.X. Funk says in regard to this text that "apparet, haereticos istos non ab omni eucharistia abstinuisse, sed ab <u>eccle-</u>
<u>siastica</u> tantum. Similiter quoad orationem seu preces res
se habere videtur." Cf. <u>PA</u> 1, 281.

44. Cf. <u>ad</u> <u>Ephes</u> 5,2; <u>PA</u> 1,216: ἐὰν μή τις ᾖ ἐντὸς τοῦ θυσιαστηρίου, ὑστερεῖται τοῦ ἄρτου τοῦ θεοῦ.

45. It would seem that Ignatius' concept of "ordination" would
logically have to be bound up with his notion of <u>specific</u> delegation. Therefore, not even one of the presbyters or deacons could hold a "valid" Eucharist without at least the implicit approval of the bishop.

breaking the power of Satan and of overcoming heresy. For this
reason, the Bishop and Martyr advises the Ephesians:

> Make an effort, therefore, to come together more fre-
> quently for (the celebration of the) Eucharist of God and
> his praise. For, when you often gather into one place, the
> powers of Satan are broken, and his ruinous influence is de-
> stroyed by your unanimity of faith.[46]

The second purpose of the Eucharist is eschatological; namely,
it is the φάρμακον ἀθανασίας and ἀντίδοτος which insures the recipient's eternal life in Christ (ad Ephes 20,2). Ignatius' firm
faith in this aspect of the Eucharist enabled him to face his
martyrdom with anticipation rather than with fear and resignation
(ad Rom 7,2). Accordingly, he writes to the Romans:

> I delight neither in corruptible food nor in the pleasures
> of this life. I desire the bread of God, which is the flesh
> of Jesus Christ, who is of the seed of David; and I want to
> drink his blood, which is immortal love.[47]

In view of this statement, it is impossible to accuse Ignatius
of having magical notions concerning the Eucharist. It is ultimately the love of Christ alone that counts. However, it is necessary that one return this love to Christ, and that is not possible
unless one loves Jesus' passion and death--which the Docetic heretics do not do (ad Philad 3,3). But the Eucharist is the sacramental form of Jesus' passion and death, and, therefore, this sacrament has a special character which brings one into a loving union

---

46. Cf. ad Ephes 13,1; PA 1, 224: Σπουδάζετε οὖν πυκνότερον
συνέρχεσθαι εἰς εὐχαριστίαν θεοῦ καὶ εἰς δόξαν. ὅταν γὰρ πυκ-
νῶς ἐπὶ τὸ αὐτὸ γίνεσθε, καθαιροῦνται αἱ δυνάμεις τοῦ σατανᾶ,
καὶ λύεται ὁ ὄλεθρος αὐτοῦ ἐν τῇ ὁμονοίᾳ ὑμῶν τῆς πίστεως.

47. Cf. ad Rom 7,3; PA 1, 260: οὐχ ἥδομαι τροφῇ φθορᾶς οὐδὲ
ἡδοναῖς τοῦ βίου τούτου. ἄρτον θεοῦ θέλω, ὅ ἐστιν σὰρξ
Ἰησοῦ Χριστοῦ, τοῦ ἐκ σπέρματος Δαυίδ, καὶ πόμα θέλω τὸ
αἷμα αὐτοῦ, ὅ ἐστιν ἀγάπη ἄφθαρτος.

with Christ. Whereas the heretic has only the χαρακτῆρα of this world, the faithful Christian, because of his love, has the χαρακτῆρα of God the Father through Jesus Christ, who gave us his love through his suffering (ad Magn 5,2). Ignatius does not, however, maintain that the heretic is so far beyond the reach of love that he can no longer be reached by love and be saved. Rather, in the spirit of 1 Jn 3,14, he says of those heretics who refrain from the Eucharist because they do not confess it to be flesh of Jesus Christ the Saviour who died and rose from the dead: "It is better to love them, so that even they might rise (from the dead)."[48]

It is now possible to see Ignatius' eucharistic ecclesiology in its proper perspective. In brief, he only wants to say that a person is a Christian, not because he participates in the bishop's Eucharist, but rather because he loves Jesus Christ in his entire existence and therefore loves his passion and death as well and shows this love by partaking of the Eucharist which professes to be Jesus Christ's body and blood which died and rose for all people. But since such a Eucharist could only be guaranteed when authorized by the bishop--a man who has been elected to his divinely established office because of his orthodoxy and upright life--, the Bishop of Antioch is able to use one's exclusive adherence to the ecclesiastical Eucharist as the empirical criterion for one's unity with Christ and the Church. Consequently, he goes on to say:

> Whoever is within (the precinct of) the altar is clean;
> but whoever is outside of (the precinct of) the altar is not
> clean. That is, anyone who does anything without the bishop
> and the presbyterium and the deacons is not clean of con-

---

48. Cf. ad Smyrn 7,1; PA 1, 280-82: συνέφερεν δὲ αὐτοῖς ἀγαπᾶν,
ἵνα καὶ ἀναστῶσιν.

science.[49] Therefore, whoever does not come to the gathering
has already become proud and has judged (i.e., condemned)
himself.[50]

d. The treatment of heretics.

The expressions concerning uncleanness and self-judgment are
to be interpreted from an eschatological point of view. Nowhere
does Ignatius outline a course of ecclesial punishment as such for
the nonorthodox. He does, however, say that it is proper to avoid
such persons and not even to discuss them in private conversation
or in an open colloquium (ad Smyrn 7,2). But these measures are
meant more for the protection of the orthodox than as punishment
of the offenders, who lack love of neighbor and neglect the works
of mercy (ad Smyrn 6,2). They are like wild animals and mad dogs
that bite unexpectedly and inflict wounds which are difficult to
heal (ad Ephes 7,1). They are like noxious plants that bring immediate death to those who eat of them (ad Trall 6,1; 11,1).
Therefore, the Christian should not listen to anyone who preaches
Judaism (ad Philad 6,1), and must flee from all false teaching
and schism (ad Philad 2,1); for schism is the beginning of evil
(ad Smyrn 7,2).

The significance of this last statement can be seen only if
one keeps the Eucharist in mind. That is, schism eventually leads

---

49. Cf. ad Trall 7,2; PA 1, 246-48: ὁ ἐντὸς θυσιαστηρίον ὢν καθαρός ἐστιν· ὁ δὲ ἐκτὸς θυσιαστηρίου ὢν οὐ καθαρός ἐστιν· τοῦτ᾽
ἔστιν, ὁ χωρὶς ἐπισκόπου καὶ πρεσβυτερίου καὶ διακόνων πράσσων
τι, οὗτος οὐ καθαρός ἐστιν τῇ συνειδήσει.

50. Cf. ad Ephes 5,3; PA 1, 218: ὁ οὖν μὴ ἐρχόμενος ἐπὶ τὸ αὐτό,
οὗτος ἤδη ὑπερηφανεῖ καὶ ἑαυτὸν διέκρινεν. The concept of
self-judgment or self-condemnation of certain types of sinners is frequent in patristic literature. It points to the
seriousness of the sin, but does not mean that the Church cannot or will not take steps of her own against the offenders.

to one's separation from the ecclesiastical Eucharist. The schismatic stands outside of the unity of the Church that is effected by the Eucharist, which unites the eucharistic assembly with Christ.[51] The unity that proceeds from the Eucharist precedes and transcends unity with the bishop; for, without the Eucharist and the other ecclesial functions, there is no meaning in the concept of unity with the bishop. Nevertheless, Ignatius does not consider it possible for anyone to bypass the bishop in order to achieve unity with Christ; "for such as belong to God and Jesus Christ are also with the bishop."[52]

By now, it should be clear that St. Ignatius' concept of unity in Christ and the Church is not the logical consequence of the hierarchical structure which he attributes to the Church. Rather, it is just the opposite. The hierarchical structure of the Church is the logical consequence of his description of the Church's unity with Christ in the various ecclesial functions and especially in the Eucharist as the sacrament of love and union in Christ's death and resurrection.

However, in spite of the well-structured picture of the Church that Ignatius presents, it is not clear just to what extent the bishop took part in the exclusion of heretics from the Church other than be advocating avoidance of them. The Martyr's seven letters give no explicit indication that excommunication was to be imposed by the ecclesial authorities. Instead, it is simply assumed that the separation from the Church flowed from the nature of the offense.

51. Cf. Aloys Scheiwiler, Die Elemente der Eucharistie in den ersten drei Jahrhunderten, in: Forschungen zur christlichen Literatur- und Dogmengeschichte 3/4 (Mainz, 1903) 23-35.

52. Cf. ad Philad 3,2; PA 1, 266: ὅσοι γὰρ θεοῦ εἰσιν καὶ Ἰησοῦ Χριστοῦ, οὗτοι μετὰ τοῦ ἐπισκόπου εἰσίν.

In his letter to the Philadelphians (3,1), Ignatius describes the Church's avoidance of the "noxious plants" as a process of cleansing or purification (ἀποδιΰλισμός). W. Doskocil[53]
is of the opinion that this term "necessarily indicates an event
(ein Geschehen) in the public action of the community, which
apparently has taken the initiative in the process." However,
this judgment does not seem justified. First of all, ἀποδιΰλισμός
means to be purified by having the impure elements filtered off.
Ignatius only indicates that this is to be done by avoiding the
offenders. Moreover, the context shows that the Bishop chose
the expression in anticipation of an objection that avoidance of
such persons would only create divisions and schism within the
Church. Therefore, he says that the Philadelphians should avoid
the heretics "not that I (might) find a division among you, but
rather, filtered purity."[54] The image is well-chosen since a
filtered liquid is purified in the process of filtration but is
not divided in the sense that, for example, pruning as a process
of purification removes a portion of the plant itself by division.

The main interest of Ignatius in his treatment of heretics
and the like is that they repent and return to the Church (ad
Philad 3,2). Therefore, even though the Christian should go so
far as to avoid meeting such persons on the street if possible,
he should pray for their conversion since some of them might,
through the power of Jesus Christ, repent (ad Smyrn 4,1). At
least the works of the Christian should edify the heretics and
pave the way for their conversion (ad Ephes 10,1). The Christian

---

53. Op. cit., 138.
54. Cf. ad Philad 3,1; PA 1, 266: οὐκ ὅτι παρ' ὑμῖν μερισμὸν
εὗρον, ἀλλ' ἀποδιΰλισμόν.

should meet their angry attacks with mildness, their boasting
with humility, their blasphemies with prayers, their floundering
in error with steadfastness in the faith, and their boorish man-
ners with civility (as Ephes 10,2). Such wayward persons are
never completely abandoned to their ways, but remain the loving
concern of the Church.

4. Polycarp of Smyrna

St. Polycarp, Bishop and Martyr, may have been born as early
as A.D. 69 and died about A.D. 155. He was a close friend of St.
Ignatius and a disciple of John. But it is disputed if this was
"John the son of Zebedee" or "John the Presbyter." Polycarp was
involved in the earliest phase of the Easter controversy between
Rome and the East. However, this will be dealt with more fully
in connection with Irenaeus of Lyons. The Smyrnian Bishop also
supposedly wrote a number of letters, but only his Epistle to
the Philippians has not been destroyed or lost.[55] This letter
was written about 135. Very probably, paragraph 13 of the letter
was originally a brief note written shortly before Ignatius'
death. It was Polycarp's personal note to a collection of Ignatius' letters which the Philippians had requested to be sent
to them.

Although the letter contains no information on the Eucharist,
it forms a good complementary work to Ignatius' thoughts on the
treatment of Christians who have somehow gone astray. Paragraph
11 is concerned with the relapsed presbyter, Valens, of whom nothing is known beyond what Polycarp says of him in the letter.

---

55. Since the Greek MSS break off after 9,2, only the Latin translation is complete.

The Bishop of Smyrna is deeply grieved over Valens' unfortunate state. Apparently, the presbyter had given in to greed
and avarice, which Polycarp equates with idolatry.[56] By this,
the Bishop seems to mean that Valens has, as it were, returned
to paganism since the Lord will judge him along with the gentiles
who know not God (11,2); that is, they do not know God's plan of
salvation and what he requires of man (Jer 5,4).

But rather than pronounce condemnations, Polycarp asks that
the Lord grant Valens and his wife true repentance. Such persons
should not be treated as enemies. Instead, they should be considered as suffering members which need to be recalled to the
Church so that the body can be made whole again.[57] Already in
6,1 of the letter, the directive is given that the presbyters[58]
should mercifully lead back those who have gone astray. Perhaps
it is with Valens in mind that Polycarp says this.

---

56. Cf. Eph 5,5, where Paul defines avarice as a form of idolatry.
This fluid use of terms led St. Augustine (de Serm Dom in
Monte 1,12,36; 16,46) to declare that avarice constitutes
grounds for divorce since Paul calls this sin idolatry, which,
in turn, is often called adultery, and adultery is grounds for
divorce. This same sort of "word-association theology" may
also be behind Polycarp's statement in 11,1: "Moneo itaque ut
abstineatis vos ab avaritia et sitis casti veraces." Cf. PA
1, 309. At any rate, there is no reason to believe that
Valens was also guilty of unchaste conduct.

57. Cf. ad Philip 11,4; PA 1, 311: "Valde ergo, fratres, contrist-
or pro illo et pro coniuge eius, quibus det dominus paeni-
tentiam veram. Sobrii ergo estote et vos in hoc; et non sicut
inimicos tales existimetis, sed sicut passibilia membra et er-
rantia eos revocate, ut omnium vestrum corpus salvetis. Hoc
enim agentes vos ipsos aedificatis."

58. It seems that the Philippians were ecclesially governed only
by a presbyterium or were at least without a bishop when this
letter was written.

In the case of false teachers, however, the aged Bishop's feeling for orthodoxy and perhaps previous experiences lead him to be very cautious. These ψευδαδέλφοι hypocritically bear the name of Christ and should be avoided since they easily lead "empty men" (κενοὶ ἄνθρωποι) into error.[59] Obviously, Polycarp has Docetics in mind; for he immediately explains that those who do not confess that Jesus Christ has come in the flesh are anti-Christs, and those who reject Christ's death are of the devil, and whoever denies the resurrection and the judgment is the πρωτό-τοκος τοῦ σατανᾶ (7,1).

According to St. Irenaeus of Lyons (adv Haer 3,3,4), Polycarp used the expression "first-born of Satan," in reference to Marcion, whose heresies were not yet fully developed or systematized. His rejection of the entire Old Testament and most of the New Testament precipitated a reaction within the Church that ultimately led too far in the opposite direction with the result that much of the Church experienced a resurgence of "neo-Judaism" long after the Church's ties with Judaism had been thoroughly broken. This aspect will be examined more closely later on in this study.

---

59. Cf. ad Philip 6,3. According to Pastor Hermae (Mand 11,13), the κενοί are those who are uncertain and unconvinced about faith and are therefore open to the deception of false teachers.

THE CALL TO REPENTANCE

1. The Epistle of Barnabas

During the second century, several important writings of uncertain authorship appeared which sought to prepare for the second
coming of Christ by calling upon the Christian to take care to reform his life and, when necessary, to fend himself against false
teachers. The earliest of these works to be presented here is
the Letter of Barnabas. The actual author is unknown; but tradition ascribed it to Paul's companion, Barnabas. The date is equally uncertain. However, its strong polemic against the Jews suggests that it was composed during Hadrian's time (117-138), when
the Jews were given greater freedom to become a renewed threat to
Christians.[1] The use of the allegorical method in the letter suggests Alexandria as the place of composition.

Although a call to repentance is not the main purpose of the
work, an important part of the author's message is devoted to such
exhortations. However, the accent lies on the negative side, emphasizing the avoidance of evil persons and situations. The belief that the last of the "last days" had just about arrived, and
his own love for his fellow Christians, motivated the author to
counsel his readers to conduct themselves accordingly (4,9.14).
One should not join himself to those who walk ἐν ὁδῷ θανάτου.[2]
The sinner is to be avoided lest those who associate with him become like him (4,2; 10,5). However, Barnabas never says what effect such action should have on the sinner; nor does he say any-

---

1. Cf. Johannes Quasten, Patrology 1 (Utrecht-Antwerp, 1960) 91.
2. Cf. Bar 19,2c. The Epistle of Barnabas, like the Didache,
    speaks of the "Two Ways," but generally as the ways of light
    and darkness.

thing about the possibility of receiving the serious sinner back
into the Church. Perhaps such questions did not really interest
the writer just as they were not considered by the author of the
Letter to the Hebrews, with whom Barnabas shares similar ideas
concerning the fate of certain types of sinners.

To illustrate the Christian significance of the call to repentance, the author recounts how Jesus chose as his Apostles men
more impious than sin itself in order to emphasize that he came
to sinners rather than the just (5,9). But those who turn to the
"way of darkness" after having received knowledge of the "way of
righteousness" deserve to perish (5,4). This is reminiscent of
the "willful sin" in Heb 10,26, but now refashioned in accordance
with the teaching of the "Two Ways." Barnabas compares such sinners to swine, which the Old Testament declared unclean. This
symbol is chosen, because, just as pigs are no longer concerned
about their master once they have been given fill of food,
these evildoers likewise forget the Lord once they have tasted
the delights of life (10,3).

As regards discipline surrounding the eucharistic service of
the Church, very little if anything is said. Probably 15,9 is
meant to refer especially to the Eucharist when the writer contrasts the Christian day of worship (ἡ ἡμέρα ἡ ὀγδόη) with the
Jewish Sabbath and declares that Christians celebrate their day
as the day in which Jesus rose from the dead, was made manifest
and ascended into Heaven.

Another text (19,4) speaks limitedly, so it seems, of the excommunication of certain sinners from the Christian assembly.
After mentioning that Christians must avoid adultery, fornication,
and sodomy, Barnabas adds that "you shall not let the word of God

proceed from you in the impurity of any men."[3] Apparently, this is an order that libertines should not be permitted to hear the words of the Gospel at Christian worship.

On the more positive side, the author of the epistle instructs his readers to love their neighbor more than their own life (19,5), not to cause schisms, but to reconcile those who have disputes with each other, to confess their sins, and not to go to prayer with an evil conscience; for this is the way of light.[4] This is, of course, reminiscent of the Didache (4,3.14); as is also the case in 4,10, where Barnabas says Christians should come together for their own common spiritual good rather than to retire apart as if one were already justified (Di 4,2).

2. The Second Epistle of Clement
to the Corinthians

Generally, this pseudo-Clementine work is dated around the year 150. A. von Harnack[5] ascribes it to Soter of Rome (about 166-174). Others (e.g., J. B. Lightfoot think the letter or homily was written by someone in Corinth. Still others detect Alexandrian elements in the work and suggest this city as the place of origin.

This epistle is an outstanding witness to the early Church's concern about proper Christian conduct that is born of love. The

---

3. οὐ μή σου ὁ λόγος τοῦ θεοῦ ἐξέλθῃ ἐν ἀκαθαρσίᾳ τινῶν. Cf. PA 1, 90.

4. Cf. Bar 19,12; PA 1, 92-94: οὐ ποιήσεις σχίσμα, εἰρηνεύσεις δὲ μαχομένους συναγαγών. ἐξομολογήσῃ ἐπὶ ἁμαρτίαις σου. οὐ προσήξεις ἐπὶ προσευχὴν ἐν συνειδήσει πονηρᾷ. αὕτη ἐστὶν ἡ ὁδὸς τοῦ φωτός.

5. Die Chronologie der altchristlichen Literatur bis Eusebius, 1, (Leipzig, 1897) 438ff.

usefulness of repentance is emphasized along with the need to help weaker persons to turn once more to Christ. Love is the motive force for all of the Christian's actions, including repentance. Also, as will be presently seen, the writer sees an essential connection between love and eternal life through the resurrection of the flesh. In this respect, his theology is very similar to St. Ignatius'.

Chapter 9 of the work is directed against those who deny the resurrection of the flesh. By way of rebuttal, the author reminds his readers that salvation has come through the flesh which Christ, previously a spirit, assumed at his birth into his earthly life. Therefore, Christians, who were called in the flesh, will also be rewarded in the flesh (9,4f). The immediate lesson for practical Christian conduct that is immediately drawn from this pronouncement is that Christians should love one another so that they may all enter the kingdom of God (9,6).

The connection that is made bewteen Christ's coming in the flesh and loving one another for the sake of the kingdom must be considered in view of the false teaching which the writer is attacking. Those who denied bodily resurrection offended against charity by teaching others to prefer present bodily pleasures to the promises of the future (10,3). Perhaps the concrete implication is that these persons were leading others to apostasize from the faith rather than to face the prospect of martyrdom.[6] The result is that they and their followers will receive a double judgment.[7] That is to say, they will be condemned in the present

---

6. Cf. R. Knopf, op. cit., 159f.
7. Cf. 2 Clem 10,5; PA 1, 196: ὅτι διασὴν ἕξουσιν τὴν κρίσιν.

as well as eschatologically. The connection between love and salvation is thus made by way of proper conduct of life built upon correct doctrine concerning the resurrection.

The hope that the kingdom will soon come is still very pronounced, but the writer does not think it can come until Christians have learned to speak with one another in truth, to characterize their lives through good works, and not to consider each other as either male or female (14,1ff). Very probably, this means that once Christ's followers have learned to live in complete harmony with each other and to express love by way of good works rather than just sexually, then God will see it fit to bring his kingdom to men.[8] But since this is not yet the state of things, there is need for repentance (13,1). This means especially to turn toward one another in love; for, when it is seen that Christians hate those that hate them and hate perhaps even those who love them, then the outsiders are scandalized and blaspheme the name of Jesus (13,4).

The Christian has a mission of love to the world and to his fellow Christian. If it is his duty to lead men away from idols and to instruct them in the faith, then it is all the more his duty to help a weaker soul that already knows God but has gone astray so that all might be saved (17,1f). From this, it is obvious that 2 <u>Clement</u> does not see Christians as "the perfect" or

---

8. The great question of early Christianity was: "When will the kingdom come?" Many early Christian writers were eventually led to believe that a sort of "disinterested union or harmony" among Christians must be first achieved. The hope for this unity was often very mystically formulated around such New Testament passages as Eph 2,14; Gal 3,28; Mt 6,3. Cf. F.X. Funk <u>PA</u> 1, 198f, where several such examples from early Christian literature are cited.

"the saved," but rather as those who are striving for perfection and salvation. In this light, the writer humbly confesses his own weaknesses and entanglements with the devil as he continues to strive for righteousness in fear of the coming judgment (18,2). Such a humble admission would certainly encourage others to confess their own faults and to correct them as best they can.

Although the letter gives no direct insights into the writer's concept of eucharistic discipline, it must be noted that a confession of one's sins arose especially out of the eucharistic liturgy, where it was meant to re-establish the proper relationship of love among Christians before the actual celebration of the Eucharist. As the oldest extant Christian homily, this work may have been originally delivered in a eucharistic context as a part of the preparation for the reception of the Eucharist. However, as a written work, the confession of one's sinfulness becomes, as it were, a "literary form." It is even more pronounced in Hermae Pastor, where the writer gives a brief "confessio" of his own life and failings before going on to give his instructions and advice concerning Christian repentance. The most outstanding and classical example of such writing is, of course, St. Augustine's Confessiones.[9]

3. The Shepherd of Hermas

a. Paenitentia secunda.

This work, an apocryphal apocalypse, was composed or finally redacted probably shortly after 150 during the time of the Roman

---

9. The significance of the appearance of such "confessional litera-ture" should not be underestimated, for it was a development which ultimately meant the separation of the confession of sins

bishop, Pius I (140-155). According to the Fragmentum Muratorianum, Hermas was Pius' brother. The permissibility of a second
marriage (Man 4,4,1f) and the possibility of the forgiveness of
even serious sins committed after Baptism (Man 4,3,4-6) may indicate that the writer intended to counteract Gnostic elements and
Montanistic rigorism in the Church.[10] This work is not only a
call to repentance, but it is also the oldest existent document
to present the early Church's penitential discipline in systematic form with some theological reflection. However, its complicated and obscure imagery leaves many questions unanswered.

One of the more perplexing problems which this work presents
is the apparent contradiction found between verses 1f and 4-6 of
Mandatum 4,3. In the first part of this paragraph, the Angel of
Repentance[11] admits that Hermas has correctly heard that Christians know of no other repentance unto the forgiveness of their
sins except Baptism; for Christians should thereafter sin no more.
But then he immediately changes his position and admits of a
single additional repentance after Baptism. The solution to the
problem is that Hermas probably knew of a double teaching on the
forgiveness of sins. The more stringent view was perhaps taught
to the catechumens before their Baptism, while the milder teaching

---

from its immediate eucharistic or liturgical context. Although these writers did not intend it or were even aware of
it, they were preparing the way for the transferral of the
confession of sins from the sanctuary to the back of the
church.

10. Montanism itself probably emerged just two or three years
after the Shepherd of Hermas, if this work was actually written before the death of Pius I.

11. The Angel of Repentance is most probably an idealized picture
of the bishop. Cf. Karl Rahner, Die Busslehre im Hirten des
Hermas, in: ZKT 77 (1955) 421.

was applied to those Christians who had sinned in such matters as adultery and apostasy but now regretted their action and sought full communion with the Church again.[12]

This possibility of a second forgiveness gives Hermas the opportunity to legislate concerning some aspects of Christian marriage. An adultress wife who repents and wishes to return to her husband after he has released her (μετὰ τὸ ἀπολυθῆναι) can and must be reaccepted since a second forgiveness is possible. It is for this reason, according to Hermas, that the husband may not marry another. Or, if the husband has been unfaithful, the wife may not remarry since her adulterous husband can still repent and be forgiven (Man 4,1,7f). Unfortunately, the writer does not consider the possibility of remarriage any further. That is, he does not discuss what the outcome would be when the repentant wife or husband again proved unfaithful after being once reaccepted.

The one forgiveness for serious sins committed after Baptism is not absolutely the final forgiveness that one can receive from God. Rather, Hermas is apparently speaking of ecclesial forgiveness and reacceptance; for he says that if a Christian sins again after the second forgiveness, such a one does penance in vain and will live with difficulty.[13] The writer has no doubt that one

---

12. Cf. G. Rauschen, op. cit., 151; B. Poschmann, op. cit., 161; Otto Bardenhewer, Geschichte der altkirchlichen Literatur, 1 (Freiburg im Breisgau, 1913) 481.

13. Cf. Man 4,3,6; PA 1,480: μετὰ τὴν κλῆσιν ἐκείνην τὴν μεγάλην καὶ σεμνὴν ἐάν τις ἐκπειρασθεὶς ὑπὸ τοῦ διαβόλου ἁμαρτήσῃ, μίαν μετάνοιαν ἔχει· ἐὰν δὲ ὑπὸ χεῖρα ἁμαρτάνῃ καὶ μετανοήσῃ, ἀσύμφορόν ἐστι τῷ ἀνθρώπῳ τῷ τοιούτῳ· δυσκόλως γὰρ ζήσεται. It is especially interesting to note that this passage speaks of sinning ὑπὸ χεῖρα, which Karl Rahner, Busslehre im Hirten

who receives the Church's forgiveness is truly forgiven. But since he believes that a Christian can be granted such forgiveness only once after Baptism, then he also holds that it is useless for a Christian to seek readmittance into the Church a second time. His uncertain salvation is no longer something which the Church can repair.

<u>b</u>. The <u>classification</u> <u>of</u> <u>sinners</u>.

Another problem that appears in the Angel's explanation of forgiveness is the question of the "sin unto death." In verse 1 of <u>Similitudo</u> 9,19, the Angel says there is no repentance, but

---

des <u>Hermas</u>, 405, hesitatingly defines as "continual" ("<u>fort</u> <u>während</u>") sinning. However, the more likely explanation is that the expression means "willful" sinning as has already been explained in connection with Heb 10,26 and Nm 15,30. Cf. above, p. 140. K. Rahner (<u>ibid</u>.) is nevertheless correct in so far as he sees that <u>Hermas</u> considers a relapse into serious sin as "<u>Verstocktheitssünde</u>." Thus, "continual sinning" is included, but not exclusively intended by the author. Rather, <u>Hermas</u> is very probably at this point combatting a Montanistic or rigoristic interpretation of Heb 10,26 and Num 15,30 which would have <u>unequivocally</u> excluded "willful" sinners from repentance and salvation. Consequently, <u>Man</u> 4,3,6b might not be actually concerned about the fate of those who relapse after having performed <u>paenitentia</u> <u>secunda</u>. Instead, the passage might only wish to express the difficult situation that "willful" sinners in general face in repenting and regaining access to salvation since they sin entirely of their own choice, without the devil's having first to tempt them. Thus, the author is not making a statement of discipline-- namely, that backsliders are to be excluded from ecclesial penance; rather, he is simply commenting on the fact that those whose sin is ὑπὸ χεῖρα in contrast to those who sin ὑπὸ τοῦ διαβόλου face the greater moral-psychological disadvantage in remaining open to receive God's salvation. Their sin is therefore probably the "sin unto death" as explained below on pp. 231f.

only death, for apostates, blasphemers against the Lord and those
who betray God's servants. By this, the writer does not mean
that the Church would be unwilling to receive such persons back
into her fold if they repented. Rather, he means that, as a
general rule, such persons will refuse to repent even if God gave
them the grace to do so. But since God foresees that such persons will abuse and scorn his grace, he withholds it from them.[14]

In Sim 6,2,2, Hermas is told that there are two classes of
sinners who forget God's commandments and walk corrupted in vain
and delightful pleasures. Some do so "unto death" (εἰς θάνατον);
others, "unto perversion" (εἰς καταφθοράν). The difference is
that the former are so steeped in their pleasures that they per-

---

14. Cf. Sim 8,6,2. From this point of view, it is possible to see
why the writer is able to assume that the nonrepeatable character of the second repentance is not an element of rigorism.
That is, he considers the call to repentance as a real manifestation of God's mercy. Cf. Vis 1,3,2. Hermas does not
present a unified explanation for his limitation of ecclesial
penance to one time in an individual's life. First and most
important of all is his belief that the end of the world is so
near that there is scarcely time for even the one penance
still allowed to Christians. On the other hand, a relapse into serious sin places the sinner's sincerity for repentance
in such a bad light that the Church feels she cannot rightfully grant the backslider another opportunity for ecclesial
repentance. Furthermore, paenitentia secunda is seen as a
parallel to Baptism, which can be undertaken only once (Man
4,3,3f). Finally, the Church must refuse to grant further
forgiveness of sins whenever she doubts that God will grant
his forgoveness. Thus, the author does not treat penance
merely as a matter of ecclesial discipline. Rather, the "Einmaligkeit der Busse vor Gott" becomes "ein kirchenrechtliches
Prinzip der Einmaligkeit der Busse vor der Kirche"--a principle that becomes especially evident in Tertullian. Cf. K.
Rahner, Busslehre im Hirten des Hermas, 404-07.

manently separate themselves from God. There is no place for repentance in them, because they are given up to their sins and
blaspheme[15] God's name. The latter group of sinners, however,
are not so carried away by their sins that they also blaspheme
against the Lord. At least the hope of repentance is in them
(Sim 6,2,3f). But since Hermas has never observed that apostates,
blasphemers and betrayers did penance, he concludes that they are
not lost (Sim 8,6,4). The only sin that really brings death is
the sin of nonrepentance (Sim 8,6,6). Nevertheless, this does
not mean that the writer would say that a person is a blasphemer
because he is nonrepentant. Rather, he is nonrepentant because,
as already seen in Sim 8,6,2, he is a blasphemer and therefore
not given the grace of repentance, which he would not use anyway.
Thus, in the case of apostates, a distinction is made between
those who denied Christ from their heart and those who did not.
For the latter, there is the possibility of repentance (Sim 9,26,
3-6). It is "hardness of heart" that makes one an apostate who
cannot repent.

But even in the case of these apostates, the writer does not
want to pass final judgment. Instead, he only declares that he
does not know if they can obtain life (Sim 9,26,5). The author
immediately adds, however, that his distinction applies only to
those who apostasized in the past; for now that the seriousness
of apostasy has been made apparent, repentance will be denied to
all who deny the Lord. It is impossible for them to be saved.[16]

---

15. A blasphemer is probably someone who has reached a hardened
    state of separation or apostasy from the Church. Cf. Joseph
    Grotz, Die Entwicklung des Busstufenwesens in der vornicäni-
    schen Kirche, (Freiburg, 1955) 376.

16. Cf. Sim 9,26,6; PA 1, 622: καὶ τοῦτο οὐκ εἴω ταύτας τὰς

The implication is, of course, that anyone who denies the Lord
from now on, does so with full knowledge of what he is doing and
therefore does it from the heart. This is essentially the same
as "willful sin" spoken of in Heb 10,26. This attitude is in
harmony with Hermas' teaching that wickedness in those who have
heard the truth is much more damaging than it is in those who
have not yet heard (Sim 9,18,1f).

The treatment of persons which Pastor Hermae accuses of being
hypocrites who bring false teachings (Sim 8,6,5) must be noted at
this point. Interestingly, such persons are not at once placed
in the category with blasphemers, etc. Rather, since Hermas has
seen that many of them have been moved to do penance, he is willing to admit that they can be saved if they actually repent (Sim
8,6,5f). These persons are probably the false prophets spoken of
in Mandatum 11. Such persons are to be distinguished from the
true prophets by their way of life. The false prophet is proud,
talkative, luxurious, prophesies only when paid, avoids the assembly of righteous men, but cleaves to those who are undecided
and infirm in their convictions. He speaks according to the desires of his listeners, but is dumb before the righteous (Man 11,
12-14). Those who are strong in the faith do not have anything
to do with such false spirits and therefore avoid them (Man 11,4.
21). To consult such men is idolatry since the Spirit that comes
from God speaks without need of being asked, while the spirit of
false prophets speaks only when questioned and responds only according to the lusts of the listeners; for such a spirit has no

---

ἡμέρας λέγω, ἵνα τις ἀρνησάμενος μετάνοιαν λάβῃ· ἀδύνατον
γὰρ ἐστι σωθῆναι τὸν μέλλοντα νῦν ἀρνεῖσθαι τὸν κύριον
ἑαυτοῦ.

power of its own (Man 11,4f). However, since these false prophets are at least not blasphemers or traitors, repentance is
open to them. But they must act quickly or else die with the
apostates, blasphemers and traitors (Sim 9,19,2f).

c. An ecclesiastical penitential system.

The writer not only distinguishes between repentance and nonrepentance, but also between those who are quick to repent and
those who do so only slowly. This latter distinction plays an
important role in the author's most unusual picture of the Church
as a tower surrounded by a wall. Those sinners who turn quickly
to do penance for their sins will get a position in the tower;
whereas, those who are slow to do penance will only get a position
in the wall, while those who refuse entirely to do penance will
die and remain in death (Sim 8,6,6; 8,7,3.5; 8,8,3; Vis 3,7,6).

The image of the Church which Hermas presents is indeed sui
generis. G. Rauschen[17] proposes what seems to be a fairly satisfactory solution. He suggests that Pastor Hermae is both an attack
on and a compromise with rigorist elements of perhaps Montanist
origin or nature. Accordingly, the tower would correspond to the
"pure Church" of the Montanists, but the wall would represent the
"real Church" as she is existentially experienced in the world,
where she still embraces the ranks of those struggling against
sin and doing penance for their past serious lapses. Those who
perform penance quickly and sincerely can even come into the tower.
Montanism could never admit of this. The image of the wall, however, enables Hermas to keep the "pure Church" separated from sinners and the less zealous penitents.

---

17. Op. cit, 154.

Although the Shepherd of Hermas says nothing of the Eucharist, its value in this study is that it shows the early development of a tendency to see Church-membership in terms of "degrees." This made it possible to place various disciplines and degrees of penance and excommunication[18] upon those Christians who did not conform to the ideal picture of the Church. Hermas may have been somewhat of a rigorist himself, but his teaching is milder than that of certain ecclesial circles which he may have known. His was at least an attempt to paint a picture of the Church with a variety of colors, and not just in black and white.

4. The Epistola Apostolorum

This work, also known as the Dialogues of Jesus with his Disciples after the Resurrection, was originally written in Greek, but is preserved only in an Etheopian and a badly mutilated Coptic translation. Both the time and place of composition are disputed.[19] The aim of the work is, among other things, to defend the faith against Gnosticism, which this basically apocalyptic work typifies through Simon Magus and Cerinth. They are portrayed as having come in order to wander through the world as the enemies of Christ and to mislead his followers. Christians are

---

18. Cf. K. Rahner, Busslehre im Hirten des Hermas, 412-18, 421
    In this article, Rahner corrects J. Grotz' (op. cit.,) interpretation of Hermas' penitential discipline.

19. B. Altaner (p. 83) places the work around 140 or 170 in Egypt or Asia Minor. Other commentators prefer a date shortly before 150. Carl Schmidt, whose text of the epistle was consulted for the present study, sees the Epistola Apostolorum as part of the literature that sprang from the Easter Controversy, and therefore places it between 160 and 170 in Syria. Cf. Carl Schmidt and Isaak Wajnberg, Gespräche-apostolisches Sendschreiben des 2. Jahrhunderts, (Leipzig, 1919) 492.

therefore advised to be on their guard lest they fall prey to them and end in the death of ruin and judgment (A̲e̲ 32,8ff/K̲o̲ I,7ff).

The cardinal question of this apocryphal writing is: "Who will be saved and who will be lost?" The author, placing words in Jesus' mouth, does not hesitate to answer:

> Those who violate my commandment and teach something else or subtract or add to it and work only for their own exaltation and lead astray those who in simplicity believe in me-- these will I hand over to destruction (A̲e̲ 90,8ff/K̲o̲ XXIII, 13ff).

> Whoever believes in me, however, and in spite of his faith in my name still does not keep my commandment, this will be of no avail to him. In vain has he preferred that which seemed to him to be especially excellent. He is destined to an end in ruin, punishment and great pain since he has transgressed my commandment (A̲e̲ 86,9ff/K̲o̲ XXXII,4ff).

The author's object, however, is not to refute the Gnostics, but rather to confirm the faith of the faithful. To this end, he instructs his readers to "correct, discipline and convert" someone ensnared by sin or false doctrine (A̲e̲ 151,1). These measures are to be taken with complete impartiality (A̲e̲ 148,12ff/K̲o̲ XL,1ff). This action is for the good of all parties concerned; for "if his neighbor has reprimanded him, and he (the wrongdoer) has been converted, he will be redeemed; and the one who did the reprimanding will acquire eternal life" (A̲e̲ 148,4ff/K̲o̲ XXXIX,10ff). The writer also considers the possibility of real excommunication in the case of someone who refuses to repent:

> If you see, with your eyes, how your brother sins, correct him alone. If he obeys you, then you have won him. But if he does not listen to you, then punish your brother two or three times. If he still does not listen to you, then let him be like a gentile or publican.[20]

---

20. Cf. A̲e̲ 150,4ff/K̲o̲ 11ff; Mt 18,15-17. It is puzzeling that C.

Special concern about the final exclusion of sinners from the
kingdom upon the Lord's Parousia is expressed in the epistle's
version of the parable of the ten virgins (Ae 136ff/Ko XXXIVff).
At the conclusion of the parable, the Apostles are distressed
over the fate of the five foolish virgins, and, commenting from
the viewpoint of the five wise virgins, they say: "O Lord, it is
seeming to your splendor that grace also be conferred upon their
sisters." But Christ answers: "This is none of your affair, but
his who sent me; and I agree with him" (Ae 144,10ff/Ko XXXVIII,
5ff). Whether or not the writer is to be accused of rigorist tendencies depends on determining if the Apostles' statement represented his own sentiment, which he could only resolve by faith in
Christ's answer, or if he meant Christ's answer as a cold warning
to those who do not agree with the views presented in the letter.

Schmidt (op. cit., 378) can say: "Von der Kirche als einem
Bussinstitut weiss der Verfasser der Epistola nichts." The
charge of "rigorism" that he makes against the epistle's
author (378ff) is obviously not justified. Cf. B. Poschmann,
op. cit., 105.

CHAPTER TEN

ECCLESIA DOCTA DOCENS

1. Preliminary Remarks

A child seldom turns to intellectual pursuits unless he is properly coaxed and motivated--which is just a nice way of saying "pressured." It was scarcely any different with the youthful Church. The "second coming" that just would not come forced her to reflect on her role in the world and to prepare for a long future. Civil hostility continued to mount and spread. The dangers of heresy and schism from within created a critical situation as the Gnostics systematized their beliefs into elaborate concepts of life and the universe. By about the middle of the second century, it was "do or die" for the Church; and she arose splendidly to the situation. In short time, she learned the other three "R's" in addition to Religion. Her book shelves suddenly began to fill with the large volumes that flowed forth from her pen. The codification of Scriptures became a major concern. In brief, she joined the intelligentsia. This meant that the Church had to view the world in a different perspective. She could no longer see herself as a tiny boat of refuge floating in the massa damnata. Indeed, the doctrine of extra ecclesiam nulla salus est must wait another century before it is clearly formulated. But the Church's attitude toward the world itself began to change as she became more fully aware of her catholic nature. These alterations in the early Church's policies were not only calculated to insure her survival, but they also prepared the way for the year 313 and Constantine the Great. However, since many of these changes in the Church of the second century were the result of her reaction toward Gnosticism, it would be useful to take a quick look at the foe before we examine some of the works of the Christian writers of the period now under consideration.

The syncretistic nature of Gnosticism was carried to the fullest at this time, with the result that its thoughts pervaded all levels of society in even the remotest regions of the Empire and "in all provinces of literary expression."[1] Although only a few groups actually called themselves "Gnostics," Irenaeus of Lyons classified any number of sects which shared some general characteristics as "Gnostics wrongly so called."[2]

It is now commonly known that the roots of Gnosticism well predate Christianity even though the Church Fathers looked upon the systems that they refuted as Christian heresies. This was not totally unjustified since some systems such as Valentinianism did arise as a sect from within the Church, while other systems came from without but attempted to syncretize certain elements of the Christian faith with their own teachings. Sometimes this threat came by way of Jewish elements already infected with false gnosis.

These systems considered "knowledge" of God rather than faith in him as the means to salvation. This knowledge was to be achieved by various mystic and nonrational methods; and, in systems like Valentinianism, it was not only the means to salvation, but itself man's ultimate perfection and salvation. Obviously, such concepts of gnosis could not possibly be given Christian approval since

---

1. Cf. Hans Jonas, The Gnostic Religion, (Boston, 1958) 25. Except when otherwise stated, the information that is presented here on Gnosticism has been taken from the aforementioned work, or else from H. Jonas' other outstanding work, Gnosis und Spätantiker Geist, (Göttingen, 1954), which still awaits completion.

2. The full title of Irenaeus' adversus Haereses is Ἔλεγχος καὶ ἀνατροπὴ τῆς ψευδωνύμου γνώσεως. Cf. Eusebius, HE 5,7.

Christianity, or "the true gnosis,"[3] requires that one form a
real personal relationship of love with God rather than merely
acquire "knowledge" of certain "cosmic facts and formulae" which
ultimately mean that salvation rests solely in one's faith in
himself. Love of neighbor likewise becomes meaningless in such
a philosophy of life.

The Gnostic concept of the universe (i.e., its cosmology)
made it a natural consequence that salvation could not be a question of achieving a personal relationship with God in "this world,"
which was supposedly the evil creation of a demiurge or other low-
ly powers. Salvation meant "escaping" from this world by way of
gnosis. Only then could there be any question of a relation of
any sort with the God of Goodness, who is absolutely transmundane
and alien to the universe. Man was separated from this god by
the spheres of the planets and the fixed stars that surrounded
the earth. Generally, seven or eight such spheres were counted;
but Basilides multiplied them to 365. Moreover, it was not only
spatial distance and physical barriers that separated man from
God, it was also a matter of demonic forces which inhabited the
various spheres. It was the purpose of gnosis to "trick" the
forces into letting one pass through the various spheres to God.

The natural result of this cosmological dualism was a moral
dualism that expressed itself in the extremes of asceticism and
libertinism. Both extremes rested upon the common principle that
one should exercise his freedom from the norms of this earth,

---

3. In *Fragment* 35 (*Harvey* 2, 498), Irenaeus supposedly identifies knowledge of the mystery of the cross as "true knowledge."
However, this is one of the so-called *Pfaff Fragments*, which
have been shown to be forgeries. Cf. A. von Harnack, *TU* 20,
3, 1900.

which is to be despised and violated as the work of Archons, Eons, and demons. This was a radical rejection of the classical Greek concept of "cosmos" as divine order that is to be imitated--a basic notion in Stoicism and one which was readily accepted by Christianity; for it harmonized well with the Christian understanding and application of the Old Testament. But, as regards the early Church, it was precisely here--in the Old Testament--that the crux of the problem lay. This aspect became especially evident in Marcion of Sinope, whom St. Justin Martyr said the devils had promoted (1 Apol 58).

Marcion was the most "Christian" of the outstanding heretics of his time, and his system occupied a unique position in Gnostic thought and the life of the early Church. He alone of the Gnostics, if he is really to be classified with them, accepted Christ's death as of salvific value even though he held that Christ's body was but a phantom. His sober teaching rejected all the mythological fantasy of the other Gnostic systems. In fact, it was his insistence upon realism that led him and his school to reject the allegorical method of exegesis which enabled the young Church to see positive evidence of the history of salvation in the Old Testament.[4] But Marcion dismissed the entire Old Testament as the work of the God of Justice, but not the God of Love who revealed himself through Jesus of Nazareth. Consequently, his search for the "literal meaning" of the Gospel prompted him to present Christianity with a

---

4. For example, Apelles, one of Marcion's students and very much influenced by Aristotelian logic, noted in his Syllogisms that Noah's Ark was so small that it could scarcely accommodate four elephants--not to speak of all the other animals. Therefore, the story must be false and could not possibly come from God. Consequently, the Old Testament is likewise false and not from God. Cf. Origen, Hom in Gen 2,2.

very limited canon of inspired writings consisting of Luke, Acts and ten Pauline letters. Even these works were purged of Jewish elements and altered according to his teachings.

This heretic, excommunicated by his own father, the Bishop of Sinope,[5] likewise made faith rather than gnosis the means to salvation. This would seem at first to absolve Marcion of Gnosticism's most essential and most perverted teaching. However, this is not so; for he felt that "faith was supposed to have some secret mysterious charm that ensured the salvation of even the most reprobate."[6] Such a concept of faith was simply another form of Gnosticism, and was certainly not what St. Paul meant when he preached salvation by faith.

Gnosticism's influence upon Marcion is also evident in his anti-cosmic dualism which caused him to believe that matter was wholly evil and the work of an oppressive creator. As a result, he was unable to see that the principles of justice and goodness must be united in one God. This dualism led him to a Docetic Christology which declared that Christ, rather than being born of woman, first appeared in Galilee as a man of about 30 years of age without the least bit of pre-history in Judaism or the Prophets.[7]

From now on, the Fathers will stress the one God who is both just and good. The Old Testament will eventually acquire a new importance in many parts of the Church, with the result that some

---

5. This occurred probably about 138. About 139, Marcion was given a friendly reception in Rome, but was also excommunicated from the Roman community during the autumn of 144.

6. Cf. Harvey 1, cxlix.

7. Cf. Tertullian, adv Mar 1,19; 4,7; Epiphanius, Haer 42; Hippolytus, Phil 8,32.

Fathers will try to apply many elements of the Old Law directly to Christian life without proper respect either for Christian revelation or for the conditions which produced the legislation of the Old Testament.

2. Justin Martyr

With the conversion of St. Justin, the Church was given her most important apologist of the second century. Born of a pagan Greek family (perhaps about 115) at Flavia Neapolis (Sichem) in Palestine, he spent his younger years in various philosophical schools, until his restless search for knowledge brought him into contact with Christianity--probably near Ephesus. After his conversion to Christianity, he traveled extensively to spread and defend the faith. Finally he established a school at Rome, where he was probably beheaded in 165.

His education in Greek philosophy was used well in the service of his faith even though much of what he taught is no longer acceptable doctrine. His teaching in regard to the Eucharist is the Church's earliest effort to explain this mystery in terms of contemporary Greek philosophy. By identifying Jesus Christ with the Logos of Greek philosophy, Justin sought to demonstrate that the Eucharist is the λογικὴ θυσία and thus the long awaited spiritual sacrifice.[8] In addition to his speculative approach to the Eucharist and theology, the Martyr Saint offers much in the way of practical explanation concerning the early Church's eucharistic discipline. Of particular interest here are his First Apology and the Dialogue with Trypho.[9]

---

8. Cf. Dial 41. The canon of the Roman Mass speaks of the Eucharist as the "oblatio rationabilis," which corresponds quite well to Justin's concept of sacrifice. Cf. J. Quasten, Patrology 1, 218.

9. The First Apology was written to Caesar Antonius Pius about

In 1 <u>Apol</u> 65, Justin explains that the Eucharist concludes the initiation ceremony of Baptism and that it was also carried to those who could not attend. Following this, he enumerates the major conditions necessary for participation in the Euchar- ist:[10]

> And this food is called Eucharist among us. No one is allowed to partake of it except the one who believes that the things taught by us are true, and who has been washed with the bath for the remission of sins and unto regenera- tion, and who is so living as Christ taught.

These conditions for the reception of the Eucharist are imme- diately grounded in the nature of the sacrament itself:

> For we do not take these things as (if they were) common bread and common drink; but just as Jesus Christ our Saviour, having become flesh through God's word, had both flesh and blood for our salvation, so in like manner have we been taught that the food that is blessed ("eucharisticised") by the pray- er of his word, and from which our blood and flesh are nour- ished by transmutation, is the flesh and the blood of that Jesus made flesh.[11]

150-155. The <u>Second</u> <u>Apology</u> may be part of the <u>First</u> <u>Apology</u>; but this is a much disputed question. Besides the <u>Apologies</u>, only the <u>Dialogue</u> <u>with</u> <u>Trypho</u> and some fragments are generally accepted as genuine writings of Justin Martyr. The <u>Dialogue</u> was written after 1 <u>Apol</u>. But if ever such a debate did ac- tually take place, it was probably at Ephesus about 132-135 during the revolt of Bar-Cochba. Cf. B. Altaner, <u>Patrology</u>, 122f.

10. Justin almost always refers to this sacrament as εὐχαριστία. But sometimes he calls it μυστήριον. Cf. O. Casel, <u>Eucharis-</u> <u>tielehre</u> <u>des</u> <u>hl.</u> <u>Justinus</u> <u>Martyr</u>, 154.

11. Cf. 1 <u>Apol</u> 66; <u>CAC</u> 1, 180-82: Καὶ ἡ τροφὴ αὕτη καλεῖται παρ' ἡμῖν εὐχαριστία, ἧς οὐδενὶ ἄλλῳ μετασχεῖν ἐξόν ἐστιν ἢ τῷ πιστεύοντι ἀληθῆ εἶναι τὰ δεδιδαγμένα ὑφ' ἡμῶν, καὶ λουσαμένῳ τὸ ὑπὲρ ἀφέσεως ἁμαρτιῶν καὶ εἰς ἀναγέννησιν λουτρόν, καὶ οὕτως βιοῦντι ὡς ὁ Χριστὸς παρέδωκεν. Οὐ γὰρ ὡς κοινὸν ἄρτον οὐδὲ κοινὸν πόμα ταῦτα λαμβάνομεν· ἀλλ' ὃν τρόπον διὰ λόγου

In Dial 41, the nature of the Eucharist and its relation to Baptism are further explained. Accordingly, the offering of flour that one had to make after being cleansed of leprosy (Lv 14,10) prefigured the Eucharist, which Jesus prescribed in remembrance of his death in behalf of those who are purified in soul. It is the pure sacrifice foretold in Mal 1,10-12. Dial 117 adds that the prophecy of Malachi is especially fulfilled in the Eucharist, because it is universal and not confined to the temple as are the Jewish sacrifices which it replaces. Here, the purpose of the above-mentioned prerequisites for participation in the Eucharist is made clear; namely, it is similar to the Didache's command that Christians should confess their sins so that their sacrifice may be pure. Similarily, Justin remarks: "That indeed prayers and the giving of thanks, when offered by worthy men, are the only perfect and well-pleasing sacrifices to God, I also admit."[12] However, Justin Martyr nowhere directly treats the relationship of the nonorthodox to the Eucharist. Nevertheless, he has a number of things to say concerning the Church's relation to such persons.

In Dial 34, the Saint maintains that Christians prefer death to the eating of meat offered to idols. Trypho replies that he knows of people who call themselves Christians, but still eat such meat (Dial 35). Justin admits that this is so, but that such per-

---

θεοῦ σαρκοποιηθεὶς 'Ιησοῦς Χριστὸς ὁ σωτὴρ ἡμῶν καὶ σάρκα καὶ αἷμα ὑπὲρ σωτηρίας ἡμῶν ἔσχεν, οὕτως καὶ τὴν δι' εὐχῆς λόγου τοῦ παρ' αὐτοῦ εὐχαριστηθεῖσαν τροφήν, ἐξ ἧς αἷμα καὶ σάρκες κατὰ μεταβολὴν τρέφονται ἡμῶν, ἐκείνου τοῦ σαρκοποιηθέντος 'Ιησοῦ καὶ σάρκα καὶ αἷμα ἐδιδάχθημεν εἶναι.

12. ῞Οτι μὲν οὖν καὶ εὐχαὶ καὶ εὐχαριστίαι, ὑπὸ τῶν ἀξίων γινόμεναι, τέλειαι μόναι καὶ εὐάρεστοί εἰσι τῷ θεῷ θυσίαι, καὶ αὐτός φημι. Cf. CAC 2, 418.

sons were foretold in the Gospel and by Paul (Mt 7,15; 24,11; 1 Cor 11,19). With these heretics, "we have nothing in common since we know that they are atheists, impious, unjust and sinful, and confessors of Jesus in name only, instead of being his worshippers."[13] The men are immediately identified as Marcians (Marcionites?), Valentinians, Basilidians, Saturnilians and others.

Besides describing the attitude of orthodox Christians towards the Gnostics who styled themselves as Christians, Justin also has something to say about the problem of Jewish Christians who still observe the Law of Moses (Dial 47). Accordingly, Trypho wants to know if a Jewish Christian who practices the Law can be saved even though he believes that the Law does not justify. Justin feels that such a one can be saved as long as he does not try to impose the Law on others; although, there are other Christians who refuse to associate at all with Law-observing Jewish Christians. But Justin does not approve of their action. On the other hand, he does not believe that one who simply relapses from the Christian faith to return to Judaism can be saved; nor does he think a Jew who dies without first confessing Jesus as the Christ can be saved. This harsh judgment is given because of the curse that the synagogue pronounces upon all that is Christian. But, as Justin explains later (Dial 96 and 133), Christians should still pray for the Jews and love those that hate them (i.e., the Christians) and bless those that curse them.

3. Irenaeus of Lyons

a. The Eucharist and heretics.

The "Father of Catholic Dogmatics" may have been born in Syria about the middle of the second century. He became Bishop of Lyons

13. Cf. Dial 35; CAC 2, 118: ὧν οὐδενὶ κοινωνοῦμεν, οἱ γνωρίζοντες

in Gaul sometime during the latter quarter of that century. In his younger days, he supposedly was a disciple of the aged Polycarp. Neither the date nor the cause of Irenaeus' death is known.

His major work, adversus Haereses, has been only partially preserved in its original Greek. A Latin translation has come down in the manuscripts. But "of the Latin Version it is sufficient to say, that the Celt who made it was in every way inferior to the work that he undertook; independently of the barbarisms and solecisms with which his style abounds, he frequently is totally unable to catch the author's meaning."[14] However, it is necessary to add that Irenaeus' Greek is also sometimes obscure and uncertain. It may be that Greek was not his native language; for his use of scriptures betrays his acquaintance with a Syriac version.

Probably sometime between 182 and 188, St. Irenaeus wrote his refutation of heresies upon the request of a friend.[15] In the course of the work, it becomes clear that the Bishop's treatment of the Eucharist was prompted by circumstances similar to those which urged St. Ignatius (ad Smyrn 7,1) to write on the Eucharist--namely, the difficulty that the heretics had in harmonizing their eucharistic practices and beliefs with their rejection of the resurrection of the body. Their errors were, of course, the result of their fundamentally Gnostic dualism, which interposed a radical division between spiritual beings and material things, between the "real God" and the creator of the universe, and be-

---

ἀθέους καὶ ἀσεβεῖς καὶ ἀδίκους καὶ ἀνόμους αὐτοὺς ὑπάρχοντας, καί, ἀντὶ τοῦ τὸν Ἰησοῦν σέβειν, ὀνόματι μόνον ὁμολογεῖν.

14. Cf. Harvey 1, clxiv.
15. Ibid., civii.

tween the Mosaic Law and the new dispensation. The Bishop of
Lyons accuses them of attempting to place themselves above the
Apostles and of having lost the love of God (adv Haer 3,12,12).

Through his use and explanation of the Eucharist, Irenaeus
develops a very basic approach in refuting these Gnostic errors
and in defending the reality of Christ's human nature and the
bodily resurrection.[16] He points to the eucharistic practice
of the heretics and asks:

> How can they be consistent with themselves (and still
> maintain) that the bread over which thanks have been given
> is the body of their Lord, and the chalice his blood, if
> they do not say that he himself is the Son of the Creator
> of the world--that is, his Word?...Moreover, how can they

---

16. In adv Haer 5,33,1; Harvey 2, 415f, Irenaeus takes Mt 26,27-
29 as the theological basis for the connection which he makes
between the Eucharist and the resurrection: "Propter hoc
autem ad passionem veniens, ut evangelisaret Abrahae, et iis
qui cum eo, apertionem haereditatis, cum gratias egisset ten-
ens calicem, et bibisset ab eo, et dedisset discipulis, dice-
bat eis: 'Bibite ex eo omnes. Hic est sanguis meus novi Testamenti, qui pro multis effundetur in remissionem peccatorum.
Dico autem vobis, a modo non bibam de generatione vitis hujus,
usque in diem illum, quando illum bibam vobiscum novum in regno Patris mei.' Utique haereditatem terrae ipso novabit, et
reintegrabit mysterium gloriae filiorum; quemadmodum David
ait: 'Qui renovavit faciem terrae' (Ps 103,30). Promisit
bibere de generatione vitis cum suis discipulis, utrumque ostendens, et haereditatem terrae in qua bibitur nova fenera-
tio vitis, et carnalem resurrectionem discipulorum ejus.
Quae enim nova resurgit caro, ipsa est quae et novum percepit
poculum. Neque autem sursum in supercoelesti loco constitutus cum suis, potest intelligi bibens vitis generationem;
neque rursus sine carne sunt, qui bibunt illud: carnis enim
proprium est et non spiritus, qui ex vite accipitur potus."
The system of citation that is used here for Irenaeus' adv
Haer follows Massuet rather than Harvey since Massuet's system is more familiar and is also given in the margins of
Harvey's edition.

say that the flesh becomes corrupt and does not partake of
the life that is nourished with the Lord's body and blood?
Therefore, let them either alter their opinion or else cease
to offer the aforementioned things.[17]

Although Ignatius declared that the Eucharist of heretics was, as
it were, invalid because it did not have the bishop's approval,
Irenaeus bases his objection to such liturgical gatherings on the
heterodoxy of the heretics. That is, whatever the Church offers
to God is a pure offering; whereas, the offering of the Jews and
the heretics is unacceptable because the former have rejected
God's Word, and the latter insult the Father through their dual-
istic cosmology (adv Haer 4,18,4). Therefore, orthodoxy in belief is an essential precondition for the celebration of the
Eucharist. It is not a question of the "Church over the Eucharist," but of the "Eucharist over the Church":

> But our opinion is in harmony with the Eucharist, and the
> Eucharist in turn confirms our opinion. For we offer to Him
> what belongs to Him,[18] and announce consistently the fellow-

---

17. Cf. adv Haer 4,18,4f; Harvey 2, 204f: "Quomodo autem consta-
    bit eis, eum panem in quo gratiae actae sint, corpus esse
    Domini sui, et calicem sanguinis ejus, si non ipsum fabrica-
    toris mundi Filium dicant, id est Verbum ejus, per quod lig-
    num fructificat, et effluunt fontes, et terra dat primum qui-
    dem foenum, post deinde spicam, deinde plenum triticum in
    spica?" Πῶς...τὴν σάρκα λέγουσιν εἰς φθορὰν χωρεῖν, καὶ μὴ
    μετέχειν τῆς ζωῆς, τὴν ἀπὸ τοῦ Κυρίου καὶ τοῦ αἵματος αὐτοῦ
    τρεφομένην; ῍Η τὴν γνώμην ἀλλαξάτωσαν, ἢ τὸ προσφέρειν τὰ
    εἰρημένα παραιτείσθωσαν. Cf. also adv Haer 5,2,3, where
    Irenaeus asks how the heretics can deny that the flesh is
    able to receive eternal life after being nourished as a mem-
    ber of the Lord's body (Eph 5,30) by means of his eucharistic
    body and blood.

18. This is in reference to the Gnostic belief that all matter,
    having been created by a being other than God, is totally
    alien to God. Therefore, when God redeemed mankind, he was

ship and union of the flesh and the spirit. For as the bread, which is from the earth, when it receives the invocation of God, is no longer common bread, but Eucharist, consisting of two realities, earthly and heavenly, so also our bodies, receiving the Eucharist, are no longer corruptible but have the hope of the resurrection unto eternity.[19]

From this, it seems that Irenaeus does not mean to say simply that the Eucharist of the heretics is *per se* "defective." Rather, he implies that they receive in the Eucharist whatever their defi-

---

"buying back" something that never belonged to him in the first place. Again, this reduces the Eucharist of the heretics to absurdity; for, in their denial that God became man in Jesus Christ, they would have to admit, if they were to be logical, that Christ's blood could not and did not redeem man. Cf. adv Haer 5,2,1.

19. Cf. adv Haer 4,18,5; Harvey 2, 205-08: Ἡμῶν δὲ σύμφωνος ἡ γνώμη τῇ εὐχαριστίᾳ, καὶ ἡ εὐχαριστία βεβαιοῖ τὴν γνώμην. Προσφέρομεν δὲ αὐτῷ τὰ ἴδια, ἐμμελῶς κοινωνίαν καὶ ἕνωσιν ἀπαγγέλλοντες (καὶ ὁμολογοῦντες) σαρκὸς καὶ πνεύματος (ἔγερσιν). Ὡς γὰρ ἀπὸ γῆς ἄρτος προσλαμβανόμενος τὴν ἔκκλησιν (i.e., ἐπίκλησιν) τοῦ θεοῦ, οὐκέτι κοινὸς ἄρτος ἐστὶν, ἀλλ' εὐχαριστία, ἐκ δύο πραγμάτων συνεστηκεῖα, ἐπιγείου τε καὶ οὐρανίου· οὕτως καὶ τὰ σώματα ἡμῶν μεταλαμβάνοντα τῆς εὐχαριστίας, μηκέτι εἶναι φθαρτά, τὴν ἐλπίδα τῆς εἰς αἰῶνας ἀναστάσεως ἔχοντα. In analysing this text, Harvey holds the words in the first two parentheses to be interpolations. This seems to be the case; for, by "announcing consistently the fellowship and union of the flesh and spirit," Irenaeus is again attacking the Eucharist of the heretics since their Christology renders their Eucharist absurd. That is, they cannot maintain that the Eucharist is the Lord's body and blood since they cannot admit that Jesus Christ is the Son of the Creator of the world. Consequently, they cannot admit the real and essential unity of the divine Logos with the real human body. The Church's Eucharist is thus in harmony with the eucharistic mystery, because the Church confesses faith in the unity (or union) of the Logos with the Lord's body and blood, and she expresses this article of faith in the sacrament of the Eucharist. Cf. Johannes Döllinger, Die Eucharistie in den drei ersten Jahrhunderten, (Mainz, 1826) 32.

cient faith admits--that is, in accordance with their beliefs.
Therefore, their Eucharist cannot benefit them as regards the resurrection. Likewise, the Bishop declares that the Ebionites,
who use water in place of wine in the Eucharist, do not receive
the union of God and man in this sacrament, but only remain in
the old Adam rather than coming into the new Adam, who is Christ.[20]

b. Heretics and the bishop.

Although Irenaeus discredits the Eucharist of heretics on the
grounds of their insufficient faith rather than their disunity

---

20. Cf. adv Haer 5,1,3; Harvey 2, 316f: "Vani autem et Ebionaei,
    unitionem Dei et hominis per fidem non recipientes in suam
    animam, sed in veteri generationis perseverantes fermento...
    Reprobant itaque hi commixtionem vini coelestis, et sola aqua
    secularis volunt esse, non recipientes Deum ad commixtionem
    suam: perseverantes autem in eo qui victus est Adam, et pro-
    jectus est de paradiso, non contemplantes, quoniam quemadmo-
    dum ab initio plasmationis nostrae in Adam ea quae fuit a
    Deo adspiratio vitae unita plasmati animavit hominem, et
    animal rationabile ostendit; sic in fine Verbum Patris et
    Spiritus Dei, adunitus antiquae substantiae plasmationis
    Adae, viventem et perfectum effecit hominem, capientem per-
    fectum Patrem: ut quemadmodum in animali omnes mortui sumus,
    sic in spiritali omnes vivificemur." Cyprian of Carthage,
    writing about 254, addresses himself to the question of the
    Eucharist where water is used in place of wine. He points
    out that Jesus used wine at the Last Supper, referring to it
    as his blood. Cyprian concludes: "unde apparet sanguinem
    Christi no offerri, si desit uinum calici, nec sacrificium
    dominicum legitima sanctificatione celebrari, nisi oblatio et
    sacrificium nostrum responderit passioni." Cf. ep 63,9; CSEL
    3/2, 708. In Cyprian's mind both wine and water must be used
    in the Eucharist: "quando autem in calice uino aqua miscetur,
    Christo populus adunatur et credentium plebs ei in quem credi-
    dit copulatur et iungitur...sic autem in sanctificando calice
    Domini offerri aqua sola non potest quomodo nec uinum solum
    potest, nam si uinum tantum quis offerat, sanguis Christi in-
    cipit esse sine nobis. si uero aqua sit sola, plebs incipit

with the Church as such, he does not mean to imply that their separation is only of an accidental nature or that union with the Apostolic successors is of little consequence for orthodoxy in faith. In the first place, union with the Church is to be identified as "true knowledge" and is thoroughly bound up with episcopal succession. Irenaeus thus writes:

> True knowledge is the teaching of the Apostles--the manifestation of the body of Christ according to the succession of bishops, to whom they have handed down that Church which exists in every place and which has come even unto us (and has been) preserved without forging of scriptures (but) by a very complete credo, receiving neither addition nor subtraction; and (true knowledge is) reading without falsification, and a legitimate and diligent exposition in accordance with Scriptures, both without danger and without blasphemy; and (it is) the pre-eminent gift of love, which is more precious than knowledge, more glorious than prophecy, and excels all other gifts.[21]

Irenaeus makes it clear that union with the bishops is necessary--not that they are anything in themselves, but rather because they are in possession of the truth which the risen Christ explained in the light of the Scriptures to the Apostles (adv Haer 4,26,1). He then continues:

esse sine Christo. quando autem utrumque miscetur et adunatione confusa sibi inuicem copulatur, tunc sacramentum spiritale et caeleste perficitur." Cf. ep 63,13; CSEL 3/2, 711f.

21. Cf. adv Haer 4,33,8; Harvey 2, 262f: Γνῶσις ἀληθής, ἡ τῶν ἀποστόλων διδαχή· καὶ τὸ ἀρχαῖον τῆς ἐκκλησίας σύστημα κατὰ παντὸς τοῦ κόσμου· "et character corporis Christi secundum successiones episcoporum, quibus illi eam quae in unoquoque loco est Ecclesiam tradiderunt, quae pervenit usque ad nos custodita sine fictione scripturarum tractatione plenissima, neque additamentum neque ablationem recipiens, et lectio sine falsatione, et secundum Scripturas expositio legitima et diligens, et sine periculo et sine blasphemia: et praecipuum dilectionis munus, quod est pretiousius quam agnitio, gloriousius autem quam prophetia, omnibus autem reliquis charismatibus supereminens."

Wherefore, it is necessary for those who are in the Church to obey the presbyters, who, as I have shown, have succession from the Apostles, and who have received--according to the pleasure of the Father--the certain charism of truth together with their succession in the episcopate. But (it is also necessary) to hold in suspicion any others who refrain from the primitive succession and assemble elsewhere, (considering them) either as heretics with evil intentions, or as schismatics[22] elated and self-gratifying, or else as hypocrites acting thus for the sake of monetary gain and vainglory. All of these have fallen away from the truth. Indeed, the heretics, who bear strange fire to God's altar-- namely, strange doctrines--shall be consumed by the fire from heaven, as were Nadab and Abiud (Lv 10,1f). Such as rise up against the truth and exhort others against the Church of God (shall) remain apud inferos, being taken away by an earthquake, as were those around Korah, Dathan and Abiron (Nm 16,33). And those who split and separate the unity of the Church (shall) receive from God the same punishment as Jeroboam did (1 Kgs 14,10).[23]

---

22. Irenaeus is the first of the Christian writers to use the term "schismatic" in today's sense--that is, someone split from the main body of the Church, but still holding to the fundamental doctrines of the faith. But later Church fathers (e.g., Cyprian) did not always make the distinction, and used the terms "heretic" and "schismatic" interchangeably. Cf. H.W. Fulford, Schism, in: ERE 11, 232.

23. Cf. adv Haer 4,26,2; Harvey 2, 236: "Quapropter eis qui in Ecclesia sunt presbyteris obaudire oportet, his qui successionem habent ab Apostolis, sicut ostendimus; qui cum episcopatus successione charisma veritatis certum secundum placitum Patris acceperunt: reliquos vero qui absistunt a principali successione, et quocunque loco colliguntur, suspectos habere, vel quasi haereticos et malae sententiae, vel quasi scindentes et elatos et sibi placentes, aut rursus ut hypocritas, quaestus gratia et vanae gloriae hoc operantes. Omnes autem hi deciderunt a veritate. Et haeretici quidem alienum ignem afferentes ad altare Dei, id est alienas doctrinas, a coelesti igne comburentur, quemadmodum Nadab et Abiud. Qui vero exsurgunt contra veritatem, et alteros adhortantur adversus Ecclesiam Dei, remanent apud inferos, voragine terrae absorpti, quemadmodum qui circa Chore Dathan

However, in adv Haer 4,26,3, Irenaeus lets it be known that even those in the hierarchical service of the Church are to be judged according to their deeds and integrity of life. He compares the unjust presbyters with evil servants (Mt 24,48 and par.). Such persons will be convicted by the Word of God himself, who is not deceived by outward appearances:

> Therefore, one is obliged to avoid such men and to adhere to those who, as we have said before, keep the doctrine of the Apostles, and who, together with the order of the priesthood, display sound speech and nonoffensive conduct for the edification and correction of the others.[24]

Apostolic tradition is the "touchstone" of orthodoxy for Irenaeus, and this is found only within the Church. Thus, those churches which were established by the Apostles, or had direct and continuous intercourse with them, are of special importance. On the other hand, the subsequent emergence of heresies and heretical groups at a later date is "proof" of their non-apostolicity (adv Haer 3,4,3; Clement of Alexandria, Stromata 7,17,106-08). As a result, even barbarian nations without a written record of Scriptures or traditions preserved their orthodoxy since they were able to distinguish false doctrine simply by comparing it with the ancient tradition they had received from the Apostles and their successors (adv Haer 3,4,2).

---

et Abiron. Qui autem scindunt et separant unitatem Ecclesiae, eandem quam Hieroboam poenam percipiunt a Deo."

24. Cf. adv Haer 4,26,4; Harvey 2, 237: "Ab omnibus igitur talibus absistere oportet; adhaerere vero his qui et Apostolorum, sicut praediximus, doctrinam custodiunt, et cum presbyterii ordine sermonem sanum et conversationem sine offensa praestant, ad conformationem et correctionem reliquorum."

c. Heretics and the Church.

Irenaeus realizes that it is simply not enough to refer to
Apostolic tradition without, at the same time, giving meaningful
content to the principle. Basically, and in view of the nature
of the heresies which the Bishop has in mind, the Apostolic tradition upon which all other Christian doctrines follow almost as
if by analogia fidei is summed up in the Christian belief that
the Old Covenant and the New Covenant have one and the same God--
the Father of Jesus Christ--as their author. The Old Covenant is
a true foreshadowing of the New--that is, the Church--, and both
Covenants were given for the benefit of those who believe in God
(adv Haer 4,32,2). But the essential ecclesiological principle
is that the New Covenant is not simply a parallel of the Old.
Rather, it replaces the Old Covenant. Therefore, the true Christian, while himself above judgment from anyone else--for how can
that which is less judge the greater?--will serve to judge all
others: the gentiles who serve the creature instead of the Creator
(Rm 1,21), the Jews who prefer enslavement in place of Christian
liberty, Marcion for his doctrine of two gods which contradicts
the Eucharist,[25] the Valentinians who confess one God and Father
but think that the creator is the fruit of apostasy or defect
from God, the Gnostics, th Ebionites and those who do not admit
the Incarnation, false prophets who lie against God, schismatics
who without love destroy the Church's unity, and he will judge

---

25. Cf. adv Haer 4,33,2; Harvey 2, 257: "Examinabit autem et doc-
    trinam Marcionis,...Quomodo autem juste Dominus, si alterius
    patris exsistit, hujus conditionis quae est secundum nos acci-
    piens panem suum corpus esse confitebatur, et temperamentum
    calicis suum sanguinem confirmavit?"

all those outside of the Church as those outside of the truth
(adv Haer 4,33,1-7).

However, this judgment is not effective of the condemnation
of the judged persons. Rather, Christians, as the norm upon
which the judgment is based, simply affirm the condemnation
which the others receive from God. But even then, it is not
God who is ultimately responsible for their unfortunate outcome.
Rather, he merely imposes the separation from himself which such
persons have already chosen for themselves (adv Haer 5,27,2).
Wherefore, Irenaeus says that those who fall away from the Church
in order to follow the fables of false teachers are truly αυτοκα-
ταϰϱιτοι, whom Christians should avoid after one or two warnings
(Ti 3,10). In fact, one should not even wish such persons "good-
speed";[26] for that would make one a partaker of their wrongdoing
(2 Jn 10f); but it is the Lord's will that the ungodly find no
"good-speed" (Is 48,22). Therefore, such as hold Gnostic opinions should be shunned (adv Haer 1,16,3). Playing upon the idea
of knowledge (i.e., gnosis), Irenaeus compares the Gnostic notions to the tree of knowledge of good and evil, which is in the
midst of paradise (i.e., the Church), but must be avoided (adv
Haer 5,20,2). In adv Haer 3,3,4, the Bishop refers to concrete
historical examples of such treatment of heretics. For example,
John, the disciple of the Lord, immediately left the bath house
at Ephesus--although he had not finished bathing--when he saw
Cerinth, "the enemy of truth," come in.[27] And on another occasion,

---

26. Βουληθείς (ave). To greet someone in ancient times meant to
bless (Ps 129,8) and wish the person well and successful in
all of his endeavors. Cf. 2 Sm 11,7, where the word shalom is
used in the sense of "successful conduct of affairs" even in
matters of war.

27. According to W. Speyer (Fluch, in: RAC 7, 1248), early Christ-

Marcion approached Polycarp and asked him: "Do you recognize us
(ἐπιγινώσκεις ἡμᾶς)?" By this, Marcion meant to inquire whether
or not Polycarp recognized him and his followers as fellow Christians.[28] However, the aged Saint plays on the notion of "recognize," and answers: ἐπιγινώσκω (σε) τὸν πρωτότοκον τοῦ Σατανᾶ [29]

Besides the instructions to avoid false teachers and the like,
Irenaeus gives evidence that he knows of a real excommunication
formally pronounced by the Church acting through the bishop perhaps together with the presbyters or community. This seems to be
the case in adv Haer 4,32,1, where it is stated that a heretic who
distinguishes between the creator and the real God:

> must of necessity fall into much inconsistency and many con-
> tradictions for which he will (be able to) give no explana-
> tions (that can be regarded) as either probable or true. And
> it is for this reason that those who introduce other doctrines
> hide from us the opinion which they themselves hold regarding
> God; for they recognize the shaky and absurd nature of their
> teaching, and they are afraid lest, having been vanquished,
> their salvation will be endangered.[30]

---

ians were of the opinion that heretics were so filled with
"magischem Fluchstoff" that no true believer would want to
use the same bath water with a heretic.

28. Cf. Harvey 2, 14, n. 1.
29. In adv Haer 4,41,1-3, Irenaeus explains that the expression,
    filius or angelus diaboli, means especially those who have re-
    lapsed from the faith since the devil is their teacher, for a
    teacher's students are often referred to as his "sons."

30. "Si enim semel quis transmoveatur a factore omnium, et conce-
    dat ab aliquo altero, aut per alium factam conditionem quae
    est secundum nos, multam incongruentiam et plurimas contradic-
    tiones necesse est incidat hujusmodi: ad quas nullas dabit
    rationes, neque secundum verisimile, neque secundum veritatem.
    Et propter hoc hi qui alias doctrinas interunt, abscondunt a
    nobis quam habent ipsi de Deo sententiam, scientes quassum et
    futile doctrinae suae, et timentes ne victi salvari pericli-

Further insight into the process of ecclesial excommunication is given when Irenaeus points to Cerdon, Marcion's predecessor, as a concrete example of how the Church deals with heretics:

> Often coming into the church and making public confession (of orthodoxy), he thus persisted, sometimes teaching in secret, and then again making public confession; and finally being denounced for evil teaching, he was excommunicated from the assembly of the brethren.[31]

But whether a person is excommunicated for ethical or doctrinal reasons, the Bishop of Lyons supplies ample indication that reconciliation with the Church is possible.[32] In one instance, he relates the story of a deacon's wife who was deceived by the trickery of a certain charlatan who often gave love potions to his women followers and sexually abused them. The wife of the deacon was finally persuaded to return to the Church, where she did penance in sorrow and tears (adv Haer 1,13,5).

---

tentur." Cf. Harvey 2, 254. Apparently, the Christian teaching that the Church embraces those who are to be saved had made such an impression on the syncretistic Gnostics that they were reluctant to leave the Church or to expose themselves to the possibility of formal excommunication even though their personal beliefs were completely contrary to Christian beliefs.

31. Cf. adv Haer 3,4,3; Harvey 2, 17: εἰς τὴν ἐκκλησίαν ἐλθὼν καὶ ἐξομολογούμενος, οὕτως διετέλεσε, ποτὲ μὲν λαθροδιδασκαλῶν, ποτὲ δὲ ἐλεγχόμενος ἐφ' οἷς ἐδίδασκε κακῶς, καὶ ἀφιστάμενος τῆς τῶν ἀδελφῶν συνοδίας. It should be noted, the Latin translation renders ἀφιστάμενος "abstentus est," which, in Cyprian (e.g., ep 3,2) means formal excommunication. Cf. N. München, Das Kanonische Gerichtsverfahren und Strafrecht, 2 (Köln, Neuss, 1866) 139, 200f.

32. Cf. Karl Rahner, Die Sündenvergebung nach der Taufe in der Regula fidei des Irenäus, in: ZKT 70 (1948) 450-55. Irenaeus does not indicate how often forgiveness of serious sins is possible; but since he considers Pastor Hermae to be a part of Scriptures (adv Haer 4,20,2), he probably shared the opinion that such forgiveness can be granted only once.

As regards those caught up in false beliefs, Irenaeus says: "Etenim si non facile est ab errore apprehensam resipiscere animam, sed non omnimodo impossibile est errorem effugere apposita veritate" (adv Haer 3,2,2). In adv Haer 1,31,3, mention is made of some followers of Valentinus who, when confronted with the perverted nature of their heresy, were converted to the true God and Creator of the universe, thus being able to be saved ("salvari possint").[33] Indeed, it is the Church's prayer that heretics may not remain trapped in their own trenches, but rather that they return to the Church of God, who actually loves these people better than they love themselves.[34]

d. The Eucharist in the light of the Old Testament.

One other aspect of Irenaeus' theology must yet be treated-- namely, his tendency of nearly equating the Old Testament with the new "legislation" in Christ. In reality, Irenaeus is far from actually doing this. Nevertheless, he does react strongly to the

---

33. Cf. also adv Haer 3,3,4, where Irenaeus states that Polycarp was able to win back many heretics to the Church during his visit to Rome. In adv Haer 3,16,8, the Bishop of Lyons informs his readers that those who do not confess Jesus as the Christ and the only begotten Word and Saviour are "extra dispositionem." In the Greek Fathers, this was rendered ἔξω τῆς οἰκονομίας, and indicated that such heretics "alieni sunt a gratia incarnationis Filii Dei." Cf. MG 7, 926. The statement is thus not strictly ecclesiastical. Nevertheless, it does indicate the underlying motive for the Church's excommunication and exclusion of heretics. And by contrast, it indicates what the effect of the conversion of heretics implies in terms of grace.

34. Cf. adv Haer 3,25,7; Harvey 2, 137: "Nos autem precamur non perseverare eos in fovea, quam ipsi foderunt...et legitime eos generari conversos ad Ecclesiam Dei...Haec precamur de illis, utilius eos diligentes, quam ipsi semetipsos putant diligere."

Gnostic rejection or depreciation of the Old Testament, with the result that he sometimes "plays down" certain aspects of the New Covenant in order to emphasize the importance of the Old Covenant.[35] This is especially apparent when the Bishop explains the Old Testament's sacrifices in relation to the Eucharist.

As is usual among the Fathers, Irenaeus likewise identifies the Eucharist with the "pure oblation" predicted in Mal 1,11 (adv Haer 4,17,5). But in very obscure terms, the Church Father explains:

> The genus of oblations has not been rejected; for there are oblations there (in Judaism), and there are oblations here (in Christianity). There are sacrifices among the (Jewish) people as well as sacrifices in the Church: but that the species only has been changed in that it is now offered by freemen rather than slaves (Gal 4,21-31). For the Lord is one and the same; however, the character of a servile oblation (has its own) peculiarity, just as (the oblation) of freemen (has its own) peculiarity, so that an indication of the liberty (of the Christian dispensation) may be set forth by means of the oblations as well.[36]

In his polemic against the heretics who reject the Old Testament, Irenaeus is careful to keep the offerings and sacrifices of the Old Law in a favorable light. Consequently, he does not want

---

35. Irenaeus does not "overapply" the Old Testament as did e.g. Cyprian and the Council of Elvira in a number of matters. But his reaction to the heretical disregard for the Old Testament can be seen as opening the way for the direct transferral of many elements of the Old Law--especially as regards cult-- into the Church.

36. Cf. adv Haer 4,18,2; Harvey 2, 201: "Et non genus oblationum reprobatum est; oblationes enim et illic, oblationes autem et hic: sacrificia in populo, sacrificia et in Ecclesia: sed species immutata est tantum, quippe cum jam non a servis, sed a liberis offeratur. Unus enim et idem Dominus; proprium autem character servilis oblationis, et proprium liberorum, uti et per oblationes ostendatur indicium libertatis."

to place the Eucharist in a better light than the comparison demands. That is, he does not present all the differences, but only makes it clear that the oblations of the Old Testament were, in spite of their more external nature, types of the eucharistic offering of the New Covenant. This he manages to do by resorting to the distinction between genus and species. It is the exclusively external character of the Old Law's offerings that Irenaeus rejects or finds reprehensible. The objection is not against the external nature of these sacrifices--for the Eucharist has also its external character--, but against the lack of a corresponding internal disposition that should accompany an offering:[37]

> Thus, sacrifices do not sanctify the man--for God does not need a sacrifice--, but the conscience of the person who offers sanctifies the sacrifice when it (the conscience) is pure (Di 14; 4,14), and moves God to accept (the offering) as if from a friend.[38]

Yet, Irenaeus is careful to explain that the Eucharist, even though accepted by God as a pure sacrifice, is not offered to supply God's needs--for he has none--, but for the benefit of those who do the offering in simplicity and innocence, and thus do not appear empty-handed before the Lord.[39]

---

37. Cf. A. Scheiwiler, op. cit., 54.
38. Cf. adv Haer 4,18,3; Harvey 2, 203: "Igitur non sacrificia sanctificant hominem; non enim indiget sacrificio Deus: sed conscientia ejus qui offert sanctificat sacrificium, pura existens, et praestat acceptare Deum quasi ab amico."
39. Cf. adv Haer 4,18,1f; Harvey 2, 201: "Igitur Ecclesiae oblatio, quam Dominus docuit offerri in universo mundo, purum sacrificium reputatum est apud Deum, et acceptum est ei: non quod indigeat a nobis sacrificium, sed quoniam is qui offert, glorificatur ipse in eo quod offert, si acceptetur munus ejus. Per munus enim erga regem, et honos, et affectio ostenditur: quod in omni simplicitate et innocentia Dominius volens nos

4. Excursus: The Easter Controversy

a. The historical facts.

Strictly speaking, the so-called Easter controversy of second century Christianity was not a question about the date of Easter (i.e., Christ's resurrection) or whether or not it should be celebrated consistently on a Sunday. The basic issue concerned the nature of the feast both as to its origins and its content.

It is chiefly through Eusebius of Caesarea (HE 5,23-25) that anything at all is known of the actual Easter controversy that arose between Rome and Asia Minor. Unfortunately, however, the underlying motives for the seriousness with which the question was taken are not at all clear in Eusebius' account. One could wish that the great Church historian might have reported more facts less partially. Instead, he seems to ignore or play down certain aspects of the controversy.[40]

The question first came up during the Laodicean controvery (ca. 164-166) when Polycarp went to Rome. At that time, Anicetus, the Bishop of Rome, tried to convince Polycarp that Asia Minor should keep the feast of Easter at the same time as did the west-

---

offerre, praedicavit dicens: 'Cum igitur offers munus tuum ad altare, et recordatus fueris, quoniam frater tuus habet aliquid adversum te, dimitte munus tuum ante altare, et vade primum reconciliari fratri tuo, et tunc reversus offeres munus tuum' (Mt 5,23f). Offerre igitur oportet Deo primitias ejus creaturae, sicut et Moyses ait: 'Non apparebis vacuus ante conspectum Domini Dei tui' (Dt 16,16); ut in quibus gratus exstitit homo, in his gratus eis deputatus, eum qui est ab eo percipiat honorem."

40. Cf. Bernhard Lohse, Das Passafest der Quartadecimaner, (Beiträge zur Förderung christlicher Theologie 54, ed. by Paul Althaus et alii), (Gütersloh, 1953) 134-37.

ern church.[41] But neither side could convince the other to change its practice. Nevertheless, the confrontation remained fraternal and peaceful, and Polycarp departed from Rome with the unity between the East and the West still fully intact and unthreatened. However, after a few years, the question was raised again--but this time in Asia Minor itself.[42] By 190, the issue had spread to Rome when Polycrates of Ephesus and Pope Victor I confronted each other in their letters on the subject (HE 5,24). In Victor's time, the question of the date and nature of Easter may have had certain heretical overtones not yet present or prevalent under Pope Anicetus. But the real issue at stake between Polycrates and Victor remains clouded.

b. Probable misunderstandings.

The controversy between the East and the West on the question of Easter was perhaps due to a number of basic misunderstandings about the issue itself, so that the matter was confused to such an extent that even those most deeply involved were, in all likelihood, unaware of the fundamental differences or positions being argued.

41. In all probability, the Roman custom of celebrating the Lord's resurrection especially on "Easter Sunday" began early in the second century in Rome under Pope Xystus (ca. 115-125). This western feast, borrowing heavily from the already established eastern practice and possibly also from the "Mystery Cult," then spread rapidly among gentile Christians. Eventually, feeling began to build up against the eastern practice until it reached a climax at the Council of Nicea (325) when a general excommunication was pronounced against the Quartodecimans, who then went into a decline and dwindled totally away by the end of the fifth century. Cf. B. Lohse, op. cit., 117-22, 140.

42. Cf. Ferdinand Christian Baur, Das Christianthum und die christliche Kirche der drei ersten Jahrhunderte, 1, (Stuttgart-Bad Cannstatt, 1966, originally 1853) 156f.

In the <u>Epistola Apostolorum</u>, a Quartodeciman[43] work, the celebration of the "Easter Eucharist" is called the "Pasch," and is to
be kept in remembrance of Christ's death until he returns from the
Father (<u>AE</u> 52ff/<u>Ko</u> VII,13-IX,1). As simple as this may seem, it
immediately raises a whole complex of problems surrounding the actual dating of Jesus' Last Supper and death and the purpose of the
feast itself. In keeping the feast at the same time as the Jewish
Passover,[44] the eastern church claimed it was only following the
tradition given to it by the Apostles John and Philip (<u>HE</u> 5,23,1;
5,24,2f).

This custom would certainly have been cherished by the Jewish
Christians, not, however, due to any real Judaizing tendencies on
their part. Rather, they were adamant that they were not celebrating the Jewish Passover as such; for Christ was their Passover
Lamb. Their custom stemmed from the practice of the earliest communities of Jewish Christians, who observed the time of the Jewish
Passover by fasting for the rest of their people who had rejected
Christ.[45] However, with the passage of time, the original intentions began to grow somewhat blurred as Christianity moved ever
farther away from its Jewish roots. For one thing, even among the
Quartodecimans, the Aramaic etymology of the word πάσχα was forgotten and often confused with the Greek word for "suffer," πάσχειν.[46]

---

43. This name was eventually applied to those who kept the 14th of
    Nisan as the day for commemorating Christ's Pasch.

44. In reality, the eucharistic celebration of the Quartodecimans
    was held at about 3:00 a.m. on the 15th of Nisan. Cf. B.
    Lohse, <u>op. cit.</u>, 32, 44f 49.

45. <u>Ibid.</u>, 139.
46. <u>Ibid.</u>, 15f, 53.

To these persons--and a *fortiori* to the gentile Christians of the
western church--, the feast of Easter as celebrated in the Asia-
tic church would appear to be associated only with Christ's death.
But this attitude soon led to other problems arising from the differences between the Johannine and the Synoptic accounts and chro-
nologies of Christ's Last Supper and death. Furthermore, there
would appear to be no reason for the Asiatics (either at home or
while abroad) to break off their fasting after the 14th day of
Nisan instead of prolonging it until Easter Sunday as in the western church.[47]

If, as suggested earlier in this study, a distinction is to be
made between the "supper of betrayal" and the actual Last Supper
with the institution of the Eucharist, then it is easy to see how
the confusion over the origin and content of the eastern practice
could be further compounded. Moreover, the East did not make the
same sharp distinction that was made in the West between Christ's
death and his glorification (i.e., resurrection and ascension).
The eastern celebration did not exclude the commemoration of
Christ's resurrection, but it was viewed from the perspective of
his death; whereas, the West commemorated Christ's death separate-
ly from his resurrection. By concentrating solely on the resurrection and by celebrating the feast of Easter always on a Sunday,
the western church avoided all the complications inherent in the
eastern practice, which may have been rooted to some extent in a
tradition that Christ died and rose on the same day.[48]. But this
aspect was probably unknown or disregarded in the western church.

---

47. Cf. F. Chr. Baur, op. cit., 162.
48. Cf. C. Schmidt, op. cit., 651-53; Didascalia Apostolorum 21.

c. Rome's reaction and reasons.

Although there is no direct evidence, it is possible that Rome looked disfavorably upon the eastern observance of Easter as being an encouragement to various heretical elements that were then threatening the Church. For one thing, there were numerous Gnostic sects which would have been more than eager to see the Eucharist and Easter celebrated in commemoration of Christ's death exclusive of any notion of a real bodily resurrection to follow. As a result, the eastern practice would have received their hearty support, but for unorthodox reasons. From the Collection of 32 Heresies, written perhaps by Pope Zephyrinus or Hippolytus but found attached to Tertullian's de Praescriptione, it is learned that a certain Blastus was charged with trying to introduce a disguised form of Judaism into the Church. However, it still remains to be shown that "suspicion of heresy" was really involved at the actual time of the controversy. Such a charge becomes less founded in view of the fact that Blastus was probably chosen to lead the Quartodecimans in Rome only after they had been excommunicated by Victor, and so, of necessity, had to form themselves into their own autonomous church in order to survive.[49]

The real root of the problem must be sought elsewhere--namely, in Victor's zeal to Latinize the Roman church and to secure a monarchical episcopate by expanding his sphere of "legal" influence both quantitatively and qualitatively while, at the same time, rooting out all Greek and oriental elements that in any way conflicted with the Roman church's Latinization program. These motives were probably already present in Pope Anicetus, but his pru-

---

49. Cf. B. Lohse, op. cit., 126.

dence led him to discontinue his campaign.[50] At any rate, the
differences between the two traditions were considered to be more
than just variations in customs. This is confirmed by the fact
that Epiphanius of Salamis (d. 403) included the Quartodecimans in
his list of heresies even though he only points out their different fasting practice as reprehensible (Panarion 30 [50]).

At the time of Polycarp and Anicetus, the differences in traditions did not disturb the intercommunion of the eastern and western churches, and their lack of unity in the issue was permitted
to exist as a matter of legitimate plurality within the Church.
However, Victor reacted by denouncing the church of Asia Minor as
unorthodox and sought to break off all communion with it.

It is certainly only in a very qualified sense that modern historians can speak of excommunication of the Asiatics by Victor.
In the mind of the early Church, excommunication of a person or a
group of persons indicated that he or they ceased to belong to
the Church of God, with the consequence that the sacraments performed by the excommunicated were partially or wholly defective.
But Victor introduced a new concept into the process of excommuni-
cation--namely, that of isolation rather than expulsion from the
Church as such.[51] The action which the Roman Bishop took meant
the end of the eucharistic sharing between himself and the eastern church. This would seem to be the major ecclesial effect of
this communication.

---

50. Ibid., 62, 125-27; George La Piana, The Roman Church at the
    End of the Second Century, in: Harvard Theological Review 18
    (1925) 218.

51. Cf. Nikolai Afanassieff, Una Sancta, in: Irénikon 36 (1963)
    460f.

It must not be overlooked that Rome's refusal to accept the eastern tradition already at Anicetus' time was of great importance due to Rome's priority and importance, which Irenaeus, who so sharply objected to Victor's action against the eastern church (HE 5,24,9-13), fully recognized (adv Haer 3,3,2). But it was also equally significant that Anicetus continued to tolerate the Quartodeciman practice and sent a portion of his Eucharist to those in Rome who observed the eastern tradition (HE 5,24,14f). This indicates Rome's relation to the Eucharist as a sign of the universality of the one Church. That is, the unity of the Church is founded in and through the Eucharist itself rather than in the centralization of governing powers in the Bishop of Rome. Nevertheless, he appears as the foremost protector of the "purity" of this eucharistic unity. Consequently, the theological foundation of his primacy is located in the Eucharist.[52] But, as regards Victor's action, it seems that one must agree with those bishops who urged him to seek peace, union and charity with the eastern church since, as Irenaeus pointed out, the unity of the faith does not depend on the uniformity of custom and practice; rather, the unity of faith is enhanced by such differences (HE 5,25,10-13).

5. Clement of Alexandria

a. The Christian Gnostic and paenitentia secunda.

Probably born in Athens about 150, Titus Flavius Clemens became well-educated in the philosophy, sciences and literature of his times. After his conversion to Christianity, his extensive travels brought him to Alexandria, where he became a pupil of

---

52. Cf. Joseph Ratzinger, Das Neue Volk Gottes, Entwürfe zur Ekklesiologie, (Düsseldorf, 1969) 88f.

Pantaenus, the first known rector of the famous school of theology in that city. Clement was installed at the head of the school around the year 200. However, within two or three years, he was forced to leave Egypt for good due to the persecution instigated by Septimius Severus. He died in Cappadocia (south central Asia Minor) shortly before 215.

His extensive learning and writing has earned him the title of "the first Christian scholar." With the aid of the allegorical method of exegesis, he sought to teach a true Christian Gnosticism which was to be achieved by means of a moral life rather than by knowledge of certain "facts." The pedagogical role of the divine Logos is to improve the soul by training it in a virtuous life as opposed to intellectual pursuits (<u>Paed</u> I,1,1,4). However, Clement himself made abundant use of his knowledge in an effort to lead others to this truly moral life, the mark of the "true Gnostic."

The true Gnostic is the "perfect Christian"--that is, one who prefers his baptismal purity to all else and therefore has no need of a "second repentance." However, Clement does not indicate that even he is a true Gnostic, and his description of such a person is probably to be taken as the Christian ideal that only a very few actually achieve. Instead, most Christians must reckon with a second repentance, but the full forgiveness which it is meant to effect may be achieved only in the next life. In other words, Clement abandons the notion of an early Parousia and of the necessity of completing the second repentance in this life before Christ's second coming. This, then, means that allowances were made for a sort of "purgatory" after death so that the individual's second repentance could be completed and enable him to be saved. This was Clement's solution to soteriological problems

connected with the teaching on repentance found in <u>Pastor Hermae</u>
and the <u>Letter to the Hebrews</u>.[53]

b. Eucharist and ethics.

It would indeed be informative if Clement had treated the
Eucharist in the context of his theology of repentance. Nevertheless, he does give a few direct or indirect insights into the
questions which this study presents concerning eucharistic discipline even though his treatment of the Eucharist is relatively
sparse.

Faith is the necessary prerequisite for fruitful participation in the Eucharist, and "whoever partakes of it in faith is
sanctified in body and soul."[54] However, as one might expect,
faith for Clement always includes a strongly ethical character.
Along with St. Paul, he demands that the individual examine his
own conscience in regard to his moral disposition in order to
determine whether or not he can worthily partake of the Eucharist:

> For the best means toward correctly choosing or avoiding
> is the conscience, whose firm foundation is an upright life
> together with fitting instruction; just as the imitation of
> others who have already been approved and have conducted them-
> selves properly is a most appropriate means for grasping the
> truth and carrying out the commandments. 'So that anyone who
> shall eat the bread and drink the cup of the Lord unworthily

---

53. Cf. Heinrich Karpp, <u>Die Busslehre des Klemens von Alexandrien</u>,
    in: <u>Zeitschrift für die Neutestamentliche Wissenschaft und die
    Kunde der alteren Kirche</u> 43 (1950/1) 224-42; ----, <u>Die Busse:
    Quellen zur Entstehung des altkirchlichen Busswesens</u>, (Tradi-
    tio Christiana: Texte und Kommentare zur patristischen Theo-
    logie 1), (Zurich, 1969) xix.

54. Cf. <u>Paed</u> II,2,20,1; <u>CB</u> 12, 168: ἧς οἱ κατὰ πίστιν μεταλαμβάν-
    οντες ἁγιάζονται καὶ σῶμα καὶ ψυχήν. Cf. also 1 Cor 11,30;
    1 Thes 5,23.

shall be guilty of the body and the blood of the Lord. However, let a man examine himself, and thus let him eat of
the bread and drink from the cup' (1 Cor 11, 27f).[55]

Clement of Alexandria makes only one other direct mention of
the Eucharist--this time, in reference to the "Hydroparastates,"
a sect which substituted water for the wine in the Eucharist.
The Alexandrian considered this to be contrary to the established
canon of the Church and, with the aid of allegorical exegesis,
believed he could see in their action a damnable practice predicted in the Old Testament:

> Wisdom says to those who make manifestations about their
> selective beliefs: 'I earnestly enjoin those who are lacking
> in understanding: Take gladly of the hidden loaves and of
> the sweet water of thievery' (Prv 9,16f). Whereby, Scripture
> quite clearly applies the terms 'bread and water' to nothing
> else other than to the heresies which use bread and water in
> the offering contrary to the regulation of the Church. For
> there are those who celebrate the Eucharist with mere water.[56]

Clement then goes on to Prv 9,18 and states that these heretics are to be avoided, for they do not belong to the constitution

---

55. Cf. Strom I,1,5,2f; CB 15,5: ἀρίστη γὰρ πρὸς τὴν ἀκριβῆ αἵρε-
σίν τε καὶ φυγὴν ἡ συνείδησις, θεμέλιος δὲ αὐτῆς βέβαιος ὀρ-
θὸς βίος ἅμα μαθήσει τῇ καθηκούσῃ τό τε ἕπεσθαι ἑτέροις δοκι-
μασθεῖσιν ἤδη καὶ κατωρθωκόσιν ἄριστον πρός τε τῆς ἀληθείας
τὴν νόησιν καὶ τὴν κατάπραξιν τῶν ἐντολῶν. "ὥστε ὃς ἂν ἐσθίῃ
τὸν ἄρτον καὶ πίνῃ τὸ ποτηρίον τοῦ κυρίου ἀναξίως, ἔνοχος ἔσται τοῦ σώματος καὶ τοῦ αἵματος τοῦ κυρίου. δοκιμαζέτω δὲ
ἄωθρωπος ἑαυτὸν καὶ οὕτως ἐκ τοῦ ἄρτου ἐσθιέτω καὶ ἐκ τοῦ ποτηρίου πινέτω."

56. Cf. Strom I,19,96,1; CB 15, 61f: "καὶ τοῖς ἐνδεέσι φρενῶν
παρακελεύομαι λέγουσα," φησὶν ἡ σοφία, τοῖς ἀμφὶ τὰς αἱρέσεις
δηλονότι, "ἄρτων κρυφίων ἡδέως ἅψασθε, καὶ ὕδατος κλοπῆς γλυ-
κεροῦ," ἄρτον καὶ ὕδωρ οὐκ ἐπ' ἄλλων τινῶν, ἀλλ' ἢ ἐπὶ τῶν
ἄρτῳ καὶ ὕδατι κατὰ τὴν προσφορὰν μὴ κατὰ τὸν κανόνα τῆς ἐκκλησίας χρωμένων αἱρέσεων ἐμφανῶς ταττούσης τῆς γραφῆς. εἰσὶ
γὰρ οἱ καὶ ὕδωρ ψιλὸν εὐχαριστοῦσιν.

of the Church. This conclusion is again the result of allegorical exegesis:

'But hasten away; delay not in her place!' In is the synagogue, not the Church, that is called by the equivocal name 'place.' Then she (Wisdom) says in conclusion: 'For you will thus go through strange water; since heretical baptism is not considered proper and legitimate water.[57]

This last statement is very significant; for it indicates that Clement held that heretical Baptism was invalid, or he at least had doubts about its effectiveness. From now on, the question of the genuine character of Baptisms performed by heretics will continue to come up and trouble the Church for two more centuries and even longer. However, there is no evidence that Clement of Alexandria or his contemporaries actually demanded the "rebaptism" of converted heretics. But Strom II,13,58,1 clearly states that Baptism unto repentance and the forgiveness of sins cannot be repeated. There is no question of rebaptism for one who left the Church to join a heretical group and then returned. At any rate, Clement does not exclude the possibility of the conversion of heretics, and prays that such will be the case. This he hopes to be achieved by enlightenment from his writings; and if that fails, then by the punishing visitations of God (Strom VII,16,102,2f). Even the σκληροκαρδίοι are not excluded from this hope (Strom VII,2,6,1).

c. The penitential practice.

Clement sees all sins as forgiveable except one's ultimate and unrepented rejection of God.[58] However, he has a tendency

---

57. Cf. Strom I,19,96,2f; CB 15, 62: "ἀλλὰ ἀποπήδησον, μὴ χρονίσῃς ἐν τῷ τόπῳ αὐτῆς." τόπον τὴν συναγωγήν, οὐχὶ δὲ ἐκκλησίαν ὁμωνύμως προσεῖπεν. εἶτα ἐπιφωνεῖ "οὕτω γὰρ διαβήσῃ ὕδωρ ἀλλότριον," τὸ βάπτισμα τὸ αἱρετικὸν οὐκ οἰκεῖον καὶ γνήσιον ὕδωρ λογιζομένη.

58. Cf. B. Poschmann, op. cit., 260; H. Karpp, Busslehre, 231.

toward rigorism when he speaks of only one penance after Baptism; for permission for more than that would only be permission to exercise oneself in sin (Strom II,13,56,1; II,13,58,3; Pastor Hermae, Mand 4,3). But in actual practice, it appears that he knew of and approved more than the single penance after Baptism, especially in the case of the "involuntary sins"--a very broad category in Clement's theology.[59] As in Pastor Hermae, Tertullian, Origen and Cyprian, Clement of Alexandria applies the "one" opportunity for ecclesial penance only in cases of such serious sins as murder, adultery and apostasy, which were publicly treated within the "court" of the Church.[60] That such serious sins were considered forgiveable is apparent in Clement's treatise, Quis Dives Salvetur? 42,14, where the tears of repentance shed by a young Christian who had turned highwayman and had robbed and murdered are seen as the water required in a second Baptism (βαπτιζόμενος ἐκ δευτέρου).

In the further consideration of the penitential practices outlined by the Alexandrian, evidence comes to light that he knows of a real practice of excommunication even though he never speaks expressly of its formal practice.[61] In Strom I,27,171,4, the penalties imposed by the Old Law on even lesser sins as well as capital punishment for persistent sinfulness that leads to hardened wickedness are considered good for the community. The lesser penalties train everyone in piety, and the punishment of death is compared to amputation which is performed for the good of the rest of the body. Clement then compares this to Paul's statement that

---

59. Cf. Paed I,2,4-5; B. Poschmann, op. cit., 232.
60. Cf. J. Grotz, op. cit., 341.
61. Cf. B. Poschmann, op. cit., 252; H. Karpp, Busslehre, 235.

Christians are judged by the Lord so that they may be chastened and not condemned with the world (1 Cor 11,32). This would seem to imply an actual process or practice of discipline and excommunication. Explicit mention is made in <u>Strom</u> II,14,61,2 that anyone who fails to "contain the generative word is to be punished"; for, in being similar to idle chatter, it is an irrational passion of the soul.[62] By this, Clement means that sexually incontinent persons are to be punished since those afflicted with gonorrhoea were avoided in the Old Law, as he has just previously pointed out.

d. Heretics and sexual conduct.

More than any previous Christian writer, Clement treats at length the perveted sexual view of the heretics, who tended either toward a false asceticism or toward the opposite extreme, libertinism. It is especially in regard to the sexual license of the heretics that the Alexandrian scholar comes closest to speaking of actual excommunication. Such persons are the "old leaven" that must be put away (1 Cor 5,7); for no one should converse with a fornicator (1 Cor 5,11) since such do not belong to the body of the Lord (1 Cor 6,13), nor will they inherit the kingdom (1 Cor 6, 9-11; <u>Strom</u> III,18,106-07). The unclean animals of the Old Testament prefigured them and, like the swine, portray them as lustful people to be avoided (<u>Paed</u> II,10,83,4f; III,9,75,3).

However, Clement is perfectly clear about the fact that heretics are called such, not for their unethical lives, but rather for their selective use of Scripture, using only those parts and

---

62. τῷ ὄντι γὰρ κολαστέος ὁ ἀκρατὴς τοῦ γονίμου λόγου, ὃ καὶ αὐτὸ πάθος ἐστὶ ψυχῆς ἄλογον, ἐγγὺς ἀδολεσχίας ἰόν. Cf. <u>CB</u> 15, 146.

passages which they find pleasing (Strom VII,16,93-94). By this
means, they are able to pervert the Lord's words on sexual issues
so as to make it appear that he advocated their immoral practices
and license (Strom III,4,27,4). But when Revelation is left un-
distorted, then one gets quite a different impression of the truth
on such matters. Clement thus asks of a person who advocates pro-
miscuity and adultery:

> How can this man still be considered within the body of
> our doctrine when he annuls both the Law[63] and the Gospel
> through his teachings? For indeed the one says 'you shall not
> commit adultery' (Ex 20,13), and the other says 'everyone who
> looks with desire has already committed adultery' (Mt 5,28)[64]

e. Religious categories.

In Clement's system of "Christian Gnosticism," heretics, pagans and orthodox Christians are classified according to the three
"states of mind" that they represent. The pagan is in the state
of ignorance (ἀγνοία), the heretic is founded solely on opinion
(οἴησις), but the Christian has solid understanding (ἐπιστήμη:
Strom VII,16,100,7).

From the Mosaic dietary legislation concerning "clean" and
"unclean" animals based on the empirical norms of a cloven hoof
and cud chewing, the Alexandrian finds allegorical evidence that
Christians and non-Christians (including heretics) are to be re-
spectively classified as "clean" and "unclean". Sacrificial ani-

---

63. Clement's object is to defend the Old Law and to show how it
   resembles or leads to the Gospel, and, when necessary, to apply the allegorical method of exegesis to that end.

64. Cf. Strom III,2,8,4; CB 15, 199: καὶ πῶς ἔτι οὗτος ἐν τῷ καθ'
   ἡμᾶς ἐξετασθείη λόγῳ ἄντικρυς καὶ τὸν νόμον καὶ τὸ εὐαγγέλιον
   διὰ τούτων καθαιρῶν; ὁ μὲν γάρ φησιν· "οὐ μοιχεύσεις," τὸ δὲ
   "πᾶς ὁ προσβλέπων κατ' ἐπιθυμίαν ἤδη ἐμοίχευσεν" λέγει.

mals with a cloven hoof and which chew the cud are considered pure
and pleasing to God; for the cloven hoof represents the Word of
God together with faith in the Son of the Father, and rumination
is an image for mental reflection and contemplation of the Word
and faith. The orthodox Christians are the pure offerings since
they have the Word and faith in Jesus and reflect upon these facts.
Jews are represented by the animals that ruminate, but have an un-
cloven hoof; that is, they reflect only on their own Law, but know
neither the Son nor the Father, who can only be known by way of
the Son (Jn 14,6-9). Heretics resemble animals which have a cloven hoof but do not chew the cud; for they have the Word and claim
to believe in the Son and the Father, but they are not capable of
understanding the exact meaning of the words and thereby fall into
many errors in their judgment of derived facts of faith. Finally,
those persons who are represented by the animals which neither ruminate nor have a cloven hoof are totally unclean (Strom VII,18,
109-10). Nevertheless, Clement asks that Christians love all
men--even those who are evil men and enemies of the faith, because
it is the person that is to be loved and not the evil (Strom IV,13,
93,2-3; IV,95-96,1).

CHAPTER ELEVEN

THE HERESY OF ORTHODOXY

1. Preliminary Remarks

So far, the heresies and difficulties with which the Church
had to deal were generally of a "leftist" or "liberal" nature.
That is, they were attempts to make the Church conform to standards and beliefs that came from without or were otherwise fully
foreign to her nature and purpose. As in the attempts to "Judaize" and "Gnosticize" the Church, their heterodoxy was manifest.
Therefore, it was only natural that the Church would defend herself chiefly by recourse to "Apostolic tradition." But this principle is effective only in cases where the tradition is clear and
uniform and when the opposition does not attempt to support its
stand by citing what it believes is likewise Apostolic tradition.
The so-called Easter controversy is a good example of the outcome
when both sides are convinced of their Apostolic orthodoxy. Moreover, the principle is not without its own inherent dangers in
that it can "stagnate the faith" at a certain point of development by absolutizing and dogmatizing legitimate elements or struc-
tures of the past which are themselves the outgrowth of historical
development, but which are no longer appropriate for present conditions; or it can lead to an uncritical conservatism which falls
as far wide of the mark of true orthodoxy as does any of the most
radical "liberal" heresies. This "new breed" of heresy, which presents itself as the ultimate protector and preserver of orthodoxy,
began to assert itself especially toward the end of the second century and throughout much of the third century. Such "rightist" or
"conservative" errors are generally characterized by rigorism and
legalism and by an exclusive claim that they alone are truly representative of the pure "Faith of our Fathers." Although the

title of this chapter could be expanded to include such men as
Origen and Cyprian, only two men are particularly meant here--
Tertullian of Carthage and Hippolytus of Rome.

2. Tertullian

a. The status of heretics.

No one is quite certain how Christianity came to North Africa.
But when this portion of the Church came to the attention of the
rest of the world, the Christian faith was already flourishing
there beyond all expectation. The literature and theology from
this part of the ancient world well exceeded that which Rome produced in the same period. However, the two churches--Rome and
Carthage--were then intimately connected with each other.

About 155, Tertullian was born of pagan parents in Carthage.
His conversion to Christianity came about 193, and he put his
knowledge of law, literature and philosophy into the service of
the Church. It is especially through this learned Carthaginian
that the North African church is brought into the theological
limelight. By about 207, however, Tertullian openly broke with
the Church. A definite date cannot be set if for no other reason
than that his affection for Montanism came earlier and his loss
of orthodoxy occurred in stages which are equally difficult to
date.[1] Even as a Montanist, Tertullian was able to stay in the
Church for some time since Montanism was tolerated in the West

---

1. This situation, of course, makes it difficult to evaluate
   some of Tertullian's works in regard to whether or not they
   reflect Montanist rather than Catholic views. The matter is
   further complicated by the fact that the exact order of writing is debatable. And finally, not a few authors would prefer to place Tertullian's break with the Church somewhere
   around 212.

for a number of years after it was condemned in ecclesial synods held in the East (<u>HE</u> 5,16,9f). The ebbing hope for Christ's second coming, plus the loss of prophetism in the Church coupled with the emergence of "states of holiness" among Christians rather than the continued reference to <u>all</u> Christians as ἅγιοι contributed greatly to the rise of Montanism as a conservative, heretical reaction from within the faith, and which considered itself as the saviour of the Church.[2]

Tertullian was the most prolific Latin author preceding Constantine's reign. Many of his works or treatises have been lost. But those writings which have survived offer many insights into the discipline surrounding the Eucharist. Tertullian also makes some significant new developments in this regard.

In his great work, <u>adversus</u> <u>Marcionem</u>, the African theologian, as other ecclesial writers before him, attacks the Docetic Christology of the heretic by referring to the Eucharist. After explaining how Jesus knew of the time for his death from various Old Testament statements and predictions (<u>adv</u> <u>Mar</u> 4,40,1f), Tertullian continues:

> And so, having expressed that he earnestly desired to eat the Passover as his own--for it is not proper that God should desire something foreign--, he made the bread which had been taken and distributed to the disciples (into) his own body by saying 'this is my body,' that is, 'a figure of my body.' A figure, however, would not have been possible unless there had been in fact a body (to begin with). Besides that, an empty thing, because it is a phantasm, could not receive a figure. But if, for that reason, he (merely) pretended that the bread was for him a body, because he was in truth lacking a body,

---

2. Cf. Pierre de Labriolle, <u>La</u> <u>Crise</u> <u>Montaniste</u>, (Paris, 1913) 108, 122, 330; Adolf von Harnack, <u>Die</u> <u>Mission</u> <u>und</u> <u>Ausbreitung</u> <u>des</u> <u>Christentums</u> <u>in</u> <u>den</u> <u>ersten</u> <u>drei</u> <u>Jahrhunderten</u>, 1, (Leipzig, 1924⁴) 416ff.

then he should have (simply) delivered up bread for us. He
was (if that were the case) acting according to Marcion's
vain theory so that bread might be crucified. But then why
does he call his body bread and not rather the melon which
Marcion had in place of a heart since he (Marcion) failed to
understand that it was that ancient figure of the body of
Christ speaking through Jeremiah: 'Come, let us cast wood
upon his bread' (Jr 11,19 LXX)--that is, is it not, the cross
upon his body? And this, the one who shed his light upon the
ancient (Law and Prophets) declared plainly enough what he
then meant the bread to signify when he called his own body
'bread.' So, he likewise affirmed the reality of his body
when he mentioned the chalice and established the testament
sealed in his own blood. For no blood can belong to a body
without flesh.[3]

---

3. Cf. adv Mar 4,40,3f; CC 1,656f: "Professus itaque se concu-
    piscentia concupisse edere pascha ut suum,--indignum enim, ut
    quid alienum concupisceret deus--acceptum panem et distribu-
    tum discipulis corpus suum illum fecit 'hoc est corpus meum'
    dicendo, id est 'figura corporis mei.' Figura autem non fuis-
    set nisi ueritatis esset corpus. Ceterum uacua res, quod est
    phantasma, figuram capere non posset. Aut si propterea panem
    corpus sibi finxit, quia corporis carebat ueritate, ergo panem
    debuit tradere pro nobis. Faciebat ad uanitatem Marcionis, ut
    panis crucifigeretur. Cur autem panem corpus suum appellat et
    non magis peponem, quem Marcion cordis loco habuit, non intel-
    legens ueterem fuisse istam figuram corporis Christi dicentis
    per Hieremian: 'aduersus me cogitauerunt cogitatum dicentes:
    uenite, coiciamus lignum in panem eius,' scilicet crucem in
    corpus eius? Itaque inluminator antiquitatum, quid tunc uolu-
    erit significasse panem, satis declarauit corpus suum uocans
    panem. Sic et in calicis mentione testamentum constituens
    sanguine suo obsignatum substantiam corporis confirmauit. Nul-
    lius enim corporis qualitas non carnea opponetur nobis, certe
    sanguinem nisi carnea non habebit." In adv Mar 1,14,3, Ter-
    tullian defends the natural elements used in the sacraments
    and says that the Creator disdains neither the water of Bap-
    tism "nec panem, quo ipsum corpus suum repraesentat." It is
    not the purpose of the present study to explain how such terms
    as "figura" or "repraesentare" relate to "real presence" and
    "transubstantiation" in regard to the Eucharist. However, it
    is clear from other texts that Tertullian did not consider the
    Eucharist as ordinary food, as is evident in de Corona 3,3,4:

As one might expect in view of Tertullian's legal training, the Carthaginian makes his most original contributions to an understanding of the Eucharist when he has occasion to refer to this sacrament in a juridical context. He finds this opportunity in the Church's stipulation that only the baptized may partake of the Eucharist. It is upon this disciplinary practice that he is able to level charges against the heretics, who do not distinguish between the baptized and the unbaptized at their worship:

> I must not omit a description of the actual conduct of the heretics: how futile, earthy and (purely) human it is, lacking seriousness, authority and discipline--as suits their creed. In the first place, it is uncertain who is a catechumen and who is a believer; they (all) have equal access, and listen and pray as peers. Even if heathens happen to come in among them, they will throw that which is holy before dogs, and pearls--but not real ones, to be sure--before swine (Mt 7,6).[4]

"Calicis aut panis etiam nostri aliquid decuti in terram anxie patimur."

4. Cf. de Praescriptione Haereticorum 41,1f; CC 1, 221: "Non omittam ipsius etiam conuersationis haereticae descriptionem quam futilis, quam terrena, quam humana sit, sine grauitate, sine auctoritate, sine disciplina ut fidei suae congruens. Inprimis quis catechumenus, quis fidelis incertum est, pariter adeunt, pariter audiunt, pariter orant; etiam ethnici si superuenerint, sanctum canibus et porcis margaritas, licet non ueras, iactabunt." According to Tertullian, Baptism is the pact with God that admits one to the Eucharist. This is clear from de Pudicitia 9,15f, where the writer, now a Montanist, interprets the return of the Prodigal Son (Lk 15,11-31) as the conversion of the pagans, who are admitted to the feast (i.e., the Eucharist) after receiving the ring (i.e., the seal of faith in Baptism). But cf. de Paenitentia 8,6-8, where Tertullian, still a Catholic, interprets the same story as an indication of the reconciliation of lapsed Christians with the Church.

Although "pearls" can mean even the daily conversation of Christians as in ad Uxorem 2,5, it is obvious that the term in the above text refers to the specially sacred functions, very probably including the Eucharist.[5] More will be said later concerning Tertullian's treatment of the Eucharist. But first it is necessary to complete the issue on the validity or nonvalidity of heretical religious actions.

It is more evident in Tertullian than in any previous Christian writer that there were doubts and actual denials in the early Church that heretics could still be considered Christians. In Apologeticum 46,17, Tertullian answers the hypothetical objection that someone might make about Christians who fail to maintain correct discipline in their lives. To this, the African replies: "Desinum tamen Christiani haberi penes nos."[6] Although this passage is meant to apply directly only to those who fail in disciplinary matters ("excidere a regula disciplinae"), heretics are not excluded, but rather a fortiori included for their lack of "doctrinal discipline":

---

5. However, at least the Marcionites practiced an ecclesial discipline which generally excluded married persons from Baptism and the Eucharist. Cf. adv Mar 4,34,5: "nec coniungens marem et feminam nec alibi coniunctos ad sacramentum baptismatis et eucharistiae admittens, nisi inter se coniurauerint aduersus fructum nuptiarum." Cf. CC 636.

6. For Tertullian, it is God's will rather than ecclesial law that sinners, heretics and various religious dissenters should be excommunicated in order to preserve the Church's honor, holiness and unity--that is, integrity of doctrine. In addition, such action was meant to safeguard other Christians and to dispose the offender for reconciliation with God and the Church. Cf. Clement Chartier, L'Excommunication ecclésiastique d'après les écrits de Tertullien, in: Antonianum 10 (1935) 304-10.

For, since they (i.e., the heretics) are still seeking (the truth), they hold to nothing yet; and since they do not yet hold to anything, they have not yet believed; and since they have not yet believed, they are not Christians. But even though they indeed maintain and believe (something), they say, nevertheless, that is is necessary to inquire so that they may make a defense (of their position). But before they make their defense, they deny what they believe since they (must) confess that they have not yet come to believe as long as they are seeking. Therefore, when people are not Christians even in their own eyes, how much more (is that the case) from our point of view?[7]

From this, it is clear that Tertullian's supreme principle for judging the nature of heretics is faith.[8] He feels that a defection in faith as seen in the heretics vitiates all of their religious functions. All that they have and do comes from the devil, with the result that there is no real distinction to be made between heresy and idolatry.[9] Without the least bit of equivocation, Tertullian thus declares heretical Baptism to be of no avail:

---

7. Cf. de Praescr Haer 14,10-13; CC 1, 199: "Cum enim quaerunt adhuc, nondum tenent; cum autem nondum tenent, nondum crediderunt; cum autem nondum crediderunt non sunt christiani. At cum tenent quidem et credunt, quaerendum tamen dicunt ut defendant. Antequam defendant, negant quod credunt, confitentes se nondum credidisse dum quaerunt. Qui ergo nec sibi sunt Christiani, quanto magis nobis?"

8. Cf. Adolf Kolping, Sacramentum Tertullianeum, (Part One: Untersuchungen über die Anfänge des christlichen Gebrauches der Vokabel sacramentum), Regensburg, Münster, 1948) 71f.

9. Cf. de Praescr Haer 40,1-4; CC 1, 220: "sed quaeritur a quo intellectus interpretetur eorum quae ad haereses faciant? A diabolo scilicet, cuius sunt partes interuertendi ueritatem qui ipsas quoque res sacramentorum diuinorum idolorum mysteriis aemulatur. Tingit et ipse quosdam utique credentes et fideles suos; expositionem delictorum de lauacro repromittit; et, si adhuc memini Mithrae, signat illic in frontibus milites suos. Celebrat et panis oblationem et imaginem resurrectionis inducit et sub gladio redimit coronam."

We have but one Baptism, according to the Lord's Gospel as well as the Apostle's letters, inasmuch as (he says) there is one God, and one Baptism, and one Church in the heavens (Eph 4,4-6). But one is certainly justified in considering what rules must be observed in regard to the heretics; for the assertion was made to us. However, heretics have no part in our discipline, and the very fact of their being excepted from fellowship attests that they are indeed outsiders. I am not duty-bound to recognize in them something that is prescribed for me; for they do not have the same God as we do, nor one and the same Christ. Therefore, their baptism is not one (with ours) either, because it is not the same (baptism). And since they do not have it in the proper manner, there can be no doubt that they do not have it at all; nor is that which one does not have capable of being counted. Thus, they cannot receive it since they do not have (it to give).[10]

b. The status of Christian discipline.

Within the Church, Baptism can be administered by all males.[11] However, this should be done in accordance with the bishop and the

---

10. Cf. de Baptismo 15,1f; Evans, 32: "Nescio si quid amplius ad controversiam baptismi ventilatur. sane retexam quod supra omisi, ne imminentes sensus videar intercindere. unus omnino baptismus est nobis tam ex domini evangelio quam et apostoli litteris, quoniam unus deus et unum baptisma et una ecclesia in caelis. sed circa haereticos sane quae custodiendum sit digne quis retractet. ad nos enim editum est: haeretici autem nullum consortium habent nostrae disciplinae, quos extraneos utique testatur ipsa ademptio communicationis. non debeo in illis cognoscere quod mihi est praeceptum, quia non idem deus est nobis et illis, nec unus Christus, id est idem: ergo· nec baptismus unus, quia non idem. quem cum rite non habeant sine dubio non habent, nec capit numerare quod non habetur; ita nec possunt accipere, quia non habent."

11. Tertullian looks disdainfully upon the concept of women fulfilling any ecclesial or sacramental functions; for that is characteristic of the lack of order and discipline found among the heretics. Cf. de Praescr Haer 41,5; CC 1, 221: "Ipsae mulieres haereticae, quam procaces! quae audeant docere, contendere, exorcismos agere, curationes repromittere, fortasse

rest of the hierarchically structured clergy. Nevertheless, the basic principle remains that all Christians are priests and that what one can receive, one can also give.[12] Unfortunately, Tertullian never elaborates on this principle in regard to the Eucharist. But as long as he was a member of the Church, he maintained that the laity should not presume to perform sacramental functions since that would lead to disorder and schisms in the Church, for, as the African theologian puts it, "episcopatus aemultio schismatum mater est" (de Bapt 17,2). Thus, the goal of the hierarchy is to enable the Church to function as a unity in matters of religion and discipline.[13]

----

an et tingere." In Marcionism, women were permitted to baptize. Cf. W. Bauer, op. cit., 47, n. 3. Tertullian may have had this fact in mind. In de Bapt 17,4f, such functions are forbidden to a woman out of regard for tradition and the Pauline regulation that women must keep silent in the assembly and consult their husbands at home. Cf. 1 Cor 14,34f.

12. Cf. de Bapt: "Quod enim ex aequo accipitur ex aequo dari potest." As a Catholic, Tertullian was careful not to confuse the line between clergy and lay people, mainly because it was a means to keep order as well as a mark of the heretics to grant ecclesial offices to the laity at random and temporarily. Cf. de Praescr Haer 41,8; CC 1,222: "Itaque alius hodie episcopus, cras alius; hodie diaconus qui cras lector; hodie presbyter qui cras laicus. Nam et laicis sacerdotalia numera iniungunt." Even as a Montanist--assuming that Tertullian had already broken with the Church about 211 when he probably wrote de Corona--, he insisted upon order and distinction since he declared that the Eucharist should only be accepted from one who presides over the service. Cf. de Cor 3,3; CC 2, 1043: "Eucharistiae sacramentum, et in tempore uictus et omnibus mandatum a domino, etiam antelucanis coetibus nec de aliorum manu quam praesidentium sumimus."

13. Cf. Apol 39,1; CC 1, 150: "Corpus sumus de conscientia religionis et disciplinae unitate et spei, foedere."

The Christian gathering is not only for prayers and other religious functions, it is also the time and place for the exercise
of discipline, including formal excommunication. In Apol 39,4,
Tertullian explains that the Christian assembly is the place for
"castigationes et censura diuina" as well as "exhortationes."
This work of judging is done with great gravity, especially when
it has been established that someone has sinned so seriously that
he is to be deprived of all Christian association in prayer or in
the assembly.[14] Yet, as long as the Carthaginian remained attached to the Church, he held that all sins could be forgiven and that
the reconciliation of a repentant sinner with the Church was possible.[15] He even mentions that Marcion supposedly repented of his
errors and was doing penance with a view to being reaccepted into
the Church, when death intervened to prevent the completion of the

---

14. "Ibidem etiam exhortationes, castigationes et censura diuina.
    Nam et iudicatur magno cum pondere, ut apud certos de Dei con-
    spectu, summumque futuri iudicii praeiudicium est, si quis ita
    deliquerit, ut a communicatione orationis et conuentus et om-
    nis sancti commercii relegetur." Cf. CC 1, 150.

15. Cf. B. Poschmann, op. cit., 482. As a Catholic, Tertullian's
    list of matter that should normally compel one to undergo
    ecclesial penance is rather large and included even one's most
    secret sins. Cf. de Paen 3,4ff; 10,8. As a Montanist, this
    list of sins that immediately excommunicated one from the
    Church is limited to the three or four "capital sins" defined
    in early Christianity. (Cf. the consideration of Acts 15 in
    this study, pp. 83f). However, in actual practice, as is also
    the case today, there were always more theoretical reasons and
    instances of excommunication than cases of actual excommunica-
    tion. Even in Tertullian's Catholic days, actual expulsion
    from the Church was probably limited to the "capital sins."
    Cf. Karl Rahner, Zur Theologie der Busse bei Tertullian,
    (Abhandlungen über Theologie und Kirche: Festschrift für Karl
    Adam), (Düsseldorf, 1952) 142-44.

period of penance and the actual granting of reconciliation (<u>de</u> <u>Praescr</u> <u>Haer</u> 30,3).

In his Catholic days, Tertullian shared the view characteristic of his time that there was only one opportunity to do penance for serious sins after Baptism. But even this one chance
for penance was a source of embarrassment for the severe theologian, and he is reluctant to inform catechumens of the <u>paeniten-</u>
<u>tia</u> <u>secunda</u> since he has found that some catechumens, with an eye
on the forgiveness of sins granted in Baptism, felt that the time
just before Baptism was a splendid occasion to commit sin. It
would thus be undesirable to give such persons the impression
that the time after Baptism was likewise a good occasion for sinning just because one would have the opportunity to have even
these sins forgiven. Therefore, Tertullian rightly points out
that sincere repentance must precede actual Baptism if the sacrament is to have its proper effect (<u>de</u> <u>Paenitentia</u> 6,14-733).
However, in the remaining chapters of his work on penance, the
African Father exhorts those who need to undertake the <u>paeniten-</u>
<u>tia</u> <u>secunda</u> to do so unhesitatingly.[16]

---

16. In <u>de</u> <u>Paen</u> 9,1-4; <u>CC</u> 1, 336, the procedure for this second re-
    pentance is described as follows: "Huius igitur paenitentiae
    secundae et unius quanto in arto negotium est tanto operosior
    probatio ut non conscientia sola praeferatur, sed aliquo et-
    iam actu administretur. Is actus, qui magis Graeco uocabulo
    et exprimitur et frequentatur, exomologesis est qua delictum
    nostrum domino confitemur, non quidem ut ignaro, sed quatenus
    satisfactio confessione disponitur, confessione paenitentia
    nascitur, paenitentia deus mitigatur. Itaque exomologesis
    prosternendi et humilificandi hominis disciplina est conuer-
    sationem iniungens misericordiae inlicem de ipso quoque ha-
    bitu atque uictu: mandat sacco et cineri incubare, corpus sor-
    dibus obscurare, animum maeroribus deicere, illa quae peccant

c. Eucharistic discipline.

After turning to Montanism, Tertullian's rigoristic attitude toward sin hardened, and he came to the conclusion that certain sins were altogether unforgiveable. This is most evident in his treatment of the sins of impurity. Such offenders are to be excommunicated; and it is especially out of regard for the Eucharist that this action is to be undertaken. In de Pudicitia 18,8, the convert to Montanism attacks the Church's practice of readmission of certain categories of repentant sinners to the Eucharist as a profanation of this sacrament and a flagrant violation of St. Paul's instructions in 1 Cor 5,6.9-11 to avoid eating with fornicators, defrauders and the like. Quoting and simultaneously commenting on the Pauline passage, Tertullian says:

> 'But now I write to you, if any brother among you is named a fornicator or idolator' (for what is so intimately joined together?) 'or a defrauder' (for what is so much akin?) and so on, 'not even to take food with such persons,' not to mention the Eucharist! For, as a matter of fact, even 'a bit of leaven spoils the entire lump.'[17]

tristi tractatione mutare; ceterum pastum et potum pura nosse, non uentris scilicet sed animae causa; plerumque uero ieiuniis preces alere, ingemiscere, lacrimari et mugire dies noctesque ad dominum deum tuum. presbyteris aduolui, et aris dei adgeniculari, omnibus fratribus legationem deprecationis suae iniungere." At what point the penitent is fully readmitted, and by what liturgical function, is not directly stated by Tertullian. But it seems that it must have been by the laying on of hands since he interprets the laying on of hands from 1 Tm 5,22 in this manner. Cf. de Pud 18,9.

17. "'Nunc autem scribe uobis, si quis frater nominatur in uobis fornicator aut idololatres' (quid enim tam coniunctum?) 'aut fraudator' (quid enim tam propinquum?) et cetera, 'cum talibus ne cibum quidem sumere,' nedum eucharistiam; quoniam scilicet et 'fermentum modicum totam desipit consparsionem.'" Cf. CC 2, 1318. In de Pud 9,11, Tertullian explains that it is impossible to readmit apostates into the Church and to the Eucha-

Already as a Catholic, Tertullian expressed his leaning to the excommunication of fornicators when he explains that Paul's instructions concerning a pagan marriage partner (1 Cor 7,12-14) does not mean that a Christian is free to marry a pagan. Again, the thought of the Eucharist seems to be foremost--even if only implicitly stated--in the theologian's mind. Pointing to Paul's statement that impurity cannot have any part in that which is holy (Eph 5,5; 1 Thes 4,7), Tertullian writes:

> If these things are so, then it stands to reason that believers who contract marriages with gentiles[18] are guilty of lustful license and are to be excluded from all communication with the brotherhood in accordance with the letter of the Apostle, who says that not even food should be taken with such a one.[19]

---

rist since that would be the same as immolating Christ anew. Obviously, this was not generally the view of the Catholic Church, which admitted such persons to penance even though they might have to perform penance for the rest of their lives. Nevertheless, admission to penance at least presupposed the bishop's intention of eventually granting the pax. Cf. C. Chartier, art. cit., 339, 344.

18. It is worthwhile noting that Tertullian technically defines "gentile" in the following way: "Superest gentile illud genus inter populos deorum quos libidine sumptos, non pro necessitate ueritatis, docet priuata notitia." Cf. ad Nationes 2,8, 1; CC 1, 53. However, he generally uses the term simply to distinguish Christians from non-Christians. This demonstrates how the early Church, consciously or unconsciously, regarded herself as the new Israel. Moreover, this was in many instances, as in Tertullian, more than a mere formal distinction or term indicating the mass of unbaptized persons. Rather, it was a derogatory term used to express such persons' sinful state of separation from God and, consequently, subjection to Christian judgment and censure in spite of what St. Paul said about his lack of right or ability to judge those outside of the Church. Cf. 1 Cor 5,13.

19. Cf. ad Ux 2,3,1; CC 1, 387: "Haec si ita sunt, fideles genti-

Soon after this statement, the African writer goes on to explain what the main objections are--from the practical point of view--to a pagan partner in marriage. Such a partner will make it difficult for the Christian party to attend to the various duties and practices of religion such as the observance of certain fasts or attendance at certain religious vigils at night (ad Ux 2, 4-5,3). Finally, a pagan partner would not understand what the bread (i.e., Eucharist) means which the Christian partner took before meals.[20] Even a "tolerant" non-Christian partner is more than Tertullian can permit since his tolerance would mean that he was familiar with the Christian practices which should normally remain unknown to pagans (ad Ux 2,5,4).

It is also with special reference to the Eucharist that the Carthaginian proceeds against all professions that in some way render a service, direct or indirect, to the idolatry of the pagans. In de Idololatria 7, a work generally included as one of Tertullian's Montanist writings, he writes concerning those Christians who somehow cooperate in promoting pagan worship:

> In this regard, the zeal of faith will direct its pleadings and bewail that a Christian should come from the idols

---

lium matrimonia subeuntes stupri reos constat esse et arcendos ab omni communicatione fraternitatis, ex litteris apostoli dicentis cum eiusmodi ne cibum quidem sumendum."

20. Cf. ad Ux 2,5,2f; CC 1, 389: "'Nolite,' inquit, 'margaritas uestras porcis iactare, ne conculcent eas et conuersi uos quoque euertant.' Margaritae uestrae sunt etiam quotidianae conuersationis insignia. Quanto curaueris ea occultare, tanto suspectiora feceris et magis scrutanda gentili curiositate. Latebisne tu, cum lectulum, cum corpusculum tuum signas, cum aliquid immundum flatu explodis, cum etiam per noctem exurgis oratum? Et non magiae aliquid uideberis operari? Non sciet maritus, quid secreto ante omnem cibum gustes? Et si sciuerit panem, non illum credet esse, qui dicitur?"

into the church, or come from the workshop of the foe into
the house of God and raise to God the Father the hands which
are the mothers of idols, and pray to God with those hands
which, outside (of the church), are employed in adoration
opposed to God--and then apply to the Lord's body those hands
which confer bodies upon demons? Nor does that suffice!
Supposing it is a slight matter if they receive from other
hands that which they contaminate; but those same hands even
distribute to others what they (i.e., the hands) have contaminated. The manufacturers of idols are even chosen for
an ecclesiastical office. What an outrage! Once only did
the Jews lay hands upon Christ; these scoundrels tear his
body to pieces every day! O hands to be cut off! By now
they should have perceived whether or not it was said (merely) by way of metaphor, 'If your hand scandalizes you, cut
it off' (Mt 18,8). What hands could be more rightfully am-
putated than those in which the body of the Lord is impli-
cated in scandal?[21]

Apparently, some Christians had found (or retained) an occu-

pation in the manufacture of idols. But Tertullian equates this

with idolatry itself, maintaining that, even if God had not ex-

21. "Ad hanc partem zelus fidei perorabit ingemens: Christianum
    ab idolis in ecclesiam uenire, de aduersaria officina in
    domum dei uenire, attollere ad deum patrem manus matres ido-
    lorum, his manibus adorare, quae foris aduersus deum adorantur,
    eas manus admouere corpori domini, quae daemoniis corpora con-
    ferunt? Nec hoc sufficit. Parum sit, si ab aliis manibus ac-
    cipiant quod contaminent, sed etiam ipsae tradunt aliis quod
    contaminauerunt. Adleguntur in ordinem ecclesiasticum arti-
    fices idolorum. Pro scelus! Semel Iudaei Christo manus in-
    tulerunt, isti quotidie corpus eius lacessunt. O manus prae-
    cidendae! Viderint iam, an per similitudinem dictum sit: 'si
    te manus tua scandalizat, amputa eam.' Quae magis amputandae
    quam in quibus domini corpus scandalizatur?" Cf. CC 2, 1106.
    Due to the thorough integration of pagan religion and public
    life in the Roman Empire, Tertullian felt it necessary to for-
    bid Christians to hold public offices, to attend plays or
    other public entertainment or to hold a number of other occu-
    pations which were somehow incompatible with the faith. Cf.
    C. Chartier, art. cit., 321f.

plicitly forbidden the making of idols (Ex 20,4), "we would conclude from our sacrament itself that such arts are opposed to the
faith."[22] Although "sacrament" seems to refer especially to the
"baptismal promises" in this particular text,[23] the Eucharist is.
by no means excluded. That is, Baptism and the Eucharist were intimately associated in practice and thought in the early Church.[24]
It is also clear that this is the case in the passage now in question since Tertullian's progression of thought brings him to dis-

---

22. Cf. de Idol 6,1; CC 2, 1105: "Si nulla lex dei prohibuisset
    idola fieri a nobis, nulla uox spiritus sancti fabricatoribus
    idolorum non minus quam cultoribus comminaretur, de ipso sac-
    ramento nostro interpretaremur nobis aduersas esse fidei eius-
    modi artes." Implicitely, Tertullian distinguishes between
    direct and indirect idolatry. The former is considered a
    "capital sin"; whereas, the latter is viewed as less serious.
    Cf. C. Chartier, art. cit., 323f.

23. In the very next sentence (de Idol 6,2), Tertullian says:
    "Quomodo enim renuntiauimus diabolo et angelis eius, si eos
    facimus?" In de Cor 3,2; CC 2, 1042, the renunciation of the
    devil and his angels is described as part of the baptismal
    rite: "Denique, ut a baptismate ingrediar, aquam adituri ibi-
    dem, sed et aliquanto prius in ecclesia sub antistitis manu,
    contestamur nos renuntiare diabolo et pompae et angelis eius."
    However, it has been amply shown that "sacramentum" is often
    used by Tertullian to refer to the Eucharist--although, not in
    the sense of "Blessed Sacrament." Cf. Evans, xxxix. A. Kol-
    ping, op. cit., 62, defines Tertullian's eucharistic use of
    the term as follows: "Das Brot in der anwendung der Figural-
    prophetie wie auch das eucharistische Brot heissen als Andeu-
    tung des Herrenleibes sacramentum." Finally, in adv Mar 4,34,
    5, Baptism and the Eucharist are spoken of almost as if they
    were a single sacrament: "ad sacramentum baptismatis et euch-
    aristiae."

24. It will be seen later (in Cyprian) how Baptism was a conglo-
    merate" sacrament still in the 3rd century. That is, Penance
    and Confirmation were likewise not clearly distinguished from
    the actual Baptism itself.

cuss the Eucharist in this context just a few lines later on in
de Idol 7, which has been cited above.

Finally, notice must still be taken of Tertullian's witness
to the fact that already in his day some Christians came to the
eucharistic service at times without partaking of the Eucharist.
Although these persons were not under any sort of censure--but
were only misguided by their concern about keeping a fast--, their
action was certainly preparing the day when the Church would permit certain persons to attend the eucharistic worship in part or
in full, but now allow them to partake of the Eucharist itself.
Perhaps this was the situation with penitents already during Tertullian's day.[25]

The African theologian apparently became aware of the fact
that some persons were refraining entirely from attendance at the
Eucharist during times of their more or less private fasts; for
they felt that the reception of the Eucharist would prematurely
end their abstinence from food. After denouncing the practice of
those who come to prayer but refuse to give the kiss of peace--
therewith revealing to all that they were fasting[26]--, Tertullian
seeks a solution to the problem of the noncommunicating faithful
and offers a sort of compromise in which he suggests that the

---

25. C. Chartier (art cit., 341f) is of the opinion that the peni-
    tents, whose place was in the vestibule and who had to do pub-
    lic penance "in ecclesia" (de Paen 7,10; de Pud 13,7), were
    permitted to attend the eucharistic service apart from the
    rest of the faithful, but were excluded from reception of the
    Eucharist. However, positive proof that this was actually the
    case is lacking.

26. Tertullian sees the refusal to give the kiss of peace on such
    occasions as an over-extension of the Good Friday practice in
    which the kiss was omitted since everyone was expected to fast
    at that time. Cf. de Oratione 18,7.

fasting person at least come to the service and take the Eucharist home with him for reservation until after the fast:

> Similarly (i.e., like those who omit the kiss of peace while fasting), as concerns the days of the stations (i.e., certain days of fasting), not a few think that they must absent themselves from the sacrificial prayers, because the reception of the Lord's Body would put an end to the station. Does the Eucharist therefore cancel a service devoted to God, or does it bind it all the more to God? Won't your station be more solemn if you likewise take your 'station' at the altar of God? After one has received and then reserved the Lord's Body, both one's participation at the sacrifice as well as one's fulfillment of duty (in fasting) is secured.[27]

3. Hippolytus of Rome

a. Schism at Rome.

Born possibly in Alexandria about the year 170, Hippolytus is known to the modern historian especially as a presbyter at Rome, the first known antipope,[28] and as a Saint. This ambitious presbyter found himself at odds already with Pope Zephyrinus (c. 198-217) and his archdeacon, Callistus, over the Christological

---

27. Cf. de Orat 19,1-4; CC 1, 267f: "Similiter et de stationum diebus non putant plerique sacrificiorum orationibus interueniendum, quod statio soluenda sit accepto corpore Domini. Ergo deuotum Deo obsequium eucharistia resoluit an magis Deo obligat? Nonne sollemnior erit statio tua, si et ad aram Dei steteris? Accepto corpore Domini et reseruato utrumque saluum est, et participatio sacrificii et exsecutio officii."

28. According to Dix, xxvii, "Hippolytus was not the first or only anti-Pope in Rome in his own lifetime, nor necessarily the most important in the eyes of contemporaries." However, it could also be argued that Novatian was the first antipope in the strict sense in as much as he tried to win support well beyond Rome for his usurped office and even appointed bishops to take over the sees of other bishops who refused to acknowledge his claims.

questions raised by the Monarchians. Callistus' accession to the papacy upon Zephyrinus' death precipitated a schism between Hippolytus and the Roman Church. Although the smarting presbyter claimed to be the lawful Bishop of Rome, he does not mention the circumstances or time of his election. Perhaps his group of sympathizers acted very swiftly when it became apparent that Callistus would be elected to become Zephyrinus' successor, and held their own electoral assembly in anticipation of the official election.[29] The split that resulted continued through the reign of the next two popes, but was definitively settled when the fanatic persecutor of Christians, Maximinus Thrax, exiled Hippolytus and Pope Pontianus to the dreadful mines of Sardinia. Here both men, well advanced in years, quickly succumbed to their woeful lot and died in 235. Pontianus had previously resigned his office, and Hippolytus reconciled himself with the Church, who remembers him as a martyr for the faith rather than as a schismatic.

Besides the Christological differences that separated Hippolytus from Rome, there was also the question of penance and reconciliation of certain types of sinners with the Church. When Pope Callistus issued a decree affirming the belief that even all sins of the flesh could be forgiven within the Church,[30] Hippolytus

---

29. Cf. Dix, xxvi.
30. It has been generally accepted that Tertullian (de Pud 1,6) and Hippolytus (Philosophumena 9,12,20ff) attack the same decree and the same person--namely, Callistus and his stand on the readmission of adulterers and fornicators to communion with the Church. However, many recent scholars believe that Tertullian is assailing some African bishop (perhaps Agrippinus of Carthage) for a similar decree on the reconciliation of sinners. Cf. J. Quasten, Patrology, 2, 234f; B. Altaner, Patrology, 178; Josef Ludwig, Der Heilige Martyrerbischof Cyprian von Karthago, (Munich, 1951) 15f. This last mentioned

felt he had even greater reason for his bitter opposition toward
the duly elected Bishop of Rome.[31]   From this time on, his writings, including the famous Traditio Apostolica,[32] become a polemic

author notes the unusually strong emphasis on the first person
singular in the decree as quoted by Tertullian ("Ego et moe-
chiae et fornicationis delicta poenitentia functis dimitto")
as an indication of the episcopal struggle against Montanism
in the claim over who could forgive what sins within the
Church.

31. Unlike Tertullian, who left the Church upon what he felt were
genuinely theological grounds, Hippolytus seems to be offended
by Callistus' stand on repentance for deeply personal rather
than doctrinal reasons.   To be sure, Hippolytus is eager to
make the issue appear a matter of his zeal for orthodoxy.   He,
like Novatian a few decades later, attempts to hide his personal ambitions behind a veil of attacks against the Bishop of
Rome, charging him with both personal and doctrinal failings
in his willingness to receive repentant sinners against purity
back into the Church.   The charge of "laxity" becomes a cover-
up for Hippolytus' disappointment that his own rigorous stand
has failed to attract a following as large as Callistus' milder and more realistic position.   Cf. J. Quasten, Patrology, 2,
205f; Dix, xv-xvii.   One should also not overlook the social
difference between Hippolytus and his rivals.   Callistus was
slave-born, while the ambitious presbyter had been raised on
Greek sophistication.   The waning of Greek influence, language
and culture in the Roman see plus the waxing Latinization of
Rome and the papacy would have appeared to be a barbarization
of the Church to Hippolytus, thus adding salt to his wounds.

32. It may be, as Dix, xxxv-xxxvii, suggests, that Hippolytus
wrote the Tr Ap during Zephyrinus' closing years as an attempt
to steer the Bishop of Rome away from his archdeacon, Callistus.   If the original text of this work could be reconstructed
with more certainty, then it would be somewhat easier to as-
sign a date of composition to it.   The recovery of the text
even in its present "nondefinitive" form represents one of the
greatest and most difficult feats of modern paleographical research.   In this present study, Gregory Dix's text from 1937
has been consulted and correlated with the text provided by
Bernard Botte, La Tradition Apostolique de Saint Hippolyte,

against Callistus, whom he accuses of Sebellianism and of unjustified departure from tradition in his leniency toward sinners. As
far as Hippolytus is concerned, Callistus is a heretic and therefore an atheist,[33] or, at best, a reprehensible "teacher" of a
"school against the Church."[34]

Essai de Reconstitution, in: *Liturgiewissenschaftliche Quellen
und Forschungen* 39 (Münster, 1963). However, G. Dix's method
of division and ordering of the text has been followed in the
present study since his system is more familiar among English-
speaking students and scholars and allows for a more precise
citation of the text. Nevertheless, the textual quotations
used here are provided with B. Botte's page and line number
whenever his text is employed. Finally, it should be pointed
out that it can not be expected that Hippolytus is describing
Roman ecclesial life and liturgy just as it was when he wrote
the Tr Ap. Rather, his conservative reaction to the latest
developments within the Roman church probably led him to describe many things as they were in bygone days, but still
within the living memory of many persons. The title of this
work itself indicates the nature of Hippolytus' reaction and
what he hoped to achieve by it. But to what exact extent he
may have been induced to describe the past as he knew it or
thought it should have been can not be very well determined as
long as the date and circumstances of composition are uncertain.

33. Although Hippolytus equates heretics with atheists, he does
not mean that such persons hold that there is no God. Rather,
they are "godless" because they are "blasphemers" of the truth.
Cf. Phil proemium. Most likely, the term is simply Hippolytus'
answer to Callistus' charge that the schismatic and his followers are "ditheists." Cf. Phil 9,11,3; 9,12,16.

34. Cf. Phil 9,12,20; CB 26, 249: τοιαῦτα ὁ γόης τολμήσας συνε-
στήσατο διδασκαλεῖον κατὰ τῆς ἐκκλησίας οὕτως διδάξας, καὶ
πρῶτος τὰ πρὸς τὰς ἡδονὰς τοῖς ἀνθρώποις συγχωρεῖν ἐπενόησε,
λέγων πᾶσιν ὑπ' αὐτοῦ ἀφίεσθαι ἁμαρτίας. ὁ γὰρ παρ' ἑτέρῳ
τινὶ συναγόμενος καὶ λεγόμενος Χριστιανὸς εἴ τι ἂν ἁμάρτῃ,
φασίν, οὐ λογίζεται αὐτῷ ἡ ἁμαρτία, εἰ προσδράμοι τῇ τοῦ Καλ-
λίστου σχολῇ.

The significance of this last mentioned charge must be understood in the light of the general situation within the Church at
Rome during this period of history. Some insight into these facts
is also necessary for a proper appreciation of Hippolytus' contribution to the present study.

<u>b</u>. The <u>conditions</u> <u>of</u> <u>the</u> <u>Roman</u> <u>church</u>.

Rome, the center and capital of the ancient world, was likewise the center and capital of religious and social syncretism
where nearly every philosophical whim could establish a school.
Yet, for reasons that are still not entirely clear, Christianity
was under the constant threat or fact of persecution; although,
there were periods of civil tolerance. The situation was especially precarious for the Christians of Rome, where the appearance
of a strong monarchical episcopacy came rather belatedly. But
herein lay the tensile strength of the Roman church, whose presbyterate and hierarchy was set up with sufficient flexibility so
that the election of a new bishop could be easily postponed for a
period of time, frustrating the attempts of civil authorities to
destroy the unity of the Church by removing her leaders.[35] Often
it was possible to consider the provinces such as North Africa as
lands where nearly every village had its own bishop and where the
Church led a public existence in spite of the occasional persecutions.[36] But the Roman church remained a relatively less rigidly

---

35. For example, Pope Fabian was supposedly martyred in January
    of 250, but his successor, Cornelius, was not chosen until
    March of the following year, after the persecution had sub-
    sided. Cf. Edward Benson, <u>Cyprian:</u> <u>His</u> <u>Life,</u> <u>His</u> <u>Times,</u> <u>His</u>
    <u>Work</u>, (London, 1897) 271.

36. Cf. J. Ludwig, <u>op</u>. <u>cit</u>., 8. Actually it would be another cen-
    tury before North Africa would see any Christian "temples" or

organized body with no buildings or public sanctuaries[37] set aside
for religious life.

Under these conditions, the Roman διδάσκαλοι could open a lec-
ture hall with ecclesial approval, but operate as private individuals rather than as officials of the Church. Their lectures were
attended by baptized and unbaptized alike. The hierarchy intervened in the case of catechumens only at the last stage of instruction in order to prepare them directly for Baptism.[38] The Roman
church was unusually tolerant in the more speculative areas of religion, with the result that persons such as Marcion or Montanists
often found at least temporary acceptance and refuge in the church
of the capital city, although they were under censure from other

churches in the modern sense. Also, the Church at Carthage
was organized as a funerary association much as the Church in
Rome. However, the location of Carthage on the sea coast
ruled out the construction of the catacombs that offered the
Roman church some measure of privacy. The ecclesial life of
the Carthaginian church thus centered around the home of the
bishop and the "funerary chapels" located in the above-ground
cemeteries. Cf. Paul Monceaux, *Histoire Littéraire de L'*
Afrique Chrétienne depuis les Origines jusqu'à L'Invasion
Arabe, 1, (Paris, 1901, reprint: Brussels, 1966) 11-17. The
result of this situation seems to be that Christian life in
Carthage was so open to the public eye that Tertullian could
say in a writing addressed to the pagan population: "Quod
sciam, et conversatio notior facta est, scitis et dies con-
ventuum nostrorum, itaque et obsidemur et opprimimur et in
ipsis arcanis congregationibus detinemur." Cf. *ad Nationes*
1,7.

37. The Roman church seems to have acquired its first cemetery
during the archdeaconship of Callistus and was probably regis-
tered with the state as a funerary association. However, such
associations were private in most other respects. Cf. La
Piana, *op. cit.*, 254f.

38. Cf. *Dix*, 81f.

churches. Even the Gnostic, Valentinus, supposedly came very near to being elected the Bishop of Rome at one time (Tertullian, adv Valent 4). "Only when a teacher had demonstrated beyond a doubt that his creed really did differ in essentials from that of the Roman Church did 'the presbyters' expel him from Communion."[39] Thus, Hippolytus' sneer at "the school of Callistus" is tantamount to a charge of false faith and philosophy whereby adulterers, twice married clergy and free women married to slaves[40] could still find acceptance in the Church. Hippolytus, however, would exclude all such persons (Phil 9,12,25).

---

39. Cf. Dix, xxvii. This situation furnishes a likely explanation for Hermas' tolerance toward false teachers even though he by no means sympathizes with them. Cf. Sim 8,6,5f; 9,22.

40. Since Roman law did not recognize a union between a free person and a slave as a proper marriage, the Church undoubtedly ran into difficulties in this regard. Apparently, Hippolytus felt that the Church should abide by civil law on this point. In A.D. 52, a Senatus-consultum Claudianum led to the ruling that a free woman who continued to have sexual relationships with a slave against the master's wishes also became a slave. Cf. Gaius, Institutes 3,12 (Digest 29,5); Tacitus, Annals 12, 53; Tertullian, ad Ux 2,8; A reliable modern reference to this legislation can be found in Adolf Berger's Encyclopedic Dictionary of Roman Law, (Transactions of the American Philosophical Society 43/2), (Philadelphia, 1953) 697. Juvenal (c. 60-140) gives several indications in his satire on women (Satire 6, 362 and 592f) that many women of his day carried on love affairs with slaves, often preferring eunuchs since that eliminated the danger of unwanted children. In other cases, where pregnancy did occur, it was not uncommon for the women to resort to abortion in order to escape the undesirable social consequences of their illegal union with slaves. Therefore, Hippolytus did not hesitate to lay the charge of murder at Callistus' feet in view of the decree permitting a Christian free woman to marry a slave. Cf. Phil 9,12,24.

c. Christian discipline and the Eucharist.

Besides the above mentioned classes of persons, the reaction-
ary presbyter provides a list of personal occupations or other
conditions that can result in excommunication from the Church or
even from obtaining membership through Baptism. A slave must
have his master's permission and good recommendation before he
may take instructions in the faith (Tr Ap 2,16,4). But if the
slave's master is a heathen, then such permission cannot be very
well sought. Apparently, Hippolytus is ready to accept such a
slave for instruction into the faith, but he makes a point of saying that this slave must be instructed to please his master lest
scandal or blasphemy be the outcome (Tr Ap 2,16,5). A supposedly
possessed person must be exorcized before being admitted to instructions (Tr Ap 2,16,8). Panderers, sculptors or painters of
idols, actors, circus performers (e.g., charioteers and gladia-
tors), pagan priests and servants of the pagan state (e.g., sol-
diers), harlots, castrates, sodomites, magicians, teachers of
secular subjects and men with concubines are all mentioned as
either disqualified per se and permanently, or, in some cases,
at least until they desist in the practice of their profession.[41]

---

41. Cf. Tr Ap 2,16,9-25. Apparently disqualified per se are castrates, harlots, sodomites, magicians and catechumens or
Christians who volunteer for military service. In Tr Ap 2,16,
20, it is stated that the first three mentioned categories are
to be refused admission into the Church because they are impure: "Meretrix vel homo luxuriosus vel qui se abscidit, et
si quis alius facit rem quam non decet dicere, reiciantur; im-
puri enim sunt." Cf. Botte, 36, 14. Hippolytus undoubtedly
had a heightened sense of cultic purity as is made clear from
his general instructions concerning exorcisms, ablutions and
the quasi-isolation of catechumens. Cf. Tr Ap 2,18,1; 2,20,
3-5.8 and text below. It is quite possible that he meant that

Catechumens must remain apart from the faithful during prayer (<u>Tr</u> <u>Ap</u> 2,22,5; 2,18,1f); nor is it permitted to give them the kiss of peace; "<u>nondum enim osculum eorum sanctum est</u>."[42] Consequently, they must first undergo numerous exorcisms (<u>Tr</u> <u>Ap</u> 2,20, 3f; 2,21,7f.10), and are not permitted to eat anything with the faithful except "<u>panis exorcizatus</u>" in addition to the cup which each one has for himself (<u>Tr</u> <u>Ap</u> 2,26,4.11). Special care must be taken that catechumens and unbaptized persons--along with mice and other animals--be kept from partaking of the Eucharist. Therefore, great caution must be exercised lest a portion fall to the floor where it could be licked up even by a strange spirit.[43]

In the absence of the bishop, apparently no Eucharist can be held.[44] However, at a meal or agape without the Eucharist, the

---

even repented and reformed harlots, sodomites and the like remained permanently impure and therefore could not be accepted as candidates for Baptism.

42. Cf. <u>Tr</u> <u>Ap</u> 2,18,3; <u>Botte</u> 40,5.
43. Cf. <u>Tr</u> <u>Ap</u> 2,32,2-4; <u>Botte</u>, 84,1ff: "Omnis autem festinet ut non infidelis gustet de eucharistia, aut ne sorix aut animal aliud, aut ne quid cadeat et pereat de eo. Corpus enim est Christi edendum credentibus et non contemnendum. Calicem in nomine enim dei benedicens accepisti quasi antitypum sanguinis Christi. Quapropter nolite effundere, ut non spiritus alienus, uelut te contemnente, illud delingat. Reus eris sanguinis, tamquam qui spernit praeputium quod conparatus est."

44. The <u>Tr</u> <u>Ap</u> does not say this directly, but describes the bishop alone as president of the eucharistic service, while the rest of the clergy simply assists in the distribution of the Eucharist. Cf. <u>Tr</u> <u>Ap</u> 2,23,7. Unlike Tertullian, Hippolytus emphasizes the difference between clergy and laity on the one side, and the differences among the various ranks of clergy on the other side. In <u>Tr</u> <u>Ap</u> 1,9,7, he states that a presbyter can only receive Ordination, but only the bishop can bestow this sacrament. However, as regards the holding of a

presbyters or deacons may distribute the blessed bread (ευλογιον) when the bishop is not there (Tr Ap 2,26,11). But this bread is not the Eucharist (Tr Ap 2,16,2). Likewise, the bishop has the presidency over Baptism; but a presbyter or even a deacon may, in cases of necessity, baptize (Tr Ap 2,26,14f).

It is not possible to say from available data what Hippolytus thought of the effectiveness of sacraments performed by heretics. He scoffs at their eucharists--which are more like magic shows-- and their attempts to forgive sins by means of a second Baptism (Phil 6,39-41; 9,15,1.3-6). Most probably, his rigorism and pro-nounced hierarchical ordering of the Church made it self-evident that no sacraments, and in particular the Eucharist, could exist outside of this religious structure.[45] Hippolytus presupposes

---

eucharistic service, the presidency of a bishop was probably not considered so absolute that the death of the bishop pre-cluded the Eucharist until the election of a new bishop, or that a visiting bishop had to preside over the Eucharist when-ever the local bishop was hindered from attending. This would seem to be a conclusion that can be drawn from Tr Ap 2,24,1-3, where it is stated that the bishop should, if possible, dis-tribute Communion to all who are present for the Eucharist. But, on other days, "recipient secundum mandatum episcopi." Cf. Botte 60, 10. This may indicate that the presbyters and deacons could hold an ordinary weekday Eucharist in the bish-op's absence as long as they had his approval.

45. The writing, περὶ τοῦ Πάσχα 6,4, states that the Paschal lamb had to be eaten in one house and could not be borne without since this was all a figure of the Church and the Eucharist, which could not be borne outside of the one house of the Church. This work was originally attributed to Chrysostom (MG 59, 735-46), and then ascribed to Hippolytus by Ch. Martin in 1926. In 1950, P. Nautin ascribed it to the 4th century. Cf. J. Quasten, Patrology, 2, 178f. But, as Cyprian shows in de Unitate 8, this interpretation of the Paschal lamb is found already in the 3rd century. R. Cantalamessa, op. cit., 25-65,

a community of faith for the valid execution of the Eucharist
even though the Eucharist also develops this faith.[46]

453-55, 461-53, ascribes the work to a Quartodeciman writer
of the second half of the 2nd century in Asia Minor. His arguments for this place and date are very convincing and seem
conclusive.

46. Cf. B. Cooke, art cit., 345f. The object of this author is
to show that even in Hippolytus there is some room to justify
today's efforts toward better relations between Catholics and
non-Catholics through possible intercommunion.

CHAPTER TWELVE

THE ZENITH OF ALEXANDRIAN THEOLOGY

1. Origen

a. Biographical background.

Few if any writers would disagree that the "man of steel" ('Αδαμάντιος), as Eusebius called Origen (HE 6,3,7), was the most outstanding theologian of Christian antiquity. He is the first of the Church Fathers whose life is known in any appreciable detail. Born into a fervent Christian home in Alexandria about 185, he was given charge of the city's famous school for catechumens at the age of 18, when Clement of Alexandria was forced to flee in the face of persecution. About 216, the school was forcefully closed by Caracalla (Marcus Aurelius Antonius), and Origen removed to Palestine. Here, several bishops invited the famous theologian and orator to preach. Upon accepting the invitation, Origen was ordered back to Alexandria by his own bishop, Demetrius, who objected that only an ordained person may preach.

Fifteen years later, Origen was sent to Greece to refute the heretics. But in passing through Caesarea, Bishops Alexander of Jerusalem and Theoctistus of Caesarea ordained him in hopes of avoiding any further difficulties concerning the relationship of his lay state and his theological forensics. Again, Bishop Demetrius took a dim view of this action, and refused to acknowledge Origen's ordination on the grounds that the theologian's earlier physical castration disqualified him for the priesthood.[1] De-

---

1. Origen's self-inflicted emasculation (c. 202-203) resulted from his all too literal understanding of Mt 19,12. He apparently realized his lack of discretion later, at which time, Demetrius encouraged him not to let the irreversible mistake

metrius called together a synod and excommunicated Origen from the Alexandrian Church. Sometime after 232, this sentence was repeated by Heraclas, Demetrius' successor and Origen's former assistant. This marked the second period of Origen's adult life; for he then withdrew to Caesarea in Palestine, where his censure was ignored by the local bishop.

For the next 20 years, Origen presided over the new school of theology which he founded in Caesarea. He died at the age of 69 in 253 at Tyre, his health broken by the sufferings he courageously underwent during his imprisonment in the Decian persecution.

In Origen, the allegorical method was carried to its ultimate development, even being applied to the New Testament. This subjective method of exegesis[2] did indeed lead Origen into many errors of doctrine, but his own personal zeal for orthodoxy and his love for the truth offer the modern Christian ample compensation. Moreover, thanks to Origen and men like him, the Church was led to realize that a literal, fundamentalist interpretation of Scrip-

---

depress him or interfere with his holy aspirations. The Bishop's use of Origen's error as grounds for not recognizing the latter's ordination may have been motivated more by his envy of Origen than by his concern for a proper application of revelation to Christianity. But even if that is the case, the incident nevertheless demonstrates a growing propensity of the Church's hierarchy to interpret the nature of its priesthood with the help of Old Testament categories and regulations.

2. Although one may say that this method of exegesis is subjective, it does not necessarily follow that it is arbitrary. Such a charge made against Origen would be especially unjustified; for, in his Platonic view of reality, where all things perceived by the senses are "symbols" which not only signify but also participate in a "higher reality," Origen could feel justified in interpreting certain things allegorically.

tures, including the New Testament, was incapable of uncovering and defining in any acceptable way the truths of faith. The Church found her first truly systematic and theoretical theologian in Origen--in contrast to Tertullian who proceeded casuistically and juridically. Origen's great personal learning and fine sense of theology enabled him to apply the allegorical method with unusually keen perception. His exegesis was not merely an imitation of Hellenistic allegory and Philo, but included elements of Jewish spiritualization as well.[3]

As early as about 300, the doctrinal errors that resulted from the Alexandrian's method of exegesis and Platonism (e.g., the preexistence of souls) gave rise to "Origenistic controversies."[4] The polemics were revived again in about 400 and 550. In the first period of controversy, the matter remained in the literary sphere, and the Church took no official position. But the second period led to Origen's posthumous condemnation by Epiphanius and Pope Anastasius. Origen himself apparently held that a person's work should be burned and scattered along with his ashes if that one is posthumously found to be nonorthodox.[5] However, the coun-

---

3. Cf. Rolf Gögler, Zur Theologie des biblischen Wortes bei Origenes, (Düsseldorf, 1963) 16.

4. These "controversies" have been carried on into very recent times with the result that many authors of the last century and even w thin this century have made unjust, uncomplimentary statements about Origen. Cf. Henri de Lubac, Histoire et Esprit, L'Intelligence de l'Écriture d'après Origène, in: Théologie 16 (1950) 13-20; Walther Völker, Das Vollkommenheitsideal des Origenes, Eine Untersuchung zur Geschichte der Frömmigkeit und zu den Anfängen christlicher Mystik, in: Beiträge zur historischen Theologie 7 (1931) 1-21.

5. Cf. in Nm hom 9,1; CB 30, 54, where, commenting on the death of Moses' challengers in Nm 16, Origen says: "Manifeste quo-

cil at Constantinople in 543 probably sensed that this was a
questionable practice even in regard to Origen, and so compromised by pronouncing 15 anathemas against some of Origen's doctrines but not against Origen himself.

The vast majority of the Alexandrian's works have been lost
or destroyed--perhaps not a little due to later questions concerning his orthodoxy. Moreover, later copyists often abridged
many of Origen's lengthier works;[6] and much of what Origen wrote
or dictated is now accessible only in questionable Latin transla-
tions from several sources, especially from St. Jerome (died c̲.
420) and Rufinus of Aquileis (died in 410). Both men attempted
to correct Origen's works according to their own respective concepts of Christian orthodoxy. The results from the historical-
literary point of view are very regrettable; and even from the
point of view of orthodoxy, the outcome remained somewhat less
than felicitous. Therefore, a caveat lector is not out of place
wherever only a Latin translation of Origen's works can be provided.

b. Eucharistic doctrine and discipline.

The great theologian's doctrine on the Eucharist presents several new aspects which are pertinent to the present study. To

---

dam in loco Dominus per prophetam dicit: 'non sunt consilia
mea sicut consilia vestra nec cogitationes meae sicut cogitationes vestrae.' Si apud homines hodie iudicaretur haec
causa et apud ecclesiarum principes haberetur examen de his,
verbi gratia, qui diversa ab ecclesiis docentes divinae vin-
dictae pertulerint ultionem, nonne iudicaretur, ut, si quid
locuti sunt, si quid docuerunt, si quid etiam scriptum re-
liquerunt, universa pariter cum ipsorum cineribus deperirent?
Sed non sunt iudicia Dei sicut iudicia nostra."

6. Cf. R. Gögler, op. cit., 17-28.

begin with, he is clearly antagonistic toward any concept of the
Eucharist which would make it appear that this sacrament produces
beneficial effects (either spiritual or physical) in an automatic,
material manner. On the one hand, Origen treats the Eucharist
within the notional context of the "bread of life" (Com in Mt 11,
14); yet, he never connects the Eucharist with the resurrection of
the dead--an idea so popular among earlier Fathers in their struggles against Gnosticism, but one which is already absent in Tertullian and, so to speak, systematically avoided by Origen. His
doctrine of the Ἀποκατάστασις, which implies ultimate salvation
for everyone including the demons and Satan himself, greatly reduces and minimizes the eschatological character of the sacraments.[7]
Thus, there is scarcely any way or reason for Origen to consider
the Eucharist in the light of the resurrection. Moreover, the
present material body is not the subject of resurrection according to him. Rather, resurrection involves the changing of the
present body into a glorious spiritual body (de Princ 1,6,1; 3,40

---

7. Cf. Georg Teichtweier, Die Sündenlehre des Origenes, (Studien
   zur Geschichte der katholischen Moraltheologie 7), (Regensburg,
   1958) 153, 168f, 172f. As regards the Eucharist, the nearest
   Origen even comes to giving this sacrament any sort of eschatological character is in in Mt com ser 86. Commenting on
   Christ's interpretation of food and the kingdom of Heaven, the
   Alexandrian says: "ergo inplebitur 'in regno dei' hoc pascha
   et manducabit eum Iesus cum discipulis suis et bibet; et quod
   dicit apostolus: 'nemo vos iudicet in esca et in potu et cetera quae sunt umbra futurorum' (Col 2,16f), revelationem habet ad futura mysteria de escis et potibus spiritalibus, quo-
   rum umbra fuerunt quae de escis et potibus in lege fuerant
   scripta. manifestum est autem quoniam veram escam et verum
   potum manducabimus et bibemus 'in regno dei,' aedificantes per
   ea et confortantes verissimam illam vitam." Cf. CB 38, 198.

6). In view of these facts, it is difficult to determine wherein Origen sees the specificum and real function of the Eucharist.[8]

Although the exact role of the Eucharist both from the ecclesial as well as the soteriological aspect remains rather indeterminate in the otherwise thorough theologian, he does ascribe a sanctifying character to this sacrament if it is partaken of sincerely:

> But as for us, we give thanks to the Master of all things, and, with thanksgiving and prayer for blessings received, we eat the bread that has been offered, and which, having become a certain holy body by way of the prayer, sanctifies those who take of it with a wholesome purpose.[9]

---

8. A Struckmann's (op. cit., 201f) contention that Origen believed that worthy reception of the Eucharist was somehow connected with one's glorious resurrection in a spiritualized body which "will radiate in splendor like the angels and the stars" is an unfounded assumption. In de Oratione 27, Origen indeed speaks of the bread that gives its recipient eternal life. However, he is speaking here of Christ's life-giving doctrine--which Struckmann also admits (171). But Struckmann also sees a real reference to the Eucharist in this passage, and concludes that Origen is actually combining the promise of eternal life with the Eucharist (171-73). Struckmann's mistake stems from his failure to see that Origen ascribed a "real presence" to Christ in his word that is just as "substantial" as his real presence in the Eucharist. For Origen, Scriptures are a phase ("façon") of the Word's incarnation. Cf. Henri Crouzel, Origène et la Structure du Sacrement, in: Bulletin de Littérature Ecclésiastique 63 (1962) 94. And even if de Orat 27 does allude to the Eucharist, one is by no means forced to say that Origen made a connection between the Eucharist and one's resurrection. At most, it might be said that the sanctifying effects of worthy communion insures "quicker" salvation after death. But this still does not show the specific effect of the Eucharist itself, especially in view of the fact that Origen does not make a precise distinction between the proper operation of a sacrament and one's disposition. Ibid., 96.

9. Cf. Contra Celsum 8,33; CB 3, 249: ἡμεῖς δὲ τῷ τοῦ παντὸς

When Origen speaks of the Eucharist as a "body," one must
avoid seeing in this an affirmation of the doctrine of real presence as formulated in the hylomorphic interpretation of material
reality in Aristotelian philosophy. Indeed, Origen refers to the
Eucharist as the "corpus Domini" (in Ex hom 13,3), but he also interprets the eucharistic body and blood of the Lord as Christ's
teaching which nourishes the soul.[10] On the other hand, however,
the Alexandrian's understanding of the Eucharist's symbolical nature must be considered from two aspects: 1. from the Platonic
concept of reality and symbolism, 2. dialectically in view of Origen's reaction to a popular, contemporary understanding of the
Eucharist which he justly considered gross and misleading. This
latter situation apparently resulted from a belief in the real
presence of Christ which looked upon the sanctifying effects of
the Eucharist in the same "automatic" way in which the Jews felt
one contracted impurity by eating "impure" food. Origen refuses
to make room for any such naive and external religion in his theo-

---

δημιουργῷ εὐχαριστοῦντες καὶ τοὺς μετ' εὐχαριστίας καὶ εὐχῆς
τῆς ἐπὶ τοῖς δοθεῖσι προσαγομένους ἄρτους ἐσθίομεν, σῶμα γενομένους διὰ τὴν εὐχὴν ἅγιόν τι καὶ ἁγιάζον τοὺς μετὰ ὑγιοῦς
προθέσεως αὐτῷ χρωμένους.

10. Cf. in Mt com ser 85; CB 38, 196f: "Panis iste, quem deus
    verbum corpus suum esse fatetur, verbum est nutritorium ani-
    marum, verbum de deo verbo procedens et panis de pane caeles-
    ti...et potus iste, quem deus verbum sanguinem suum fatetur,
    verbum est potans et inebrians praeclare corda bibentium...
    Non enim panem illum visibilem quem tenebat in manibus corpus
    suum dicebat deus verbum, sed verbum in cuius mysterio fuerat
    panis ille frangendus. nec potum illum visibilem sanguinem
    suum dicebat, sed verbum in cuius mysterio potus ille fuerat
    effundendus. nam corpus dei verbi aut sanguis quid aliud po-
    test esse, nisi verbum quod nutrit, et verbum quod 'laetifi-
    cat cor'?"

logy, and remarks: "Likewise, it is not that which goes into the stomach that sanctifies the person even though that which is called bread of the Lord is thought by simpler folk[11] to effect sanctification (in this way)!"[12] In other words, the Eucharist does not produce holiness irrespective of the recipient's personal moral life.[13]

The great theologian's more "spiritual" concept of the Eucharist comes to light especially in his Logos-theology with its Platonic overtones.[14] On one occasion, Origen asks that Christians

---

11. Similar to Tertullian, Origen sees the Church as composed of "simple Christians" and "perfect Christians" (πνευμάτικοι). Cf. G. Teichtweier, op. cit., 253. Although this latter class holds a pre-eminent place in the Church, there is no reason to believe that Origen thinks of them as exclusively constituting the Church or as being so "perfect" that they are no longer bound to the visible, hierarchical Church. Cf. Aloisius Lieske, Die Theologie der Logosmystik bei Origenes, (Münsterische Beiträge zur Theologie 22), (Münster, 1938) 76-79, 83-86.

12. Cf. Com in Mt 9,14; CB 40,57: Εἴποι δ' ἄν τις κατὰ τὸν τόπον γενόμενος ὅτι, ὥσπερ οὐ τὸ εἰσερχόμενον εἰς τὸ στόμα κοινοῖ τὸν ἄνθρωπον, κἂν νομίζηται εἶωαι ὑπὸ 'Ιουδαίων κοινόν· οὕτως οὐ τὸ εἰσερχόμενον εἰς τὸ στόμα ἁγιάζει τὸν ἄνθρωπον, κἂν ὑπὸ τῶν ἀκεραιοτέρων νομίζηται ἁγιάζειν ὁ ὀνομαζόμενος ἄρτος τοῦ κυρίου.

13. The situation which Origen has in mind here is similar to the problem which Tertullian explains in de Paen 7,1-3, where the Carthaginian theologian speaks critically of those catechumens who used the time before Baptism for sinning rather than for reforming their lives in preparation for entering the Church.

14. For a proper understanding of the analogy which Origen draws between the Eucharist and the Word, it is necessary to take a brief look at the Logos-theology that Origen took over especially from Plotinus (i.e., the neo-Platonic principle that a word has meaning and significance due to its supposed metaphysical participation in the "ideal reality" which the word signifies) and developed in the light of Jewish Torah-theology.

adhere to Christ's blood, which is the blood of the New Testament
that gives reconciliation with the Father. In this context, he
draws a parallel between the Eucharist and the Word:

Not a little did the prologue of the Fourth Gospel bring Origen to this form of theology. Already Ignatius had called
the Gospel as well as the Eucharist the σάρξ of Jesus. Cf.
ad Philad 5,1; ad Smyr 7,1. Just as the Alexandrian considers the Holy Spirit to be the "hypostasis" (which approxi-
mates St. Thomas' concept of substance) in the water of Baptism, so does he consider the "person of the Word" to be the
"hypostasis" of the bread and wine in the Eucharist. Cf. H.
Crouzel, op. cit., 101. For Origen, "der Buchstabe des biblischen Wortes und das Fleisch Christi sind Parallelen in der
einen grossen inkarnatorischen Offenbarungsökonomie." Cf. R.
Gögler, op. cit., 301. That is, the Word of God in his flesh
and Jesus Christ as present in the word of Scriptures "stehen
als zwei gleicherweise vorläufige und verhüllte (sakramentale)
Daseinsweisen des Logos nebeneinander." Ibid., 303. Thus,
the parallel which Origen makes between the Eucharist on the
one hand and the Scriptures and the Logos on the other are
logical consequences of his Logos-theology, whereby both the
Eucharist and the word are ways of making Christ actually present as the Logos. Ibid., 376. However, "word-presence" had
a certain priority over eucharistic presence in so far as Origen holds that the divinity of Christ is more immediately present by way of the word; whereas, the Eucharist, being a "less
spiritual" symbol, is not to be considered as the divinity itself. Cf. H. de Lubac, op. cit., 366f. For Origen, the body
of Christ is present in three ways: in Scriptures, the Eucharist, and the Church. In this triad, the Eucharist must take
the humblest position and form for the presence of Christ's
body, since it is but a sacrament and therefore transitory.
Ibid., 368f, 372. However, the doctrine of Christ's real presence in the words of Scripture does not mean that Origen in
any way denies the same for the Eucharist. "La seconde pro-
position (i.e., Scriptures as the body of Christ) ne détruit
pas la première (i.e., Christ's bodily presence in the Eucharist), elle ne nie pas ni meme ne néglige la présence dans l'
eucharistie du corps revêtu par le Logos en son incarnation:
elle introduit seulement un autre corps, analogue au premier,
plus 'vrai' en un certain sens que lui." Ibid., 364. Finally

But you--who have come to Christ, the true pontifex who, by his own blood, has made God propitious towards you and has reconciled you to the Father--should not remain fixed in the blood of the flesh; but learn rather the blood of the word, and hear it saying to you: 'this is my blood, which has been poured out for you into the remission of sins' (Mt 26,28). He who has been instructed in the mysteries knows both the flesh as well as the blood of the Word of God. Therefore, let us not remain in those things which are known to the instructed and cannot be disclosed to the ignorant.[15]

As would be expected in the case of someone who thinks basically in Platonic categories, Origen is less interested in the esse of the Eucharist, and is more concerned with its essentia, which is to be found especially in the "function" of the Eucharist.

---

any discussion of Origen's doctrine of the bodily presence of the risen Christ must not overlook the Alexandrian's belief that the present material body is changed into a glorious spiritual body by means of the resurrection. Cf. de Princ 1, 61; 3,4-6. This, of course, is the result of Origen's neo-Platonism, whereby everything is somehow characterized as an image and likeness of the Logos: "En conséquence, l'Église a aussi une structure sacramentelle en tous ses éléments (Christ, Église visible, Écriture, Hiérarchie, Culte, Sacrements); On y distingue une 'couche' extérieure, celle des signes (corps historique de Jésus, lettre de l'Écriture, hiérarchie externe, sacrifice visible, corps eucharistique, baptême d'eau, etc.), qui introduit à la réalité spirituelle présente en eux, agissant en eux et par eux." Cf. Karl Rahner, La Doctrine d'Origène sur la Pénitence, in: Recherches de Science Religieuse 37 (1950) 50.

15. Cf. in Lv hom 9,10; CB 29, 438: "sed tu, qui ad Christum venisti, pontificem verum, qui sanguine suo Deum tibi propitium fecit et reconciliavit te patri, non haereas in sanguine carnis; sed disce potius sanguinem verbi et audi ipsum tibi dicentem quia: 'hic sanguis meus est, qui pro vobis effundetur in remissionem peccatorum.' Novit, qui mysteriis imbutus est, et carnem et sanguinem verbi Dei. Non ergo immoremur in his, quae et scientibus nota sunt et ignorantibus patere non possunt."

In this regard, the Eucharist is given a basic role in determining the character of other aspects concerning the Church and the faith. It serves as a sort of "essential idea" (Platonically understood) or "canon" (i.e., "measuring rod") for many other elements that make up Christianity. This is especially clear in the relationship between the Word and the Eucharist according to Origen. Noting the care and caution that accompanies the handling of this sacrament, he finds in this a reason for being equally careful about the treatment given to God's word by those entrusted with the care of the Church's liturgy and teaching:

> You who are accustomed to partake of the divine mysteries know how you take care with all due precaution and reverence whenever you receive the body of the Lord lest anything from the consecrated gift fall (to the floor) and be lost as a result of too little concern. For you believe, and rightly so, that it is a serious matter if anything fall to the ground through neglect. But if you take such care as regards the preservation of the body--and it is proper that you do that--, how do you consider it to be less a sin to neglect the word of God than his body?[16]

Elsewhere, Origen sees in the Eucharist an occasion for the Christian to keep his moral life in order since participation in the Eucharist requires a proper moral disposition. However, the idea does not remain at that point, but is used to exhort presbyters[17] to a good life:

---

16. Cf. in Ex hom 13,3; CB 29, 274: "nostis, qui divinis mysteriis interesse consuestis, quomodo, cum suscipitis corpus Domini, cum omni cautela et veneratione servatis, ne ex eo parum quid decidat, ne consecrati muneris aliquid dilabatur. Reos enim vos creditis, et recte creditis, si quid inde per negligentiam decidat. Quod si circa corpus eius conservandum tanta utimini cautela et merito utimini, quomodo putatis minoris esse piaculi verbum Dei neglexisse, quam corpus?"

17. That is, if the participation in the Eucharist requires that one be of upright character, then that is all the more reason

For, if one receives the Eucharist unto judgment when he receives it unworthily (1 Cor 11,29), then how much more does the one who sits in the presbyterium with a befouled conscience stain the assembly of Christ? For which devout person sitting with him will dare to say: 'I have not sat in the assembly of vanity' (Ps 25,4 LXX)[18]

Although Origen has no sympathy for an external, nonpersonal concept of religious purity, he does consider it incompatible with the "purity" of the Church for certain types of sinners to remain in full communion with her. They are apt to bring spiritual harm to others. This is hinted at when he speaks of a presbyter whose sinful conscience "stains" the rest of his religious associates.[19]

Through an allegorical exegesis of a New Testament text in the light of the Old Testament concept of purity, the Alexandrian theologian is able to develop a theology of excommunication. Accordingly, he sees the removal of Jesus and his disciples from the upper room to Gethsemane after the Last Supper as an act that had the mystical meaning of excommunication, because it would have been inappropriate had Jesus permitted himself to be arrested in

---

for a presbyter to be of pure conscience not only for his own sake, but for the sake of the entire Church. The significance of this latter aspect is emphasized by the fact that, even though it is the bishop who pronounces a formal excommunication, the entire community takes part in the expulsion of a clerical offender. Cf. in libro Jesu Nave 7,6; G. Teichtweier, op. cit., 255.

18. Cf. selecta in Jr 29,21; MG 13, 580: Εἰ γὰρ ὁ ἀναξίως τις μεταλαμβάνων Εὐχαριστίαν εἰς κρῖμα λήψεται, πόσῳ μᾶλλον ὁ καθεζόμενος ἐν πρεσβυτερίῳ συνειδότι μεμιασμένῳ, καὶ τὸ Χριστοῦ κολύνων συνέδριον; Τίς γὰρ αὐτῷ συγκαθήμενος εὐλαβὴς λέγειν τολμήσει τὸ, Οὐκ ἐκάθισα μετὰ συνεδρίου ματαιότητος, καὶ τὰ ἐπὶ τούτοις.

19. Cf. above, note 17.

the same place where he had celebrated the Supper with his disciples. However, since he wished to pray after the meal, it was
proper that he should select a "locum mundum ad orationem" before
his arrest. Origen then goes on to point out that Jesus was only
acting in accordance with Jewish mentality concerning the biblical concept of purity (Ex 3,5; Ps 17,6 LXX). However, it is not
that Jesus himself held that places could be holy or unholy, but
rather that "place" is here meant to symbolize "person"; for it
is persons who are either clean or unclean--that is, holy or unholy. That is why Jesus put out the mourners before raising
Jairus' daughter from the dead (Mk 5,21ff. and pars.) and carefully selected the witnesses to his transfiguration (Mk 9,2-9 and
pars.). Origen concludes his explanation:

> Propter hoc enim et in ecclesiis Christi consuetudo
> tenuit talis, ut qui manifesti sunt in magnis delictis, ei-
> ciantur ab oratione communi, ne 'modicum fermentum' non 'ex
> corde mundo' orantium totam unitatis conspersionem et consen-
> sus corrumpat.[20]

However, formal excommunication is just that--a mere formal-
ity in so far as the actual excommunication is the result of the
sin itself rather than the Church's sentence delivered by the
bishop of the community (in Lv Hom 12,6; 14,2). Consequently, it
also follows that if one is unjustly expelled from the Church,
then he suffers no harm from the formal excommunication. "Et ita
fit ut interdum ille, qui foras mittitur, intus sit et ille foris
sit, qui intus retineri videtur."[21] But one who is justly out-

---

20. Cf. Com in Mt ser 89; CB 38, 204f. In the same place, Origen
    explains the action further: "sed quia melius est cum nullo
    orare quam cum malis orare."

21. Cf. in Lv hom 14,3; CB 29, 483; J. Grotz, op. cit., 232f.

side of the Church is likewise "segregatus a consortio et unanimitate fidelium" (in Lv Hom 14,2).

From this, it becomes clear that communion in the Eucharist and in the Church are inseparable elements in Origen's theology.[22] For his own good, therefore, the serious sinner should withdraw from the Church at least to the extent of voluntarily placing himself in the ranks of the penitents.[23] For to remain hypocritically in full communion would only invite the ills which St. Paul speaks of in 1 Cor 11,30 in regard to unworthy participation in the Eucharist:

> Do you disregard the Church warning you and the judgment of a threatening God? Do you not fear the body of Christ when you approach the Eucharist as if you were clean and pure, as if there were nothing unworthy in you? And in all these things, do you think that you will escape the judgment of God? Do you not recall that which is written, that 'for this reason there are many infirm and sick among you and many have fallen asleep'? Why many infirm? Because they do not judge themselves and examine themselves, nor do they understand what it is to communicate with the Church, or what it is to approach such a great and exalted sacrament.[24]

---

22. Ibid., 264.
23. Ibid., 283f.
24. Cf. selecta in Pss 37, hom 2,6; MG 12, 1386: "Judicium Dei parvipendis, et commonentem te Ecclesiam despicis? Communicare non times corpus Christi accedens ad Eucharistiam, quasi mundus et purus, quasi nihil in te sit indignum, et in his omnibus putas quod effugias judicium Dei? Non recordaris illud quod scriptum est, quia 'propterea in vobis infirmi et aegri et dormiunt multi'? Quare multi infirmi? Quoniam non se ipsos diiudicant, neque seipsos examinant, nec intellegunt quid est communicare Ecclesiae, vel quid est accedere ad tanta et tam eximia sacramenta." In commenting on this passage, J. Grotz (op. cit., 264) says that the close association of "communicare Ecclesiae" and "accedere ad tanta et tam eximia sacramenta" attests that communio in the full sense includes not only the right to participate in prayer, but also the right to

The implication is that Origen believes that a number of his contemporary Christians are unworthily partaking of the Eucharist. These are apparently loveless hatefilled persons, who are compared to Judas Iscariot: "Tales sunt omnes in ecclesia, qui insidiantur fratribus suis, cum quibus ad eandem mensam corporis Christi et ad eundem potum sanguines eius frequenter simul fuerunt.[25]

receive the Eucharist. However, J. Grotz continues, this does not mean that the right to participate in prayer necessarily gave one a rightful claim to receive the Eucharist. "Wenn es nämlich In Ier. 12,5 heisst, dass der Sünder 'nach seiner Sünde um die communio bittet', so ist dabei an die Gemeinschaft mit den Gläubigen überhaupt zu denken, noch night an den Empfang der Eucharistie; denn es wäre unvorstellbar, dass einer, der ob seiner schweren Sünde gerade von der gesamten Gemeinde ausgeschlossen werden sollte, die Stirn hätte, um die Erlaubis des Eucharistieempfangs zu bitten." But the question remains whether or not the readmission of the penitent was actually carried out in Alexandria in such a way that a person was first granted the right to partake in prayer and then later the right to receive the Eucharist. Ibid., 268,n. 1.

In Com in Mt 10,24, Origen explains that the weak, the sick and those who have fallen asleep (died) represent different degrees of the seriousness of sins on the part of those who unworthily took part in the Eucharist at Corinth. Each type of sin has its own devil in charge of it (W. Völker, op. cit., 36f), and just as the holy person has union with Christ and God, so the sinner has union with a devil. Cf. A. Lieske, op. cit., 149. The unworthy communicant receives only "le corps 'typique', qui est accessible à tous. Mais cet acte sacrilège ne l'unit pas à l'Eglise, parce qu'il ne se prolonge pas en une manducation spirituelle du Christ lui-même, de cette chair et de ce sang du Logos qui sont la vie de l'Eglise et qu'on reçoit dans l'intelligence spirituelle des Ecritures." Cf. H. de Lubac, op. cit., 368.

25. Cf. Com in Mt ser 82; CB 38, 194. In his Com in Jn 32,24 (16), Origen says that Judas took the eucharistic bread (although he is not at all sure that Judas actually ate it) and left, thereby receiving the Eucharist unto judgment as in 1 Cor 11,28. Cf. H. Crouzel, op. cit., 97f.

However, Origen is careful to point out that the necessity of a proper moral disposition for the reception of the Eucharist derives from the relationship or quasi-identity which this sacrament has with the Word. The great theologian seeks to prove this thesis by way of an allegorical interpretation of the loaves of propitiation, which must be kept in a clean place (Lv 24,5-9). The mystical meaning of the text is that the word of God must be received into a "clean place"--that is, into the recipient's undefiled soul. But the relationship between the Word and the Eucharist also implies that one should receive the Eucharist into a pure soul:

> Wherefore, this law (concerning the loaves) is presented also in like manner to you, so that, when you receive the mystic bread, you might eat it in a clean place; that is, that you do not receive the sacrament of the body of the Lord into a befouled soul polluted with sins: 'for whoever eats the bread and drinks the chalice of the Lord unworthily, is guilty of the body and blood of the Lord. However, let each one examine himself and then eat from the bread and drink from the chalice' (1 Cor 11,27f).[26]

The period of penance that sinners must undergo has the obvious function of preparing them once more for full communion with the Church. But this means more than just inducing a changed and repentant heart within the sinners so that the rest of the Church may "safely" associate with them. Rather, it is meant to prepare them especially to participate worthily in the Eucharist. Origen

---

26. Cf. in Lv hom 13,5; CB 29, 477: "Unde simili modo etiam tibi lex ista proponitur, ut, cum accipis panem mysticum, in loco mundo manduces eum, hoc est ne in anima contaminata et peccatis polluta dominici corporis sacramenta percipias: 'quicunque' enim 'manducaverit' inquit 'panem et biberit calicem Domini indigne, reus erit corporis et sanguinis Domini. Probet autem se unusquisque, et tunc de pane manducet, et de calice bibat.'"

uses the image of Lazarus still wrapped in bonds as an allegorical example of the penitent who must first be freed of all "bonds"
before he can take his place at table with Christ.[27]

In another instance, the great master of allegory joins the
image of Jesus raising his eyes towards heaven just before calling Lazarus forth from the dead (Jn 11,44) with the image of the
Publican's unwillingness to raise his eyes in the temple (Lk 18,
13) and St. Paul's command that each one should examine himself
before approaching the Eucharist (1 Cor 11,28); and those who find
that their conscience orders them to abstain from the Eucharist
must likewise refrain from lifting up their eyes. Origen interprets this to mean that such Christians must remain outside of
the house of God and the assembly of Christians. He concludes:

> Therefore, just as it is not proper that everyone not use
> that bread and not drink from that chalice, and not be far
> from the house of God and from the Church; so is it not pro-
> per that everyone be unwilling to raise up his eyes.[28]

---

27. Cf. Com in Jn 28,7; CB 10, 398: 'αλλ' ἐπὰν εἰπόντος 'Ιησοῦ
τοῖς λῦσαι αὐτὸν δυναμένοις, διὰ τὴν πρόσταξιν ὡς δεσπότου
τοῦ Χριστοῦ, τὸ "Λύσατε αὐτὸν" καὶ "ἄφετε αὐτὸν ὑπάγειν"
λυθῇ τοὺς πόδας καὶ τὰς χεῖρας, καὶ ἀποθῆται τὸ ἐπικείμενον
αὐτοῦ τῇ ὄψει κάλυμμα ἀφαιρεθέν, προεύεται τοιαύτην πορείαν,
ὥστε φθάσαι αὐτὸν ἐπὶ τὸ ἕνα καὶ αὐτὸν γενέσθαι τῶν συνανακει-
μένων τῷ 'Ιησοῦ. In view of this evidence, one must agree
with K. Rahner (La Doctrine d'Origène, 272) when he says of
excommunication as explained by Origen: "Cette séparation
signifie plus précisément l'exclusion de l'eucharistie." Cf.
also J. Grotz (op. cit., 304-07) for a more detailed explanation of Origen's eucharistic use of Jn 12,2.

28. Cf. Com in Jn 28,4; CB 10, 393: ὥσπερ ⟨οὖν⟩ οὐ παντὶ καθῆκει
μὴ χρῆσθαι τῷ ἄρτῳ καὶ μὴ πίνειν ἐκ τοῦ ποτηρίου καὶ [μὴ]
πόρρω εἶναι τοῦ οἴκου τοῦ θεοῦ, καὶ τῆς ἐκκλησίας οὕτως οὐ
παντὶ καθῆκει τὸ μὴ θέλειν ἐπᾶραι τοὺς ὀφθαλμούς. J. Grotz

Or, to state it positively: It is proper that those who make use of the Eucharist also be in a state free from serious sin, so that they may rightly "lift up their eyes"--that is, join the assembly of Christians in the house of God. Thus, participation in the Eucharist means also participation in the prayer-service; and, as far as Origen is concerned, there is no such thing as a right to the prayer-service without a corresponding right to the Eucharist.[29] The Eucharist, in its relationship to the Word, holds a central position in the Church's reasoning behind the whole or partial exclusion of sinners and penitents from the prayer-service until such a time when she judges that the excluded person has again acquired the proper moral state for readmission to full membership.

It is especially due to the common priesthood of Christians[30] that Origen concludes that they must lead sinless lives:

> For he has commanded that we know how we are to approach the altar of God--for it is an altar upon which we offer our prayers--and that we know how we should make an offering; namely, that we put aside the 'soiled garments' (Ze 3,4)--that is, the foulness of the flesh, moral vices, and the defilements of lust. Or are you unaware that the priesthood has been given also to you--that is, to the whole Church of God and nation of believers?[31]

(op. cit., 285f) thinks Origen may have been prompted to write this passage in answer to those who were either overly eager about receiving sacramental absolution, or who became impatient during long worship services and so left at the same time that the penitents were dismissed.

29. Cf. J. Grotz, op. cit., 286.
30. Cf. Darwell Stone, A History of the Doctrine of the Holy Eucharist, 1, (London, 1909) 52f.
31. Cf. in Lv hom 9,1; CB 29, 418: "praecepit enim ut sciamus, quomodo accedere debeamus ad altare Dei. Altare est enim,

The reference to the fact that prayers are offered upon the altar of God is fully in keeping with Origen's desire to emphasize that it is not the mere reception of the Eucharist that sanctifies the one who offers it:

Just as it is not the food, but rather the conscience of the one who eats with doubt that defiles the eater (for 'he who doubts is condemned if he eats, because it is not done out of faith' [Rm 14,23]); and, just as nothing is pure to the defiled and unbelieving person--not indeed per se, but rather due to the contaminated and unbelieving state of that party--, likewise does that which is sanctified 'through the word of God and prayer' (1 Tm 4,5) not of itself sanctify the user. For, if that were the case, it would have sanctified even the one who ate the bread of the Lord 'unworthily,' and no one would have become ill or feeble or died on account of

---

super quod orationes nostras offerimus Deo, ut sciamus, quomodo debeamus offerre, scilicet ut deponamus 'vestimenta sordida,' quae est carnis immunditia, morum vitia, inquinamenta libidinum. Aut ignoras tibi quoque, id est omni ecclesiae Dei et credentium populo, sacerdotium datum?" This text is very similar to in Ex hom 11,7, where Origen explains that one should hear the word of God and receive the Eucharist only after being sanctified in body and spirit and after one's garments have been washed. In other words, one should participate in these only in a state corresponding to one's original baptismal purity. To act otherwise is to render impure ("immunda") what God has cleansed ("mundavit"). Origen supports his theology here by referring to the directive given in Ex 19,15 that the men of Israel, now assembled at Mount Sinai, should abstain from sexual relations for three days prior to the making of the Covenant, which Origen refers to in this text as "verbum Dei." In this passage, the Alexandrian makes a clear distinction between hearing the word and receiving the Eucharist. Cf. A. Struckmann, op. cit., 147. Unfortunately, Origen's intelligence and ability to apply the allegorical method of exegesis did not prevent him from actually believing that marital relationships had sullying effects so that one who participated in the Eucharist shortly thereafter polluted the sacrament (τὰ ἅγια ποιεῖ φυρμόν). Cf. selecta in Ez 7.

this food; for Paul teaches such a thing in these words: 'Therefore there are many infirm and weak among you, and many have fallen asleep' (1 Cor 11,30). Accordingly then, as concerns the bread of the Lord, the user receives its beneficial effect whenever he partakes of this bread with an undefiled mind and a pure conscience. Thus, we are not 'deprived' of any good by not eating--that is, due to our not eating from the bread consecrated by the word of God and prayer--, nor do we 'derive' any advantage merely by eating it. For the cause of deprivation is Evil and sins; and the cause of deriving is justice and uprightness, in as much as this was said by Paul in the following statement: 'We do not derive (any advantage) if we eat, nor are we deprived (of anything) if we do not eat' (1 Cor 8,8). But if everything that comes into the mouth goes into the belly and is cast into the privy (Mt 15,17 and par.), then the food that is blessed 'by the word of God and prayer' goes, according to its material nature, into the belly and is cast into the privy. But according to the prayer which accompanies it 'as regards the proportion of faith' (Rm 12,6), it becomes something beneficial and a source of the mind's perception when it sees the advantage in it. Furthermore, it is not the material of the bread--but the prayer offered over it-- that helps the one who does not eat it while being 'unworthy' of the Lord. Indeed, these things (were said) concerning the typic and symbolic body. But many things must be said about this Word which became 'flesh' and 'true food'; and all who eat it 'shall live forever' (Jn 6,58); although, no evil person can eat it. For, if one could, while remaining evil, eat the Word which has become flesh and which is living bread, it simply would not stand written that 'all who eat this bread will live forever.'[32]

---

32. Cf. Com in Mt 11,14; CB 40,57f: ὥσπερ οὐ τὸ βρῶμα, ἀλλ' ἡ συνείδησις τοῦ μετὰ διακρίσεως ἐσθίοντος κοινοῖ τὸν φαγόντα ("ὁ" γὰρ "διακρινόμενος ἐὰν φάγῃ κατακέκριται, ὅτι οὐκ ἐκ πίστεως"), καὶ ὥσπερ οὐδὲν καθαρὸν οὐ παρ' αὐτό ἐστι τῷ μεμιασμένῳ καὶ ἀπίστῳ, ἀλλὰ παρὰ τὸν μιασμὸν αὐτοῦ καὶ τὴν ἀπιστίαν, οὕτως τὸ ἁγιαζόμενον "διὰ λόγου θεοῦ καὶ ἐντεύξεως" οὐ τῷ ἰδίῳ λόγῳ ἁγιάζει τὸν χρώμενον. εἰ γὰρ τοῦτο, ἡγίαζεν ἂν καὶ τὸν ἐσθίοντα "ἀναξίως" τοῦ κυρίου, καὶ οὐδεὶς ἂν διὰ τὸ βρῶμα τοῦτο ἀσθενὴς ἢ ἄρρωστος ἐγίνετο ἢ ἐκοιμᾶτο (τοιοῦτον γάρ τι ὁ Παῦλος παρέστησεν ἐν τῷ "διὰ τοῦτο ἐν ὑμῖν πολλοὶ ἀσθενεῖς καὶ ἄρρωστοι καὶ κοιμῶνται ἱκανοί"). καὶ ἐπὶ τοῦ ἄρτου τοίνυν

c. Christian discipline and excommunication.

Origen's program for inducing Christians to a holy life and to
guard them against external, formalistic concepts of sanctification begins previous to one's Baptism into the faith. Candidates
for Baptism are carefully screened in order to prevent the admission of those with reprehensible lives and conduct. Very much the
same procedure is applied to sinners within the Church. The Alexandrian describes this process when he explains to Celsus that
Christians exhort the masses to a good life; whereas, the philosophers indiscriminately allow all comers to enter their circles:

> But, as far as they can, Christians previously examine
> the souls of those who want to hear them, and test them indi-
> vidually beforehand...Some are appointed to inquire into the

---

τοῦ κυρίου ἡ ὠφέλεια τῷ χρωμένῳ ἐστίν, ἐπὰν ἀμιάντῳ τῷ νῷ καὶ
καθαρᾷ τῇ συνειδήσει μεταλαμβάνῃ τοῦ ἄρτου. οὕτω δὲ οὔτε ἐκ
τοῦ μὴ φαγεῖν, παρ' αὐτὸ τὸ μὴ φαγεῖν ἀπὸ τοῦ ἁγιασθέντος λόγῳ
θεοῦ καὶ ἐντεύξει ἄρτου, "ὑστερούμεθα" ἀγαθοῦ τινος οὔτε ἐκ
τοῦ φαγεῖν "περισσεύομεν" ἀγαθῷ τινι. τὸ γὰρ αἴτιον τῆς ὑστε-
ρήσεως ἡ κακία ἐστὶ καὶ τὰ ἁμαρτήματα, καὶ τὸ αἴτιον τῆς περισ-
σεύσεως ἡ δικαιοσύνη ἐστὶ καὶ τὰ κατορθώματα· ὡς τοιοῦτο εἶναι τὸ παρὰ τῷ Παύλῳ λεγόμενον ἐν τῷ "οὔτε ἐὰν φάγωμεν περισσεύομεν, οὔτε ἐὰν μὴ φάγωμεν ὑστερούμεθα". εἰ δὲ πᾶν τὸ εἰσ-
πορευόμενον εἰς τὸ στόμα τὴν κοιλίαν χωρεῖ καὶ εἰς ἀφεδρῶνα
ἐκβάλλεται, καὶ τὸ ἁγιαζόμενον βρῶμα "διὰ λόγου θεοῦ καὶ ἐντεύξεως" κατ' αὐτὸ μὲν τὸ ὑλικὸν εἰς τὴν κοιλίαν χωρεῖ καὶ εἰς
ἀφεδρῶνα ἐκβάλλεται. κατὰ δὲ τὴν ἐπιγενομένην αὐτῷ εὐχὴν
"κατὰ τὴν ἀναλογίαν τῆς πίστεως" ὠφέλιμον γίνεται καὶ τῆς τοῦ
νοῦ αἴτιον διαβλέψεως, ὁρῶντος ἐπὶ τὸ ὠφελοῦν· καὶ οὐχ ἡ ὕλη
τοῦ ἄρτου ἀλλ' ὁ ἐπ' αὐτῷ εἰρημένος λόγος ἐστὶν ὁ ὠφελῶν τὸν
μὴ "ἀναξίως" τοῦ κυρίου ἐσθίοντα αὐτόν. καὶ ταῦτα μὲν περὶ
τοῦ τυπικοῦ καὶ συμβολικοῦ σώματος. πολλὰ δ' ἂν καὶ περὶ αὐτοῦ λέγοιτο τοῦ λόγου, ὃς γέγονε "σάρξ" καὶ "ἀληθινὴ βρῶσις",
ἥντινα ὁ φαγὼν πάντως "ζήσεται εἰς τὸν αἰῶνα", οὐδενὸς δυνα-
μένου φαύλου ἐσθίειν αὐτήν· εἰ γὰρ οἷόν τε ἦν ἔτι φαῦλον μέν-
οντα ἐσθίειν τὸν γενόμενον σάρκα λόγον, ὄντα καὶ ἄρτον ζῶντα,
οὐκ ἂν ἐγέγραπτο ὅτι "πᾶς ὁ φαγὼν τὸν ἄρτον τοῦτον ζήσεται εἰς
τὸν αἰῶνα".

the lives and conduct of those who want to join the community
in order that they may prevent those who indulge in secret sins
from coming to their common gathering...They follow a similar
method also with regard to those who fall into sin, and especially with the licentious, whom they drive from the community..
the renowned school of the Pythagoreans constructed cenotaphs
to those who turned away from their philosophy, reckoning them
to be dead. But they (i.e., Christians) mourn as for dead men
over those who have been overcome by licentiousness or some
foul crime--(they are mourned) as men who have perished and
died to God. And, after a period of time more prolonged than
required of those who are joining for the first time, they admit them as though they had risen from the dead, provided they
show sincere conversion. But they do not enroll those who have
fallen after their conversion to the Word for any office or
post in the Church of God, as it is called.[33]

From the preceding quote, it is clear that serious sins could be

forgiven at least once within certain limits.[34] Lesser offenses

---

33. Cf. con Cel 3,51; CB 2, 247f: Χριστιανοὶ δὲ κατὰ τὸ δυνατὸν
αὐτοῖς προβασανίσαντες τῶν ἀκούειν σφῶν βουλομένων τὰς ψυχὰς
καὶ κατ' ἰδίαν αὐτοῖς προεπᾴσαντες,...παρ' οἷς εἰσι τινές τε-
ταγμένοι πρὸς τὸ φιλοπευστεῖν τοὺς βίους καὶ τὰς ἀγωγὰς τῶν
προσιόντων, ἵνα τοὺς μὲν τὰ ἐπίρρητα πράττοντας ἀποκωλύσωσιν
ἥκειν ἐπὶ τὸν κοινὸν αὐτῶν σύλλογον...Οἷα δ' ἐστιν αὐτοῖς ἀγω-
γῇ καὶ περὶ ἁμαρτανόντων καὶ μάλιστα τῶν ἀκολασταινόντων, οὓς
ἀπελαύνουσι τοῦ κοινοῦ...Καὶ τὸ μὲν τῶν Πυθαγορείων σεμνὸν διδασκαλεῖον κενοτάφια τῶν ἀποστάντων τῆς σφῶν φιλοσοφίας κατε-
σκεύαζε, λογιζόμενον νεκροὺς αὐτοὺς γεγονέναι· οὗτοι δὲ ὡς
ἀπολωλότας καὶ τεθνηκότας τῷ θεῷ τοὺς ὑπ' ἀσελγείας ἤ τινος
ἀτόπου νενικημένους ὡς νεκροὺς πενθοῦσι, καὶ ὡς ἐκ νεκρῶν ἀνα-
στάντας, ἐὰν ἀξιόλογον ἐνδείξωνται μεταβολήν, χρόνῳ πλείονι
τῶν κατ' ἀρχὰς εἰσαγομένων ὕστερόν ποτε προσίενται· εἰς οὐδε-
μίαν ἀρχὴν καὶ προστασίαν τῆς λεγομένης ἐκκλησίας τοῦ θεοῦ κα-
ταλέγοντες τοὺς φθάσαντας μετὰ τὸ προσεληλυθέναι τῷ λόγῳ ἐπται-
κέναι.

34. It is highly disputed as to just how great a power of forgiveness of sins Origen ascribes to the Church. Cf. G. D'Ercole,
Penitenza, 116; ---, Communio, 227; B. Poschmann, op. cit., 280),
in reference to in Lv hom 15,2, would limit to once the number
of times a person could be admitted to penance after excommunication from the Alexandrian Church or wherever Origen's theology

could be readily forgiven; and it seems that this was primarily
a matter between the parties involved. A brother who is worthy
of receiving forgiveness and asks for it should not be refused.
And one should not come to prayer until he has granted the forgiveness under these conditions (de Orat 8,1f). Nevertheless,
the true Christian is free of the serious sins which are generally found among pagans and even philosophers:

> Such (sins) do not, generally speaking, exist among
> Christians, if you carefully examine who is a Christian. Or
> if such are actually found, then at least it would not be
> among those who assemble and come to the common prayers and
> are not excluded from them. [35]

held sway. K. Rahner affirms this, but points out that Origen fails to reconcile this position with his contention that
God always forgives a repentant sinner. Perhaps repeated ecclesial reconciliation was refused for practical reasons--
that is, to avoid scandal--, or because the Church felt that
God still forgave the sinner who relapsed and then again repented. Cf. K. Rahner, La Doctrine d'Origène, 427f. But even
more difficult to reconcile to Origen's contention that all
sins can be forgiven is his attitude toward apostasy, which
seems to be an unforgivable sin even to the extent of contradicting Origen's theory of ἀποκατάστασις. In his Com in Mt
ser 114; CB 38, 239, the learned theologian says: "Propterea
'communem' putare 'sanguinem testamenti' (Heb 10,29) pretio-
sissimum et iniuriare spiritum gratiae, omnibus peccatis de-
terius est, ita ut 'nec in hoc saeculo nec in futuro' (Mt 12,
32) remissionem possimus accipere, si dei filium denegemus
...Et hoc attende, quoniam ante galli cantum, et ante spiritum sanctum et in tempore noctis profundae, etiamsi frequenter denegavit quis, vivere potest; quod manifestum est ex eo
quod ter denegavit Petrus. Si autem post galli cantum, vel
semel in quocumque periculo constitutus denegavit quis, 'impossibile est eum renovare in poenitentia, ut iterum cruci-
figat sibi filium dei'" (Heb 6,4.6). The loss of the Greek
text is here especially regrettable since such rigorism is
often more characteristic of Origen's translators than of
Origen himself.

35. Cf. con Cel 4,27; CB 2, 296: ἤτοι δὲ οὐδ' ὅλως ὑπάρχει ἐν

On the other hand, Origen is careful to note that the sin must be manifestly serious beyond reasonable doubt before <u>formal</u> excommunication[36] can be imposed: "<u>Ubi</u> <u>peccatum</u> <u>evidens</u> <u>non</u> <u>est</u>, '<u>eicere</u>' <u>de</u> <u>ecclesia</u> <u>neminem</u> <u>possumus</u>, '<u>ne</u> <u>forte</u> <u>eradicantes</u> <u>zizania</u> <u>eradicemus</u> <u>simul</u> <u>cum</u> <u>ipsis</u> <u>etiam</u> <u>triticum</u>'" (Mt 13,29).[37] This is part of the conclusion which Origen draws from his commentary on Jos 15,63 concerning the Jebusites in Jerusalem whom the Israelites were supposed to drive out, but were unable to do. The Jebusites allegorically represent those who should be excommunicated from the Church for their manifest sins. Christians are thus admonished:

> Sed sit vobis summi studii summaeque cautelae, ne quis in hanc sanctam congregationem vestram pollutus introeat, ne quis Iebusaeus habitet vobiscum...Eiciamus saltem quos pos-- sumus, quorum peccata manifesta sunt.[38]

Χριστιανοῖς, εἰ κυρίως ἐξετάζοις, τίς ὁ Χριστιανός, ἢ εἰ καὶ εὑρεθείη, ἀλλ' αὔτι γε ἐν τοῖς συνεδρεύουσι καὶ ἐπὶ τὰς κοινὰς εὐχὰς ἐρχομένοις, καὶ μὴ ἀποκλειομένοις ἀπ' αὐτῶν

36. The bishop alone is the active subject of excommunication. Cf. K. Rahner, <u>La Doctrine d'Origène</u>, 262. A sin is <u>manifestly</u> serious either when it is publicly known or when the sinner confesses his sin to the bishop, who then must judge the seriousness of the wrong committed. If he determines that a serious sin has been committed, then the offender is formally excommunicated and must undertake a period of penance in preparation for reconciliation and readmission into full communion by the bishop. The excommunication and subsequent reconciliation are viewed as but phases of the entire penitential process. <u>Ibid.</u>, 441. The formal exclusion of the sinner is not seen as vindictive, but rather it is "<u>le médicin par excellence</u>" because it places one in the grace of God's immediate judgment. <u>Ibid.</u>, 442.

37. Cf. <u>in Jesu Nave hom</u> 21,1; <u>CB</u> 30, 429.
38. <u>Ibid.</u>

Commenting on Jos 16,10 ("<u>Et non disperdidit Effrem Chanana-</u><u>eum, qui habitabat in Gazer; et habitavit Chananaeus in Effrem</u><u>usque in hodiernum diem</u>"), the Alexandrian theologian improvises a couple of etymologies and applies allegory in order to explain a type of nonformal excommunication that requires the avoidance of the offending party even though he is not formally excommunicated:

> 'Effrem' interpretatur fructification (פרה). Qui ergo fructificat et crescit in fide, 'non potest exterminare Chananaeum,' semen pessimum, semen maledictum, semen semper mobile (נוע), semen incertum; hoc enim interpretatur 'Chananaeus'...Sed tu si vere fructificas in Deo et vides talem aliquem inquietum, turbidum, mobilem, scito quia 'Chananaeus' est. Et si non potes eum eicere de ecclesia, quia 'non potuerunt filii Effrem disperdere Chananaeos,' illud observa, quod Apostolus commendat dicens: 'Substrahite vos ab omni fratre inquiete ambulante' (2 Thes 3,6).[39]

However, it may happen that one sins so secretly that it can be noticed by no one in the Church. Such a sinner is also in reality excommunicated in that he is handed over to Satan directly by God rather than through the hands of the Church. After mentioning that those who preside over the Church have the power of loosening and binding in view of 1 Cor 5,2 where Paul orders the offender to be handed over to Satan for the destruction of the flesh so that his spirit may be saved, Origen continues:

> Alio autem modo quis 'traditur Zabulo' cum peccatum eius manifestum non fit hominibus, Deus autem, 'qui videt in occultio,' perspiciens eius mentem et animos vitiis ac passionibus servientes et in corde eius non se coli, sed aut avaritiam aut libidinem aut iactantiam vel alia huiusmodi, istum talem ipse Dominus 'tradit Satanae.' Quomodo eum 'tradit Satanae'? Discedit a mente eius et avertit se et refugit a cogitationibus eius malis et desideriis indignis et derelin-

---

39. Cf. <u>in Jesu Nave hom</u> 21,2; <u>CB</u> 30, 430.

quit 'domum' cordis eius 'vacuam.' Et tunc complebitur in
illo homine, quod scriptum est: 'cum autem immundus spiritus
exierit ab homine, circuit loca arida; et si non invenerit re-
quiem, redit ad domum suam; et inveniens eam vacantem et mun-
datam, assumit secum septem alios nequiores se spiritus, et
intrans habitat in domo illa; et tunc fient hominis illius no-
vissima peiora prioribus' (Mt 12,43-45). Hoc ergo modo intel-
legendum est Deum 'tradere,' quos tradit, non quia ipse tradat
aliquem, sed ex eo quod derelinquit indignos, eos scilicet,
qui se non ita excolunt et a vitiis purgant, ut libenter in
iis habitet Deus. Ipso refugiente atque avertente se ab anima,
quae in immunditia ac vitiis posita est, tradita dicitur ex eo,
quod Deo vacua invenitur et invaditur ab spiritu nequam.[40]

Besides holding that a sinner is to be excommunicated for his

own good--so that, being shamed into repentance, he may yet be

saved--, Origen also maintains--and very emphatically--that the

serious and manifest sinner must be expelled lest his presence

blight and destroy others in the Church. Thus, the Alexandrian

theologian strongly denounces those ecclesiastical leaders who he-

sitate to carry out Christ's instructions given in the Gospel and

in Paul's letters to expel certain sinners and those who refuse to

repent after the three-fold warning. Apparently, Origen has spe-

cific instances in mind, where the bishop's desire to maintain his

popularity has led him to be overly lenient to the sinner. But

Origen objects:

> What sort of kindness and mercy is that, to be sparing to
> one person and to lead everyone else into a crisis? For the
> people are then polluted by the one sinner. Just as the en-
> tire flock is infected by one diseased sheep, so is the whole
> multitude likewise polluted by one fornicator or by one who
> commits any other serious offense whatsoever...We do not say
> these things so that someone may be cut off for a slight of-
> fense. But, if by chance someone has been warned and correc-
> ted for a fault once and again and a third time, and shows not
> a wit of amendment, let us use the doctor's discipline. If

---

40. Cf. in Libr Judicum hom 2,5; CB 30, 478f.

we have annointed with oil, if we have soothed with pads, if
we have softened with malagmate, and the harshness of the
tumor still does not yield to medications, there then remains
only the remedy of surgical operation. For thus says the
Lord: 'If your right hand scandalizes you, cut it off and
cast it away' (Mt 5,30). Does not the hand of our body sometimes scandalize us so that the Gospel says concerning the
hand of the body: 'cut it off and cast it away'? But, that
is what it says, so that I--who seem to be your right hand
and am named presbyter and appear to preach the word of God--
if I perform anything contrary to ecclesial discipline and
the rule of the Gospel, with the result that I scandalize you
and the Church, then let the entire Church breathing in one
consent cut me off--her right hand--and cast me forth from
herself.[41]

The return of the excommunicated person to the fold of the
Church depends on his undertaking positive works directed toward
his reconciliation:

---

41. Cf. in Jesu Nave hom 7,6; CB 30, 332-34: "Quae ista bonitas,
    quae ista misericordia est, uni parcere, et omnes in discri-
    men adducere? Polluitur enim ex uno peccatore populus. Si-
    cut ex una ove morbida grex universus inficitur, sic etiam uno
    vel fornicante vel aliud quodcunque sceleris committente plebs
    universa polluitur...Haec non ideo dicimus, ut pro levi culpa
    aliquis abscidatur; sed si forte commonitus quis et correptus
    pro delicto semel et iterum ac tertio nihil exmendationis
    ostenderit, utamur medici disciplina. Si oleo perunximus, si
    emplastris mitigavimus, si malagmate mollivimus nec tamen ce-
    dit medicamentis tumoris duritia, solum superest remedium de-
    secandi. Sic enim et Dominus dicit: 'si dextera manus tua
    scandalizaverit te, abscide eam et proice abs te.' Nunquid-
    nam manus corporis nostri aliquando scandalizat nos aut de
    hac manu corporis Evangelium dicat: 'abscide eam, et proice
    abs te'? Sed hoc est, quod dicit, ut ago, qui videor tibi
    manus esse dextera et presbyter nominor et verbum Dei videor
    praedicare, si aliquid contra ecclesiasticam disciplinam et
    evangelii regulam gessero, ita ut scandalum tibi, et eccle-
    siae, faciam, in uno consensu Ecclesia universa conspirans
    excidat me dexteram suam, et proiciat a se." Obviously, Ori-
    gen is describing a more radical form of formal excommunica-
    tion than explained above in note 36, where it is assumed

Let the one thrown out of Jerusalem (i.e., the Church)
know that if he does (not) do the things required within sufficient time while he is carrying on outside of the Church,
he will not return to Jerusalem. Whoever sins is indeed expelled, even if he is not expelled by men. It is necessary
that he not neglect to build a house and plant a garden while
he is outside (of the Church); for in not doing these things
and in failing to fulfill the symbolic number of 70 years--
which lead to Sabbath and rest--, he will not return to communicate with the Church; but he will continue to stay outside of Jerusalem as a condemned person.[42]

Here, Origen says that a person who has been excommunicated--
either formally or at least by his own sins--must take care to
cultivate a virtuous life[43] just the same, and that this must be
carried out over a period of time (70 years being symbolic for
the "fulfilled time") before he can think of obtaining full reconciliation with the Church. In any case, the reconciliation is
not to be granted too readily; for that would encourage crimes and
endanger the entire Church:

---

that the excommunicated sinner immediately and voluntarily en-
ters the ranks of the penitents.

42. Cf. selecta in Jr 29,4; MG 13, 577: Ἴστω δὲ ὁ τῆς ᾿Ιερουσα-
λὴμ ἐκβληθείς, ὡς ἐὰν μὲν ποιήσῃ χρόνον αὐτάρκη πράττων ἔξω
τῆς ᾿Εκκλησίας ἃ δεῖ, οὐκ ἐπάνεισιν ἐπὶ τὴν ᾿Ιερουσαλήμ· ἐκβάλλεται δέ τις ἁμαρτάνων, κἂν μὴ ὑπ' ἀνθρώπων ἐκβληθῇ. Δεῖ
δὲ αὐτὸν ἔξω γεγονέναι τοῦ μὴ ἀμελεῖν τοῦ οἰκοδομεῖν οἰκίαν
καὶ φυτεύειν παραδείσους· ταῦτα γὰρ μὴ ποιῶν, μηδὲ πληρώσας
τὸν συμβολικὸν ἀριθμὸν τῶν ἐτῶν τῶν ἑβδομήκοντα, Σαββάτου καὶ
ἀναπαύσεως ὄντα, οὐκ ἐπάνεισι κοινωνήσων τῇ ᾿Εκκλησίᾳ, μένει
δὲ καταδεδικασμένος ἔξω εἶναι τῆς ᾿Ιερουσαλήμ.

43. Origen's allegorical use of the term "house" refers to some
singular virtue such as simplicitas or timor Dei. Cf. K.
Rahner, La Doctrine d'Origène, 71. It also seems that the reference to "garden" indicates virtues; for, in de Plantatione
viii,35-ix,37, Philo allegorically interprets the Garden of
Eden as the soul of a person in which God plants a "garden of
virtues" which bring the soul to complete happiness.

If someone has sinned, then, after the sin, a request is made for communion. But if it is granted quickly,[44] the common (bond of unity) is undone--the sin of others is stimulated to grow. But if with rational deliberation--and not as an unmerciful and cruel judge, but as one who, while concerning himself about a single party, is still more concerned about the many apart from the one--he sees the immanent destruction of the common (welfare) as a result of the communion of the one and as a result of the concession made to his sin, then it is clear that he will cast out the one in order to save the many.[45]

d. The nature and fate of heretics.

Finally, it is necessary to see what Origen's attitude is toward heretics. In this regard, the Alexandrian's main concern is with the heresies and heretics within the Church.[46] If one must find a "worst sin" in Origen's eyes then it would be found in turning away from the faith to apostasy and heresy.[47] This would seem to be because the sin of heresy vitiates all that the heretic does and renders his every act sinful. The great theologian draws this conclusion from Paul's statement in Rm 14,23 that all that is done without faith is sin. Origen thus seeks to show that heretics act without faith:

---

44. At this point, the Latin translation furnished by St. Jerome (MG 13, 386) fails to render "quickly" (τάχιον), thus betraying St. Jerome's rather than Origen's tendency toward rigorism.

45. Cf. in Jr hom 12,5; CB 6, 92: ἡμαρτέ τις, ἐδεήθη μετὰ τὴν ἁμαρτίαν περὶ κοινωνίας. ἐὰν τάχιον ἐλεηθῇ, ἐπιτρίβεται τὸ οὐχ ὡς ἀνελεήμων, οὐδ' ὡς ὠμὸς ⟨ὁ⟩ δικαστὴς, ἀλλ' ὡς προνοούμενος καὶ τοῦ ἑνὸς, πλεῖον δὲ προνοούμενος τῶν πολλῶν παρὰ τὸν ἕνα σκοπάσῃ τὴν ἐσομένην ζημίαν τῷ κοινῷ ἐκ τῆς κοινωνίας τοῦ ἑνὸς καὶ τῆς συγχωρήσεως τοῦ ἁμαρτήματος αὐτοῦ, δῆλον ὅτι ποιήσει ἐκβαλεῖν τὸν ἕνα, ἵνα σώσῃ τοὺς πολλούς.

46. Cf. R. Gögler, op. cit., 204f.
47. Cf. G. Teichtweier, op. cit., 272ff.

However, someone might ask if also the things which heretics do are considered to be done out of faith since they act
in accordance with their belief; or, since their faith is defective, should whatever they do be pronounced a sin because
it does not come about by faith. I personally think that
their state is to be designated as credulity rather than faith.
Just as false prophets are sometimes incorrectly called 'prophets' and false knowledge is called 'knowledge' and false wisdom is wrongly named 'wisdom,' so is the credulity of heretics
likewise called 'faith'--but by way of incorrect nomenclature.
Wherefore, it is necessary to see to it that no good work per-
chance appear to be performed among them as well; and because
it is not done out of faith, it is turned into sin just as it
was said in regard to a certain person: 'Let his prayer become sin' (Ps 108,7 LXX).[48]

In his commentary on the Letter to Titus, Origen defines a
heretic as follows:

Omnis qui se Christo credere confitetur, et tamen alium
Deum legis et prophetarum, alium Evangelorum dicit, et Patrem
Domini nostri Jesu Christi non eum dicit esse qui a lege et
prophetis praedicatur, sed alium nescio quem ignotum omnibus
atque omnibus inauditum, hujusmodi homines haereticos desig-
namus.[49]

However, this definition does not exhaust all the possible
ways in which one may become a heretic. Orthodoxy also includes
confessing the virgin birth and Christ's pre-existence, his divine

---

48. Cf. Com in Ep ad Rm 10,5; MG 14, 1256: "sed requirat aliquis
si et haeretici quae faciunt, quia secundum hoc quod credunt
faciunt, ex fide facere credantur: an quia fides apud illo
mala est, omne quod faciunt peccatum pronuntiandum sit, quia
non fit ex fide. Ego puto illorum credulitatem appellari magis quam esse fidem. Sicut enim pseudoprophetae falso nomine
interdum prophetae appellantur; et falsa scientia, scientia
dicitur; et falsa sapientia, sapientia abusive nominatur: ita
et haereticorum credulitas falso nomine fides appellatur. Unde videndum est ne forte etiam si quid boni operis apud illos
geri videtur, quia non fit ex fide, convertatur in peccatum,
sicut et de quodam dictum est: 'Fiat oratio ejus in peccatum.'"

49. Cf. MG 14, 1303.

nature as well as his humanity, and that Jesus was truly the Son--
and not the Father in a human person.[50] Besides these errors concerning various Trinitarian aspects,[51] Origen also enumerates several anthropological concepts that are contrary to the faith and
therefore to be rejected as heretical: the claim that not all human souls have the same nature and the denial of free will, for
instance, are to be condemned as "perniciosa dogmata."[52] The
Alexandrian theologian concludes:

> Si quis ergo horum aliquid quae supra exposuimus, commu-
> tare vel subvertere conatur, velut perversus, et a semetipso
> damnatus (Ti 3,11) secundum sententiam Apostoli, etiam a
> nobis praecepto obsequentibus ejus similiter habendus est.[53]

To define the nature of the heretic himself, Origen finds a
number of scriptural texts or ideas that he applies allegorically
in order to describe such persons. Since circumcision was meant
to distinguish the true Israelite in the Old Testament, the heretic, therefore, is uncircumcised in heart because his heart is
full of blasphemous ideas that contradict the wisdom of Christ.
Those who are circumcised in heart have pure faith and a sincere
conscience. Thus, the Lord says in Mt 5,8 that the pure of heart
will see God.[54]

Heretics are like the wooden poles which Yahweh forbade Israel
to plant next to his altar (Dt 16,21), for these were the sacred

---

50. Ibid., 1304.
51. Cf. R. Gögler, op. cit., 205-07.
52. Cf. in Ep ad Ti; MG 14, 1305.
53. Ibid.
54. Cf. in Gn hom 3,6; CB 29, 47: "Sed et qui haereticos sensus
mente continet et blasphemas assertiones contra scientiam
Christi disponit in corde, hid 'incircumcisus' est 'corde.'
Que vero puram fidem in conscientiae sinceritate custodit,
iste circumcisus est corde; de quo dici potest: 'Beati mundo
corde, quia ipsi Deum videbunt.'"

poles of the pagans and were totally opposed to the worship of
Yahweh--just as the heretic is opposed to the true nature of the
Church and her worship to God (in Jer Hom 4,4). Should a Christian happen to hear a heretic's doctrine, he must "vomit it from
his conscience" (de Prin 3,3,4). Even the name of a heretic is to
be avoided, and there is to be no participation in his prayer.[55]
Heretics, like fornicators, idolators, etc., (Gal 5,19-21) will
not possess the kingdom of God.[56] In short, Origen sees the heretic as someone "impure," who introduces nonorthodox philosophy into the Church in order to create sects and to "pollute every church
of the Lord."[57] Unfortunately, Origen says nothing explicitly
about the possibility or impossibility of the reacceptance of a
former heretic into the Church.

2. Dionysius of Alexandria

Born of pagan parents around the beginning of the third century, Dionysius was converted to Christianity through his wide
reading and diligent search for truth. He is the best known and
most famous of Origen's students at Alexandria, and around 231 he
took over the headpost of the catechetical school from Heraclas.
Upon the latter's death (c. 247), Dionysius was elected to fulfill
his post as bishop of Alexandria. He took an active role in the
internal ecclesiastical difficulties of his time--that is, especially in the schism of Novatian and the baptismal controversy, in

---

55. Cf. in Ep ad Ti; MG 14, 1303: "ita etiam nomen devitare, ne-
    que cum talibus orationis societate miscere."

56. Ibid.

57. Cf. in Jesu Nave hom 7,7; CB 30, 335: "Furti sunt isti 'lin-
    guas aureas' de Hiericho et philosophorum nobis non rectas in
    ecclesias introducere conati sunt sectas et polluere omnem ec-
    clesiam Domini."

the problems created by chiliastic unrest, and in the Trinitarian
controversies. His constant concern and efforts for the faith
earned him the name of "Dionysius the Great." He died of illness
about 264. Of his many works, the very few to survive are mostly
preserved in the sixth and seventh books of Eusebius' Ecclesiastical History.

In this Alexandrian, the Church appears to find her first real
penitential system with distinct degrees of penance. Perhaps in
reaction to the rigoristic elements of his time--a matter to be
taken up more fully in the chapter on Cyprian--, Dionysius is
quite willing to reconcile sinners with the Church.[58] However,
his system of penance was indeed rigid by today's standards, especially in the case of former apostates. Such a person must
spend three years as a "listener," and then ten years as a "kneeler."[59] The penitent could hear the word of God, but not partake
of the Eucharist. Most probably, this meant that the penitent,
either a "listener" or a "kneeler," was not permitted to remain
for the actual eucharistic service, since participation or presence at this service without reception of the Eucharist would
have been an anomaly then, and the reception of the Eucharist was

---

58. In his Letter to Conona, Dionysius orders that the repentant
    apostates (lapsi) not be refused absolution in articulo mor-
    tis, nor is the absolution to be withdrawn if such persons
    should happen to recover. In a fragment concerning repentance,
    the Alexandrian Bishop asks that penitents be not thrust out,
    but rather they should be gladly received back and numbered
    with the steadfast; and thus whatever is lacking in them is
    made up: μὴ οὖν ἀποπεμπώμεθα τοὺς ἐπιστρέφοντας, ἀλλ' ἀσμένως
    δεχώμεθα, καὶ τοῖς ἀπλάνεσιν ἐναριθμῶμεν, καὶ τὸ ἐλλεῖπον ἀνα-
    πληρῶμεν. Cf. Feltoe, 64.

59. Cf. B. Poschmann, op. cit., 474.

granted normally only at the termination of the whole penitential period.[60]

On the other hand, this rigid penitential system was not considered absolutely inflexible as Dionysius himself attests in the case of those repentant apostates who had obtained a "letter of recommendation" from a martyr[61] and were thus given almost immediate readmission into the Church. In his letter to Fabius of Antioch (HE 6,42,5f), the Alexandrian Bishop expresses his uncertainty about how he should react to this new development, whereby the Christian community, without any special consultation with the bishop, spontaneously reaccepted the lapsi whom the martyrs felt had already done sufficient penance or had shown sufficient evidence of real interior repentance. Dionysius writes:

> Therefore, the divine martyrs themselves who are among us, and who are now magistrates of Christ and share the fellowship of his kingdom and take part in his decisions and judge along with him, have espoused the cause of certain fallen brethren who became answerable for the charge of sacrificing; and, seeing their conversion and repentance, they judged that it (i.e., their repentance) had the power to prove acceptable to him who has no pleasure at all in the death of the sinner, but rather in his repentance (2 Pt 3,9). And so they received and admitted them to the worship of the Church as "consistentes" (i.e., those in full communion), and gave them fellowship in their prayers and feasts. What do you counsel us, brethren, on these matters? What should we do? Are we to be of like opinion and mind with them, uphold their decisions and concessions and deal kindly with those whom they pitied? Or shall we consider their decision unjust, and set ourselves up as critics of their opinion, cause grief to kindness, and do away with their arrangement?[62]

---

60. Ibid.
61. In the early Church, the term "martyr" included not only those who died for the faith, but also those who were imprisoned or underwent other suffering (e.g., torture) for the faith.
62. Cf. HE 6,42,5f: Schwarz, 260f: αὐτοὶ τοινὺν οἱ θεῖοι μάρτυρ-

Clearly, Dionysius shows a sympathetic leaning toward the action taken by the community under his charge. No clash develops between him and the martyrs, who, however, were more selective in Alexandria than elsewhere at this time. For instance, Cyprian felt it necessary to raise his voice in rebuke against the martyrs in North Africa for their indiscretion when issuing their letters of recommendation. It is thus clear that the penitential discipline of the third century, especially in the East where the modern distinction between mortal and venial sin was unknown, was very flexible when pastoral needs demanded.[63] Moreover, the practice of immediate readmittance to full communion showed that the importance or function of penance was considered a relative matter.

Apparently, Fabius of Antioch felt equally sympathetic about the readmission of apostates; for, in a letter to Dionysius (HE 6, 43,44,2-6), he recounts an incident wherein Serapion, an apostate

---

ες παρ' ἡμῖν, οἱ νῦν τοῦ Χριστοῦ πάρεδροι καὶ τῆς βασιλείας αὐτοῦ κοινωνοὶ καὶ μέτοχοι τῆς κρίσεως αὐτοῦ καὶ συνδικάζοντες αὐτῷ, τῶν παραπεπτωκότων ἀδελφῶν τινας ὑπευθύνους τοῖς τῶν θυσιῶν ἐγκλήμασιν γενομένους προσελάβοντο, καὶ τὴν ἐπιστροφὴν καὶ μετάνοιαν αὐτῶν ἰδόντες δεκτήν τε γενέσθαι δυναμένην τῷ μὴ βουλομένῳ καθόλου τὸν θάνατον τοῦ ἁμαρτωλοῦ ὡς τὴν μετάνοιν δοκιμάσαντες, εἰσεδέξαντο καὶ συνήγαγον καὶ συνέστησαν καὶ προσευχῶν αὐτοῖς καὶ ἑστιάσεων ἐκοινώνησαν. τί οὖν ἡμῖν, ἀδελφοί, περὶ τούτων συμβουλεύετε; τί ἡμῖν πρακτέον; σύμψηφοι καὶ ὁμογνώμονες αὐτοῖς καταστῶμεν καὶ τὴν κρίσιν αὐτῶν καὶ τὴν χάριν φυλάξωμεν καὶ τοῖς ἐλεηθεῖσιν ὑπ' αὐτῶν χρηστευσώμεθα, ἢ τὴν κρίσιν αὐτῶν ἄδικον ποιησώμεθα καὶ δοκιμαστὰς αὐτοὺς τῆς ἐκείνων γνώμης ἐπιστήσωμεν καὶ τὴν χρηστότητα λυπήσωμεν καὶ τὴν τάξιν ἀνασκευάσωμεν;

63. The "great sins" of idolatry, apostasy, murder and adultery were the only offenses subjected to formal ecclesiastical discipline and which excluded one from the reception of communion. Cf. John Quinn, The Lord's Supper and Forgiveness of Sin, in: Worship 42 (1968) 289.

excommunicated for his religious defection during the persecution under Decius, is readmitted into the Church under unusual circumstances. In this case, the pastoral need and the role of the Eucharist are exceptionally obvious:

> There was a certain Serapion among us, an old man of faith, who lived blamelessly for a long time, but then fell in the trial. This man often besought (absolution), but no one heeded him; for he did, as a matter of fact, make the sacrifice. And, falling ill, he remained speechless and unconscious for three successive days. But on the fourth day, he rallied a bit, and, calling his grandson to him, he said: 'How long, my child, will ye refuse me? Haste ye, I beg, and grant me a speedy release. Do thou summon one of the presbyters for me.' And, after saying these things, he again became speechless. The boy ran to the presbyter; but it was night, and the latter was ill. Thus, on the one hand, he could not come; but on the other hand, since an order had been given by me that those who were departing from this life, if they requested it and especially if they had previously made supplication, should be absolved so that they might depart in hope, he gave the lad a small portion of the Eucharist, prescribing that he soak it and let it fall a drop at a time into the aged gentleman's mouth. The boy came back carrying it, and as he drew near--just before actually entering--, Serapion revived again and said: 'Hast thou come, child? Indeed, the presbyter could not come; but do thou quickly what he has directed and let me depart.' The lad soaked it and at once poured it into his mouth; and when he had swallowed a bit, he straightway gave up the spirit. Consequently, was it not plain that he was preserved and remained alive until he obtained release so that, with his sins blotted out, he might be acknowledged for all the good things he had done?[64]

---

64. Σεραπίων τις ἦν παρ' ἡμῖν, πιστὸς γέρων, ἀμέμπτων μὲν τὸν πολὺν διαβιώσας χρόνον, ἐν δὲ τῷ πειρασμῷ πεσών. οὗτος πολλάκις ἐδεῖτο, καὶ οὐδεὶς προσεῖχεν αὐτῷ· καὶ γὰρ ἐτεθύκει. ἐν νόσῳ δὲ γενόμενος, τριῶν ἑξῆς ἡμερῶν ἄφωνος καὶ ἀναίσθητος διετέλεσεν, βραχὺ δὲ ἀνασφήλας τῇ τετάρτῃ προσεκαλέσατο τὸν θυγατριδοῦν, καὶ "μέχρι με τίνος" φησίν "ὦ τέκνον, κατέχετε; δέομαι, σπεύσατε, καί με θᾶττον ἀπολύσατε, τῶν πρεσβυτέρων

This story demonstrates how the Bishop of Antioch considered admission to the Eucharist as the ultimate and real act of reconciliation; although, the formal reconciliation by way of hand-imposition has not yet been granted by the bishop. Such a formal reconciliation was apparently not considered essential, but was only a matter of discipline.[65] Finally, the story shows that excommunication was at least implicitly thought of in terms of one's relationship with the Eucharist since, when pastoral needs required it, the intermediate steps in the process of reconciliation could be passed by and the repentant party could be readmitted to the Church by way of the Eucharist rather than by the immediate intervention of the hierarchy.

The course which Dionysius and Fabius struck was indeed an enlightened pastoral practice in times that were often otherwise excessively rigid. But less enlightened was Dionysius' attitude toward the religious activity of women in their monthly period:

The question concerning women in the time of their separation--that is, whether it is proper for them to enter the

μοί τινα κάλεσον." καὶ ταῦτα εἰπών, πάλιν ἦν ἄφωνος. ἔδραμεν ὁ παῖς ἐπὶ τὸν πρεσβύτερον· νὺξ δὲ ἦν, κἀκεῖνος ἠσθένει. ἀφικέσθαι μὲν οὐκ ἐδυνήθη, ἐντολῆς δὲ ὑπ' ἐμοῦ δεδομένης τοὺς ἀπαλλάττομένους τοῦ βίου, εἰ δέοιντο, καὶ μάλιστα εἰ καὶ πρότερον ἱκετεύσαντες τύχοιεν, ἀφιέσθαι, ἵν' εὐέλπιδες ἀπαλλάττωνται, βραχὺ τῆς εὐχαριστίας ἔδωκεν τῷ παιδαρίῳ, ἀποβρέξαι κελεύσας καὶ τῷ πρεσβύτῃ κατὰ τοῦ στόματος ἐπιστάξαι. ἐπανῆκεν ὁ παῖς φέρων, ἐγγύς τε γενομένου, πρὶν εἰσελθεῖν, ἀνενέγκας πάλιν ὁ Σεραπίων "ἧκες" ἔφη "τέκνον; καὶ ὁ μὲν πρεσβύτερος ἐλθεῖν οὐκ ἠδυνήθη, σὺ δὲ ποίησον ταχέως τὸ προσταχθὲν καὶ ἀπάλλαττέ με." ἀπέβρεξεν ὁ παῖς καὶ ἅμα τε ἐνέχεεν τῷ στόματι καὶ μικρὸν ἐκεῖνος καταβροχθίσας εὐθέως ἀπέδωκεν τὸ πνεῦμα. ἆρ' οὐκ ἐναργῶς διετηρήθη καὶ παρέμεινεν, ἕως λυθῇ καὶ τῆς ἁμαρτίας ἐξαλειφθείσης ἐπὶ πολλοῖς οἷς ἔπραξεν καλοῖς ὁμολογηθῆναι δυνηθῇ; Cf. Schwarz, 266f.

65. Cf. B. Poschmann, op. cit., 278.

house of God when they are in such a condition--I consider a
superfluous inquiry. For I do not think that believing and
pious women will themselves be rash enough in such a condition either to approach the holy table or to touch the body
and blood of the Lord. For the woman who had the flow of
blood for 12 years and eagerly sought a cure did not touch
(the Lord) himself, but only the hem of his cloak, for the
sake of (obtaining) a cure (Mt 9,20 and par.). For, on the
one hand, to pray in whatever situation one may find himself,
and to be mindful of the Lord in accordance with one's disposition, and to present one's petitions to obtain help, are
completely irreprehensible. But on the other hand, the individual who is not entirely clean in soul and in body shall be
prevented from entering the Holy of Holies.[66]

The influence of Origen's allegorical method as applied to the
New Testament is obvious here in its effects on Dionysius.[67] However, he does not apply such elements of Old Testament legislation
with equal consistency and rigidity. In the case of what might be

---

66. Cf. Ep ad Basilides, c 2; Feltoe, 102f: Περὶ δὲ τῶν ἐν ἀφέδρῳ
    γυναικῶν, εἰ προσῆκεν αὐτὰς οὕτω διακειμένας εἰς τὸν οἶκον
    εἰσιέναι τοῦ θεοῦ, περιττὸν καὶ τὸ πυνθάνεσθαι νομίζω. οὐδὲ
    γὰρ αὐτὰς οἶμαι, πιστὰς οὔσας καὶ εὐλαβεῖς, τολμήσειν οὕτω
    διακειμένας ἢ τῇ τραπέζῃ τῇ ἁγίᾳ προσελθεῖν, ἢ τοῦ σώματος καὶ
    τοῦ αἵματος τοῦ χριστοῦ προσάψασθαι. οὐδὲ γὰρ ἡ τὴν δωδεκαετῆ
    ῥύσιν ἔχουσα πρὸς τὴν ἴασιν σπεύδουσα ἔθιγεν αὐτοῦ, ἀλλὰ μόνου
    τοῦ κρασπέδου. προσεύχεσθαι μὲν γὰρ ὅπως ἂν ἔχῃ τις, καί,
    ὡς ἂν διάκειται, μεμνῆσθαι τοῦ δεσπότου, καὶ δεῖσθαι βοηθείας
    τυχεῖν, ἀνεπίφθονον· εἰς δὲ τὰ ἅγια καὶ τὰ ἅγια τῶν ἁγίων ὁ
    μὴ πάντη καθαρὸς καὶ ψυχῇ καὶ σώματι προσιέναι κωλυθήσεται.

67. It is quite possible that Dionysius misunderstood Origen's in-
    terpretation of Mt 9,20 and Mk 5,27. In in Lv hom 4,8, Origen
    says that the woman did not dare touch Christ himself because
    she had not yet been cleansed ("nondum enim mundata fuerat").
    However, in touching his garment, she is cleansed because her
    faith drew sanctifying virtue from Christ's flesh. By this,
    Origen means that faith and the cleansing action of Baptism
    are prerequisite to the reception of the Eucharist. Cf. A.
    Struckmann, op. cit., 188-90.

considered the analogous situation for men--that is, nocturnal emissions--, he does not accept the view of the Old Testament that this automatically renders one impure (Lv 15,16; Dt 23,11; 1 Sm 20,26). Rather this matter should be settled within the person's own conscience:

> Let those who are overtaken by an involuntary flux at night follow the testimony of their own conscience, and judge for themselves whether or not they have doubts in this matter. And (Paul) tells us that he who doubts in the matter of meats 'is damned if he eats' (Rm 14,23). In these matters, therefore, let everyone who approaches God be of good conscience and of proper confidence so far as his own judgment is concerned.[68]

The treatment of Dionysius' theological position in regard to eucharistic discipline is not complete without an investigation of his contribution in the baptismal controversy between Pope Stephen and the North African church. However, this material is best considered in the chapter on Cyprian, where Dionysius' position can be seen in its proper context.[69]

---

68. Cf. *Ep* *ad* *Basilides*, c 4; *Feltoe*, 104: Οἱ δὲ ἐν ἀπροαιρέτῳ νυκτερινῇ ῥύσει γενόμενοι, καὶ οὗτοι τῷ ἰδίῳ συνειδότι κατακολουθησάτωσαν, καὶ ἑαυτούς, εἴτε διακρίνονται περὶ τούτου εἴτε μή, σκοπείτωσαν. ὡς ἐπὶ τῶν βρωμάτων ὁ "διακρινόμενός," φησιν, "ἐὰν φάγῃ, κατακέκριται," καὶ ἐν τούτοις εὐσυνείδητος ἔστω καὶ εὐπαρρησίαστος κατὰ τὸ ἴδιον ἐνθύμιον πᾶς ὁ προσιὼν τῷ θεῷ.

69. At this point, a word should be said about another of Origen's students--namely, Gregory Thaumaturgus (died c. 270), whose *epistola* *canonica* addressed to an unknown bishop offers some important facts concerning penitential discipline as practiced during Gregory's time. However, there are some doubts concerning the letter's authenticity. Canons 5 and 8f indicate that certain offenders are to be excluded from prayer and included in a determined order of penitents. In canon 11, several types or "orders" of penitents are described: 1. the "weeping" who stand outside of the church door to ask the prayers of those who enter, 2. the "listening" who stand with-

in the portico and leave the with the catechumens, 3. the
"kneeling" or "prostrating" are permitted to enter the door,
but must likewise leave with the catechumens, 4. the "standing" remain with the faithful throughout the service, but may
not partake of the Eucharist. Cf. MG 10, 1048; G. D'Ercole,
Penitenza, 85f. The authenticity of this canon, however, is
even more doubtful than for the rest of the letter. Cf. MG
10, 967f.

CHAPTER THIRTEEN

THE DIDASCALIA APOSTOLORUM

1. The Anti-Judaizing Program

Written probably by a Jewish Christian Bishop for a North
Syrian church sometime during the third century,[1] the Didascalia
is modelled to some extent on the Didache, borrows from several
sources including possibly the Pastor Hermae and Irenaeus, and
forms the basis of the first six chapters of the Apostolic Constitutions (c 380). The original Greek text has been lost;[2] however,
the work has been preserved in a Syriac translation and some Latin
fragments. The main motive of the document, which attempts to
give the impression that it is a direct recording of Apostolic

---

1. A. von Harnack (Geschichte der altchristlichen Literatur bis
   Eusebius, 2/2, 490f) feels that the treatment which Didasc 6
   (cf. note 5 below on the method of citation) prescribes for
   serious sinners could not have been written before the Novatian controversy in the latter half of the 3rd century. Therefore, he dates the document--or at least the penitential pas-
   sages--within the latter 50 years of the 3rd century. However,
   it appears that the author of the Didascalia wrote his work,
   including the penitential sections, exclusively for the North
   Syrian Church and did not have a sect in mind. Thus, it is
   more probable that it was written during the first half of the
   3rd century. Cf. R. Hugh Connolly, Didascalia Apostolorum,
   the Syriac Version Translated and Accompanied by the Verona
   Latin Fragments, (Oxford, 1929) xxxvii, whose translation is
   used in this study.

2. F. X. Funk, Didascalia et Constitutiones Apostolorum, 1,
   (Paderborn, 1905), attempts a reconstruction of the Greek text.
   text. However, his main purpose is to reproduce the original
   Greek text of the Apostolic Constitutions with the help of
   the Didascalia. To this end, Funk's Greek rendition of the
   Didascalia is good, but it does not necessarily represent an
   accurate reconstruction of the original document as such.

instructions, is to supply "an elementary treatise on Pastoral Theology,"[3] especially in the face of the confusion created in the Church by heresies, schisms and "neo-Judaizing" tendencies. The author of the Didascalia felt called upon to defend the Old Testament against the Gnostic heretics on the one side, but at the same time, he must somehow "devaluate" the Old Legislation so as to counteract the latest attempts to Judaize the Church. Caught in this dilemma, the writer seeks to solve the problem by resorting to compromise. Accordingly, he gives special prominence to the Law and the Prophets apart from the ceremonial ordinances and the like, which he refers to as the "second legislation" (δευτέρωσις). This is the law which the prophets rejected and which Christ abolished by fulfilling the Law itself.

Besides the distinction between the "pure Law" (i.e., the Decalogue and the precepts preceding the Israelite worship of the golden calf) and the Deuterosis--which was not part of God's original plan, but was imposed upon the Jews as a sort of punishment for their sin of idolatry--, the author also interprets certain elements of the Old Law to be merely figures of spiritual and better things to come. However, a clear division of the above defined categories is not easily made.[4]

The Christian, since he has been liberated by Jesus Christ, must not take up the burdens of the Old Law again. Rather, he should content himself in reading the "simple Law," the Gospel, the Prophets and the Book(s) of Kings for the sake of encouraging his growth in the faith and of improving his personal life.[5]

---

3. Cf. R. H. Connolly, Didascalia, xxvii.
4. Cf. ibid., lvii-lxxv for a fuller treatment of the Didascalia's use of the Old Testament.
5. Cf. Didasc 2 (Connolly, 14,20-23;11,16-18; Funk, i 5f). The

But whoever subjects himself to the "second legislation" shares
in the Israelite guilt for idolatry toward the golden calf. Moreover, such a person calls down God's wrath upon himself in as much
as he asserts the curse of the _Deuterosis_ against the Saviour and
thus becomes the enemy of God. In addition to that, he also calls
down the curse of the Law upon himself since the Jews, who are under gentile rule, cannot carry out all the prescriptions of the
second legislation and therefore, according to Dt 27,26 (cf. also
Gal 3,10), come under the curse and condemnation of the Law (26,
233,2-6, 240,1-4; vi 18f).

Obviously, the author of the _Didascalia_, unlike many previous
Christian writers, finds the tendency toward Judaization to be
such a vexing and dangerous problem, that he is unable to consider even a pious and peaceful observation of the _Deuterosis_ in
whole or in part as a merely neutral practice that could at least
be tolerated in the Church. The reason for this uncompromising
attitude is not that the writer is anti-Jewish--for he is not
that--, but rather it is due to his immediate pastoral problems.
He readily sees that the observation of the second legislation
contains an implicit annulment of the effects of Baptism and the
Holy Spirit within the Christian. For example, this legislation

---

exact location of all cited texts is given according to Connolly, who has followed the chapter divisions established by
H. Achelis and J. Flemming, _Die Syrische Didascalia_, (_TU_),
(Leipzig, 1940). The general location is given in _Funk_ to
facilitate anyone's wanting to see what the probable Greek
construction of the text originally was. To simplify the
method of citation, the present writer has chosen to give
Connolly's location first, followed by Funk's. Thus, the
above citation, written in this manner, appears as (2, 14,20-
23;11,16-18; 1 5f).

includes, among other things, the prescription that sexual intercourse in marriage or the menstruation of a woman requires one's
temporary withdrawal from certain religious practices and associations. The author thus remarks:

> Let them tell us, in what days or in what hours they keep
> themselves from prayer and from receiving the Eucharist, or
> from reading the Scriptures--let them tell us whether they are
> void of the Holy Spirit. For through baptism they receive the
> Holy Spirit, who is ever with those that work righteousness,
> and does not depart from them by reason of natural issues and
> the intercourse of marriage, but is ever and always with those
> who possess Him, and keeps them (26, 242,11-19; vi 21).

That the author does not present this as a mere hypothetically
logical conclusion becomes quickly evident. He has actual cases
of such needless, self-imposed abstinence from religious functions
in mind. He continues:

> For if thou think, O woman, that in the seven days of thy
> flux thou art void of the Holy Spirit; if thou die in those
> days, thou wilt depart empty and without hope. But if the
> Holy Spirit is always with thee, without (just) impediment
> dost thou keep thyself from prayer and from the Scriptures
> and from the Eucharist. For consider and see, that prayer
> also is heard through the Holy Spirit, and the Eucharist
> through the Holy Spirit is accepted and sanctified, and the
> the Scriptures are the words of the Holy Spirit, and are holy.
> For if the Holy Spirit is in thee, why dost thou keep thyself
> from approaching the works of the Holy Spirit? (26, 244,3-13;
> vi 21)

Whether or not one is "clean" and properly disposed to partake
of the Eucharist or to perform other religious functions depends
on whether or not one has the Holy Spirit, whom the Christian receives through Baptism and retains as long as he continues in good
works. The heathen, on the other hand, are filled with unclean
spirits and their works only _appear_ at most to be good works. One
is either filled with unclean spirits, or else one is filled by
the Holy Spirit through Baptism and can give no room to evil spir-

its as long as no serious sin has been committed. But it is precisely for this reason that the author is so concerned about those
who want to observe the Deuterosis:

> Thou then, O woman, according as thou sayest, if in the
> days of thy flux thou art void, thou shalt be filled with un-
> clean spirits. For when the unclean spirit returns to thee
> and finds him a place, he will enter and dwell in thee always
> (Mt 12,43-45): and then will there be entering in of the un-
> clean spirit and going forth of the Holy Spirit, and perpetual
> warfare. Wherefore, O foolish (women), these misfortunes be-
> fall you because of your imaginings; and because of the obser-
> vances which you keep, and on account of your imaginings, you
> are emptied of the Holy Spirit and filled with unclean spirits:
> and you are cast out from life into the burning of everlasting
> fire. But again I will say to thee, O woman: In the seven
> days of thy flux thou accountest thyself unclean according to
> the Second Legislation: after seven days, therefore, how canst
> thou be cleansed without baptism? But if thou be baptized for
> that which thou supposest, thou wilt undo the perfect baptism
> of God which wholly forgave thee thy sins, and wilt be found
> in the evil plight of thy former sins; and thou shalt be de-
> livered over to eternal fire. But if thou be not baptized,
> according to thy own supposition thou remainest unclean, and
> the vain observing of the seven days has availed thee nothing,
> but is rather hurtful to thee; for according to thy supposi-
> tion thou art unclean, and as unclean thou shalt be condemned
> (26, 246,29-248,23; vi 21).

The writer then explains how, if the observers of the Second
Legislation were fully logical, they would have to be constantly
washing their clothes and couches and be wary of stepping on a
mouse or a bone and so on. To emphasize the fact that such external things do not make one unclean, the author orders that his
Christian readers gather even in the cemeteries to celebrate the
Eucharist:

> But do you, according to the Gospel and according to the
> power of the Holy Spirit, come together even in the cemeteries,
> and read the holy Scriptures, and without demur perform your
> ministry and your supplication to God; and offer an acceptable
> Eucharist, the likeness of the royal body of Christ, both in

your congregations and in your cemeteries and on the depar-
tures of them that sleep--pure bread that is made with fire
and sanctified with invocations--and without doubting pray
and offer for them that are fallen asleep...And Elisha the
prophet also, after he had slept and was a long while (dead),
raised up a dead man (2 Kgs 13,21); for his body touched the
body of the dead and quickened and raised it up. But this
could not have been were it not that, even when he was fallen
asleep, his body was holy and filled with the Holy Spirit.

For this cause therefore do you approach without restraint
to those who are at rest, and hold them not unclean. In like
manner also you shall not separate those (women) who are in
the wonted courses; for she also who had the flow of blood was
not chidden when she touched the skirt of our Saviour's cloak,
but was even vouchsafed the forgiveness of all her sins.[6]

To explain the source of the difficulties which the Church
faces in trying to eliminate nonorthodox elements, the author of
the _Didascalia_ places the blame upon Satan, who has now left the
Jews and has gone to the Church to stir up troubles, heresies and
schisms (23, 200-02; vi 7f). The schismatic and his followers are
to be avoided like fire, for they will inherit the fire that God
brought upon Korah, Dathan and Abiram and their followers (23,
194,7-16;196,5-13; 197,19-21; vi 1 and 3-5):

But as for heresies, be unwilling even to hear their names,
and defile not your ears (with them); for not only do they in
no wise glorify God, but they verily blaspheme[7] against Him.
Wherefore, the heathen are judged because they have not known,

---

6. Cf. _Didasc_ 26, 252,6-15.20-254,5; vi 22. Perhaps Dionysius of
Alexandria was purposely trying to rebutt this argument when
he insisted on pointing out and emphasizing that the woman in
Mt 9,20-22 only touched Christ's cloak. Cf. the end of the
previous chapter. This may be an indication that the _Didasca-
lia_ predates Dionysius' _Letter to Basilides_.

7. J. Grotz (_op. cit._, 376) defines the blasphemers meant by the
Didascalia as those "welche 'endgültig' abgefallen sind."

but the heretics are condemned because they withstand God
(23, 197,22-27; vi 5).

At the eucharist assembly, a deacon is to stand by the door
and guard against the entrance of any heretics:

> But if any brother or sister come from another congrega-
> tion, let the deacon question her and learn whether she is
> married, or again whether she is a widow (who is) a believer;
> and whether she is a daughter of the Church, or belongs per-
> chance to one of the heresies; and then let him conduct her
> and set her in a place that is suitable for her (12, 120,28-
> 33; ii 58).

Here, the author assumes that the interrogated party is found
to be orthodox. Unfortunately, he does not describe the procedure
to be taken if the person proves to hold unorthodox beliefs. But,
if the Didascalia is older than Tertullian, then this reference,
which is undoubtedly implied, that certain apparently heterodox
elements must be kept from entering into the eucharistic assembly
of "orthodox" Christians is the earliest witness that baptized
persons were to be actively excluded from the eucharistic worship
of the Church if they proved to be "nonorthodox" in faith. Although such excommunication--including the explicit reference to
the Eucharist--may not have been radically new at the time of the
Didascalia's composition, it cannot be said a priori that this
was not a new procedure for the intended readers of this work.
If Walter Bauer's[8] thesis that the original representatives of
Christianity in many areas sprang from heretical sects has any
validity at all (and this can scarcely be doubted), then it may
very well be that the Didascalia is only giving witness to the
fact that a group of Christians of some North Syrian community
has, with the development of a strong episcopacy, finally taken

---

8. Op. cit.

the upper hand over the opponents and is able to exclude them from its ecclesial gatherings.[9] The apocryphal nature of the Didasca-lia Apostolorum may itself be a strong indication that this was actually the case. That is, as W. Bauer more or less convincingly shows throughout his book, apocryphal works were often employed or even composed by bishops in order to add weight to their claims that their teachings, in contrast to other teachings of the area, can be traced back to the Apostles themselves and are, consequently the exclusively valid (orthodox) doctrines of the Church.

2. Christian Ethics and Discipline

a. The treatment of sinners.

Besides Judaizers, schismatics and heretics, there is still another category of "questionable Christian" that the author of the Didascalia treats--namely, the serious sinner and his relation-ship to the Church. The writer is not a rigorist, and he is aware of the fact that all men are sinners (7, 55,13-56,1; ii 18). How-ever, this does not free the Christian from the obligation of achieving and maintaining certain ethical standards. "For if any man run after iniquity and be contrary to the will of God, the same shall be accounted unto God as heathen and ungodly" (1, 15-17; i 1). As a consequence, Christians are not permitted to at-tend the amusements of the pagans; for, in doing so, they with-draw themselves from the assembly of the Church and are therefore to be accounted as heathens (13, 127,12-128,23; ii 61f). On the other hand, there are those who withdraw from the Church simply

---

9.   Cf. what Georg Stecker has to say in his appendix to Walter
     Bauer's work (op. cit., 248f).

out of neglect and lack of concern for spiritual things. Such persons are even worse than the Jews and heathen gentiles, who are most diligent in keeping their religious observances and assemblies even though they profit to nothing (13, 126,25-31; ii 60).

A Christian who has been found blameworthy is to be handled according to the prescriptions of the Gospel. At first, a private admonition should be given, and then, if that is of no avail, two or three witnesses are to attend the next admonition. If the offender still does not repent, he is to be reproved before the whole assembly. And if he still does not obey, then he is to be treated as a "heathen and a publican":[10]

> For the Lord has commanded you, O bishops, that you should not henceforth receive such a one into the Church as a Christian, nor communicate with him. For neither dost thou receive the evil heathen or publicans into the Church and communicate with them except they first repent, professing that they believe and henceforth will do no more evil works: for to this end did our Lord and Saviour grant a place for repentance to those who have sinned (10, 102,24-103,5; ii 38).

Whoever has been exposed as an evildoer, but remains unrepentant, is to be considered a liar rather than a Christian and is to be avoided (5, 38,19-23; ii 8). Even the gifts for the support of the Church from such persons should be sternly and completely refused lest the beneficiaries be deceived into offering prayers for some hypocrite who refuses to repent. It would be better for the various communities of Christians to starve in poverty than to allow themselves to be supported in this manner (18, 159,9-31; iv 7).

---

10. Cf. Didasc 10, 102,9-24; ii 38; Mt 18,15-17; Lk 17,3; Dt 19, 15. Cf. also Didasc 5, 38,19-23; ii 8, where the author explains that the Christian refusal to mix and communicate with the pagans arouses the latter to hatred and blasphemy towards Christians. Thus, the Didascalia attests to the fact that Christians did actually make an effort to avoid pagans in normal life.

On the other hand, the Christian community should not hesitate to receive a repentant sinner back into the fold. In giving this instruction, the author of the Didascalia knowingly and intentionally sets himself up against the rigorists who would wish to prevent the reacceptance of a sinner for fear that such a person would somehow defile the others.[11] The writer rebuts their naive argument by pointing out that God will not kill the sons on account of the sins of the father, and vice versa (Dt 24,16). In fact, a sinful and wicked nation will be spared if only a few righteous men are found there (Ez 14,12-14). Nor did Judas bring any sort of harm upon the other Apostles even though they prayed together with him (6, 43,9-44,2). However, the reacceptance of the repentant is to be accomplished through a prescribed penitential system consisting of several stages, which the Didascalia describes as follows:

---

11. The author is, however, not fully consistent in such matters since he also believes that sinners "stain" the Church. At any rate, the Church must at least expel certain sinners so that she might remain unstained. Cf. Karl Rahner, Busslehre und Busspraxis der Didascalia Apostolorum, in: ZKT 72 (1950) 259. The Didascalia, because it does not accept the western practice of a single paenitentia secunda, can "afford" to consider a greater number of sins as serious enough to warrant one's excommunication from the Church. Ibid., 260f, 268-72, 275f, 278-80. Excommunication shuts one out from salvation until he is again reconciled with the Church. Again, however, the author is inconsistent in that he at one time holds that an unjust excommunication has no validity in God's view, and, on the other hand, he warns the bishop that an unjust excommunication that is not followed by reconciliation does more damage to the excommunicated person than the murder of a just person can cause; for even an unjust excommunication can cast the expelled person into hell. Ibid., 266f.

'As a heathen,' then, 'and as a publican let him be accounted by you' (Mt 18,17) who has been convicted of evil deeds and falsehood; and afterwards, if he promise to repent--even as when the heathen desire and promise to repent, and say 'We believe,' we receive them into the congregation that they may hear the word, but do not communicate with them until they receive the seal and are fully initiated: so neither do we communicate with these until they show the fruits of repentance. But let them by all means come in, if they desire to hear the word, that they may not wholly perish; but let them not communicate in prayer, but go forth without. For they also, when they have seen that they do not communicate with the Church, will submit themselves, and repent of their former works, and strive to be received into the Church for prayer; and they likewise who see and hear them go forth like the heathen and publicans, will fear and take warning to themselves not to sin, lest it so happen to them also, and being convicted of sin or falsehood they be put forth from the Church.

But thou shalt by no means forbid them to enter the Church and hear the word, O bishop; for neither did our Lord and Saviour utterly thrust away and reject publicans and sinners, but did even eat with them. And for this cause, the Pharisees murmured against Him, and said: 'He eateth with publicans and sinners.' Then did our saviour make answer against their thoughts and their murmuring, and say: 'They that are whole have no need of a physician, but they that are sick' (Mk 2,16f and pars.). Do you therefore consort with those who have been convicted of sins and are sick, and attach them to you, and be careful of them, and speak to them and comfort them, and keep hold of them and convert them. And afterwards, as each one of them repents and shows the fruits of repentance, receive him to prayer after the manner of a heathen. And as thou baptizest a heathen and then receivest him, so also lay hand upon this man, whilst all pray for him, and then bring him in and let him communicate with the Church. For the imposition of hand shall be to him in the place of baptism: for whether by the imposition of hand, or by baptism, they receive the communication of the Holy Spirit (10, 103,19-104,26; ii 39-41).

It is apparent that excommunication is in the process of taking on a special reference to the Church's eucharistic worship; whereas, excommunication from the Church as such no longer is interpreted as complete exclusion from all ecclesial activity. This growing awareness of the role of the Eucharist in cases of excommunication receives still further development in the <u>Didascalia</u>. However, it must be kept in mind that the author does not introduce anything radically new, but only wishes to apply the principles already laid down in the New Testament writings.

<u>b</u>. The <u>settlement</u> <u>of</u> <u>quarrels</u>.

When a quarrel arises between two "parties"--for they are not called "brothers" until peace has been restored between them (11, 112,26f; ii 49)--, and they insist upon taking the matter to court, they are to bring their differences before the bishop for judgment rather than to air their disagreements in the courts of pagans (11, 109,19-110,10; ii 45f). The process before the bishop should begin on Monday so that there may be the greatest possibility of a settlement and reconciliation between the quarreling parties by the time of the next eucharistic gathering of the faithful on the following Sunday (11, 111,16-20; ii 47). In order to insure the acceptability of the congregation's oblations and prayers, the bishop should take care that the deacon asks with a loud voice in church: "Is there any man that keepeth aught against his fellow?" (11, 117,14f; ii 54) At this, those with quarrels should, through the bishop's entreaty, make peace with each other. The implication would seem to be that those who still refused to come to terms would also be refused the right to remain in the assembly for prayers and the Eucharist:

> He who is contentious, or makes himself an enemy to his neighbor, diminishes the people of God. For either he drives out of the Church him whom he accuses, and diminishes her and deprives God of the soul of a man which was being saved, or by his contention he expels and ejects himself from the Church, and so again he sins against God...Wherefore thou art no help-

er with God for the gathering together of the people, because thou art a disturber and a scatterer of the flock, and an adversary and enemy of God. Be not therefore forever embroiled in contentions and quarrels, or wrangling, or enmity, or lawsuits, lest thou scatter someone from the Church (11, 118, 11-24; ii 56).

If someone keeps his quarrel secret and refuses to make peace, his prayers and Eucharist will prove unacceptable. This is the reason why Mt 5,23f requests that one leave his gift before the altar and go first to be reconciled to his brother before returning to offer his gift.

Now the gift of God is our prayer and our Eucharist. If then thou keep any malice against they brother, or he against thee, thy prayer is not heard and thy Eucharist is not accepted; and thou shalt be void (both) of prayer and Eucharist by reason of the anger thou keepest (11, 116,15-19; ii 53).

Such as are contentious and ever bringing accusations against others, either falsely or truly, should be given to know "that everyone who searches out such things for the purpose of accusing or slandering any man, is a son of wrath: and where wrath is, God is not; for wrath is of Satan, and through these false brethren he never suffers peace to be in the Church" (10, 101,22-102,3; ii 37). Terminology such as "sons of wrath" and "false brethern" may be used here somewhat rhetorically, but the indication is that the author really does not consider such persons to be rightful members of the Church.

c. The theology and purpose of excommunication.

The theological basis upon which the Didascalia builds its practice of excommunication is in the complete incompatibility of sin with the Christian's baptismal purity:

For we believe not, brethern, that when a man has (once) gone down into the water he will do again the abominable and filthy works of the ungodly heathen. For this is manifest and known to all, that whosoever does evil after baptism, the same is already condemned to the Gehenna of fire (5, 38,2-7; ii 7).

This, however, is not to be construed to mean that every failing of a Christian is of such a serious nature or that the condemnation is so binding that the sinner can no longer escape even if he repents.

In the case of a serious offense, the excommunication that is imposed is meant to serve a twofold purpose: to move the sinner to repentance, and to preserve the purity of the rest of the community:

> But if he who sins sees that the bishop and the deacons are clear of reproach, and the whole flock pure: first of all he will not dare to enter the congregation, because he is reproved by his conscience; but if it should happen that he is bold and comes to the Church in his arrogance, and he is reproved and rebuked by the bishop, and looking upon all (present) finds no offence in any of them, neither in the bishop nor in those who are with him: he will then be put to confusion, and will go forth quietly, in great shame, weeping and in remorse of soul; and so shall the flock remain pure. Moreover, when he is gone out he will repent of his sin and weep and sigh before God, and there shall be hope for him. And the whole flock itself also, when it sees the weeping and tears of that man, will fear, knowing and understanding that everyone who sins perishes (5, 40,5-19; ii 10; cf. also 11, 113,22-27; ii 49; 11, 114,5-12; ii 50).

However, the treatment that heretics receive--that is, avoidance--is aimed first of all at the preservation of the purity of the Church:

> Do you therefore avoid all heretics, who follow not the Law and the Prophets, and obey not Almighty God, but are His enemies; and who abstain from meats, and forbid to marry, and believe not in the resurrection of the body; who moreover will not eat and drink, but would fain rise up demons, unsubstantial spirits, who shall be damned everlastingly and punished in unquenchable fire. Fly and avoid them, therefore, that you may not perish with them (26, 240,22-242,5; vi 20).

If normal daily associations with the expelled are to be avoided, then certainly all forms of communicatio in sacris are a fortiori forbidden. This is made amply clear by the author of the Didascalia, but his motives are for the best pastoral reasons that his situation can afford:

> Now whosoever prays or communicates with one that is ex-pelled from the Church, must rightly be reckoned with him; for these things lead to the undoing and destruction of souls. For if one communicate and pray with him who is expelled from the Church, and obey not the bishop, he obeys not God; and he is defiled with him (that is expelled). And moreover he suf-fers not that man to repent. For if no one communicate with him, he will feel compunction and weep, and will ask and be-seech to be received (again); and he will repent of what he has done, and will be saved (15, 140,25-34; iii 8).

As regards those Christians who have been imprisoned by the state for some crime such as theft or murder, other Christians are to avoid visiting with them in prison even though the greatest of concern and care for the imprisoned brethren should normally be given. In this case, however, the reason for the avoidance is not so much for the sake of shunning sinners, but rather to forestall the possibility that the visiting Christian might fall into a trap of having to confess that he is "like that man"--that is, a Christ-ian. However, the state may then understand the visitor's affirma-tive reply to mean that he is a thief or a murderer "like that man," and thus imprison the visitor on false charges. Or else, if the visitor responds negatively to the question, "Are you like that man?", then there is the danger that he will be understood as denying that he is a Christian. However, the Christian should not hesitate to visit and comfort those of the brotherhood who have been "violently and unjustly" thrown into prison (19, 162,20-163, 5; v 2).

It is already clear from many of the aforesaid facts that the Didascalia knows of and advocates temporary excommunication that

can be imposed with various degrees of severity. Likewise, reconciliation is generally achieved by several steps including
fasting and acts of humiliation (6, 52,10-53,13; ii 16).

> And when he that sinned has repented and wept, receive
> him (O bishop); and while the whole people prays over him,
> lay hands upon him, and suffer him henceforth to be in the
> Church (7, 56,13-17; ii 18).

Formal excommunication itself should only be undertaken as a
last resort--like the amputation of a limb infested with gangrene:

> But if the gangrene assert itself and prevail even over
> the burnings, give judgment; and then, whichever member it be
> that is putrified, with advice and much consultation with
> other physicians, cut off the putrified member, that it may
> not corrupt the whole body. Yet be not ready to amputate
> straightway, and be not in haste to have recourse at once to
> the saw of many teeth; but use first the knife and cut the
> sore, that it may be clearly seen, and that it may be known
> what is the cause of the disease that is hidden within; so
> that the whole body may be kept uninjured. But if thou see
> that a man will not repent but has altogether abandoned him-
> self, then with grief and sorrow cut him off and cast him
> out of the Church (10, 105,8-20; ii 41).

This is not to be construed immediately as permanent excommunication. Nevertheless, the author seems to prescribe a more or
less permanent excommunication in the case of someone, who after
having been once excommunicated and then reconciled, relapses
again. At least, this appears to be the case of someone expelled
a second time from the Church for attempting to bring false charges against his fellow Christians:

> If then he is found to be such (i.e., a maker of false
> charges), expel him from the Church with great denunciation
> as a murderer; and after a time, if he promise to repent,
> warn him and correct him sternly; and then lay hands upon him
> and receive him into the Church. And be wary and guard such
> a one, that he no more disturb any other. But if, after he
> is come in, you see that he is still contentious and minded to
> accuse others also, and mischievous and designing, and making

false complaints against many: drive him out, that he may no further disturb and trouble the Church. For such a one, though he be within, yet because he is unseemly to the Church, he is superfluous to her, and there is no profit in him. For we see that there are some men born with superfluous members to their bodies, as fingers or other excessive flesh; but these, though they pertain to the body, are a reproach and a disgrace both to the body and to the man, because they are superfluous to him. Yet when they are removed by the surgeon, that man recovers the comeliness and beauty of his body; and he suffers no defect by the removal from it of that which is superfluous, but is even the more conspicuous in his beauty... For when he has gone forth twice from the Church, he is justly cut off; and the Church is more beautiful in her proper form, forasmuch as peace has been restored to her, which (before) was wanting to her; for from that hour the Church remains free from blasphemy and disorder (10, 106,28-107,20;108,7-12; ii 43).

d. Heresy and repentance.

Whether or not the <u>Didascalia</u> intends this form of excommunication to be applied to other types of relapsed sinners in the Church is not directly indicated, unless, perhaps, in the case of heretics. In this regard, the author places the following words in the mouths of the Apostles:

Now let those who have not erred, and those also who repent of their error, be left in the Church. But as for those who are still held fast in error and repent not, we have decreed and enjoined that they be put forth from the Church and be separated and removed from the faithful, because they are become heretics; and that the faithful be commanded wholly to avoid them, and not to communicate with them either in speech or in prayer (25, 210,19-26; vi 14).

It seems to be the nonrelenting position that a person takes in regard to doctrinal error rather than the error itself that classifies one as a heretic. It is in regard to this category of sinners that the <u>Didascalia</u> comes closest to affirming anything like a "sin unto death" which cannot be forgiven since it constitutes blasphemy against the Holy Spirit:

But those who blaspheme God Almighty, those heretics who receive not His holy Scriptures, or receive them ill, in hypocrisy with blaspheming, who with evil words blaspheme the Catholic Church which is the receptacle of the Holy Spirit: it is they who, before the judgment to come and before ever they can make a defence, are already condemned by Christ. For that which he said, 'It shall not be forgiven them' (Mt 12,31f), is the stern sentence of condemnation which goes forth for them (25, 212,27-214,4; vi 14).

Clearly, the worst offense is the refusal to repent of some wrong. The possibility of sincere heretics was not generally a subject for speculation among the Church Fathers--or even throughout most of the Church's history. The author of the Didascalia apparently feels that convinced heretics are really hypocrites. Yet, even if such persons should happen to repent, it is probable that they would have been reaccepted into the Church; for the Didascalia calls idolatry the worst sin, and yet it can also be forgiven:

You have heard, beloved children, how Manasseh served idols evilly and bitterly, and slew righteous men; yet when he repented God forgave him, albeit there is no sin worse than idolatry. Wherefore, there is granted a place for repentance (7, 74,15-19; ii 23).

Apparently, the author of the Didascalia sets no time limit within a person's lifetime for repentance. However, since no one knows the number of his days, he should not put off repenting; for, in Sheol, no one confesses God (Ps 6,6)--which the Didascalia interprets to mean that there is no more opportunity after death for repentance (6, 42,17-22; ii 13).

Because the author finds repentance a real possibility, he warns the bishop not to be unduly harsh in correcting sinners; and above all, not to hide the doctrine of repentance from them. To do so is to run the risk of making the evil only worse by en-

couraging offenders to go over to the heresies.[12] It is for this
reason, then, that he is so eager to give the sinner the opportunity to repent and be reconciled with the Church. Thus, he says
to the bishop:

> If thou deal harshly with thy lay fold, and correct them
> 'with force,' and thrust and drive out and receive not (back)
> them that sin, but harshly and without mercy hide away repen-
> tance from them, and become a helper for the return of evil,
> and for the scattering of the flock 'for meat of the beasts
> of the field' (Ez 34,5), that is, to evil men of this world:
> nay, not to men in truth, but to beasts, to the heathen and
> to heretics. For to him who goes forth from the Church they
> presently join themselves, and like evil beasts devour him as
> meat. And by reason of thy harshness, he who goes forth from
> the Church will either depart and enter among the heathen, or
> will be sunk in the heresies; and he will become alien alto-
> gether, and will depart from the Church and from the hope of
> God (7, 64,22-66,4; ii 21).

The bishop who refuses to reaccept a repentant sinner, likewise becomes a sinner (7, 76,11-18; ii 24). Rather, love is to be
the ultimate motive and norm for all the judgments which the bishop must make; for God will judge bishop and layman alike to see if
bishop has loved bishop and if layman has loved layman, and if the
bishop has loved his people and if the people have loved the bishop (7, 60,18-62,7; ii 19f).

Christians are to pray and intercede for the conversion of
all, especially of the Jews (21, 186,3-187,4; v 17). Out of
love, they are to fast and offer prayers for everyone's conversion
for the disobedience of the Jews has made it possible for the message of Christ to come to the gentiles (21, 184,16-31; v 14).
Finally, love and charity in contributing for the support of the

---

12. At this point, it becomes clear that the author is thinking in
    terms of the principle "extra ecclesiam nulla salus est."

visitors of a church is seen in the <u>Didascalia</u> as a special motive for coming to the eucharistic assembly:

> And not with the lips only shall you love the Lord, as
> did that People, to whom upbraiding them He saith: 'This
> people honoureth me with their lips, but their heart is very
> far from me' (Is 29,13; Mt 15,8); but do thou love and honour
> the Lord 'with all thy strength' (Mk 12,30; Lk 10,27; Dt 6,5),
> and offer His oblations ever at all times.
>
> And hold not aloof from the Church; but when thou hast re-
> ceived the Eucharist of the oblation, that which comes into
> thy hands cast (in), that thou mayest share it with strangers:
> for this is collected (and brought) to the bishop for the en-
> tertainment of all strangers (9, 100,16-25; ii 36).

In conclusion, it can be said that the <u>Didascalia</u> consciously
attacks rigoristic elements within the Church, and, inspired by a
real concern for Christian charity, proposes a reasonable approach
for dealing with the Church's imperfect members. In this context,
much is done to develop a penitential system that shows very well
some of the motives that eventually led to explicit eucharistic
excommunication.

CHAPTER FOURTEEN

CYPRIAN OF CARTHAGE

1. The Calm before the Storm

a. The historical background.

Born of pagan parents around the year 200, Cyprian became
Bishop of Carthage early in 249--perhaps within just three years
of his Baptism. In choosing him for their bishop, the Christians
of this Roman city gave themselves a spiritual leader of great
dignity and influence in regard to both his own personal abili-
ties and his family. However, he was also a man whom many senior
clerics considered an ecclesial upstart. Consequently, he had
to contend with an opposition party from the beginning of his
episcopacy (ep 43). The results of this situation will become
evident in the course of this chapter.[1]

The early days of the Carthaginian's bishopric were marked
only by the "routine" matters of his office; although, a percep-
tive eye could see the lowering clouds of persecution gathering
on the horizon. In April of 248, Rome began the celebration of
the millenium of its founding; and it was decreed that each citi-
zen of the empire prove his patriotism by making a formal and
public offering to the gods of Rome.[2] Lists were kept of those
who offered, and the offerer received in return a certificate

---

1. Due to the wealth of biographical information that can be
   gleaned from Cyprian's many works and letters, it is possible
   to develop this chapter chronologically and in direct connection with the events of the life of Cyprian and his contemporaries.

2. Cf. J. Ludwig, op. cit., 28. Most historians, however, point
   to the threat which enemies then presented to the Empire as
   the decisive factor behind Rome's decree demanding that all
   citizens and subjects of the Empire offer a sacrifice.

(<u>libellus</u>) as proof of his act. Those who refused to comply were to be imprisoned and put on trial for their "crime." Torture and even death was therefore the fate of many Christians. Others preferred to flee, either selling their property previous to flight or else simply allowing it to be confiscated by the state. But there were also thousands of Christians throughout the empire who either performed the prescribed sacrifice--thus earning the name "<u>sacrificati</u>"--or otherwise had themselves enrolled in the lists and acquired a <u>libellus</u> by various and devious means (e.g., through special friends and bribery) without ever actually making the sacrifice. But the Church did not appreciate their subterfuge, and the <u>libellatici</u>, as they were called, found themselves excluded from the Christian community along with the <u>sacrificati</u>. However, all this required time, and it was a matter of two or three years before all parts of the empire were affected by the decree. Hence, Cyprian had a brief period of peace at the beginning of his episcopacy, and during this time, he wrote several letters or works which are of interest to the present study.[3]

<u>b</u>. <u>Church</u> and <u>Eucharist</u>.

In a letter to the clergy and people of Furnos (some distance south-west from Carthage), the Bishop notes that Paul ordered Timothy not to become entangled in worldly matters (2 Tm 2,4); therefore, clerics should not get involved in certain secular

---

3. These works include the three <u>Testimonia</u> <u>ad</u> <u>Quirinum</u> and letters 1 through 4. The <u>de</u> <u>Oratione</u> <u>Dominica</u> is dated around 252 by P. Monceaux, <u>op</u>. <u>cit</u>., 258. However, Michel Réveillaud, <u>Saint</u> <u>Cyprian</u>, <u>L'Oraison</u> <u>Dominicale</u> (<u>Etudes</u> d' <u>Histoire</u> <u>et</u> <u>de</u> <u>Philosophie</u> <u>Religieuses</u> 58), (Paris, 1964) 39, places the final form of <u>de</u> <u>Or</u> during the first four months of 250. But cf. below, note 8.

affairs (ep 1,1). Cyprian then proceeds to pronounce a posthumous excommunication over a cleric who had named another cleric
to be the testator of his will, thereby causing a cleric to leave
his work at the altar to involve himself in secular juridical
matters. The effect of this excommunication is that no priest is
to offer the Eucharist in behalf of the dead cleric or pray for
him.[4]

In ep 2, Cyprian informs a fellow bishop, Eucratius, that a
certain former theater actor turned Christian must not only give
up the stage (which the actor had done upon conversion), but also
that it is not permissible for him to train others for the stage
even though this may be his only means of making a living. Under
such conditions, the community should take care of the man's
needs, if he is truly unable to find another profitable occupa-
tion. In his tract ad Donatum 8, the Carthaginian Bishop explains
that acting is a shameful profession because the scenes are shameful in themselves, the gods are portrayed, and men are made to
dress and act like women when on stage. In the letter to Eucratius, Cyprian seems only to be concerned with the last mentioned
objection to the acting profession; for the Law of Moses (Dt 22,5)
forbids men to put on women's apparel.[5] Such action supposedly

---

4. Cf. ep 1,2; CSEL 3/2, 467: "non est quod pro dormitione eius
   apud uos fiat oblatio aut deprecatio aliqua nomine eius in
   ecclesia frequentetur, ut sacerdotum decretum religiose et
   necessarie factum seruetur a nobis, simul et ceteris fratribus detur exemplum, ne quis sacerdotes et ministros Dei altari eius et ecclesiae uacantes ad saecularem molestiam
   deuocet."

5. Cf. ep 2,1; CSEL 3/2, 468: "nam cum lege prohibeantur uiri
   induere mulierebrem uestem et maledicti eiusmodi iudicentur,
   quanto maioris est criminis non tantum muliebria indumenta

pleases the devil, who takes pleasure in seeing men artificially change into women and thus disgrace the body which is made in God's likeness (ep 2,2).

The importance of this epistle is that it demonstrates how Cyprian, along with many other early Christian leaders and writers, used the Old Testament in defining the limits of the Church. Moreover, his ruling in this matter led later generations of Christians to exclude actors as a profession from the Eucharist.[6]

When attention is focused on the Eucharist itself, one sees that it has an important role for Cyprian in defining the Church. In fact, it is precisely the Eucharist which distinguishes the Christian from the Jew: "Quod panem et calicem Christi et omnem gratiam eius amissuri essent Iudaei, nos uero accepturi, et quod Christianorum nouum nomen benediceretur in terris."[7] To prove this thesis, the African Bishop points out that Isaiah foretold that Yahweh would withdraw from the Jews and go to the gentiles (Is 65,13.15f; 5,26f; 3,1). Then, he uses Ps 33,9 ("Gustate et uidete, quoniam suauis est Dominius," etc.) as a lead to Jn 6,35 ("Ego sum panis uitae," etc.) as well as Jn 7,37f and 6,53 to show that the transferral of Yahweh from the Jews to the gentiles has been made by way of the Eucharist, without which one cannot have life (Test 1,22). Unfortunately, Cyprian seems to think that Yahweh brought most of the Mosaic Law with him when he came to the gentiles--a fact that will become presently evident. Not

---

accipere sed et gestu quoque turpes et molles et muliebres magisterio inpudicae artis exprimere?"

6. Cf. Georg May, Die kirchliche Ehre als Voraussetzung der Teilnahme an dem eucharistischen Mahle, (Erfurter Theologische Studien 8), (Leipzig, 1960) 25, n. 45.

7. Cf. Test 1,22; CSEL 3/1, 57f.

only is the Eucharist the major difference between Christians and Jews, it is also about the only real difference from a theological rather than ethnic point of view.

One of the Carthaginian's more involved explanations of the theology of the Eucharist and consequent discipline is found in his tract de Oratione Dominica 18, and bears lengthy quotation here:[8]

> For the bread of life is Christ, and this bread does not belong to all but only to us. And just as we say 'our Father,' because he is the father of the understanding and believing, so do we also say 'our bread,' because Christ is the bread of those (of us) who touch his body. But we ask that this bread be given to us daily, lest, by the intervention of a serious fault, we who are in Christ and receive his Eucharist daily as the food of salvation be separated from the body of Christ, who declares and says: 'I am the bread of life which is coming down from heaven; if anyone eat from my bread, he will live forever; however, the bread which I will give is my flesh for the life of the world' (Jn 6,48-52); (for) as long as we are excommunicated and not in communion[9]

---

8. The present writer is more inclined to accept P. Monceaux's chronology for de Or, or at least for the passage now under consideration, since Cyprian speaks here of eucharistic excommunication and of touching the body of Christ. This sounds very much like a reference to the state of affairs following the persecution that began in 250. Moreover, Cyprian's concern at this point about the necessity of the Eucharist for salvation may indicate a time after the Carthaginian council of 252, which discussed this matter.

9. "dum abstenti et non communicantes." Many theologians have attempted to define these terms in various ways and with various results. N. München (op. cit., 139, 198) believes that "abstinere" means temporary, formally imposed excommunication and has the same meaning as "arcere." M. Réveillaud (op. cit., 146) holds that "abstentus" is synonymous with "non communicans." J. Grotz (op. cit., 156-63) is of the opinion that "communio" ("communicatus") means the admission of the sinner to penance, while the "pax" terminates this period and

we are kept away from the heavenly bread. Therefore, when
he speaks of one's living forever if he eat his bread, so
is it manifest that those persons live who touch his body
and receive the Eucharist by right of communication. Likewise, on the other hand, it is necessary to fear and to pray
lest any excommunicant--in as much as he is separated from
the body of Christ--remain (separated) from salvation which
warns and says: 'if you do not eat the flesh of the son of
man and drink his blood, you will not have life in you' (Jn
6,53). And so we ask that we be given our daily bread which
is Christ, so that we who remain and live in Christ should
not (have to) refrain from his sanctification and body.[10]

From this passage, it is clear that Cyprian interprets separa-
ation from the Body of Christ (the Church) primarily as separation

----

admits the penitent to full communion--i.e., the Eucharist.
However, this thesis has found very little sympathy and has
given rise to sharp critique. Cf. Siegfried Hübner, Kirchenbusse und Exkommunikation bei Cyprian, in: ZKT 84 (1962) 191-
215.

10. "nam panis uitae Christus est et panis hic omnium non est sed
noster est. et quomodo dicimus pater noster, quia intelli-
gentium et credentium pater est, sic et panem nostrum uocamus,
quia Christus eorum qui corpus eius contingimus panis est.
hunc autem panem dari nobis cottidie postulamus, ne qui in
Christo sumus et eucharistiam eius cottidie ad cibum salutis
accipimus interdicente aliquo grauiore delicto, dum abstenti
et non communicantes a caelesti pane prohibemur, a Christi
corpore separemur ipso praedicante et dicente: 'ego sum panis
uitae qui de caelo descendi. si qui ederit de meo pane,
uiuit in aeternum. panis autem quem ego dedero caro mea est
pro saeculi uita.' quando ergo dicit in aeternum uiuere. si
qui ederit de eius pane, ut manifestum est eos uiuere qui
corpus eius adtingunt et eucharistian iure communicationis
accipiunt ita contra timendum est et orandum, ne dum quis abstentus separatur a Christi corpore remaneat a salute commin-
ante ipso et dicente: 'nisi ederitis carnem filii hominis et
biberitis sanguinem eius, non habetis uitam in uobis.' et
ideo panem nostrum id est Christum dari nobis cottidie peti-
mus, ut qui in Christo manemus et uiuimus a sanctificatione
eius et corpore non recedamus." Cf. CSEL 3/1, 280f.

from the Eucharist.[11] This is at least the primary disciplinary effect of excommunication, and also the factor that most threatens the salvation of anyone expelled from or not yet a member of the Church.[12] This accounts for the unusual language of the passage, whereby "corpus Christi" embraces the Church, the Eucharist and the historical Christ all at the same time, and is extended even further through the personification of the abstract concept of "salvation itself warning and saying."

2. Persecution and Apostasy

a. The problem created by the apostates.

After only about a year in office, the young Bishop fled from Carthage (perhaps to a nearby fishing village); for the persecution instigated by Decius finally broke out also in North Africa. From his place in exile, Cyprian directed his see by means of cor-

---

11. Cf. Adrien Demoustier, L'Ontologie de L'Église selon Saint Cyprien, in: Recherches de Science Religieuse 52 (1964) 569f.

12. It is clear that Cyprian feels that membership in the Church means more than merely belonging to the group of the baptized. Rather, union with the Church implies frequent reception of the Eucharist, which, as the celebration of ecclesial unity, is an essential self-execution of the Church's dymanic unity. Words can scarcely describe Cyprian's compact and all-embracing concept of ecclesial unity. Unity at its fullest in all aspects of the Church is Cyprian's main theological concern, and, for this end, all grammar and philosophy must take second place. Consequently, it would be futile to say that Cyprian's use of "corpus Christi" here and elsewhere means the Church but not (the real body of Christ in) the Eucharist. Being in the Body of Christ (the Church) is to be daily or nearly daily involved in the body of Christ (the Eucharist). For a fuller treatment of Cyprian's concept of unity, cf. A. Demoustier, art. cit., in toto, esp. 596, 587.

respondence, and addressed himself to the problems created by the various apostates (lapsi).

Obviously, the lapsi were still firmly convinced of their Christian beliefs. The persecutors, on the other hand, were not really intent upon producing a sincere following for the Olympic pantheon. "They could be content with the merest pretense of conformity because they could rely on the discipline of the Church itself to exclude from the ecclesia all who had in any way compromised."[13] But, much to the frustration of the Roman authorities, the Church responded to the crisis by an unanticipated mitigation of the severe discipline that seemed about to strangle her. Namely, she began to receive the apostates back in large numbers into her fold--but not without great opposition from conservative zealots, nor without abuses on the part of the "liberals" who were often too ready to readmit the lapsed before a real test of their sincere repentance had been made.

Cyprian never doubted that even apostates could be forgiven; but as long as the persecution was waging, he wanted to forestall the readmission of the lapsi until such a time when he could meet in council with his own people and clergy in order to establish a uniform policy for dealing with the lapsed who were clamoring for reacceptance into the Church (ep 14,4). Rather than decide the whole issue immediately and on his own, "Cyprian might well have felt that with the clergy and people all assembled, he could, by force of his authority and eloquence, appease both sides and bring them to a reasonable solution midway between rigorism and laxism."[14] As a temporary modus agendi, an exception was to be made only in

---

13. Cf. Gregory Dix, The Shape of the Liturgy, 146.
14. Cf. John H. Taylor, St. Cyprian and the Reconciliation of Apostates, in: Theological Studies 3 (1942) 37.

the case of those _lapsi_ who were in the danger of death and had
acquired a letter of reconciliation (_libellum_ _pacis_) from a martyr or confessor.[15] But the Bishop's ruling in this matter was
not always observed by his own clergy, and tension and discord
soon began to rise.[16]

---

15. Cf. _epp_ 18,1; 19,2; 20,3. These _libelli_ _pacis_, as letters
    of communion, have their roots already in 2 Cor 3,1. But
    as a "standard form and practice," they begin first with Cyp-
    rian's time and become common for Christian travelers of the
    4th century and for sometime thereafter. Cf. W. Elert, _op_.
    cit., 108-12; L. Hertling, _art_. _cit_., 102-06.

16. Sometime in the spring or early summer of 250, Cyprian sent
    a letter to the martyrs and confessors in Carthage to ask
    them to correct their overly liberal issuance of the letters
    of recommendation, which were often very inexplicit in regard
    to those to be included in the recommendation: "late enim
    patet quando dicitur 'ille cum suis' et possunt nobis et
    uiceni et triceni et amplius offerri qui propinqui et adfines
    et liberti ac domestici esse adseuerentur eius qui accepit
    libellum." Cf. _ep_ 15,4; _CSEL_ 3/2, 516. In the future, the
    martyr or confessor is to be personally acquainted with the
    letter's recipient, who must also be truly repentant and
    nearly at the end of the period of ecclesially imposed pen-
    ance: "et ideo peto ut eos quos ipsi uidetis, quos nostis,
    quorum paenitentiam satisfactioni proximam conspicitis, de-
    signetis nominatim libello et sic ad nos fidei ac disciplinae
    congruentes litteras dirigatis." Cf. _ibid_. This letter was
    quickly followed by two others, one to the clergy and one to
    the people, asking that the abuse of premature readmission be
    corrected. Cyprian complains that the martyr has scarcely
    died before some priests grant the _pax_ to any holder (i.e.,
    from among the _lapsi_) of that martyr's letter of recommenda-
    tion: "contempta Domini lege et obseruatione quam idem mar-
    tyres et confessores tenendam mandant, ante extinctum perse-
    cutionis metum, ante reditum nostrum, ante ipsum paene marty-
    rum excessum, communicant cum lapsis et offerant et eucharis-
    tiam tradant." Cf. _ep_ 16,3; _CSEL_ 3/2, 519. Cf. also _ep_ 17,
    2. But the abuses continued to multiply, and the _libelli_
    "were issued in the name of a dead confessor, or a confessor
    too illiterate to write; issued so copiously, that some thou-

The controversy, as has been already implied, originated from the action of an opposition party which probably took root at the time of Cyprian's elevation to the episcopacy and which was further aggravated by the spiritual leader's flight into exile--an act that many considered to be cowardly (epp 8; 9; 20,1). While some clerics were readmitting the apostates all too readily perhaps out of misguided opinion, others were probably doing the same with the intention of slighting their bishop. But Cyprian is less concerned about his offended authority than about the harm such premature reconciliation apparently causes the Church (ep 16,2). The essential thing is that the lapsed first perform proper penance and be duly reconciled by the bishop himself.[17] However, Cyprian does not consider this procedure just to be a matter of discipline bereft of deeper theological motives. Rather, the Eucharist--the terminus ad quem of the penitential practice-- is always foremost in the Carthaginian's mind.

b. The Eucharist and the reconciliation of apostates, phase one.

In a letter written probably sometime between April and July of 250, Cyprian informs his priests and deacons that, in view of 1 Cor 10,21, the lapsed as such have no right to the Eucharist since a Christian cannot partake of both the "table of the Lord" and the "table of the Devil" (ep 16,2). In another letter of the same period addressed to the martyrs and confessors of the faith, premature reconciliation of the lapsi is seen as a contradiction

---

sands were believed to be circulating in Africa, and the very sale of them was not beyond suspicion." Cf. E. Benson, op. cit., 93. Thus, Cyprian's growing disregard for such letters is quite understandable.

17. Cf. G. D'Ercole, Penitenza, 103.

to the Gospel and Christian life chiefly due to the requirement
that one be worthy of receiving the Eucharist (1 Cor 11,27-29)--
which the lapsed are not.[18] Addressing himself in a letter written probably in the summer of 250 to the clergy of Rome, Cyprian
explains that the *lapsi* profane the Eucharist because they have
sullied their hands and mouth by handling and eating pagan sacrifice; or at least their consciences were stained by obtaining a
libellus even if they did not actually take part in the sacrifice.[19]

A closer examination of what Cyprian means by stained mouth
and hands and a polluted conscience shows that such expressions
in his works are not merely classical rhetoric. This Church
Father's use of Scriptures indicates that he unhesitatingly employs the Old Testament, whenever it serves his purposes, with
the same force and binding power that one would otherwise do only
with the New Testament. This, however, is fully consistent with
the Martyr-Bishop's theology (esp. of the Church and the priesthood), which is more informed by Old Testament legislation than
by the New Testament.[20] Consequently, his concept of religious

----

18. Cf. *ep* 15,1; *CSEL* 3/2, 514: "illic contra euangelii legem,
    contra uestram quoque honorificam petitionem, ante aetam
    paenitentiam, ante exomologesim grauissimi adque extremi de-
    licti factam, ante manum ab episcopo et clero in paenitentiam
    inpositam, offerre pro illis et eucharistiam [dare] id est
    sanctum Domini corpus profanare audeant, cum scriptum sit:
    'qui ederit panem aut biberit calicem Domini indigne reus
    erit corporis et sanguinis Domini'" (1 Cor 11,27). Cf. also
    ep 16,2f and note 21 below.

19. Cf. *ep* 20,2; *CSEL* 3/2, 527f: "item cum conperissem eos qui
    sacrilegis contactibus manus suas adque ora maculassent uel
    nefandis libellis nihilominus conscientiam polluissent."

20. M.F. Wiles, The Theological Legacy of St. Cyprian, in: The
    Journal of Ecclesiastical History 14 (1963) 146, says that

purity approaches that of the cultic purity demanded in Judaism,
and he sees a sort of defilement in apostasy and other serious
sins that requires a definite program of penance over a fairly
lengthy period of time. Finally, the reconciliation (pax) must
be granted by the bishop and clergy before a penitent is again
rendered worthy enough to approach the Eucharist.[21]

In his tract, de Lapsis, Cyprian complains of those who come,
as it were, directly from their pagan sacrifice to the Eucharist,

---

Cyprian's major concern over schismatic ministers, who may
also have been compromising in regard to pagan sacrifice,
"was that such people had put themselves outside of the
Church and needed to seek reacceptance into its fold by penitence. Yet it is not on these grounds that he opposes the
legitimacy of their continued ministrations. Instead, he employs the old Law's insistence on the need for a priest to be
without stain or blemish. This argument fits, as we have
seen, naturally enough with his general understanding of the
ministry as fulfilling the precise role laid down for the Old
Testament priesthood." Cyprian uses 480 quotes from the Old
Testament and 454 quotes from the New Testament. Altogether,
he quotes or alludes to the Old Testament about 755 times and
the New Testament about 1035 times. Nevertheless, it is the
way in which Cyprian uses the Old Testament to prove his arguments that ultimately determines his theology and gives it a
certain neo-Judaizing character. However, he generally manages to maintain the essentially Christian aspect as well, and
no one would think of accusing him of trying to revive the
earlier errors and attitudes shared by the Judaizers that St.
Paul often faced. Moreover, Cyprian's method of exegesis was
no anomaly during his times and was generally accepted as
valid.

21. Cf. de Lapsis 16; CSEL 3/1, 248: "Spretis his omnibus adque
contemptis ante expianta delicta, ante exomologesim factam
criminis, ante purgatum conscientiam sacrificio et manu sac-
erdotis, ante offensam placatam indignantis Domini et minan-
tis uis infertur corpori eius et sanguini et plus modo in
Dominum manibus adque ore delinquunt quam cum Dominum negav-
erunt."

their hands and breath still reeking with the idolatrous food.
Thus, they assault the body of the Lord.[22] St. Paul (1 Cor 10,
21; 11,27) is quoted against these persons, and their assault on
the Lord's body is explained by way of Lv 7,19f:

> They assault the Lord's body, since divine Scripture pre-
> sents itself and declares and says: 'Every clean person will
> eat flesh; and whichever soul has eaten from the flesh of the
> sacrifice of salvation which belongs to the Lord, and the im-
> purity of that person is upon himself, that soul will perish
> from his people.'[23]

To receive the Lord's body into impure hands and mouth is a
worse crime than the act of apostasy itself.[24] Consequently,
Cyprian challenges the wisdom of premature readmission of the
lapsi to communion with the Church. Such indulgence is no real
reconciliation of the offender, but rather a hindrance to his salvation: "Non concedit pacem facilitas ista sed tollit, nec commu-
nicationem tribuit sed inpedit ad salutem."[25] It is against the
law of the Lord and of God--"irrita et falsa pax."[26] In a letter

---

22. Cf. de Lap 15; CSEL 3/1, 248: "a diaboli aris reuertentes ad
    sanctum Domini sordidis et infectis nidore manibus accedunt,
    mortiferos idolorum cibos adhuc paene ructantes exhalantibus
    etiam nunc scelus suum faucibus et contagia funesta redolen-
    tibus Domini corpus inuadunt."

23. Ibid.: "Domini corpus inuadunt, quando occurrat scriptura
    diuina et clamet et dicat: 'Omnis mundus manducabit carnem,
    et anima quaecumque manducauerit ex carne sacrificii salu-
    taris quod est Domini, et immunditia ipsius super ipsum est,
    peribit anima illa de populo suo.'"

24. Cf. note 21 above.
25. Cf. de Lap 16; CSEL 3/1, 249.
26. Cf. de Lap 15; CSEL 3/1, 247. "The invalidity of the 'recon-
    ciliation' in this case was not only due to the absence of
    adequate penance, but also to the disregard for Cyprian's
    episcopal rulings in the matter. In ep 64,1, a reconcilia-
    tion before the penance had been completed is nevertheless

to his priests and deacons, the Bishop of Carthage declares that henceforth he will excommunicate any priest or deacon who dares to grant communion to the lapsi against his will.[27]

In this same letter, written probably toward the end of 250, Cyprian expresses his approval of the excommunication of the presbyter Gaius of Dida and his deacon for their continued communion with the lapsi and for accepting their offerings for the eucharistic service.[28] Playing on both the ecclesial and secular

---

regarded as valid (though illicit), because granted by the bishop concerned." Cf. Maurice Bévenot, ACW 25, 85, n. 72. However, since ep 64 concerns the decisions of the council of 66 bishops in 253, this conclusion may be more than Cyprian would have conceded in 251 when he concurred with a council of bishops in the formal excommunication of Felicissimus and his followers for being too lax with the lapsi in spite of repeated warnings as attested in ep 59,9. According to ep 43,3; CSEL 3/2, 592, the opposition party is acting contrary to the Gospel with their "new tradition": "contra euangelicam disciplinam noua traditio sacrilegae institutionis exurgat."

27. Cf. ep 34,3; CSEL 3/2, 570: "interea si quis immoderatus et praeceps siue de nostris presbyteris uel diaconis siue de peregrinis ausus fuerit ante sententiam nostram communicare cum lapsis, a communicatione nostra arceatur, apud omnes nos causam dicturus temeritatis suae."

28. Cf. ep 34,1; CSEL 3/2, 568f: "Integre et cum disciplina fecistis, fratres carissimi, quod ex consilio collegarum meorum qui praesentes erant Gaio Didensi presbytero et diacono eius censuistis non communicandum, qui communicando cum lapsis et offerendo oblationes eorum in prauis erroribus suis frequenter deprehensi et semel atque iterum secundum quod mihi scripsistis a collegis meis moniti, ne hoc facerent in praesumptione et audacia sua pertinaciter perstiterunt." Similarly, Cyprian announces in ep 41,2; CSEL 3/2, 589 that anyone who continues to associate with the schismatic layman, Felicissimus, will also be excommunicated: "quisquis se conspirationi et factioni eius adiunxerit sciat se in ecclesia

meaning of "presbyter," the Bishop compares those priests who offer a premature pax with the two elders who tried to lead Susanna into sin (Dn 13). Such wantonness soils the purity of the Church and injures the truth of the Gospel (ep 43,4).

The hasty extension of reconciliation to the lapsed is viewed as a deception that attempts to get around the need for penance as expressed in Apc 2,5 ("Consider from where you have fallen and do penance") and Is 30,15 ("Thus says the Lord: If you convert yourself and sigh, then you will be saved, and you will know where you were"). Those who denied Christ should now ask him for forgiveness; and this means to do penance under the bishop's direction (ep 43,1.3).

It would be too simple to say that Cyprian considered premature reconciliation to be null and void merely for juridical reasons--that is, simply because he, as bishop with jurisdiction over his priests and people, had decreed against such action. Rather, he felt that anyone who did not comply with his ruling was immediately in schism with him, the bishop, and was thus immediately extra ecclesiam ubi salus non est (epp 73,21; 4,4; 55, 29). It was not, however, the mere difference of opinion between him and his subordinates that he felt sufficed for a schism. Instead, it was because he was convinced that penance must be performed under the direction of the bishop if there is to be any positive effect.[29] For this reason, then, anyone acting in a contrary manner should be rebuked and even excommunicated.

---

nobiscum communicaturum non esse." The effect of the excommunication was that such persons could not enter the church in order to take part in any religious function, especially the Eucharist. Cf. N. München, op. cit., 198f.

29. An important concrete example of Cyprian's insistence upon

But no case of expulsion of an offender from the Church is seen to be merely the result of a formal excommunication pronounced by the bishop. This is obvious from the fact that Cyprian felt that all serious sins immediately excluded the sinner from the Eucharist.[30] Readmission to this sacrament presupposed that the sinner first underwent formal penance and received the pax from the bishop.[31]

Apparently, Cyprian and many of his contemporaries felt that excommunication of the sinner from the Eucharist was not only necessary for preserving the purity of the Church, but also for the sinner's spiritual and physical well-being. In chapter 26 of de Lapsis, the Carthaginian Bishop tells of three cases where God severely punished unworthy communicants.

In the first instance, we hear of a girl who secretly joined those assisting at sacrifice. The Bishop does not specify whether or not Christian sacrifice is meant, but from the context it seems

_____

penance for serious offenses is found in the case of those lapsed who went over to the lax party led by Felicissimus in order to avoid having to perform penance. The Bishop of Carthage thereupon wrote a letter to all his subjects to inform them that those who turned back from Felicissimus could not return to the Church and communicate with the bishops and the people of Christ. Cf. ep 43,7. However, this should not be construed to mean permanent excommunication, but rather that such persons must still undergo proper ecclesial penance and reconciliation (i.e., under the bishop's direction) before they can claim the right of communion and the Eucharist. Cf. Karl Rahner, Die Busslehre des hl. Cyprian von Carthage, in: ZKT 74 (1952) 387.

30. Ibid. Cf. also note 18 above.
31. Penitential acts were viewed by Cyprian as necessary satisfaction made to God (de Lap 16) and as rendering the sinner worthy of the Eucharist. Cf. K. Rahner, Busslehre des hl. Cyprian, 412.

certain that such is the case.[32] Upon communicating, she is
seized with choking spasms and collapses as if she had swallowed
poison. He compares the incident to virtual suicide: "non cibum
sed gladium sibi sumens."[33]

In another incident, a woman whose hands were still "impure"[34]
from her pagan sacrifice was trying to open a locket in which
she had the Eucharist. However, fire suddenly flared up from it,
and she was unable to open it. Likewise, another of the lapsi
found that the Eucharist had turned to ashes in his hands. From
such incidents, Cyprian seems to conclude that Christ withdraws
from the Eucharist on such occasions.[35]

However, it is not mere guilt in itself that brings affliction upon communicants who are somehow improperly disposed to

---

32. Cf. M. Bévenot, ACW 25, 33.
33. Cf. CSEL 3/1, 256. Whether or not the girl actually died can-
    not be conclusively drawn from the text. From Cyprian's de-
    scription of the case, it appears that he was simply confront-
    ed with someone afflicted with epilepsy. At any rate, the
    story illustrates the mentality of the times in regard to un-
    worthy reception of the Eucharist. Further witness of this
    fact is found in the apocryphal work, Acta Thomae, Sect. 51,
    contemporary with Cyprian, which tells of a lad who, after
    murdering a young girl, tried to receive the Eucharist, but
    found that his hands suddenly shrivelled up so much that he
    could not bring the Eucharist to his mouth. When Thomas is
    told of the incident, he remarks that the Eucharist has ex-
    posed and convicted (ἤλεγξεν) the boy. Thus, the Eucharist
    is accredited with a power which the New Testament ascribed
    to Christ and the Holy Spirit. Cf. above, p. 130.

34. "inmundis." However, Bévenot's new text (being prepared for
    publication) will prefer the reading "indignis."

35. Cf. de Lap 26; CSEL 3/1, 256: "documento unius ostensum est
    Dominum recedere cum negatur nec inmerenti ad salutem pro-
    desse quod sumitur, quando gratia salutaris in cinerem sancto
    fugiente mutetur."

receive the Eucharist. Even in the case of an infant that had been given a bit of bread dipped in the wine of the pagan sacrificial offering of his parents--the child being too young to chew the sacrificial meat--, the reception of the Eucharist is seen to produce adverse physical effects in spite of the infant's lack of personal guilt. For, when the baby was later given the wine of the Eucharist, it choked on it and vomitted. Cyprian claims to have witnessed this himself and concludes that it was due to the infant's defiled mouth and stomach: "In corpore adque ore uiolato eucharistia permanere non potuit, sanctificatus in Domini sanguine potus de pollutis uiseribus erupit."[36]

Although Cyprian makes good use of these incidents to arouse faith and the fear of God in his listeners and readers, it may be pressing the issue too far to conclude that he really thought that one's unworthiness of the Eucharist could be so detached from actual personal guilt. Perhaps these stories "tell us more of the mentality of his flock than of himself."[37] However, such a belief in objective pollution in addition to the possibility of personal guilt for participation in pagan sacrifice is certainly not contrary to Cyprian's times, and the Bishop himself encourages the idea when he says that those parents who induced their babies and youngsters to partake of the pagan sacrifice will be accused on Judgment Day of murdering the souls of their children and of bringing them to ruin; for it was not the children who of themselves left the Lord's food and drink ("nec derelicto cibo et poculo Domini") in order to defile themselves with pagan sacrifice (de Lap 9).

---

36. Cf. de Lap 25; CSEL 3/1, 255.
37. Cf. M. Bévenot, ACW 25, 90, n. 113.

In view of the sacredness of the Eucharist, it seems clear that Cyprian fully believed in a sort of real, objective defilement that, of itself, sufficed to make one, including infants, unfit to receive the Eucharist. In de Lap 22, he emphasizes that the lapsi have defiled hands and a polluted mouth ("inquinatis manibus...ore pollute"). This is in contrast to the glorious hands and holy mouth of those who, having withstood the persecution, may rightfully receive the Eucharist.[38]

c. The Eucharist and the reconciliation of apostates, phase two.

As long as the persecution raged, Cyprian felt that those lapsi who were truly repentant should not be granted ecclesial reconciliation as long as the possibility remained of their being able to acquire the greater crown of martyrdom itself--thereby undoing their previous offense (epp 55,4; 19,2). However, the council which Cyprian held[39] in Carthage in the spring of 251 at the conclusion of the persecution decided to grant pardon to the libellatici, but insisted that the sacrificati should continue to do penance. They were to be received back into the Church only upon death (epp 55,6.17; 45,2; 57,1; 59,13).

A year later, however, when persecution was again threatening, a synod of 42 bishops meeting in Carthage ruled that the pax should be immediately granted to all the sacrificati who had been

---

38. Cf. de Lap 2; CSEL 3/1, 238: "Illustres manus, quae non nisi diuinis operibus adsueuerant sacrificiis sacrilegis restiterunt. sanctificata ora caelestibus cibus post corpus et sanguinem Domini profana contagia et idolorum reliquias respicerunt."

39. In today's terminology, we would call Cyprian a "metropolitan." He was thus responsible for calling and organizing councils (or, more accurately, synods) of bishops in northern Africa.

constant in doing penance. The purpose for relaxing the restriction of the previous year was to enable those who most needed the Church's support to get it in view of the trying days ahead. To this end, the Eucharist suddenly took the central positive role. For who could refuse this shield of protection, the blood of Christ, to those who were about to be called upon to shed their own blood for Christ? Rather, it was necessary to reconcile these penitents with the Church in order to allow them to receive the Eucharist as a means of strengthening them against further trials and temptations (ep 57,2).

Since a distinction was to be made between those lapsi who were sincerely repentant and had persevered in the practice of penance, and those who had relapsed even further and gone over to heretical or schismatic groups (ep 57,1.3), bishops should consider it an honor and glory to grant the Church's peace to the reformed lapsi. Cyprian compares this action with the Eucharist, the daily sacrifice, whereby the bishops are able to prepare victims for God by preparing these formerly lapsed persons for martyrdom: "immo episcopatus nostri honor grandis et gloria est pacem dedisse martyribus, ut sacerdotes qui sacrificia Dei cotidie celebramus hostias Deo et uictimas praeparemus."[40] The Eucharist is considered so important for these persons, that Cyprian and the assembled bishops are unwilling to let the idea of martyrdom as Baptism by blood suffice of itself.[41]

---

40. Cf. ep 57,3; CSEL 3/2, 652.
41. Cf. ep 57,4; CSEL 3/2, 653: "Nec quisquam dicat: 'qui martyrium tollit sanguine suo baptizatur, nec pax illi ab episcopo necessaria est habituro gloriae suae pacem et accepturo maiorem de Domini dignatione mercedem' primo idoneus esse non potest at martyrium qui ab ecclesia non armatur ad proelium, et mens deficit quem non recepta eucharistia erigit et accendit."

Apparently, the Bishop of Carthage had no difficulty in accepting the decisions of the council. In fact, his ability to influence and persuade very probably played a major role in forming the council's decisions. Nevertheless, the resolution to give the pax so soon to the sacrificati seems to represent an about-face in Cyprian's thinking. However, it is understandable that he felt it necessary to enforce a stricter code during the persecution itself since the readmittance of lapsi at that time would have encouraged others to apostasize and would have been belittling to those who had to suffer for the faith. Even the decision to readmit only those who had a letter of recommendation from a martyr and were in articulo mortis was probably not all too harsh under the circumstances; for such letters were apparently readily available to anyone really concerned about repenting his apostasy.[42] Yet, Cyprian admits that he has undergone some change of mind in the matter: "quod utrumque (i.e., in the cases of the libellatici and the sacrificati) non sine librata diu et ponderata ratione a me factum est."[43]

3. The Schism of the Rigorists

a. Novatian's rebellion.

As a result of the more moderate attitude of the bishops toward the lapsi, a small party of puritanical rigorists was organized and eventually proved to be far more dangerous and divisive than the former party of laxists. These rigorists thought the Church could not forgive certain sins at all--especially apostasy. As long as Cyprian himself proved to be quite strict, this party

---

42. Cf. J.H. Taylor, op. cit., 33.
43. Cf. ep 55,3; CSEL 3/2, 625.

remained in the background. The African rigorists never did get into the scene very much until after the schism in Rome between Pope Cornelius and Novatian.

Pope Fabian died a victim of Decian persecution on January 20th, 250. His successor, Cornelius, could not be elected until about March of 251 due to the persecution,[44] which ended as suddenly as it had begun when Decius had to leave Rome to defend his imperial authority against Priscus, who had proclaimed himself <u>Augustus</u> in Macedonia. During the vacancy of the bishop's chair in Rome, Novatian became the leading personage and led the Roman clergy through the persecution. During this time, he wrote Cyprian a letter[45] expressing the Roman clergy's approval of the Carthaginian's penitential discipline. But the election of Cornelius keenly disappointed Novatian and frustrated his ambitious hopes (<u>HE</u> 6,43,5-7). Apparently, it was because Cornelius favored removing the embarrassing traces of the days of persecution as quickly as possible by reconciling the <u>lapsi</u> that he was preferred to Novatian.[46] The latter, however, had a small following which included three bishops who consecrated him bishop in opposition to the duly elected Bishop of Rome. But since Cornelius' election could not be contested on canonical bases, Novatian and his following of rigorists looked upon Cornelius' attitude toward the <u>lapsi</u> as an unjustified laxism (ep 55,12). "<u>De la question de personne, on arrivait ainsi à la question de doctrine</u>."[47]

---

44. Cf. E. Benson, <u>op</u>. <u>cit</u>., 127.
45. This is <u>ep</u> 30 in the collection of Cyprianic letters. Cf. also <u>ep</u> 55,5.
46. Cf. E. Amann, <u>DThC</u> 11,837.
47. <u>Ibid</u>.

Once Cyprian had ascertained that Cornelius was the properly elected Bishop of Rome (ep 45), he began to take steps against Novatian and his efforts to attract an ever larger following. In 251, the schismatic antipope was excommunicated by the Council of Carthage (epp 44,1; 45,1.3f; 48, 2-4; 68,2). For this occasion, Cyprian may possibly have composed his famous treatise, de Unitate Catholicae Ecclesiae.

b. The schismatic's status and the Eucharist.

Very early in the treatise, the Bishop of Carthage makes it quite clear that schism or heresy (Cyprian saw very little if any difference between the two) is in every way worse than the sin of the lapsi, who sinned but once; whereas, the heretics sin daily (de Un 19). Heresy and schism are the invention of the devil (de Un 3; ep 43,6). They are especially dangerous to the unity of the faith (and for Cyprian, anyone outside of this unity is also totally outside of the faith) since they still parade under the name of "Christian" even after abandoning the Gospel (de Un 3). Novatian's schism makes him Judas Iscariot's contemporary counterpart (de Un 22).

In a letter to Fabius of Antioch (HE 6,43,5-22), Cornelius also records his sentiments and theological conclusions concerning Novatian. Since the latter suddenly fell seriously ill during his catechumenate, he received "emergency Baptism," which Cornelius considered to be the work of Satan. That is, Cornelius apparently felt that Satan caused Novatian's illness and thus became the very occasion for the schismatic's entrance into the Church. Moreover, according to Cornelius' theology of Baptism, the Holy Spirit is given by the "sealing" (i.e., imposition of hands) from the bishop and not by the pouring of the water over the candidate of Baptism. Since Novatian had not been "sealed" at the time of his Baptism, he was considered bereft of the Holy Spirit by Cornelius and others.[48] Although "clinical Baptisms" were not repeated or "solemnized" by means of the standard form of Baptism at a later date if the person recovered from his illness after the emergency Baptism, there was a general air of suspicion about such Baptisms since such hastily baptized persons were not to be ordained to any ecclesiastical order. Cornelius did not fail to bring this objection up against his opponent (HE 6,43,17).

Cyprian's confrontation with Novatian soon led him to treat the dogmatic issues concerning schismatics and heretics in the light of the nature of the Church and the Eucharist. The fact that the Church has a Eucharist is seen as the basic reason why she must be one, for the Old Testament type of the Eucharist was the Pasch which had to be eaten in one single home:

> Loquitur Deus dicens: in domo una comedetur: non eicietis de domo carnem foras. caro Christi et sanctum Domini eici foras non potest, nec alia ulla credentibus praeter unam ecclesiam domus est.[49]

Consequently, Cyprian has nothing but scorn for the Eucharist celebrated by schismatics and heretics (de Un 8) and says that "they profane the sacrament."[50]

---

48. Cf. HE 6,43,15. Cyprian, however, regarded Novatian's Baptism as complete and in order. Cf. ep 69,12.

49. Cf. de Un 8, here quoted according to Maurice Bévenot, The Tradition of Manuscripts, a Study in the Transmission of St. Cyprian's Treatises, (Oxford, 1961) 104.

50. "sacramentum profanant." Cf. de Un 15; M. Bévenot, op. cit., 113. "Sacramentum almost certainly means the Eucharist here. Cf. ----, ACW 25, 117, n. 27.

The establishment of a Eucharist apart from that of the Church's was understood as the ultimate sign and seal of revolt. Therefore, Cyprian calls the heretic:

> an enemy of the altar, a rebel against the sacrifice of Christ, perfidious instead of faithful, sacrilegious instead of religious, a disobedient servant, an undutiful son, a hostile brother...He dares to erect another altar, to pray in other than legitimate voices, to profane the reality of the divine victim with their false sacrifices.[51]

Likewise, Cornelius reacted very strongly to Novatian after the schismatic had forced his followers to receive the Eucharist from him while swearing they would, in the name of the body and blood of Christ, never return to Cornelius. This action Cornelius viewed as calling a curse down upon oneself, and as the worst of all Novatian's offenses (HE 6,43,18f).

The Carthaginian Bishop explains the relationship of schismatic to the Church in view of his interpretation of Mt 10,5. In this passage, Christ sends out his disciples before him, but orders them to avoid the cities of the Samaritans. Cyprian concludes that the order to avoid these schismatics from Judaism was the same as equating them with pagans. This, then, is to serve as the theological model for the Church's attitude toward Christian schismatics (ep 69,6). Or, as Bishop Januarius of Muzul put it in 256, "ecclesia enim et haeresis duae et diuersae res sunt."[52]

---

51. Cf. de Un 17; M. Bévenot, op. cit., 114: "Hostis altaris, adversus sacrificium Christi rebellis, pro fide perfidus, pro religione sacrilegus, inobsequens servus, filius impius, frater inimicus,...constituere audet aliud altare, precem alteram illicitis vocibus facere, Dominicae hostiae veritatem per falsa sacrificia profanare."

52. Cf. Sententiae Episcoporum 34; CSEL 3/1, 449.

4. The Question of Rebaptism

a. Ecclesial unity as the basis for rebaptism.

It has already been seen that Tertullian claimed that heretical Baptism was ineffective (de Bapt 15). In Cyprian's struggle with Novatian and his followers, the question of heretical
or schismatic Baptism is raised in the midst of the fight (epp
69-75). The problem came to the surface when some of Novatian's
converts from paganism left the schismatic and sought admission
into the Church.[53] It was the general opinion of the North
African Church that such persons must be "rebaptized." Just
exactly when and how this practice arose within the Church is
difficult to say, but Cyprian himself, although calling it an
established tradition of the Church, says the custom stemmed
from Agrippinus of Carthage (ep 71,4), who was Bishop of Carthage
next but one before Cyprian.[54]

---

53. Rebaptism never came into question for those repentant schismatics originally baptized in the Church. Cf. epp 71,2;
74,12; HE 7,7,4. However, such persons were henceforth bar-
red from taking Holy Orders. Cf. epp 67,6; 68,1-5. This
ruling was also imposed a half century later by the Council
of Elvira, c. 51.

54. P. Monceaux (op. cit., 37) holds that the practice was not
initiated by Agrippinus or his council, but was only approved
by them--the practice itself apparently stemming from Tertullian. E. Benson (op. cit., 337-39) believes it is the other
way around, and so dates the practice of rebaptism in North
Africa from about 213. Rebaptism may also have been practiced in Rome during the time of Callistus (Hippolytus, Ref
Haer 9,12), but only as a means of making it easier for the
restoration of sinners and schismatics alike--that is, as a
penitential practice and not as a sacramental necessity.
But even this practice was never really accepted by the
Church. Cf. E. Benson, op. cit., 337.

In the spring of 256, Cyprian informed Pope Stephen (254-257) of the African Church's practice (ep 72). However, Stephen's reaction was quite unexpected. He not only disapproved of the practice of rebaptism, but he even threatened to excommunicate those who refused to discontinue it (ep 74; HE 7,5). The Bishop of Rome recognized heretical Baptism because he maintained that its validity depended not on the worthiness of the minister but on Christ himself. However, Cyprian and his supporters were of the opinion that Christ and the Holy Spirit were in no way present in the sacramental actions of heretics (de Un 18; ep 74,4). Years later, the Donatists readily took up Cyprian's arguments as their own. However, it would be wrong to accuse the Carthaginian Bishop of being a real forerunner of Donatism.[55]

Cyprian sees an absolute unity between the Church and her sacraments. This unity, in turn, flows from the unity of the episcopate. Hence, there is a reciprocal relation between the unity of the Church and the unity of the bishops. Sacramentally, this union and unity is "mediated" by the Eucharist, which, first of all, relates Jesus Christ with the Holy Trinity. In turn, the local church, assembled around its bishop for the celebration of the Eucharist, is offered and joined with Christ to the Father. And finally, the whole Church is united as one through the (eucharistic) intercommunion of the episcopacy.[56]

---

55. A. d'Alès, La Théologie de Saint Cyprien, (Paris, 1922) 239f, 321, sees a real germ of Donatism and the doctrine of personal holiness in Cyprian's attitude. However, Cyprian's real concern and test for orthodoxy and validity is not so much in personal holiness as in his concept of ecclesial unity. Cf. H. von Campenhausen, op. cit., 299.

56. Cf. A. Demoustier, art. cit., 587f, 574-78; ----, Épiscopat et Union à Rome selon Saint Cyprien, in: Recherches de Science Religieuse 52 (1964) 342f.

Another altar and another priesthood are impossible (ep 43,5)
beyond the altar and priesthood found in the Church and through
which the Church is founded and maintained.[57] This unity was
signified by Christ when he founded the Church upon Peter and
gave him the power of the keys[58] and the Holy Spirit (ep 73,7).
In turn, Cyprian--and the North African bishops in general--
bound the validity of the sacraments exclusively to the bishop.
Consequently, it goes without saying, that this unity of Church,
bishop and sacraments as conceived by the theology of North
Africa precluded any possibility of valid heretical Baptism:

> Iesus Christus Dominus et Deus noster Dei patris et
> creatoris filius super Petram aedificauit ecclesiam, non
> super haeresim, et potestatem baptizandi episcopis dedit,
> non haereticis. quare qui extra ecclesiam sunt et contra
> Christum stantes oues eius et gregem spargunt baptizare
> foris non possunt.[59]

b. Baptism and the Eucharist.

From the consideration of the validity of heretical Baptism,
it is but a small step to the consideration of heretics and the
Eucharist; for it is through Baptism that one receives the Holy

---

57. Cf. S.L. Greenslade, Scripture and Other Doctrinal Norms in
Early Theories of the Ministry, in: The Journal of Theological Studies 44 (1943) 171-74; G. D'Ercole, Communio, 383f.

58. Cyprian's use of Mt 16,18 and Jn 20,23 is unusual in that he
applies the "power of the keys" to Baptism rather than Penance. Cf. G. D'Ercole, Penitenza, 92f. Thus, it is easy to
see why he could so readily demand rebaptism and place this
sacrament so entirely under the bishop's jurisdiction so as
to preclude the validity of heretical Baptism.

59. Cf. Sent Epp 17; CSEL 3/1, 444. In de Un 11, Cyprian has
the following to say about the effects of heretical Baptism:
"Non abluuntur illic homines sed potius sordidantur, nec pur-
gantur delicta sed immo cumulantur. Non Deo nativitas illa
sed diabolo filios generat." Cf. M. Bévenot, op. cit, 108.

Spirit and is given access to the Eucharist: "per baptisma autem spiritus accipitur, et sic baptizatis et spiritum sanctum consecutis ad bibendum calicem Domini peruenientur."[60] While Baptism admitted one into the Church, the Eucharist especially signified and preserved the unity of the Church. This aspect is clearly stated in ep 63 where Cyprian seeks to correct an abuse that had taken root in some African communities of Christians who used water exclusively in place of wine in the celebration of the Eucharist.[61] First and foremost, this practice is to be rejected because it fails to express the unity of Christ with the people. It is upon this aspect that Cyprian would seem to be most ready to judge such a Eucharist invalid and ineffective:

> nam si uinum tantum quis offerat, sanguis Christi incipit esse sine nobis; si uero aqua sit sola, plebs incipit esse sine Christo; quando autem utrumque miscetur, tunc sacramentum spirituale et caeleste perficitur.[62]

However, the Eucharist likewise effects and maintains the unity of Christians among themselves. In this context, Cyprian explains to his fellow bishop, Magnus, why he thinks heretics cannot be considered a part of the Church's eucharistic unity:

> In short, even the divine sacrifices themselves declare that the Christian spirit of oneness unites itself by way of firm and inseparable love. For when the Lord calls his body bread produced by the union of many grains, he is indicating the union of our people whom he was carrying: and when he calls his blood wine pressed from many bunches of grapes and brought into one, he likewise signifies our flock joined together by the intermingling of a united multitude. If Novatian is united to this divine bread, if

---

60. Cf. ep 63,8; CSEL 3/2, 707.
61. This practice in the communities Cyprian has in mind may belong to the lingering elements of Montanism. Cf. A. Scheiwiler, op. cit., 174f.

62. Cf. ep 63,13; CSEL 3/2, 711f.

even he is also intermingled in Christ's cup, it would seem
that he could likewise have the grace of the one ecclesial
Baptism, if one should grant that he maintains the unity of
the Church.[63]

In the council held at Carthage in 256, Bishop Caecilius explains why he feels the Eucharist of heretics is so outrageous
and why it is therefore so outrageous to recognize heretical Baptism:

> I know of but one Baptism in the only Church, and beyond
> the Church, there is none. This (Baptism) will be one where
> there is true hope and certain faith. For thus it is writ-
> ten: 'one faith, one hope, one Baptism' (Eph 4,5), but not
> among heretics where there is no hope and where faith is
> false, where everything is accomplished by lying, where a
> demoniac exorcizes, (where) one whose mouth and words dis-
> charge cancer asks for the oath, (where) the infidel grants
> faith, (where) the convicted criminal administers pardon for
> crimes, and (where) anti-Christ baptizes in the name of
> Christ, (where) one who has been cursed by God blesses,
> (where) a dead person promises life, (where) one who is un-
> pacified grants peace, (where) the blasphemer calls upon
> God, (where) a profane person administers the priesthood,
> (where) a sacriligious person sets up the altar. In addi-
> tion to all these things also comes that notorious evil--
> namely, as the devil's bishop, he dares to perform the
> Eucharist. Or else, those who assist them should say that
> all these things concerning heretics are false. But behold
> what nonsense it is to which the Church is then forced to
> consent and to grant communion (even to those) without Bap-

---

63. Cf. ep 69,5; CSEL 3/2, 754: "denique unanimitatem christ-
ianam firma sibi adque inseparabili caritate conexam etiam
ipsa dominica sacrificia declarant. nam quando Dominus corpus suum panem uocat de multorum granorum adunatione conges-
tum, populum nostrum quem portabat indicat adunatum: et quando sanguinem suum uinum appellat de botruis adque acinis
plurimis expressum adque in unum coactum, gregem item nostrum significat commixtione adunatae multitudinis copulatum.
si Nouatianus huic pani dominico adunatus est, si Christi
poculo et ipse conmixtus est, poterit uideri et unici eccle-
siastici baptismi habere gratiam posse, si eum constiterit
ecclesiae unitatem tanere."

tism and the forgiveness of sins. Wherefore, brother, we must flee and avoid and separate ourselves from such a great crime and hold to the one Baptism that has been granted by the Lord to the Church alone.[64]

In a letter to Cyprian, Firmilian, Bishop of Caesarea in Cappodocia, explains that the rebaptism of heretics is especially necessary in view of the Eucharist. Those who are admitted to the Eucharist without rebaptism commit a crime along with those who admitted them:

> ceterum quale delictum est uel illorum qui admittuntur uel eorum qui admittunt, ut non ablutis per ecclesiae lauacrum sordibus nec peccatis expositis usurpata temere communicatione contingant corpus et sanguinem Domini, cum scriptum sit: 'quicumque ederit panem aut biberit calicem Domini indigne, reus erit corporis et sanguinis Domini' (1 Cor 11,27).[65]

c. Heretics and their ineffective sacraments.

A fuller understanding of the North African party's attitude concerning the relationship between heretics and the sacra-

___

64. Cf. Sent Epp 1; CSEL 3/1, 436f: "Ego unum baptismum in ecclesia sola scio et extra ecclesiam nullum. hic erit unum, ubi spes uera est et fides certa. sic enim scriptum est: 'una fides, una spes, unum baptisma,' non aput haereticos, ubi spes nulla est et fides falsa, ubi omnia per mendacium geruntur, ubi exorcizat daemoniacus sacramentum interrogat, cuius os et uerba cancerem mittunt, fidem dat infidelis, ueniam delictorum tribuit sceleratus, et in nomine Christi tinguit antichristus, benedicit a Deo maledictus, uitam pollicetur mortuus, pacem dat inpacificus, Deum inuocat blasphemus, sacerdotium administrat profanus, ponit altare sacrilegus. ad haec omnia accedit etiam illud malum ut antistes diaboli audeat eucharistiam facere. aut qui illis adsistunt dicant haec omnia falsa esse de haereticis. ecce ad qualia igitur ecclesia consentire et sine baptismo et uenia delictorum communicare conpellitur. quam rem, fratres, fugere [ac uitare] debemus et a tanto scelere nos separare et unum baptismum tenere quod soli ecclesiae a Domino concessum est."

65. Cf. ep 75,21; CSEL 3/2, 823f.

ments (in as far as the sacraments were enumerated and distinguished in contemporary North Africa) requires a deeper probing
into North Africa's ecclesiology. Accordingly, the ultimate
cause and type of the Church's unity is the Trinity. "Further
than this it is impossible to go":[66]

> Qui pacem Christi et concordiam rumpit adversus Christ-
> um facit, qui alibi praeter ecclesiam colligit, Christi ec-
> clesiam spargit. Dicit Dominus: 'Ego et Pater unum sumus'
> (Jn 10,30). Et iterum de Patre et Filio et Spiritu sancto
> scriptum est: 'Et hi tres unum sunt' (1 Jn 5,7). Et quis-
> quam credit hanc unitatem de divina firmitate venientem,
> sacramentis caelestibus cohaerentem, scindi in ecclesia
> posse et voluntatum conlidentium divortio separari? Hanc
> unitatem qui non tenet, non tenet Dei legem, non tenet
> Patris et Filii fidem, vitam non tenet et salutem.[67]

As early as 220, the Council of Iconium in Phrigia declared
that heretics had no access to grace since grace is entirely and
only within the Church. Consequently, heretics cannot ordain,
baptize or administer any other sacrament whatsoever (ep 75,7).
Bishop Primus of Misgirpa summed up the opinion of North Africa
in September of 256. Heretical Baptism is invalid:

> cum sit baptisma nisi in ecclesia unum et uerum, quia et
> Deus unus et fides una et ecclesia una est, in qua stat
> unum baptisma et sanctitas et cetera. nam quae foris ex-
> ercentur nullum habent salutis effectum.[68]

According to the Carthaginian party, the whole question of
the validity or nonvalidity of heretical Baptism (and all their
sacramental and ecclesial actions) depends on whether or not the

---

66. Cf. J.F. Bethune-Baker, An Introduction to the Early History
    of Christian Doctrine to the Time of the Council of Chalcedon.
    (London, 1903) 365.

67. Cf. de Un 6; M. Bévenot, op. cit., 102f.
68. Cf. Sent Epp 2; CSEL 3/1, 437.

minister had the Holy Spirit. But since heretical dispensers of
Baptism supposedly lack the Father, the Son and the Holy Spirit,
they cannot baptize. Therefore, they must come to the Church if
they hope to be reborn through Baptism (Sent Epp 10).

Firmilian, not fully understanding Rome's sacramental theology,[69] was of the opinion that Stephen claimed that heretical
Baptism forgave sins and produced a rebirth even though heretics
lacked the Holy Spirit. The Bishop of Caesarea and former pupil
of Origen then proceeds to expose what he feels is the absurdity
of Stephen's position in view of Paul's rebaptism of those who
had only been baptized with John's baptism since they had been
baptized before the Holy Spirit had been sent (Acts 19,3-6).
Thus, a fortiori, the heretics coming to the Church must be rebaptized.[70]

---

69. The problem was caused by the diversity of meanings for the
    imposition of hands: exorcisms, blessings, Penance, Confirma-
    tion and Holy Orders. These were not always clearly distin-
    guished from one another during Cyprian's time. In Rome,
    heretics who converted to the Church received only the impo-
    sition of hands in Penance. However, Cyprian thought that
    Rome was illogically trying to repeat the Spirit-giving impo-
    sition of hands in conjunction with Baptism (i.e., Confirma-
    tion). Cf. J. Neumann, Spender der Firmung, 52, 104-15. On
    the other hand, Stephen did not distinguish well between Pen-
    ance and Confirmation, and held the illogical position that
    heretical Baptism gave grace but not the Holy Spirit since
    he considered heretical imposition of hands in the baptismal
    rite to be ineffective. However, the basic and original pur-
    pose of the Church's imposition of hands upon heretics was
    that of Penance ("Büsserhandauflegung"). Cf. K. Rahner,
    Busslehre des hl. Cyprian, 268-71. Cf. also E. Benson, op.
    cit., 420f.
70. Cf. ep 75,8; CSEL 3/2, 815: "secundum quod (i.e., the fact
    that without the Spirit there is no new birth in Baptism) et
    beatus apostolus Paulus eos qui ab Iohanne baptizati fuerant,

The logical conclusion for Cyprian and his supporters was
that, if heretical Baptism were valid, then heretics could, according to Gal 3,27, "put on Christ" (ep 74,5). But since it is
Christ himself who sends the Spirit (Jn 16,7), then there seems
to be no way of "putting on Christ" without the Holy Spirit:

> qui potest apud haereticos baptizatus Christum induere,
> multo magis potest spiritum sanctum quem Christus accipere...
> Peccata enim purgare et hominem sanctificare aqua sola non
> potest, nisi habeat et spiritum sanctum.[71]

Under the influence of the Old Testament's concept of purity,
Cyprian and his partisans came dangerously close to slipping into
Donatism when they declared:

> quomodo autem mundare et sanctificare aquam potest qui ipse
> inmundus est et apud quem sanctus spiritus non est? cum
> Dominus dicat in Numeris: 'et omnia quaecumque tetigerit in-
> mundus inmunda erunt' (Nm 19,22). aut quomodo baptizans
> dare alteri remissam peccatorum potest qui ipse sua peccate
> deponere extra ecclesiam non potest?[72]

However, in all fairness, it must be pointed out that Cyprian's real motive for such language is the protection of the
principle and unity of true faith. That is, heretics and schis-

---

priusquam missus esset a Domino spiritus sanctus, baptizauit
denuo spiritali baptismo et sic eis manum inposuit ut acciperent spiritum sanctum (Acts 19,1-6). quale est autem et
cum Paulum post Iohannis baptisma iterato discipulos suos
baptizare dubitemus? nisi si his episcopis qui nunc minor
fuit Paulus, ut hi quidem possint per solam manus inpositi-
onem daret, nisi eos prius etiam ecclesiae baptismo baptiz-
asset." Unfortunately, we do not learn how Cyprian felt
about this different view of John's baptism, since he held
that John received the Holy Spirit already in his mother's
womb precisely for the purpose of being able to baptize
Jesus in the Spirit. Cf. ep 69,11.

71. Cf. ep 74,5; CSEL 3/2, 803.
72. Cf. ep 70,1; CSEL 3/2, 767f. This text is one of the earliest
witnesses to the use of specially blessed baptismal water.

matics have broken faith with the Church and have thus become adulterers. Therefore, they have destroyed their faith and cannot receive what faith would otherwise offer them since one receives according to one's faith:

> quomodo ergo potest uideri qui apud illos baptizatur consecutus esse peccatorum remissam et diuinae indulgentiae gratiam per suam fidem qui ipsius fidei non habuerit ueritatum? si enim, sicut quibusdam uidetur, secundum fidem suam quis accipere aliquid foris extra ecclesiam potuit, utique id accepit quod credidit. falsum autem credens uerum accipere non potuit, sed potius adultera et profana secundum quod credebat accepit.[73]

The heretics may have "faith," but not the true faith; therefore, they cannot truly baptize. For, if they could validly baptize, then it seems that all other sacraments and means of grace should likewise be at their disposal.[74] However, it is also for want of a valid Eucharist that the whole of the heretical baptismal rite is ineffective; for the Eucharist is the means by which the oil used in the anointing at Baptism acquires its sanctification. But since heretics apparently could not lay claim to a real Eucharist, there could be no grace in their anointing.[75]

---

73. Cf. ep 73,5; CSEL 3/2, 782.
74. Cf. ep 73,6; CSEL 3/2, 783: "quod si secundum prauam fidem baptizari aliquis foris et remissam peccatorum consequi potuit, secundum eandem fidem consequi et spiritum sanctum potuit, et non est necesse ei uenienti manum inponi ut spiritum sanctum consequatur et signetur. aut utrumque enim fide sua foris consequi potuit aut neutrum eorum qui foris fuerat accepit."

75. Cf. ep 70,2; CSEL 3/2, 768: "ungi quoque necesse est eum qui baptizatus est, ut accepto chrismate id est unctione esse unctus Dei et habere in se gratiam Christi possit. porro autem eucharistia est unde baptizati unguntur oleum in altari sanctificatum. sanctificare autem non potuit olei creaturam qui nec altare habuit nec ecclesiam. unde nec unctio spirit-

Obviously, such a theological viewpoint precluded the faintest possibility of communicatio in sacris with heretics and schismatics, and Cyprian comes closer than any previous ecclesial writer to developing a detailed "theology of noncommunication" with those who stand beyond communion with the bishop.

d. The theological foundation for refusing communicatio in sacris.

As might almost be expected, the Bishop of Carthage finds the heart of his theology of noncommunication in the Old Testament. Accordingly, Korah, Dathan and Abiram, who rebelled against the priesthood of Aaron and Moses (Nm 16,1-35), were the prototype of all future schismatics (ep 69,8). Association with them is contrary to the divine Law, as is demonstrated by God's destruction of those who did not cease to associate with the three rebels; for their sacrifices, like their sins, are a source of contamination.[76] Cyprian calls schismatics "hostes sacerdotum,"[77] and is

---

alis apud haereticos potest esse, quando constet oleum sanctificari et eucharistiam fieri apud illos omnino non posse. scire autem et miminisse debemus scriptum esse: 'oleum peccatoris non ungat caput meum'" (Nm 19,22).

76. Cf. ep 69,9; CSEL 3/2, 758: "et quod comminatus per Moysen Dominus fuerat impleuit, ut quisque se a Core et Dathan et Abiron non separasset poenas statim pro impia communione persolueret. quo exemplo ostenditur et probatur obnoxios omnes et culpae et poenae futuros qui se schismaticis contra praepositos et sacerdotes inreligiosa temeritate miscuerunt. sicut etiam per Osee prophetam spiritus sanctus contestatur et dicit; 'sacrificia eorum tamquam panis luctus, omnes qui manducant ea contaminabuntur' (Hos 9,4), docens scilicet et ostendens omnes omnino cum auctoribus supplicio coniungi qui fuerint eorum peccato contaminanti." At this point, attention should be drawn to the fact that, as already seen in this study, the designation of Korah, Dathan and Abiram as prototypes for Christian schismatics did not originate with Cyprian.

77. Cf. ep 69,10; CSEL 3/2, 758,21.

dismayed that anyone would think of extending even a minimum of
ecclesial recognition or association to such persons:

> illud mirandum est, immo indignandum potius et dolendum,
> christianos antichristis adsistere et praeuaricatores fidei
> adque ecclesiae proditores intus in ipsa ecclesia contra ec-
> clesiam stare.[78]

In early 256 or thereabouts, Jubaianus, a bishop from Maure-
tania in northern Africa sent Cyprian a letter[79] asking him to
explain his reasons for rebaptism--especially since Novatian also
practiced rebaptism. To this, the Bishop of Carthage replied
that he may as well renounce his bishop's chair and even give up
his priestly service at the altar if Novatian's practice of rebaptizing were a valid argument against the orthodoxy of rebaptism; for Novatian also layed claim to the episcopacy and performed priestly functions at the altar.[80] From this, it is clear
that Cyprian's understanding of ecclesial unity was so rigid that
it could not allow for any part of it to exist in schism or heresy. For him to claim otherwise would mean that he must consequently concede that all other elements of the Church could exist in schism and without regard for the unity of the Church.
The analogy is that if schismatic Baptism is valid, then the
priesthood itself must exist among schismatics. Thus, if the
correct baptismal formula alone suffices to make someone a Christ-

---

78. Ibid., 759.
79. The letter is known as a result of Cyprian's reply to Jubaia-
    nus. Cf. ep 73.

80. Cf. ep 73,2; CSEL 3/2, 780: "quale est autem, ut quia hoc
    (i.e., rebaptism) Nouatianus facere audet, nos putemus non
    esse faciendum? quid ergo? quia et honorem cathedrae re-
    nuntiare debemus? et quia Nouatianus altare conlocare et
    sacrificia offerre contra fas nititur, ab altari et sacrifi-
    ciis cessare nos oportet, ne paria et similia cum illo cele-
    brare uideamur."

ian even apart from the Church, then the correct eucharistic
formula would likewise suffice for the existence of the Eucharist outside of the Church. But this is the height of absurdity,
for the Eucharist is the sacrament which effects and celebrates
the Church's absolute unity.[81] Firmilian is the one who finally
draws the logical conclusion *expressis* *verbis* from this concept
of ecclesial oneness--namely, if heretics can validly baptize,
then it would only be logical that orthodox Christians should
even celebrate the Eucharist with those who are outside of the
Church's fold:

> quae si sic magna et caelestia ecclesiae munera hereti-
> cis concedit et tribuit, quid aliud quam communicat eis qui-
> bus tantum gratiae defendit ac uindicat? et frusta iam du-

---

81. We must keep in mind Cyprian's ecclesial structure for the
validity of the sacraments in general. Accordingly, all
sacramental power and grace comes into the Church through
the bishops from the Apostles. Once someone has broken with
the Church's unity, he no longer has access to sacramental
graces in any way because he no longer is in communion with
his bishop. As a result, to admit that a heretic--whether
bishop, priest, deacon, or layman--could baptize meant that
he could perform all the sacraments since the heretics could
then also ordain, etc. Firmilian tells of an apparently
possessed woman who baptized and offered the Eucharist--all
with the correct formula: "inter cetera quibus plurimos de-
ceperat etiam hoc frequenter ausa est, ut et inuocatione
non (sine?) contemptibili sanctificare se panem et eucharistiam facere simularet et sacrificium Dominio sine sacramento
solitae praedicationis offeret, baptizaret quoque multos
usitate et legitima uerba interrogationis usurpans, ut nihil
discrepare ab ecclesiastica regula uideretur." Cf. ep 75,
10; CSEL 3/2, 818. Although Firmilian does not say it directly, he certainly must mean to imply that it is completely
ridiculous merely to point to the correctness of form as sufficient for valid Baptism and, analogously, to offer the
Eucharist--especially ridiculous here since it is being done
by a woman, which sex was not allowed even to baptize, let
alone offer the Eucharist.

bitat in ceteris quoque consentire eis et particeps esse, ut
et simul cum eis conueniat et orationes pariter cum eisdem
misceat et altare ac sacrificium commune constituat.[82]

But this is all too absurd for Firmilian; so much so, that he
finally concludes that, since heresy is worse than apostasy in
his opinion, recognition of heretical Baptism is worse than heresy: "quin immo tu (probably Stephen is meant) haereticis omnibus
peior es."[83]

Stephen had ordered compliance with the Roman tradition which
rejected rebaptism. He looked upon Cyprian's position as an in-
novation and demanded: "nihil innouetur nisi quod traditum est."[84]
However, Cyprian challenges Stephen's position and accuses him
of being the innovator since the "tradition" that his Roman opponent holds cannot be verified in the New Testament and seems
to destroy the ecclesial unity which the Lord and the Gospel demand.[85] Rather, Stephen's tradition is only and purely of human
origin which must not be placed before and in contradiction to a
divine command.[86] Moreover, there could be no authentic aposto-

---

82. Cf. ep 75,17; CSEL 3/2, 821f.
83. Cf. ep 75,23; CSEL 3/2, 824,25. Firmilian's whole mode of
    argument indicates that he presupposed that Rome felt the
    same way as he concerning the absurdity of a eucharistic
    celebration with heretics or schismatics.

84. Cf. ep 74,1; CSEL 3/2, 799,16.
85. Cf. ep 74,2; CSEL 3/2, 800: "et praecepit nihil aliud inno-
    uari nisi quod traditum est, quasi is innouet qui unitatem
    tenens unum baptisma uni ecclesiae uindicat, et non ille uti-
    que qui unitatis oblitus mendacia et contagia profanare tinc-
    tionis usurpat. nihil inmouetur, inquit, nisi quod traditum
    est. unde est ista traditio? ustrumne de dominica et euange-
    lica auctoriatate descendens an de apostolorum mandatis adque
    epistulis ueniens?"

86. Cf. ep 74,3; CSEL 3/2, 801: "quae ista obstinatio est quaeue

lic tradition in this matter since the Apostles were supposedly dead before the arrival of the heretics (epp 74,2; 75,5). Thus, Cyprian feels that, in the absence of a tradition, he must follow reason: "Non est autem de consuetudine praescribendum, sed ratione uincendum."[87]

In a burst of sharp rhetoric, Firmilian proclaims that Stephen has actually committed schism, not by disuniting himself from the head of the Church (which would have been a novel way of conceiving schism in contemporary North Africa), but by severing himself from the rest of the Church.[88] Therefore, as one bishop at the Council of Carthage in September, 256, inferred, Stephen could be considered a betrayer of the entire Church: "Qui haereticis ecclesiae baptismum concedit et prodit quid aliud quam sponsae Christi Iudas extitit?"[89]

---

praesumptio humanam traditionem diuinae dispositioni anteponere nec animaduertere indignari et irasci Deum, quotiens diuina praecepta soluit et praeterit humana traditio, sicut per Esaiam prophetam clamat et dicit: 'populus iste labiis honorificant me, cor uero eorum longe separatum est a me. sine causa autem colunt me mandate et doctrinas hominum docentes' (Is 29,13). item Dominus in euangelio increpans similiter et obiurgans ponit et dicit: 'reicitis mandatum Dei ut traditionem uestrum statuatis' (Mk 7,13).

87. Cf. ep 71,3; CSEL 3/2, 773,10.
88. Cf. ep 75,24; CSEL 3/2, 825: "lites enim et dissensione quantas parasti per ecclesias totius mundi? peccatum uero quam magnum tibi exaggerasti, quando te a tot gregibus scidisti? excidisti enim te ipsum, noli te fallere, si quidem ille est uere schismaticus qui se a communione ecclesiasticae unitatis apostatam fecerit. dum enim putas omnes a te abstineri posse, solum te ab omnibus abstinuisti."

89. Cf. Sent Epp 61; CSEL 3/1, 455. However, contrary to the opinion of most authors, Johann Ernst, Papst Stephan I. und der Ketzertaufstreit, (Forschungen zur Christlichen Literatur-

5. In Defense of Heretical Baptism

a. Rome and Alexandria.

Stephen taught that the schismatic or heretic did not lose the "ability" to baptize since it is not so much a question of right minister as of right intention and formula--that is, Baptism in the name of Christ:[90]

> Sed in multum, inquit, proficit nomen Christi ad fidem et baptismi sanctificationem, ut quicumque et ubicumque in nomine Christi baptizatus fuerit consequatur statim gratiam Christi.[91]

Consequently, it is only necessary that someone who has received heretical Baptism and later wishes to join the Church now receive the imposition of hands[92] before being admitted to communion. However, Stephen himself had no formulated theology upon which he could draw, and he could only hold to the Catholic tradition that the effectiveness of the sacraments could not be made dependent upon the moral state of the minister.[93]

---

und Dogmengeschichte 5/4) 41, 76, holds that this council took place before Pope Stephen's decree. Consequently, the council was not personally directed against Stephen.

90. Pope Benedict XII, while still a cardinal (c. 1330), held that Pope Stephen went too far in recognizing all forms of heretical Baptism as valid, and that the Council of Nicea corrected both Stephen and Cyprian by insisting that Baptism be administered according to the formula prescribed in the Gospel. Ibid., 94.

91. Cf. ep 75,18; CSEL 3/2, 822. However, the question of Cyprian and his followers was whether Novatian and heretics and schismatics in general actually baptized in Christ's name since they supposedly know neither the Father nor the Son nor the Holy Spirit. Cf. ep 69,7.

92. Cf. note 69 above.
93. Cf. A. d'Alès, op. cit., 240.

In a letter from Dionysius of Alexandria to Pope Xystus, Stephen's successor, we learn that Stephen ultimately decided to excommunicate those who rebaptized heretics (HE 7,5,4f). The actual effects of Stephen's decision are not clear; but Dionysius, in a letter to the Roman presbyter Philemon, acknowledges that the Africans did not introduce the practice for the first time. Rather, they simply had adopted the course recommended by previous bishops and the synods held in Iconium and Synnada. Thus, Dionysius is generally reluctant to condemn those who practice rebaptism (HE 7,7,5). When the question of rebaptism becomes a clear case of heresy and schism, Dionysius, in a letter to Dionysius of Rome, presbyter and later Pope, speaks out more firmly against the practice. However, it is Novatian's _rigorism_ and practice of _rebaptizing_ _even_ _the_ _Catholics_ who have come over to him that the Alexandrian bishop attacks (HE 7,8).

In his letter to Pope Xystus, Dionysius tells of a long-time member of his congregation who eventually learned that he had received his Baptism at the hands of heretics. He subsequently begged for rebaptism, and was most reluctant to communicate in prayer and at the altar with the rest. However, Dionysius felt he could not justify rebaptizing him since the party concerned had already communicated in the Eucharist for a long time. And so the Bishop of Alexandria simply exhorted the man to be of good courage and to continue in good faith (HE 7,9,1-5). It appears that Dionysius, under these conditions, sees Baptism in a relative light, and prefers to place the emphasis on proper Christian life as expressed in prayer and the Eucharist rather than on the necessity of Baptism for membership in the Church and for salvation. Otherwise, it would seem that Dionysius would have been logically forced to take the _pars_ _tutior_ and rebaptize the person in doubt. However, the Bishop is not entirely convinced of his opinion, and he submits the case to Xystus' judgment, especially since the heretically baptized party continues to lament his situation and to refrain from common prayer and the Eucharist.

b. The treatise, de Rebaptismate.

The most important document to formulate the doctrine concerning the validity of heretical Baptism during Cyprian's time is the de Rebaptismate.[94] This anonymous work, which supports Rome's position in the question of rebaptism, was possibly written before the Council of Carthage in September, 256, or else shortly thereafter. The place of composition is likewise uncertain, but Rome or North Africa itself are the most probable locations of authorship.[95]

In difficult, rugged Latin, the tract attempts to present a systematic treatment on Baptism. In addition to the introduction (c. 1) and the conclusion (c. 19), it has three divisions; chapters 2 through 6 treat Baptism from the recipient's point of view; chapters 7 through 10 discuss the sacrament in regard to the minister; and chapters 11 through 18 explain the structure of Baptism in itself. A brief summary of the document's arguments can now be given.

The author claims that he intends to interpret Baptism through the use of Scriptures (c. 1). The recipient of Baptism must be

---

94. The text used here is from G. Rauschen, Florilegium Patristicum 9 (Bonn, 1916).

95. Cf. A. von Harnack, Geschichte der altchrtl. Literatur, 2/2, 394. Hugo Koch, Die Abfassungszeit des Liber de rebaptismate: Auch ein Beitrag zur Primatsfrage, in: Internationale kirchluche Zeitschrift 14 (1924) 134-64, supports rather convincingly the thesis that de Reb was written shortly after the Council of Carthage in 256.

baptized in the Holy Spirit (c. 2), but this is not to be construed to mean that this is always and only coincidental with
Baptism by water; for the Holy Spirit is imparted rather by the
imposition of the bishop's hands. When Scriptures speak of Baptism by water and the Spirit, two separate events are actually
meant (c. 3). Moreover, the Holy Spirit may at times even be
imparted before Baptism and the imposition of hands as in Acts
10,44-48 (cc. 4f). Consequently, this means that sins can be
forgiven even before Baptism and that subsequent Baptism in this
case is "ut invocationem quoque nominis Iesu Christi acciperent,
ne quid eis deesse videretur ad integritatem ministerii et fidei"
(c. 5). The author then observes that the Apostles were baptized
("baptismate Domini fuissent baptizati") long before they were
granted the Holy Spirit at Pentecost, which was the "baptisma
spiritus sancti" and forgave the sins of the Apostles for desert-
ing the Lord during his time of need (c. 6).

Chapter 7 forms a transition to the examination of Baptism
on the part of the minister. Here, it is noted that even men
outside of the Church ("et nonnumquam aliquae etiam ab hominibus
extraneis") have performed great deeds through the invocation of
Christ's name. Therefore, the invocation of the holy name is to
be considered only as the beginning of the mystery of the Lord
at work in us (c. 7: "Idcircoque debet invocatio haec nominis
Iesu quasi initium quoddam mysterii dominici commune nobis et
ceteris omnibus accipi"). In anticipation of the objection that
his argument is not ad rem since the Apostles were not at any
rate baptized as heretics (c. 8), the author points out that,
nevertheless, the faith of the Apostles was very imperfect (i.e.,
incomplete) and weak, and yet they baptized others (c. 9; Jn 3,
22). A parallel can be drawn with those bishops who lead bad

lives or who have unsound opinions concerning the faith or who are even very ignorant of the nature of Baptism itself. Is their baptized clientele to be rebaptized? Obviously not! However, heretical Baptism should be ammended as far as possible and needful, but not repeated. Thus, when such baptized persons come to the Church, they should receive the spiritual Baptism through the imposition of the bishop's hands which is accompanied by the reception of the Holy Spirit. But a complete rebaptism itself would be disrespectful of the name of Jesus, which cannot be taken away once it is invoked (c. 10).

Now the anonymous writer turns his attention to the structure of Baptism which is itself one, but which also has more than one form. First, there is Baptism by blood (martyrdom). However, this is not effective for heretics since they both confess and deny the name of Christ at the same time (c. 11). Invocation of the Lord's name implies that one will at least strive to seek the the Lord. Consequently, the heretic must convert to the Church in order to achieve salvation (cc. 12f). Martyrdom is, however, essentially connected with Baptism by water since Christ underwent both forms, so that one who believes but is martyred before Baptism is likewise baptized in Christ's blood (c. 14). Baptism by the Spirit may precede or follow the Baptism administered by men; or, even if that is lacking, the Spirit still comes upon those who believe (c. 15: "_Ita dum cohaeret baptismati hominum spiritus aut antecedit aut sequitur vel cessante baptismate aquae incubit super eos qui credunt_"). However, the full rite of Baptism should always be observed in as far as that is possible.

Chapters 16 and 17 answer the objection of some sect that applied the expression "baptism with fire" (Lk 3,16) literally, and

so practiced trickery to produce fire upon the water when they
baptized.   But the author of de Reb responds that fire is but
another expression for the Holy Spirit as was apparent at the
time of Pentecost.

In conclusion (c. 19), the writer states that he now feels
that he has shown the folly of rebaptism. But even without the
scriptural arguments, tradition itself should hold the chief
place among all arguments: "Quamquam haec consuetudo etiam sola
deberet apud homines timorem Dei habentes et humiles praecipuum
locum obtinere."

SYNTHESIS

1. Preliminary Remarks

The martyr-death of Cyprian in 258 during the Valerian persecution marked the end of one of the most formative and produc-
tive eras of the Church's history. No really outstanding theologians or ecclesiastical personalities come upon the scene in
the East or the West for the next 100 years. Indeed, there were
many important men in the Church between St. Cyprian's time and
St. Augustine; but none could eclipse the theologians and Church-
leaders of the first half of the third century.

During this 100-year interim, the most outstanding developments in the Church were born of her newly acquired role in the
Roman Empire during and after the time of Constantine the Great.
For the Church, it was a period of peace that began with Valerian's death in 260; albeit, it was marred by Diocletian (284-305),
who carried out the last and the most intense of all the persecutions even though his own wife and daughter were Christians. During this time, however, Spain, Gaul and Britain were under the
charge of Constantius Chlorus, Constantine's father, and, although
the least Christian of all the provinces of the Empire, were
spared the fury of the persecution. Aside from this painful
trial, the general state of peace made it possible for the Church
to attend to the systematizing of her discipline[1] and to record
and document her history as was done by Eusebius of Caesarea and
others.

---

1. The Council of Elvira (c. 300), for example, gave expression
    in codified form to many aspects of eucharistic discipline of
    earlier days, but added nothing essentially new. Cf. Mansi
    2, 109-396, esp. cc. 20, 28f, 32, 51, 53.

The hiatus in the theological development of the Church during the aforementioned 100 years provides us with an appropriate point to break off further historical investigation into the topic of this study. After the long trek through the disconnected history of the emergence of eucharistic excommunication in the early Church, there still remains the task of quickly glancing back over the highlights of the study so that the material may be more easily digested and placed in the framework of the contemporary ecumenical situation. Of course, this requires a process of selection and interpretation in addition to the selection and interpretation already made in this study; and perhaps not everyone will agree that the present writer has performed this task without prejudice and preconceived conclusions. However, it is his hope that the more or less detailed historical survey of the problem in the foregoing pages contains a sufficient number and variety of <u>facta</u> <u>bruta</u> so that the reader can better compare his own impressions and conclusions with those which the writer makes in the following pages.

<u>2</u>. <u>What</u> <u>Does</u> <u>the</u> <u>Bible</u> <u>Say</u>?

<u>a</u>. <u>Judaism</u> <u>and</u> <u>early</u> <u>Christian</u> <u>discipline</u>.

It was seen at the beginning of this study that various cultic and political elements (the distinction is, for the most part, purely formal) of Jewish discipline furnished the Israelite nation with an identity that gave a specific content and formation to its doctrine and life. More important, however, is that this discipline was coupled with the doctrine that Yahweh had revealed himself to these Semite tribes in order to choose and guide them as his special people--a picture not unlike that found in the New Testament (cf. esp. Acts 5,1-11; 10-11; 15,28). This awareness of being God's chosen ones found expression in the theology of the covenant, which presented specific rights and duties to the Israelites that eventually led to definite religious limits (ethnic and geographical) within which the Jewish people and their Yahwistic cult found their self-identity. Upon this basis, the Jews were able to develop or sanction a practice of discipline and excommunication that took centuries to form and which achieved a more or less full state of development perhaps only a few decades before the birth of Christ; although, subjection to foreign powers hindered the full and free execution of the more extreme forms of discipline.

The influence that this Jewish understanding and system of discipline had upon the development of the early Church dare not be overlooked or underestimated. At the same time, however, it must also be properly interpreted, since the orthodox trend of early Christianity was always by far and wide to reinterpret elements of this discipline in the light of Christian revelation and the law of love as taught by Jesus. Nor did the early Church's understanding of herself as the "new Israel" prevent her from rejecting the legalism and formalism that oppressed contemporary Judaism. However, this was not immediately and universally understood in the Church, and the struggle against Judaizing elements was no small task for the first several generations of Christians.

The reinterpretation of Jewish discipline was influenced especially by two characteristics of the Christian faith--namely, the relaxation of all ethnic prerequisites for membership in God's newly chosen people, and the eschatological aspect. Neither of these elements, however, was created ex nihilo by Christianity.

Rather, the Old Testament statements which connected an earthly
condition with a promise or threat, blessing or curse to be realized in an eschatological future--a future that marks the beginning of the end--formed the basis for Christian religious
life and discipline.[2] At the same time, these eschatologically
oriented texts were often impressed with a catholicity that would
normally be unexpected in such an ethnic-conscious people (cf.
esp. Mal 1,11; Jl 3,1-5; Acts 2,17-20). Evidence also indicates
that the eschatological enthusiasm of such Jewish sects as the
Essenes reinforced the eschatologically oriented hopes and discipline of early Christianity. However, the external formalism
and legalism of these esoteric groups were rejected by the infant Church, who taught justification by faith rather than by
works of the Law. Yet, this is not to be construed so as to mean
faith is _the_ good work which _earns_ justification and salvation
for the believer. Rather, it is the "personal condition" whereby
the individual opens himself up (metanoia), not to serve God in
order to "earn" salvation, but to let God serve him through his
Son and Holy Spirit.[3] Those who reject Jesus cannot be justified
and are therefore "unclean."

b. The new Israel and the Eucharist.

Justification begins with repentance and Baptism, which admit the candidate to the Body of Christ and are inseparable from

---

2. Cf. E. Käsemann, Sätze, 258.
3. In Mt 20,28 (cf. also Mk 10,45; Lk 22,25; Jn 13,4-8), Christ
    states that he came to serve rather than to be served. The
    prerequisite is that one be open to receive him, as is taught
    by Jesus' demand for faith in him before he works a wonder for
    someone. Cf. e.g. Mt 9,28-30. The story of Martha and Mary
    (Lk 10,38-42) teaches the same lesson.

the votum eucharistiae since the Eucharist is the "proper cause"
of the (mystical) Body of Christ.[4] Christian life is nourished
by the Eucharist--not as something isolated from the rest of the
Church's activity,[5] but rather as the integrating action and
source of the fullness of the Church's κοινωνία.[6] Consequently,
any disciplinary measure the Church may feel called upon to take
against negligent members must touch upon this κοινωνία in one
way or another, consciously or unconsciously. Here, the Eucharist as the basis of the New Covenant is especially important.

---

4. Cf. Jérome Hamer, L'Église est une Communion, (Unam Sanctam
   40), (Paris, 1962) 84. Hamer's work, which was written without the benefit of the results of Vatican II's ecclesiology,
   attempts a "Scholastic concordance" of the ecclesiology found
   in St. Robert Bellarmine, St. Thomas Aquinas and Pius XII's
   encyclical letter, "Mystici Corporis." Consequently, it is
   critical of the ecclesiology which considers the Church to be
   the "Ursakrament" (cf. esp. Otto Semmelroth, Die Kirche als
   Ursakrament, Frankfurt, 1953), because such a definition does
   not exclude occult heretics and schismatics from the Church.
   Cf. J. Hammer, op. cit., 93. Hamer tends to see the Eucharist as the "Ursakrament." Therefore, the present writer has
   placed "proper cause" ("cause propre") in quotation marks. not
   only to indicate that he is quoting the expression, but also
   to indicate that he does not entirely agree with the term to
   the extent that it presents the Eucharist as the "Ursakrament"
   without further clarification how that is to be properly understood.

5. The Church does not "take time out" for the celebration of
   the Eucharist, nor can she "take time out" from living the
   eucharistic life in order to attend to purely "social-humani-
   tarian" matters.

6. In the New Testament, κοινωνία refers to the manner in which
   one is in the Church as the Body of Christ. Later, it came
   to mean the relation of one church to the other and of one
   Christian to the other. Cf. J. Hamer, op. cit., 173-192; W.
   Elert, op. cit., 5-22, 166ff. In the above text, both meanings are intended.

But, as is clear from 1 Cor 11,17-34, this sacrament cannot be separated from love of neighbor and a basic acceptance of the theological meaning and purpose of the eucharist.[7] Likewise, ecclesial discipline, including excommunication, is to be ultimately interpreted in view of the principle of love, which, however, includes a basic confession of faith in Jesus Christ since, as was seen in the early Church, heresy was equally an offense against love. But all this must be seen from the Church's all-important eschatological character, which gives her an ultimate meaning and goal and places her on a path that leads beyond herself without depriving her of the already "realized" elements of the eschatological age introduced by Christ.

The New Covenant is already a fact in the Church even though not yet complete. The members of the Church participate in this Covenant, and this requires freedom from the guilt which otherwise destroys one's attainment of the promises of the New Covenant. Therefore, excommunication is more than just a sign of an unfavorable future state. Rather it _is_ a loss in the present time as well. But, as an ecclesial act, it is only a ratification of the fact that the excommunicated person or persons have already rejected the privilege of belonging to the People of God.

Moral perfection is not absolutely demanded now, but is seen as a matter to be realized eschatologically. Nevertheless, cer-

---

7. It is important to note, however, that St. Paul insists upon one Eucharist _in spite of_ the existing "heresies and schisms" (tinged, perhaps, with Gnostic elements) at Corinth since the Eucharist is the effective sign that the community is living fully from the self-imparting love and grace of its Master and Lord, just as was the case when he shared his daily table with weak disciples, publicans, prostitutes and other sinners. Cf. J. Blank, _art_. _cit_., 172-76.

tain moral and doctrinal standards must be maintained if one is to hope to remain open for God's grace and salvation and for membership in the Church. This aspect is not meant to encourage "moral minimalism." Rather, it is intended to provide some degree of "empirically" observable data whereby it can be determined whether or not one can really claim to belong fully to the Body of Christ. These data do not possess absolute character, but only leave the judgment of those "outside" entirely in God's hands (1 Cor 5,12f). Consequently, the early Church's discipline in the New Testament is to be viewed as pastoral rather than as penal since it was meant to lead the offender back into the Church as an effective and living member or at least to prepare the offender for salvation outside of the circle of active membership in the Church (1 Cor 5,5). The expulsion of a serious offender was also intended to protect the rest of the community from the sinner and his faults. This was only a secondary aspect of excommunication, but it often became of primary importance when the circumstances of a case of excommunication led the community to believe that there could really be no hope for a change of heart on the part of the excommunicated person (Heb 10, 26-30; 1 Jn 5,16f). From this position, it is but a small step to the conjecture that excommunication implies certain loss of salvation since "extra ecclesiam nulla salus est." However, the door was always open--at least in principle--to the repentant sinner. It was "the sin of obdurate refusal to repent in response to brotherly admonitions" that fully excluded one from the Church.[8]

---

8. Cf. G.W.H. Lampe, Church Discipline and the Interpretation of the Epistles to the Corinthians, (Christian History and Inter-

The strong ethical accent in early Christianity was immediately and harmoniously bound to their confession of faith, which
was not an abstraction, but rather a confession of faith ordered
to love. Metanoia and Baptism thus included a personal commitment
to the faith (doctrine) and Gospel preached by the Apostles.
Purely intellectual assent was secondary and ordered to the personal commitment. Nevertheless, there were basic doctrines which
were formulated very early into doxologies and symbola, and which
were used to "test" the orthodoxy of others who came to preach to
a local church or community of Christians. The doctrine that
Jesus is the Christ who came in flesh into the world, died and
rose from the dead and returned to the Father, but who will come
again, comprised the basic confession of faith. Any other doctrines were elaborations of this, which, in turn, is but an ela-
boration of the confession that Jesus is the Christ. Excommunication followed upon a basic denial (in word or deed) of this
confession of faith since such a denial was seen as a repudiation
of all that one's Baptism stood for. Beyond that, there was great
diversity in doctrine (theology), practice and ecclesial struc-
tures--all of which did not disturb the early Church's feeling
for orthodoxy and unity.

The Church also claimed from the beginning that she had been
entrusted with the "power of the keys," which, already in the Old
Testament and contemporary Judaism, included the "pastoral office"
but was primarily directed toward the "teaching office." However,
in the Church, it is primarily pastoral; although, it is also intended to protect the corpus fidei. Yet, in this function, it

_____

pretation. Studies Presented to John Knox), (Cambridge, 1967)
345f.

still remains subordinate to the Christian principle of love and
the Church's pastoral nature and needs as, for example, is seen
in Paul's confrontation with Peter when the latter's refusal to
eat with gentiles threatened to split the Church and, as it were,
set up a second and secondary order of salvation (Gal 2,11-14).

The exercise of the Church's disciplinary power became especially forceful in a number of situations which prompted early
Christianity to define her doctrinal, moral and structural limits
of tolerance. Harsh verbal correction or excommunication were
used to establish or maintain a necessary amount of order (1 Cor
14,23f.26-40), to prevent loafing in the community (2 Thes 3,6-
15) as well as for ethical reasons (1 Cor 5,1-13) or the protection of the exclusivity of Christian communion which could not be
syncretized with Judaism or Paganism (1 Cor 10,14-22; Gal 2,11-
14). The doctrinal reasons for excommunication are especially
clear in the Pastoral and Catholic Epistles.

Although one cannot speak of excommunication from the Eucharist in the New Testament, this sacrament was certainly a major
point of reference in the practice of ecclesial discipline. But
it was not a matter of the "elements" of the Eucharist and how
they were related to other sacraments and Christian life or how
they were to be considered in themselves (a question of later
times); rather, it was a "question of the indissoluable inner connection of Sacrament and Church."[9] The Eucharist, by forming the
baptized individuals into the one Body of Christ, is the special
celebration and effective cause of this relation of Church and
Sacrament, and gives each member a special responsibility of love

---

9. Cf. G. Bornkamm, Herrenmahl, 206.

toward the other members of the Body.[10] The Eucharist is herewith appropriately given a nuptial theme since it is the condition and moment in which the Church, assembled with and in Christ
(1 Cor 10,16; 11,20.33), renews her love.[11] But with the delay
of the second coming of Christ, the first fervor of the Church
began to cool and heresy became an ever greater threat. Even
entire local churches were threatened with excommunication for
their loss of love and zeal (Apc 2,5). Such an excommunication,
however, must eventually take on a completely different character
and effect from that of an individual excommunication by raising
the problem of separate, real but non-intercommunicating Christian churches. In this case, the Eucharist is used, not to mark
the limits of the Church as the Body of Christ, but to establish
lines of demarcation within the Church. But this phenomenon does
not occur yet in the New Testament, except in so far as the later
writings of the New Testament recognize "degrees" of sinners
(1 Jn 5,16) and the fact that there are also "dishonorable vessels" within the Church (2 Tm 2,20f). The role of the Eucharist
in establishing the "external" limits of the Church to the exclusion of pagans (1 Cor 10,14-22) and Jews (Heb 13,10) is, however,
clearly indicated in the New Testament. But the warning which
St. Paul gives concerning unworthy communion in 1 Cor 11,27-32
obviously implies the role of the Eucharist in establishing
"internal" limits within the Church.

---

10. Ibid.
11. Cf. Jean-Jacques Allmen, Essai sur le Repas du Seigneur,
    (Cahiers Théologiques 55), (Neuchâtel, 1966) 60-62; J. Blank,
    art. cit., 177-82.

3. The Answer of the Fathers

a. Baptism and the Eucharist.

The noncanonical Christian literature of the first two centuries of Christianity presents a picture of ecclesial and eucharistic discipline which corresponds in large part to what is
found (explicitly or implicitly) in the New Testament. Very
early in the formation of eucharistic discipline is the explicit insistence that only the baptized may partake of this sacrament (Didache 9,5). The New Testament is not so explicit about
the necessity of Baptism before one may partake of the Eucharist.
However, the exclusion of Christians from pagan sacrifice (1 Cor
10,21) and, even more so, the exclusion of Jews from the Christian altar (Heb 13,10) certainly include this principle.[12]

The Church, as the new Israel, had to establish definite
criteria by which her members could be set apart from the "outsider" and recognized by all other members. A certain "exclusiveness" was required in spite of the catholocity of the Church
in her openness to all classes of people of all nations. Baptism, being a nonrepeatable act[13] could not be considered a
basis in itself for defining the limits of the new Israel.
Rather, there must also be some continuous act of the Church
which is open only to members in good standing and is thereby a

---

12. 1 Cor 7,14 cannot be taken as an indication that the unbap-
    tized children of Christian parents were admitted to the
    Eucharist any more than Jewish parents would have admitted
    their uncircumcised sons to partake of Jewish sacrifices.
    Cf. above, p. 17, n. 12.

13. The relationship of Christian Baptism to John's baptism, to
    Jewish circumcision, and to dying and rising with Christ to-
    gether with the Church's rejection of rebaptism even in
    cases of heretical Baptism all indicate this fact.

<u>dynamic</u> extension of Baptism and all that this sacrament implies.
The <u>Didache's</u> ruling that only the baptized could partake of the
Eucharist, which was interpreted as the new and pure oblation of
the New Covenant (Mal 1,11ff), is analogous to the practice of
the old Israel which insisted on circumcision and freedom from
(cultic) impurity before one could partake of its sacrifices.
Thus, the exclusion of the unbaptized from the Eucharist had
nothing to do with the <u>disciplina</u> <u>arcani</u>--a later practice among
Christians--nor with the secrecy of the mystery religions. Instead, it developed directly under the influence of the Old Testament concept that the unholy must be prevented from contacting
the holy.[14] When the problem of schismatic and heretical Eucharists later arose, it was not at first a question of "validity"
of this sacrament under these circumstances, but of its "integrity"--that is, the Eucharist as an expression not only of baptismal unity, but also of baptismal love, and freedom from the
sin and guilt that separate one from God.[15]

In view of the Christian understanding of love, it was at
least theoretically "self-evident" that no baptized person had
the right to partake of the Eucharist simply and exclusively on
the basis of his Baptism. Rather, his conscience had also to be
pure and unaccusing in regard to his neighbor. Thus, there is
the strong insistence that quarreling parties be reconciled before they come forth to prayer and the Eucharist. However, since

---

14. Cf. W. Elert, <u>op</u>. <u>cit</u>., 65f. For an extensive treatment of
the relationship between the "<u>communio</u> <u>sanctorum</u>" of the Creed
and the early Christian principle of τὰ ἅγια τοῖς ἁγίοις,
cf. <u>ibid</u>., 5-16, 166f.

15. <u>Ibid</u>., 68-70. Cf. also Mt 5,23f and <u>Di</u> 14,2 on the necessity
of settling quarrels and forgiving others prior to the (eucharistic) offering.

it was quite obvious that most persons hardly if ever have such
a conscience at all times, the Jewish custom of confession of
one's sinfulness or sins was applied, perhaps from the beginning,
to the preparation for participation in the Eucharist.

b. The hierarchy and the Eucharist.

The growing conflict with heretics and schismatics within
the Church eventually had effects upon her eucharistic discipline. However, it would require some time yet before the Church
would interpret herself explicitly and directly in eucharistic
categories in her opposition to these persons. In the meantime,
the relationship of the nonorthodox to the Church and the Eucharist was existentially determined and defined by the rapidly
developing hierarchy of ecclesial offices.

One of the earliest effects (by way of reaction) of the various nonorthodox movements upon the young Church's embryonic system of order and discipline was the furtherance of an institutionalized hierarchy and the eventual division of the Church into
"clergy and laity." However, it would be a mistake to ascribe
the growth of the hierarchy solely to this one cause. In this
system of ecclesial organization and with no fixed New Testament
canon yet, it is perfectly understandable that the first attempt
at determining one's orthodoxy meant determining the nature of
one's relationship with the bishop. Any party which claimed to
function religiously, but not in communion with the bishop, was
considered beyond the limit of the Church, and not simply as a
schismatic element.

As long as the bishop himself was "blameless," it was natural
to view him, the "president" of the community, as the best equip-
ped person to prevent schisms and cliques, and to restore peace,

unity and harmony as well as to preserve the purity of doctrine through his teaching, example, direction and delegation of power. As a pre-eminent successor of the Apostles, he was an especially important part in the whole complex of "apostolic elements" meant to test and preserve orthodoxy, which could no longer be regulated directly by the Apostles themselves now that they had died. As a result, churches which could claim to have had personal association with an Apostle or to be in possession of his letters were particularly influential in establishing the norms of orthodoxy.

Although the distinction often became obscured, the bishop was not meant to replace the Church or become identified with the whole Church as if he exhausted all aspects of apostolic succession so as to render all others in the Church nonessential and simply and totally subordinate to him. That is, he was not a leader who stood outside of and above the Church herself. Rather, his place was within the Church and in subordination to her through his service.

Ignatius saw a reflection of the "divine Hierarchy" in the ecclesial hierarchy, with the bishop as the image of the Father, the deacons representing Christ, and the presbyters acting as Apostles. The role of the bishop as apostolic successor is not made here by way of the bishop's office as such. That is, the hierarchy is not considered as exhaustive of apostolic succession. Rather, it is, for Ignatius, simply an earthly reflection of divine order and rule, but not the exclusive offices for apostolic succession. Orthodoxy could not be defined simply in terms of one's solid unity with the bishop. In the early Church, one's relation with the bishop was at first so strongly connected with

orthodoxy only because it was assumed that he was its most outstanding representative--both in his personal life as well as in
his office as bishop. Consequently, orthodoxy went beyond the
bishop to the Church's doctrine and worship, as is clear when Ignatius of Antioch pictures the Church harmoniously organized
around the bishop and the altar in her efforts to preserve the
purity of Christian faith.

Although this meant the suppression of the "private Eucharists"[16] of smaller groups on the basis of their nonassociation
with the bishop, the movement of "episcopalism" was not meant as
a self-goal--that is, the strengthening of the episcopacy by way
of the removal of all other elements that distracted from the
bishop's position. Rather, it was because these "private Eucharists" often represented unorthodox theology. On the other hand,
the Eucharist (or any other religious function) performed by the
bishop or at least with his permission (a sort of "nihil obstat")
was the best guarantee possible "this side of divinely assured
infallibility" that the Christian mysteries were being celebrated
in accordance with the Church's creed. To this extent, then, the
bishop's suppression of "unauthorized" Eucharists and religious
functions was a real exercise of the Church's infallibility--or
better expressed, of her "indefectibility and perennity in the
truth."[17]

---

16. These "private Eucharists" were probably attempts to extend
    the "freer form" of worship that Christians knew before the
    various local churches became too large to hold an "agape-
    Eucharist." However, as the communities increased in size,
    it proved more feasible to hold one large "simple Eucharist"
    under the bishop. Splinter groups apparently continued to
    hold their own Eucharists as they saw fit, but often came un-
    der the influence of unorthodox views. Cf. H. Lietzman, op.
    cit., 210.

17. Cf. Hans Küng, Unfehlbar? Eine Anfrage, (Zürich, Einsiedeln,
    Köln, 1970) 148f.

This principle made it possible for Ignatius and others to attack the heretics by asking them why they celebrated the Eucharist when their faith could not be harmonized with what this sacrament represented and was meant to effect. It was not the bishop's "authorization" that made the Eucharist "valid." Rather, his approval was simply "official evidence" that this or that Eucharist fully represented the integrity of the Church and was consequently valid. Thus, the Eucharist--the pre-eminent function and "element" of the Church as the Body of Christ--was a sign and function of <u>intregral</u> orthodoxy when celebrated under the bishop. However, this regulation served only to distinguish the "exterior limit" of eucharistic worship. In effect, one who had been accustomed to celebrate the Eucharist apart from the bishop needed only to discontinue and to come to the bishop's Eucharist in order to be recognized as orthodox. This was indeed a "simple system" of orthodoxy, but it was unable to furnish what Ignatius promised it would; for, 150 years later, the "arch-heretic," Paul of Samosata, is found sitting on the bishop's chair at Antioch; and 100 years after that, Antioch is being torn apart by four bishops who all claim the same chair of apostolic succession by way of Ignatius and who all mutually declare each other to be heretics or schismatics.[18] Ignatius had specific cases and conditions in mind which his "episcopal principle" was capable of correcting or preventing from getting worse.[19] To this extent,

---

18. Cf. W. Elert, <u>op. cit.</u>, 45f.
19. W. Bauer (<u>op. cit.</u>, 83) notes that the <u>Apocalypse of John</u> addresses seven Christian communities in Asia Minor; whereas, Ignatius writes only to three of these churches (Ephesus, Smyrna, Philadelphia). Bauer concludes that the other churches may have fallen prey to heretics (against whom the Apc warns) and were consequently unable to establish episcopal

his program was fully justified; but, in spite of his efforts, he was unable to abstract a permanently valid and applicable principle from the concrete situation.

A further step (of questionable value and justification) in the attempts to establish norms for orthodoxy is seen in Pope Victor's refusal of communion to an entire segment of the Church as a result of the Easter controversy between Rome and Asia Minor. Although the eastern practice of celebrating Easter at the same time as the Jewish Passover may have encouraged certain heretical groups of Christians, the controversy seems to have been essentially a matter of a particular episcopal authority attempting to establish a certain tradition in order to expand his sphere of authority and control by imposing uniformity upon the Church under the guise of maintaining a necessary and exclusive norm for orthodoxy. Apparently, this effort did not prove very successful for Victor; but it was definitely a turning point in the history of ecclesial discipline and excommunication when formerly approved pluralism in orthodox traditions suddenly became the occasion for unfriendly ecclesiastical divisions and interrupted communion. In such a case, however, there can be no question about integrity or validity of ecclesial-religious life of the excommunicated. Yet, the integrity of the life of the Body of Christ as such suffers due to the lack of harmonious communication among its members. There is a certain character of indefiniteness about this form of excommunication and closed communion that makes it difficult to define and to apply properly and justly.

---

leaders. If so, then Ignatius had no one in these communities to whom he could write and upon whose authority within the community orthodoxy could be restored.

However, it is a practice that nearly all Christian churches or confessions of modern times impose to some degree or other on each other.

It is significant to note that St. Irenaeus of Lyons, who was very much involved in the Easter controversy on behalf of Asia Minor, realized the inadequacy of St. Ignatius' "episcopal principle" of orthodoxy. As a result, he emphasized "tradition" as the ultimate test and principle. Unlike Ignatius, Irenaeus readily acknowledges that there can be unjust and even nonorthodox bishops, who will be convicted by God's Word. Consequently, Christians are to adhere only to those who preach apostolic doctrine (adv Haer 4,25,3f). This, however, as history all too soon proved, did not solve the problem of determining orthodoxy, but only "postponed" the question and shifted its point of reference from "Who is an orthodox bishop?" to "What is apostolic doctrine, both in its nature as well as in its positive expression?". Nevertheless, Irenaeus did not abandon the "episcopal principle." Rather, he clearly subordinated it to the concept of "apostolic succession." That is, Christians should show their presbyters (bishops) respect and obedience in as much as they have special apostolic succession and the "charism of truth" (adv Haer 4,26, 1f). But the "validity" of Christian religious action is not made dependent on the bishop's office as a means for handing on and guaranteeing the "powers of the priesthood."

Finally, note must be taken of the fact that men like Hippolytus and Novatian showed that even the papacy could not prevent schisms and heresy or insure orthodoxy any more effectively than the episcopal system as envisioned by Ignatius. This fact becomes perhaps most evident in Pope Honorius I's posthumous condemnation by Pope Leo II for the former's heretical or at least

heretically oriented stand in the controversy over whether or
not Jesus Christ had one or two wills.[20]

c. Communion and penance in the new Israel.

Besides the above described attempt to form norms to determine the "external limits" of Christian communion and orthodoxy,
another logical step in the development of eucharistic discipline
would be to establish "interior limits of eligibility" in regard
to participation in the Eucharist. Here, the emergence and development of the Church's penitential system is of prime importance and more or less subsumes all other aspects yet to be discussed in this chapter.

Since metanoia was meant to precede Baptism, this sacrament
could not be taken as a basis or "motive" for developing a system of ecclesial penance even though Penance was often seen as
an analogue to Baptism. But, just as Baptism was preceded by
repentance of one's sins and gave the individual admission to
the eucharistic life of the Church in the Body of Christ, so was
it reasonable that the Church would either totally expel someone
who went back on what his Baptism implied, or else at least provide the offender with an opportunity to renew these baptismal
implications and promises and insist that he do so before further
participation in the Eucharist. Consequently, the Eucharist was
the "natural" basis and motive upon which the Church could and
did develop a penitential system to meet the needs of a faithful
that was growing weary and lukewarm while waiting for Christ's
delayed second coming and the end of the world.

Probably from the very beginning, a self-examination of one's
"spiritual life" and some form of confession of sins preceded the

---

20. Cf. W. Elert, op. cit., 49.

actual reception of the Eucharist. This implies that, on occasion, someone might find it necessary in view of his reproving conscience to exclude himself from the Eucharist. From this simple form of "auto-excommunication," the next step was for the Church to impose some sort of limit on the religious activity and association of those members whose conduct or doctrine was unacceptable, but whose conscience did not reprove them for continued communion in the Church. In addition to officially imposed forms of excommunication or censures--which would of course be limited to what were considered really serious offenses--, provision was also made for members of the Church to air their disagreements and uncharitable quarrels and to arrive at reconciliation under ecclesial guidance and persuasion (Phil 4,2f; Mt 18,15-17 and par.; Didascalia 11). Ecclesially imposed excommunication from the Church or at least from prayer and the Eucharist was the result if the quarreling parties still refused to come to terms.

The development of officially imposed excommunication is, however, not an unmixed blessing. First of all, there is the possibility that the list of "serious sins" will become needlessly expanded, and there is the probability that the "officially serious sins" will become so "institutionalized" that the relative seriousness of many sins in the list will be absolutized while the circumstantial seriousness of sins not on the list will be overlooked. The principal of "willful sinning" as seen in the consideration of Heb 10,25 is all too easily forgotten and replaced by a long "examination of conscience" (printed on paper) that neatly indicates the "mortal" and "venial sins" and is routinely consulted to determine "genus, species and seriousness" of one's moral deviations. These dangers are already somewhat ac-

tualized in the Didache, which considers its commands and prohi-
bitions as the Gospel and also presents a number of rather super-
ficial ethical "tests" for the "true prophet," which, if they are
passed, remove the prophet from all further scrutiny.[21]

In Pastor Hermae, one is confronted with a penitential system that allows for several "degrees" of penitents. This development eventually had to raise the question of the relationship
of the various types of penitents to the Eucharist.[22] To a significant degree, the question was answered by the Didascalia,
which clearly states that those who have been excommunicated for
some reprehensible conduct, but who have since entered upon a
period of ecclesially imposed penance, are to be admitted only
to hear the preaching of the word. However, they are to be excluded from the rest of the community's worship--that is, prayer
and Eucharist. The penance lasted until the community, under
the guidance of the bishop, had satisfied itself that the penitent was sincere in his repentance and therefore worthy of being
readmitted to the full worship of the Church. The period of
penance and partial excommunication ended with a liturgy consisting of the imposition of hands on the penitent by the bishop
and the prayers of the community.

Tertullian likewise affirms that the Christian gathering is
also an occasion for the exercise of discipline and formal excommunication. As long as he remained in the Church, he recognized
and urged paenitentia secunda for those who had grievously sinned after Baptism. But his inclination toward rigorism led him

---

21. Ibid., 60.
22. Ibid., 73.

to equate heresy with idolatry and to reserve the Church and
sacraments for saints rather than for sanctification. Thus, he
declared heretical Baptism to be totally invalid,[23] and, as a
Montanist, refused to grant paenitentia secunda to those who
sinned seriously.

Although Tertullian employs the Church's doctrine and practice of the Eucharist in defending the physical nature of Christ
against the Docetics, he abandons the connection that the second
century Church so emphatically made between the Eucharist and
bodily resurrection. Perhaps the Church of the second century
had been too one-sided in this teaching with the result that
simpler Christians came to look upon this sacrament as an "automatic" means to salvation irrespective of the individual's moral
life and state of faith. Consequently, Tertullian formulated
the principle of faith as the foundation of sanctification. However, he defined faith as orthodoxy in doctrine, coupled with a
moral life since St. Paul maintained that all things done without faith are sin (Rm 14,23).

On the one hand, this meant emphasizing doctrinal truth over
and beyond the hierarchical structure of the Church as the norm
and guarantee of orthodoxy. Therefore, Tertullian had little
difficulty in justifying his break with the "physical" Church in
favor of a "pneumatic" church of spirituals. Undoubtedly, the
Carthaginian's theology of the common priesthood of Christians
also contributed to his defection to Montanism. In so far as
Tertullian wanted to combat the one-sidedness of the popular

---

23. In this context, "validity" is meant strictly since it is
    more than just a question of "integrity."

conception that the hierarchy more or less exhausted the priesthood of Christians and "guaranteed" orthodoxy, his reaction is
understandable and justified. However, his concept of salvation
by faith and of a church for saints only was equally one-sided,
and isolated the individual from the visible Church and from
Christ. Salvation depended on the individual's ability to maintain purity of doctrine and purity of life. The ultimate result
was a "justification by works" rather than by faith in the Pauline sense and an intollerance toward "less spiritual" Christians.
With that, the Church's catholicity is destroyed; for there is no
longer any room in her for even repentant sinners or for a legitimate theological pluralism. Everything that binds the Church
together at the personal level is dissolved into the thin air of
a purely "spiritual Church" with extremely narrow and demanding
requirements for membership.

Tertullian took orthodoxy so "seriously" and interpreted it
so narrowly that it became separated from the visible, hierarchical Church. However, the Church which he deserted did not abandon the principle of the necessity of union with the bishop for
continued orthodoxy. Nevertheless, Tertullian did effect a certain "mellowing" of this principle in the Church in as much as
her reaction to his rigorism led her to an implicit distinction
between heresy and schism and the recognition of the fact that
neither heresy nor schism necessarily placed one so totally beyond the Church that all sacramental and religions life of such
persons is without any proper effect. But the later explicit
recognition of heretical Baptism coupled with the generally accepted belief that "extra ecclesiam nulla salus est" showed that
the Church, for all practical purposes, did not really think in

terms of "degrees of nonmembership."[24] Thus, even though the
orthodox Church granted the <u>pax</u> to all penitent sinners, she
looked upon them and treated them as a type of catechumen. Indeed, they were not rebaptized, but the parallel between Baptism
and Penance was consciously and rigorously made to the extent
that <u>paenitentia</u> <u>secunda</u> was generally considered as unrepeatable as Baptism itself.

In the history of eucharistic excommunication, it is obvious
that the Church's understanding of Baptism at any given period
must be considered. Consequently, Hippolytus' contribution to a
theology of Baptism is very important for the present study; for
his interpretation took Baptism beyond the stage of "<u>paenitentia</u>
<u>prima</u>," and has had the greatest influence upon the Church's prac-
tice of Baptism throughout all subsequent centuries.

For Hippolytus, Baptism is essentially the last step in a
series of <u>exorcisms</u> which are meant to free the candidate of all
"spiritual impurity" and diabolical subjugation so that he could
participate in the life of the Church--and especially in the prayers and sacraments. Already in the <u>Didache</u> (7,2f), the instruction that <u>cold</u> <u>flowing</u> water is to be preferred in Baptism hints
at the "theology of exorcism" found in Hippolytus since, according to the ancient world's belief, demons were more effectively
removed by cold running water and were more apt to gather in still,

---

24. It should be noted that the explicit recognition of the principle, "<u>extra</u> <u>ecclesiam</u>" etc., and the explicit acceptance of
heretical Baptism arose simultaneously in the Church, but in
different areas (Rome and North Africa) then experiencing a
number of disagreements over theological differences. At
that time, the principles appeared to be mutually exclusive;
and it has been only the ecclesiological developments of recent years that have been able to reconcile these principles
with each other to some extent.

warm water.[25]   Clement of Alexandria (<u>Strom</u> III,12, 82,6) is the
first of the Church Fathers to emphasize that Christians need
not and should not bother with the cultic washings of Judaism
after marital intercourse.[26]   Yet, the later outstanding Alex-
andrians, Origen and Dionysius, placed cultic restrictions on
Christians for normal and legitimate marital intercourse or even
for the normal biological cycle associated with sexually mature
humans.   Obviously, the Old Testament concept of purity which
the New Testament so strongly opposed was making a "come back"
in the Church.   The Church's interpretation of herself as the
new Israel sometimes failed to see what the "new" really meant,
and reverted to Old Testament categories and concepts of religion and holiness.   The effects of this neo-Judaism was perhaps
most obvious in several concepts of the Christian priesthood.

Origen, seeing that Christians form a common priesthood (<u>in</u>
<u>Lv</u> <u>hom</u> 6,2), makes this the basis for determining who belongs
to the Church and who does not.   Serious sin <u>per</u> <u>se</u> excludes one
from the Church because it robs the sinner of the sanctity necessary to belong to the holy priesthood of Christians.   In this
context, the Eucharist becomes a sign of one's holiness and membership in the common priesthood, while the unworthy communicant
is compared to Judas and seen as one who invites God's judgment
upon himself.   Origen's theory of ἀποκατάστασις and thematic dis-
association of the Eucharist from the resurrection of Christians
plus his own form of "spiritual Church" leave the Eucharist without any <u>specific</u> sanctifying function within the Church of for the
future.

---

25. Cf. O. Böcher, <u>op</u>. <u>cit</u>., 204f.
26. <u>Ibid</u>., 316.

In Cyprian of Carthage, the application of Old Testament categories to the Christian priesthood reaches a climax. But, unlike Origen who rightly gave all Christians a place in the priesthood even though he still applied Old Testament categories too directly to the common priesthood, Cyprian reserved all aspects of the priesthood for the hierarchy, with the bishop acting as "highpriest." His theology of the priesthood and of the unity of the Church forced him to conclude that heretical and schismatic sacraments and religious life were totally invalid. Just as the Epistle to the Hebrews became anachronistically rigoristic in the hands of the Montanists, so did Cyprian's writings and theology of Christian holiness supply fuel for the Donatist controversy in North Africa a century later. The consideration of Cyprian's contribution to an understanding of communion and penance in the new Israel is best left for the section which presently follows.

Dionysius of Alexandria clearly indicates that the admission of a penitent to the Eucharist meant the end of the period of penitence and excommunication even when formal absolution was lacking. His readiness to forego this absolution shows that he did not consider the entire penitential process to be a "second Baptism" in the more rigid sense; although, personal repentance on the part of the sinner still remained a prerequisite for readmission to the Eucharist. For Dionysius, Baptism itself has a "relative" value at least to the extent that he recognized heretical Baptism and saw the Eucharist as the sacrament (over and beyond Baptism) in the "building up" of the Church in that it fully incorporates Christians into the Body of Christ.

d. Once again, Baptism and the Eucharist.

St. Cyprian reacted strongly to what he considered an all too
lax treatment of those apostates who sought readmission to the
Church during or after the Decian persecution. He threatened to
(and did) excommunicate those priests who did not comply with
his regulations. This disciplinary measure also fell upon those
who held communion with such priests. Foremost in Cyprian's
mind was the impropriety in readmitting the lapsi to the Eucharist before they had completed the prescribed period or conditions for repentance. The exclusion of such persons from the
Eucharist was not meant as a punishment, but was done out of respect and concern for the sacrament itself as an effective sign
of ecclesial unity and Christ's presence. In addition to that,
the refusal to admit these persons to the Eucharist all too hur-
riedly was meant to ward off both spiritual and physical harm
from them. In this case, the harmful effects could come upon
even infants whose parents had given them a bit of the pagan sacrifice.

Basically, admission to the Eucharist was a question of one's
relationship to the Church--that is, penitents were not considered real members of the Church until after they had received the
pax from the bishop. The baptismal controversy between North
Africa and Rome was essentially the same question--namely, the
relationship of heretics and schismatics with the Church and the
Eucharist.

For Cyprian, the establishment of a separate Eucharist by
heretical and schismatic parties was the ultimate sign and act
of revolt and separation from the Church. Yet his theory of the
unique unity of the Church was sprung by Rome's recognition of

-437-

the validity of heretical Baptism. Rome, however, was unable to offer any really satisfactory theological explanations to refute North Africa's practice of "rebaptism" except to say that tradition was against it. Cyprian's fellow bishop and friend, Firmilian, took the next logical step and remarked concerning the Bishop of Rome:

> If he surrenders such great and heavenly gifts of the Church and grants them to the heretics, then what else (is there for him to do) except join those for whom he defends and arrogates so much grace? But now he illogically hesitates to give in to them in the remaining matters as well and to be their fellow associate, so that all at one and the same time he might come to their gatherings and mingle his prayers with these characters and set up an altar and sacrifice in common with them.[27]

In the mind of the bishops of North Africa and their partisans, the validity of a sacrament depended on the unity of the minister and the Holy Spirit, who "confined" himself to the Church. This meant further that Baptism was considered valid only when administered by a properly ordained person still in full union with the Church--that is, a person who has been formally ordained or at least delegated by a Catholic bishop and who is not _extra_ _ecclesiam_ for any moral or doctrinal reasons. Thus, Rome's recognition of the validity of heretical and schismatic Baptism appeared tantamount to admitting the validity of the episcopal-apostolic succession and ordination of such persons, with the result that they could be lacking in nothing that is proper to the integrity of the Church. And if that is the case, then there should be no reason to refuse intercommun-

---

27. Cf. above, pp. 402f.

ion with such persons (in spite of doctrinal differences) any more than with any other local or regional church of Christendom.

These objections from third-century Africa have never been adequately answered or considered, either by way of refutation or by way of positive evaluation for whatever truth they may possibly contain. Had the questions been adequately answered, many problems of today's ecumenical efforts and situation would perhaps be already solved.

4. Why Eucharistic Excommunication?

At this point, it is possible and desirable to give a concise summary of early Christian motives for excluding one from the Eucharist. In view of all that has been said on the previous pages, it is also permissible to confine the commentary to a minimum. An ultimate classification and an exhaustive enumeration of the early Church's underlying motives for eucharistic excommunication is not the object here; for that would be well-nigh impossible due to a number of reasons, but mainly because of the divine origin of the Church and the humanness of her members, whose motives for action are not always the result of fully rational reflections.

Since the early Church made no adequate distinction between ecclesiology and soteriology--the Church being identical with those who were to be saved and were therefore already saved--the ecclesiological motives for eucharistic excommunication were often equally soteriological. Paul's insistence that love of neighbor be a prerequisite for participation in the one Eucharist of the Church is not only meant to preserve the unity of the Church as the Body of Christ, but also to prevent the unworthy communicants from incurring additional guilt by eating and drinking an unfavorable judgment unto themselves that may lead even to physical ills and death, which, in turn, is meant to put a stop to their sinning so that they may still be numbered among the saved. If one judges himself before partaking of the Eucharist, then he can be spared the "trial by ordeal" that the unworthy communicant undertakes in receiving the Eucharist. But even if one communicates unworthily, the resulting physical afflictions are the Lord's work of chastisement that put an end to the sinning so that the sinner may still be saved and "not condemned with this world" (1 Cor 11,31f). The unworthy communicant has the choice of withdrawing from the Eucharist until he has amended his life and renewed his love of neighbor, or he may continue to partake of the Eucharist and face the above mentioned consequences. The motive for eucharistic excommunication is to move one to amendment of life before the Lord has to intervene in his own way in order to save the sinner from destroying all that is qualitatively Christian in himself.

The case of the excommunicated Corinthian (1 Cor 5,5) serves to manifest the supposed association that Satan takes up with such persons. However, the positive value that Paul attached to this situation was soon forgotten, and later generations of Christians often considered the sinner (especially heretics) and non-Christians as somehow possessed by the devil and therefore as a source of diabolical influence upon the rest of the community. Moreover, the presence of such a person in the community could supposedly lessen or destroy the value of the Church's prayers and sacraments. Some Church Fathers explicitly combatted such notions, but only with qualified success.

In general, the Eucharist was withheld from those who were for any reason extra ecclesiam. This meant the exclusion of

pagans and Jews who had not yet been baptized as well as Christians who had sinned seriously enough to cast doubt upon the sincerity of their baptismal metanoia. And just as pagans and Jews
could only be admitted to the Eucharist by way of Baptism, so
was it the same with serious sinners, who could be readmitted to
the Eucharist only by way of Penance, the "second Baptism."
Underlying the (implicit or explicit) eucharistic excommunication of the nonbaptized and sinners is the concept that such persons were associates of the devil or at least nonassociates of
Christ. Eventually, both Baptism and Penance came to be viewed
and valued as forms of exorcism. This is especially obvious in
Hippolytus. On the more positive side, however, such persons
were excluded from the Eucharist out of respect for the sacrament itself as an effective sign of the unity of the Church (as
a holy priesthood) with Christ. The underlying motive for eucharistic excommunication is, in this respect, simply the belief
and practice of all religions that the "holy" and the "unholy"
must be kept apart: τα αγια τοις αγιοις. This motive, of course,
could contain a host of other derived motives, depending on the
various definitions of "holy" and "unholy."

The outcome of the Easter controversy between Rome and Aisa
Minor introduced a completely new aspect to eucharistic excommunication; although, this was not fully recognized at the time.
The refusal of one part of the Church to share its religious
(esp., eucharistic) life with another part of the Church cannot
logically (but illogically it is existentially possible as evi-
denced by history itself) build on the above mentioned motives
for excommunication. Thus, it is perfectly in order for anyone
to question in what sense and to what an extent such a situation
can really be called excommunication. However, the logic of the

situation ultimately depends on the ecclesiology (or ecclesiologies) held by the two sides. If one side refuses to recognize the ecclesiality of the other side, then the motives for excommunication may very well be those enumerated above. One of the better historical examples of this situation is found in Cyprian.

Cyprian's ecclesiology, built upon a very narrow and one-sided concept of the hierarchy, identified union with the bishop as union _with_ the Church, and the union of bishops with each other as the union _of_ the Church (both the subjective and objective genetive are meant here). In other words, _extra episcopum nulla salus est_.

The problem inherent in Cyprian's ecclesiology, however, does not really become evident until the question of a bishop's excommunication is raised. In this case, he no longer is united to the other bishops and is therefore logically outside of the union of the Church. As a further consequence, no one united to him can be thereby united to the Church. The weakness of Cyprian's ecclesiology is not all too evident as long as the excommunicated bishop's subjects can attach their allegiance to some other bishop in union with the Church. However, when one whole segment of the Church breaks off communion with the other, then the whole system of ecclesiality is thrown into question. Pope Stephen's threat to excommunicate the bishops of North Africa unless they discontinued the practice of rebaptizing heretically baptized persons who wished to enter the Church was totally incomprehensible to Cyprian and cut the basis out from under his entire system of ecclesiology.

At the time of the Easter controversy, no one believed that Rome's refusal of communion to the Church of Asia Minor meant that the latter ceased to be a real church simply due to the rupture of communion. But for North Africa, it was a different matter since these bishops felt they were the orthodox representatives of the Church, and yet Rome was threatening to excommunicate them. This not only put Cyprian's ecclesiology into question, but it led the North Africans to ask if the concept "Church" had any meaning and basis in reality at all. But aside from the weakness of North Africa's ecclesiology, the question which Firmilian asked of Rome remains a valid question even though it must be asked from a different point of view today. Namely, since it is a fact that most Christian churches (including the Roman Catholic Church) now officially recognize at least some measure of ecclesiality in the various Christian churches not in communion with each other, how can the separation of these churches be any longer "justified" and tolerated? Are the differences a real basis for further separation, or are they legitimate expressions that a truly catholic Church can and must embrace?

The question that introduced this section, "Why eucharistic excommunication?", has changed in its internal content. Originally, it was simply a question directed toward uncovering the various historical motives underlying eucharistic excommunication and excommunication in general. But already with Cyprian and his friends, that particular form or interpretation of the question could no longer be answered when it was a matter of "mutual" excommunication between entire segments of the Church. The question then came to mean: Upon what basis can a theology of excommunication and refusal to share the Eucharist with another church (!) be built? Simple and direct answers cannot be given. Eventually, an attempt must be made at giving some answers. However, as far as the main function and aim of this study are concerned, the object of the present work is completed. That is, the object was first of all to present the historical steps in the emergence of eucharistic excommunication in such a way that the facts would be made readily available to anyone interested in finding and using them in formulating <u>his</u> <u>own</u> conclusions. To this extent this study is meant to be a "handbook." Nevertheless, this need not exclude another function of the work--namely, to demonstrate how the steps in the historical development of eucharistic excommunication eventually led to the dilemma-type question which Firmilian and Cyprian presented to Rome during the baptismal controversy. Their question is still going in search of answers.

Finding the right note with which to conclude this study is even more difficult than finding the right note to start on. Undoubtedly, there are many who would like to see the present writer go on to declare unreservedly that his investigations prove that intercommunion should be liberally permitted in today's ecumenical situation. Admittedly, the present writer is not opposed to this idea, but he is most reluctant to make such a statement simply out of the results of the research contained in this work. Before that could be done, it would be necessary to analyze the present situation from a number of angles. There is not only the problem of researching all the literature that has been produced within our own generation on the question, but it would also be necessary to follow the question in its entire history from the point where this study has left it up to our own day.

It would be a great mistake to equate the nature of today's ecclesial divisions with those which the Church experienced during Cyprian's lifetime and earlier. But it would be an equally great mistake to overlook the similarities. It seems then that the results of the foregoing study can at least be applied _muta-tis mutandis_ to our modern inquiries, even though an unqualified direct application cannot be justified. However, in the ecumenical situation of our day, there are other factors to be considered before even a modified application of this study can be truly fruitful.

In many instances, these factors have a certain amount in common with other cases in history, and, in other cases, they are without parallel. The old questions--especially since the Reformation of the 16th century--concerning the nature of the Eucharist and the priesthood, the nature of the Church and the role of its leaders in the ecclesial-sacramental system are still very much with us. On the other hand, no period of history can claim to have shown so much general concern for the ecumenical questions and problems of the various Christian churches as our own generation. The mere immensity of the number of persons, Christian and non-Christian alike, from all walks of life who are somehow contributing to the present surge of ecumenical interest has created an unparalleled pastoral situation which, of itself, must enter into any consideration of the possibility of intercommunion. For those people who see the work of the Holy Spirit in present-day efforts to heal the divisions within the Church, the ecumenical movement is not merely the servant of the churches at the beck and call of their established leaders. Rather, it is a movement of the Spirit than can justly claim the hearing and attention of the churches not only at the "grass-roots" level, but also and perhaps especially at the level of their established governing organs.

It can no longer be only a matter of holding the traditional stand while trying to develop a detailed and up-dated theology of _communicatio_ in _sacris_. Instead, it is now also a question of whether or not the various established churches can _theologically_ justify continued eucharistic separation or foot-dragging in the matter when the present situation is not as in days of yore and when so many persons, particularly younger people, are no longer internally hindered by confessional name labels in meeting together for worship. The Church cannot simply tag these persons as "ecumenical fanatics" and justly turn her back on them "in the interest of truth," when the truth is that the existing differences are often no longer seen as personal hindrances to the reunification of the Church. This, of course, does not remove the differences; but it does mean that they cannot be considered in the light of a past generation when the attitude toward inter-communion was generally negative in nearly all churches. The fact that there now exists a changed and positive attitude in so many people is itself a theologically significant factor. But this fact has not been generally recognized or fully evaluated by the established authorities of the various churches.

The situation just described has given rise to another pro-blem in the modern ecumenical movement which must be dealt with before any more lasting progress can be made. This is the fact and problem of the undeniably ever-widening gap between the auth-orities of the established churches and the protagonists of the ecumenical movement. Of course, there are many in the ranks of established authority who are as enthusiastic about the progress of present-day ecumenical endeavors as anyone else. But for such persons, the problem of the widening gap is often doubly accute, when, on the one hand, they try to promote the ecumenical spirit and activity of the people entrusted to their care, but, on the other hand, find themselves unduly restricted by other ecclesial authorities over them and who often view matters from a different theological plane. Such circumstances naturally tend to keep ecumenically oriented persons from advancing or entirely out of positions of authority, so that the gap becomes ever wider and deeper by means of this vicious circle.

Gnosticism was rejected by the early Church, not because of its ridiculous cosmologies, but because it sought salvation through "knowledge" of certain esoteric facts rather than through a personal commitment to God and neighbor by way of faith and love. Is there not a danger today of "neo-Gnosticism" in many churches where "knowledge" (that is, intellectual assent to a set body of doctrine) seems to be valued more than faith and love themselves in Paul's sense? This danger would seem to be at least as real as the danger that "ecumenical enthusiasts" will reduce the Church to a loose organization of religious humanists without any use for doctrine and the truths of faith.

The outcome of the division of the East and the West in the Easter controversy has taught us that there can indeed be a cessation of fraternal communion between local churches. However, the real scandal is not that such unfortunate divisions arise from time to time, but that later generations feel somehow obligated to continue the separation. The divisions in the Church that resulted from the controversy over rebaptism have taught us that such divisions cannot reach so deep as to destroy the ecclesiality and holiness of the separated groups. Nor did the Church disintegrate at the time as a result of the differences. But this is no reason to let the divisions remain as if they did not hinder the holiness and effectiveness of the entire Church.

What role intercommunion in the Eucharist should play in the reunification of the churches cannot be stated a priori, but must be drawn from the pastoral situation of the Church at any given time and place. St. Cyprian himself furnishes us with the basic principle for such a step, namely, his about-face from his original contention that the lapsi must complete a long period of penance before they are again "pure" enough to be readmitted to the Eucharist. Why did Cyprian change his mind about this issue? He did it because he had vision enough to see that the pastoral needs of his church, about to undergo another persecution, required such a step. Nor did he take this step begrudgingly. Rather, he pointed out that the hastened readmission of the repentant apostates to the Eucharist was, under the changed circumstances, one of the most Christ-like tasks that a bishop could possibly undertake (ep 57,3).

Perhaps we cannot simply say that the very same procedure should be taken today in regard to intercommunion; but it is important to note that St. Cyprian recognized the priority of the "pastoral principle" even to the extent of reversing a former eucharistic practice of discipline that, at one time, appeared beyond the possibility of change. Modern churches should seriously consider this example as a principle of action which guides the Church in a world of change and history instead of placing her in a world of Platonic inertia. Christianity is not a religion that exists for its own sake. Instead, it exists for the sake of the sanctification of its members and all mankind. Does this not justify the priority of pastoral principles in the Church's discipline and application of her doctrine? Might it not be that the present pastoral needs of the universal Church can only be met through a greater eucharistic openness of all Christian churches even before complete unity in faith is achieved?

BIBLIOGRAPHY

I. CITED SOURCES

Corpus Apologetarum Christianorum Saeculi Secundi, ed. by Io. Car.
Th. eques de Otto, (Jena, 1876³).

Corpus Christianorum, Series Latina, (Turnhout, 1954ff).

Corpus Scriptorum Ecclesiasticorum Latinorum, (Vienna, 1866ff).

[Cyprian of Carthage]. Saint Cyprien, L'Oraison Dominicale,
(Études d'Histoire et de Philosophie Religieuses 58), ed. and
annotated by Michel Méveillaud, (Paris, 1964).

La Didachè: Instructions des Apôtres, critical text and commentary by Jean-Paul Audet, in: Études Bibliques 49 (1958).

Didascalia Apostolorum, the Syriac Version translated and accompanied by the Verona Latin Fragments, introduction and notes
by R. Hugh Connolly, (Oxford, 1929).

Didascalia et Constitutiones Apostolorum, ed. by F.X. Funk,
(Paderborn, 1905).

[Didascalia]. Die Syrische Didaskalia, (TU, neue Folge 10, Heft
2), translated and annotated by Hans Achelis and Johannes
Flemming, (Leipzig, 1904).

ΔΙΟΝΥΣΙΟΥ ΛΕΙΨΑΝΑ--The Letters and other Remains of Dionysius of
Alexandria, (Cambridge Patristic Texts, ed. by A.J. Mason),
ed. by Charles Feltoe, (Cambridge, 1904).

[Epistula Apostolorum]. Gespräche Jesu mit seinen Jüngern nach
der Auferstehung, ein katholish-apostolisches Sendschreiben
des 2. Jahrhunderts, ed., translated and annotated by Carl
Schmidt and Isaak Wajnberg, (Leipzig, 1919).

Eusebius, Kirchengeschichte (kleine Ausgabe), ed. by Eduard
Schwartz, (Leipzig, 1914²).

-451-

BIBLIOGRAPHY

<u>Die</u> <u>griechischen</u> <u>christlichen</u> <u>Schriftsteller</u> <u>der</u> <u>ersten</u> <u>drei</u>
<u>Jahrhunderte</u>, published by the <u>Kirchenväter-Commission</u> <u>der</u>
<u>köngl.</u> <u>preussischen</u> <u>Akademie</u> <u>der</u> <u>Wissenschaften</u>, (Leipzig,
1897ff).

[Hippolytus of Rome]. <u>La</u> <u>Tradition</u> <u>Apostolique</u> <u>de</u> <u>Saint</u> <u>Hip-</u>
<u>polyte,</u> <u>Essai</u> <u>de</u> <u>Reconstitution</u>, (<u>Liturgiewissenschaftliche</u>
<u>Quellen</u> <u>und</u> <u>Forschungen</u> 39), ed. and translated by Bernard
Botte, (Münster, 1963).

----. <u>The</u> <u>Treatise</u> <u>on</u> <u>the</u> <u>Apostolic</u> <u>Tradition</u> <u>of</u> <u>St.</u> <u>Hippolytus</u>
<u>of</u> <u>Rome</u> <u>Bishop</u> <u>and</u> <u>Martyr</u>, ed. with historical introduction,
textual materials and translation with critical apparatus
and critical notes by Gregory Dix, (London, 1937).

[Irenaeus of Lyons]. <u>Sancti</u> <u>Irenaei</u> <u>Episcopi</u> <u>Lugdunensis</u> <u>Libros</u>
<u>quinquae</u> <u>adversus</u> <u>Haereses</u>, ed. by W. Wigan Harvey, (Cam-
bridge, 1857 [republished in Ridgewood, New Jersey, 1965]).

<u>Patres</u> <u>Apostolici</u>, ed. by F.X. Funk, (Tübingen, 1901 and 1913).

<u>Patrologiae</u> <u>cursus</u> <u>completus</u>. <u>Series</u> <u>prima</u> <u>latina</u>, (Paris,
1844ff), <u>Series</u> <u>graeca</u>, (Paris, 1857ff), ed. by J.P. Migne.

[Plinius]. <u>C.</u> <u>Plini</u> <u>Caecili</u> <u>Secundi</u> <u>Epistularum</u> <u>Libri</u> <u>Novem</u>
<u>Epistularum</u> <u>ad</u> <u>Traianum</u> <u>Liber</u> <u>Panegyricus</u>, ed. by H. Keil,
(Leipzig, 1896).

<u>Sacrorum</u> <u>Conciliorum</u> <u>nova</u> <u>et</u> <u>amplissima</u> <u>collectio</u>, ed. by Joannes
Dominicus Mansi, (Florence, 1759ff).

<u>Tertullian's</u> <u>Homily</u> <u>on</u> <u>Baptism</u>, ed. with text, introduction,
translation and commentary by Ernest Evans, (London, 1964).

II. CONSULTED LITERATURE

Achelis, Hans. Das Christentum in den ersten drei Jahrhunderten, (Leipzig, 1925).

Afanassieff, Nikolai. Una Sancta, in: Irénikon 36 (1963) 436-75.

Allchin, Arthur M. The Eucharistic Offering, in: Studia Liturgica 1 (1962) 101-14.

Allmen, Jean-Jacques von. Essai sur le Repas du Seigneur, (Cahiers Théologiques 55, ed. by J-J von Allmen), (Neuchâtel, 1966).

Altaner, Berthold. Patrology, (New York, 1961²).

Auer, Johannes. Einheit und Frieden als Frucht der eucharistischen Mahlgemeinschaft, (Aktuelle Fragen zur Eucharistie, ed. by Michael Schmaus), (Munich, 1960) 110-55.

Ausgewählte Martyr-Akten, Sammlung Ausgewählter kirchen- und dogmen-geschichtlicher Quellenschriften, (neue Folge 3, ed. by Rudolf Knopf and G. Krüger), (Tübingen, 1929).

Bardenhewer, Otto. Geschichte der altkirchlichen Literatur, 1, (Freiburg im Breisgau, 1913²).

Barrett, C.K. A Commentary on the First Epistle to the Corinthians (BNTC), (London, 1968).

Bauer, Walter. Rechtgläubigkeit und Ketzerei im ältesten Christentum, (Beiträge zur historischen Theologie 10, ed. by Gerhard Ebeling), (Tübingen, 1964²).

Baur, Ferdinand Christian. Das Christenthum und die christliche Kirche der drei ersten Jahrhunderte, (Stuttgart-Bad Cannstatt, 1966 [1853]).

BIBLIOGRAPHY

Benoit, Pierre. Exégèse et Théologie, 1, (Paris, 1961).

Benson, Edward. Cyprian; His Life, His Times; His Work, (London, 1897).

Berger, Klaus. Zu den sogenannten Sätzen Heiligen Rechts, in NTS 17 (1970). 10-40.

Bethune-Baker, J.F. An Introduction to the Early History of Christian Doctrine to the Time of the Council of Chalcedon, (London, 1962^{12} [1903]).

Betz, Johannes. Die Eucharistie in der Didache, in: Archiv für Liturgiewissenschaft 11 (1969) 10-39.

-----. Die Eucharistie in der Zeit der griechischen Väter, (Freiburg im Breisgau, 1955).

Betz, Otto. The dichotomized Servant and the End of Judas Iscariot, Light on the dark Passages: Matthew 24,51 and parallel; Acts 1,18, in: Revue de Qumran 5 (1964) 43-58.

-----. Der Paraklet, Fürsprecher im häretischen Spätjudentum, im Johannes-Evangelium und in neu gefundenen gnostischen Schriften, (Arbeiten zur Geschichte des Spätjudentums und Urchristentums 2) (Leiden, Köln, 1963).

Bévenot, Maurice. The Tradition of Manuscripts, a Study in the Transmission of St. Cyprian's Treatises, (Oxford, 1961).

Blank, Josef. Eucharistie und Kirchengemeinschaft nach Paulus, in: Una Sancta 23 (1968) 172-83.

Bligh, John. Galatians, a Discussion of St. Paul's Epistle, (Householder Commentaries 1), (London, 1969).

Böcher, Otto. Dämonenfurcht und Dämonenabwehr, ein Beitrag zur

Vorgeschichte der christlichen Taufe, (Beiträge zur Wissenschaft vom alten und neuen Testament, 5. Folge, 10. [90.] Heft, ed. by K.H. Rengstorf and L. Rost), (Stuttgart, Berlin, Köln, Mainz, 1970).

Borig, Rainer. Der wahre Weinstock, Untersuchungen zu Jo 15,1-10, (Studien zum Alten und Neuen Testament 16, ed. by Vinzenz Hamp and Josef Schmid), (Munich, 1967).

Bornkamm, Günther. Das Anathema in der urchristlichen Abendmahlsliturgie, in: Theologische Literaturzeitung 75 (1950) 227-30.

----. Herrenmahl und Kirche bei Paulus, in: NTS 2 (1955/56) 202-06.

Brichto, Herbert. The Problem of "Curse" in the Hebrew Bible, (Journal of Biblical Literature Monograph Series 73), (Philadelphia, 1968[2] [1963]).

Brooke, A.E. A Critical and Exegetical Commentary on the Johannine Epistles, (ICC), (Edinburgh, 1957 [1912]).

Brox, Norbert. Die Pastoralbriefe, (RNT 7/2), (Regensburg, 1969).

Bruce, F.F. Commentary on the Epistle to the Hebrews, (NLCNT), (London, Edinburgh, 1964).

Bultmann, Rudolf. Die drei Johannesbriefe, (KEKNT), (Göttingen, 1967).

----. Das Evangelium des Johannes, (KEKNT), (Göttingen, 1950[2]).

----. Die Geschichte der synoptischen Tradition, (Göttingen, 1967[7]).

----. Theologie des Neuen Testaments, (Tübingen, 1968[6]).

Caird, G.B. A Commentary on the Revelation of St. John the
Divine, (BNTC), (London, 1966).

Campenhausen, Hans Freiherr von. Kirchliches Amt und geistliche
Vollmacht in den ersten drei Jahrhunderten, (Beiträge zur
historischen Theologie 14, ed. by Gerhard Ebeling), (Tübingen, 1953).

Cantalamessa, Raniero. L'Omelia "in S. Pascha" dello Pseudo-
Ippolito di Roma, Ricerche sulla Teologia dell' Asia Minore
nella Seconda Metà del Secondo Secolo, (Pubblicazioni dell'
Università Cattolica del Sacro Cuore, 3/16) (Milan, 1967).

Casel, Odo. Die Eucharistielehre des hl. Justinus Martyr, in:
Katholik 3./6. Heft (1914).

Cerfaux, Lucien. La Théologie de L'Eglise Suivant S. Paul,
(Paris, 1947).

Charles, R.H. A Critical and Exegetical Commentary on the Revelation of St. John, (ICC), (Edinburgh, 1956 [1920]).

Chartier, Clement, L'Excommunication ecclésiastique d'après les
écrits de Tertullien, in: Antonianum 10 (1935) 301-44, 499-
536.

Connolly, Hugh. Agape and Eucharist in the Didache, in: Downside
Review 55 (1937) 476-89.

----. The Didache and Montanism, in: Downside Review 55 (1937)
339-47.

Conzelmann, Hans. Der erste Brief an die Korinther, (KEKNT),
(Göttingen, 1969).

----. Die Mitte der Zeit, Studien zur Theologie des Lukas,
(Tübingen, 1954).

Cooke, Bernard. Eucharist: Source or Expression of Community?, Worship 40 (1966) 339-48.

Crouzel, Henri. Origène et la Structure du Sacrement, in: Bulletin de Littérature Ecclésiastique 63 (1962) 81-104.

Cullmann, Oscar. Early Christian Worship, (Studies in Biblical Theology 10, ed. by C.F.D. Moule et alii), (London, 1953).

----. La Signification de la Sainte-Cène dans le Christianisme Primitif, in: Revue d'Histoire et de Philosophie Religieuses 16 (1936) 1-22.

d'Alès, Adhémar; La Théologie de Saint Cyprien, (Paris, 1922).

Dekkers, Eligius. Tertullianus en de Geschiedenis der Liturgie, (Catholica 6/2), (Brussels, Amsterdam, 1947).

Demoustier, Adrien. Épiscopat et Union à Rome selon Saint Cyprien, in: Recherches de Science Religieuse 52 (1964) 335-69.

----. L'Ontologie de L'Église selon Saint Cyprien, in: Recherches de Science Religieuse 52 (1964) 554-88.

D'Ercole, Giuseppe. Communio, Collegialità, Primato e Sollicitudo omnium Ecclesiarum dai Vangeli a Costantino, (Communio 5, ed. by G. D'Ercole), (Rome, 1964).

----. Penitenza Canonico-Sacramentale, dalle Origini alla Pace Costantiniana, (Communio 3, ed. by G. D'Ercole), (Rome, 1963).

Directorium ad ea quae a Concilio Vaticano Secundo de re oecumenica promulgata sunt exsequenda, pars prima, in: AAS 59 (1967) 574-592.

Dix, Gregory. The Shape of the Liturgy, (Westminster, 1954).

Dodd, C.H. The Interpretation of the Fourth Gospel, (Cambridge, 1968 [1953]).

Dölger, Franz Joseph. Sol Salutis, Gebet und Gesang im christlichen Altertum, (Liturgiegeschichtliche Forschungen 16/17, ed. by F.J. Dölger et alii), (Münster, 1925²).

Döllinger, Johannes. Die Eucharistie in den drei ersten Jahrhunderten, (Mainz, 1826).

Doskocil, Walter. Der Bann in der Urkirche, eine rechtsgeschichtliche Untersuchung, (Münchener theologische Studien 3, kanonische Abteilung 11), (Munich, 1958).

Douglas, Mary. Purity and Danger, an Analysis of Concepts of Pollution and Taboo, (Penguin [Pelican] Books, 1970, orig. Routledge & Kegan Paul, 1966).

Dreher, Theodor. Die Zeugnisse des Ignatius, Justinus und Irenaeus über die Eucharistie als Sakrament, (Beigabe zum Gymnasialprogramm), (Sigmaringen, 1871).

Drews, Paul. Untersuchungen zur Didache, in: Zeitschrift für neutestamentliche Wissenschaft und die Kunde der älteren Kirche 5 (1904) 53-79.

Dupont, Jacques. "Gnosis". La connaissance religieuse dans les épîtres de saint Paul, (Universitas Catholica Lovaniensis. Dissertationes ad gradum magistri in Facultate Theologica consequendum conscriptae II/40), (Louvain-Paris, 1949).

Elert, Werner. Abendmahl und Kirchengemeinschaft in der alten Kirche hauptsächlich des Ostens, (Berlin, 1954).

Ernst, Johann. Die Ketzertaufangelegenheit in der altchristlichen Kirche nach Cyprian, (Forschungen zur christlichen

Literatur- und Dogmengeschichte 2/4, ed. by A. Ehrhard and
J.P. Kirsch), (Mainz, 1901).

----. Papst Stephan I. und der Ketzertaufstreit, (Forschungen
zur christlichen Literatur- und Dogmengeschichte 5/4, ed. by
A. Ehrhard and J.P. Kirsch), (Mainz, 1905).

Filson, Floyd V. A Commentary on the Gospel according to St.
Matthew, (BNTC), (London, 1960).

Fischer, Joseph A. Die apostolischen Väter, Griechisch und
Deutsch, (Munich, 1956).

Foakes-Jackson, F.J. The Acts of the Apostles, (MNTC), (London,
1931).

Fourrier, F. La Lettre de Pline à Trajan sur les Chrétiens
(X,97), in: Recherches de Théologie Ancienne et Médiévale
31 (1964) 161-74.

Frend, W.H.C. The Gnostic Sects and the Roman Empire, in: The
Journal of Ecclesiastical History 5 (1954) 25-37.

Gipsen, W.H. Het Boek Numeri, (Commentaar op het Oude Testament,
ed. by G. Aalders et alii), (Kampen, 1959).

Gnilka, Joachim. Der Philipperbrief, (Herders Theologischer Kommentar zum Neuen Testament 10/3, ed. by A. Wikenhauser et
alii), (Freiburg, Basel, Wien, 1968).

Gögler, Rolf. Zur Theologie des biblischen Wortes bei Origenes,
(Düsseldorf, 1963).

Goguel, Maurice. L'Eucharistie des Origines à Justin Martyr,
(Paris, 1910).

Greenslade, S.L. Scripture and Other Doctrinal Norms in Early

Theories of the Ministry, in: The Journal of Theological Studies 44 (1943) 162-76.

Grotz, Joseph. Die Entwicklung des Bussstufenswesens in der vornicänischen Kirche, (Freiburg, 1955).

Haenchen, Ernst. Die Apostelgeschichte, (KEKNT), Göttingen, 1959³).

Hamer, Jérome; L'Église est une Communion, (Unam Sanctam 40), (Paris, 1962).

Handbuch zum Neuen Testament, Ergänzungsband, Die Apostolischen Väter, 1, (Die Lehre der Zwölf Apostel, Die zwei Clemens-briefe, ed. and annotated by Rudolf Knopf), (Tübingen, 1920).

Harnack, Adolf von. Die Chronologie der altchristlichen Litera-tur bis Eusebius, (Leipzig, 1897 and 1904).

----. Geschichte der altchristlichen Literatur bis Eusebius, (Leipzig, 1958² [1893-1904]).

----. Die Mission und Ausbreitung des Christentums in den ersten Jahrhunderten, (Leipzig, 1924⁴).

----. Über den dritten Johannesbrief, in: TU 15/3 (1897).

Hein, Kenneth. Judas Iscariot: Key to the Last Supper Narra-tives? in: NTS 17 (1970/71) 227-32.

Hempel, Johannes. Die israelitischen Anschauungen von Segen und Fluch im Lichte altorientalischer Parallelen, in: Zeitschrift der Deutschen Morgenländischen Gesellschaft 79, neue Folge 4 (1925) 20-110.

Hertling, Ludwig. Communio und Primat, in: Una Sancta 17 (1962) 91-125. This article originally appeared in: Miscellanea historiae pontificae 7 (Rome, 1943) 3-48.

Hollweck, Joseph. Die kirchlichen Strafgesetze, (Mainz, 1899).

Horst, Friedrich. Segen und Segenshandlungen in der Bibel, in: Evangelische Theologie 7 (1947/48) 23-37.

Hübner, Siegfried. Kirchenbusse und Exkommunikation bei Cyprian, in: ZKT 84 (1962) 49-84, 171-215.

Jermias, Joachim. Die Abendmahlsworte Jesu, (Göttingen, 1960³).

-----. Zur Exegese der Abendmahlsworte Jesu, in: Evangelische Theologie 7 (1947/48) 60-62.

Jonas, Hans. Gnosis und Spätantiker Geist, (Göttingen, 1964 [1954]).

-----. The Gnostic Religion, (Boston, 1958).

Jone, Heribert. Gesetzbuch der lateinischen Kirche, 2, (Paderborn, 1952).

Jonsson, Jakob. Humour and Irony in the New Testament, illuminated by parallels in Talmud and Midrash, (Reykjavik, 1965).

Jourjon, Maurice. La Présidence de l'Eucharistie chez Ignace d' Antioche, in: Lumière et Vie 16 (1967) 26-32.

Jungmann, Joseph A. Der Gottesdienst der Kirche, (Innsbruck, 1955).

Karpp, Heinrich. Die Busslehre des Klemens von Alexandrien, in: Zeitschrift für die Neutestamentliche Wissenschaft und die Kunde der älteren Kirche 43 (1950/51) 224-42.

-----. Die Busse: Quellen zur Entstehung des altkirchlichen Busswesens, (Traditio Christiana: Texte und Kommentare zur patristischen Theologie 1, ed. by A. Benoit et alii). (Zürich, 1969).

Käsemann, Ernst. Anliegen und Eigenart der paulinischen Abendmahlslehre, in: Evangelische Theologie 7 (1947/48) 263-83.

-----. Sätze heiligen Rechtes im Neuen Testament, in: NTS 1 (1954/55) 248-60.

Kelly, J.N.D. A Commentary on the Epistles of Peter and of Jude, (BNTC), (London, 1969).

Ketter, Peter. Die Apokalypse, (HB 16/2). (Freiburg im Breisgau, 1942).

-----. Hebräerbrief, (HB 16/1), (Freiburg im Breisgau, 1950).

Kiddle, Martin. The Revelation of St. John, (MNTC), (London, 1940).

Kleist, James A. The Didache, (ACW 6, ed. by J. Quasten and J.C. Plumpe), (London, 1961).

Koch, Hugo. Die Abfassungszeit des Liber de rebaptismate: Auch ein Beitrag zur Primatsfrage, in: Internationale kirchliche Zeitschrift 14 (1924) 134-64.

-----. Kallist und Tertullian, (Sitzungsberichte der Heidelberger Akademie der Wissenschafte, 22. Abhandlung [1919]), (Heidelberg, 1920).

Kolping, Adolf. Sacramentum Tertullianeum, (Erster Teil: Untersuchungen über die Anfänge des christlichen Gebrauches der Vokabel sacramentum), (Regensburg, Münster, 1948).

Kremer, Jakob. Das älteste Zeugnis von der Auferstehung Christi, (Stuttgarter Bibelstudien 17, ed. by H. Haag et alii), (Stuttgart, 1967²).

Küng, Hans. Unfehlbar? Eine Anfrage, (Benzinger, 1970).

Kuss, Otto. Der Brief an die Hebräer, (RNT 8/1), (Regensburg, 1966).

Labriolle, Pierre de. La Crise Montaniste, (Paris, 1913).

----. Histoire de la Littérature Latine Chrétienne, 1, (Collection d'Études Anciennes, publiée sous le patronage de l'Association Guillaume-Budé), (Paris, 1947).

Lampe, G.W.H. Church Discipline and the Interpretation of the Epistles to the Corinthians, (Christian History and Interpretation: Studies Presented to John Knox, ed. by W.R. Farmer et alii), (Cambridge, 1967) 337-61.

La Piana, George. The Roman Church at the End of the Second Century, in: Harvard Theological Review 18 (1925) 201-77.

----. Foreign Groups in Rome during the First Centuries of the Empire, in: Harvard Theological Review 20 (1927) 183-403.

Lichtenstein, Ernst. Die älteste christliche Glaubensformel, in: Zeitschrift für Kirchengeschichte 63 (1950-51) 1-74.

Lieske, Aloisius. Die Theologie der Logosmystik bei Origenes, (Münsterische Beiträge zur Theologie 22), (Münster, 1938).

Lietzmann, Hans. Mass and Lord's Supper, a Study in the History of the Liturgy, (Introduction and supplementary essay by Robert D. Richardson), (Leiden, 1953ff).

Lightfoot, R.H. St. John's Gospel, a Commentary, (Oxford, 1956).

Lohfink, Norbert. Die Landverheissung als Eid, (Stuttgarter Bibelstudien 28, ed. by Herbert Haag et alii), (Stuttgart, 1967).

Lohse, Bernhard. Das Passafest der Quartadecimaner, (Beiträge zur Förderung christlicher Theologie, 2. Reihe, 54, ed. by Paul Althaus et alii), (Gütersloh, 1953).

Lubac, Henri de. Histoire et Esprit, L'Intelligence de l'Écriture d'après Origène, (Théologie 16,), (Paris, 1950).

Ludwig, Josef. Der Heilige Märtyrerbischof Cyprian von Karthago, (Munich, 1951).

Martini, Carlo M. L'esculusione dalla comunità del popolo di Dio e il nuovo Israele secondo Atti 3,23, in: Biblica 50 (1969) 1-14.

May, Georg. Die kirchliche Ehre als Voraussetzung der Teilnahme an dem eucharistischen Mahle, (Erfurter theologische Studien 8, ed. by Erich Kleineidam and Heinz Schürmann), (Leipzig, 1960).

Michel, Otto. Der Brief an die Hebräer, (KEKNT), (Göttingen, 1966[12] [1936]).

Moffatt, James. A Critical and Exegetical Commentary on the Epistle to the Hebrews, (ICC), (Edinburgh, 1924).

Molland, Einar. The Heretics Combatted by Ignatius of Antioch, in: The Journal of Ecclesiastical History 5 (1954) 1-6.

Monceaux, Paul. Histoire Littéraire de L'Afrique Chrétienne depuis les Origines jusqu'à L'Invasion Arabe, 1 and 2, (Paris, 1901/02 [Impression anastalitique, Brussels, 1966]).

Moule, C.D.F. The Judgment Theme in the Sacraments, (The Background of the New Testament and its Eschatology: Studies in honour of C.H. Dodd, ed. by W.D. Davies and D. Daube), (Cambridge, 1964) 464-81.

München, Nikolaus. Das kanonische Gerichtsverfahren und Strafrecht, 2, (Köln, Neuss, 1866).

Munck, Johannes, The Acts of the Apostles, (Anchor Bible 31),
(New York, 1967).

Neuenzeit, Paul. Das Herrenmahl, Studien zur paulinischen Eucharistieauffassung, (Studien zum Alten und Neuen Testament 1, ed.
by Vinzenz Hamp and Josef Schmit), (Munich, 1960).

Neumann, Johannes, Der Spender der Firmung in der Kirche des
Abendlandes bis zum Ende des kirchlichen Altertums, (Meiting-
en, 1963).

----. Der theologische Grund für das kirchliche Vorsteheramt
nach dem Zeugnis der apostolischen Väter, in: Münchener theologische Zeitschrift 14 (1963) 253-65.

O'Neill, J.C. The Theology of Acts in its Historical Setting,
(London, 1961).

Noth, Martin. "Die mit des Gesetzes Werken umgehen, die sind
unter dem Fluch", (In piam memoriam Alexander von Bulmerineo),
(Abhandlung der Herder-Gesellschaft und des Herder-Instituts
zu Riga 6/3 [Riga, 1938]), (now in: Martin Noth, Gesammelte
Studien zum Alten Testament, [Theologische Bücherei, Neudrucke
und Berichte aus dem 20. Jahrhundert 6]), (Munich, 1960²
[1957]) 155-71.

Pedersen, Johannes. Israel, Its Life and Culture, (London,
Copenhagen, 1926 [1920] and 1940 [1934]).

Peters, Curt. Das Diatessaron Tatians, seine Überlieferung und
sein Nachwirken im Morgen- und Abendland sowie der heutige
Stand seiner Erforschung, (Orientalia Christiana Analecta
123), (Rome, 1939).

BIBLIOGRAPHY

Peterson, Erik. Die Kirche, (München, 1929 [reprinted in: Theologische Traktate, München, 1951, 409-29]).

Poschmann, Bernhard. Paenitentia Secunda, Die kirchliche Busse im ältesten Christentum bis Cyprian und Origenes, (Theophaneia, Beiträge zur Religions- und Kirchengeschichte des Altertums, ed. by Franz J. Dölger and Theodor Klauser), (Bonn, 1940).

Quasten, Johannes. Patrology (Utrecht-Antwerp, 1964³).

Quinn, John. The Lord's Supper and Forgiveness of Sin, in: Worship 42 (1968) 281-91.

Rahner, Karl. Busslehre und Busspraxis der Didascalia Apostolorum, in: ZKT 72 (1950) 257-81.

----. Die Busslehre des hl. Cyprian von Carthago, in: ZKT 74 (1952) 257-76, 381-438.

----. Die Busslehre im Hirten des Hermas, in: ZKT 77 (1955) 385-431.

----. La Doctrine D'Origène sur la Pénitence, in: Recherches de Science Religieuse 37 (1950) 47-97, 252-86.

----. Die Sündenvergebung nach der Taufe in der Regula fidei des Irenäus, in: ZKT 70 (1948) 450-55.

----. Zur Theologie der Busse bei Tertullian, (Abhandlungen über Theologie und Kirche: Festschrift für Karl Adam, ed. by Marcel Reding), (Düsseldorf, 1952) 139-67.

Ratzinger, Joseph. Das Neue Volk Gottes, Entwürfe zur Ekklesiologie, (Düsseldorf, 1969).

Rauschen, Gerhard. Eucharistie und Bussakrament in den ersten sechs Jahrhunderten der Kirche, (Freiburg im Breisgau, 1910).

Richardson, Alan. An Introduction to the Theology of the New Testament, (London, 1958).

Ropes, James H. A Critical and Exegetical Commentary on the Epistle of St. James, (ICC), (Edinburgh, 1954).

Scharbert, Josef. "Fluchen" und "Segen" im Alten Testament, in: Biblica 39 (1958) 1-26.

Scheiwiler, Aloys. Die Elemente der Eucharistie in dem ersten drei Jahrhunderten, (Forschungen zur christlichen Literatur- und Dogmengeschichte 3/4), (Mainz, 1903).

Schelkle, Karl. Das Neue Testament, Seine literarische und theologische Geschichte, (Kevelaer Rhld., 1966).

Schlier, Heinrich. Der Brief an die Galater, (KEKNT), (Göttingen, 1965⁴).

----, et alii. Zur Frühgeschichte der Christologie, Ihre biblischen Anfänge und die Lehrformel von Nikaia, (Questiones Disputatae 51, ed. by B. Welte), (Freiburg, Basel, Vienna, 1970).

Schnackenburg, Rudolf. Christologie des Neuen Testamentes, (Mysterium Salutis 3/1, ed. by J. Feiner and M. Löhrer), (Einsiedeln, 1970) 227-383.

----. Gottes Herrschaft und Reich, (Freiburg, Basel, Vienna, 1963³).

Schürmann, Heinz. Der Abendmahlsbericht Lucas 22,7-38 als Gottesdienstordnung-Gemeindeordnung Lebensordnung, (Schriften zur Pädegogik und Katechetik 9, ed. by Th. Kampmann and R. Padberg), (Paderborn, 1955).

Secretariatus ad Christianorum Unitatem Fovendam: Déclaration sur
la position de l'Église Catholique en matière d'Eucharistie
commune entre chrétiens de diverses confessions, in: AAS
62 (1970) 184-88.

Smith, W. Robertson. Die Religion der Semiten, (translated from
the 2nd edition of Lectures on the Religion of the Semites),
(Darmstadt, 1967 [Tübingen, 1899]).

Sqicq, Celas. L'Épître aux Hébreux, (Études Bibliques 3.60),
(Paris, 1952/53).

Stanley, David. Ecumenically Significant Aspects of New Testament Eucharistic Doctrine, in: Concilium 4/3 (1967) 23-26.

Stelzenberger, Johannes. Syneidesis bei Origenes, (Abhandlungen
zur Moraltheologie 4, ed. by J. Stelzenberger), (Paderborn,
1963).

----. Syneidesis im Neuen Testament, (Abhandlungen zur Moraltheologie 1, ed. by J. Stelzenberger), (Paderborn, 1961).

Stone, Darwell. A History of the Doctrine of the Holy Eucharist,
1, (London, 1909).

Strack, H. and Billerbeck, P. Kommentar zum Neuen Testament aus
Talmud und Midrasch, 1-4, (Munich, 1922-1928).

Struckmann, Adolf. Die Gegenwart Christi in der Hl. Eucharistie
nach den schriftlichen Quellen der vornizänischen Zeit, Eine
dogmengeschichtliche Untersuchung, (Theologische Studien der
Leo-Gesellschaft 12, ed. by A. Ehrhard and F.M. Schindler),
(Vienna, 1905).

Stürmer, Karl. Das Abendmahl bei Paulus, in: Evangelische Theologie 7 (1947/48) 50-59.

Taylor, John H. St. Cyprian and the Reconciliation of Apostates, in: Theological Studies 3 (1942) 27-46.

Teichtweier, Georg. Die Sündenlehre des Origenes, (Studien zur Geschichte der kath. Moraltheologie 7, ed. by Michael Müller), (Regensburg, 1958).

Temple, Sydney. The two traditions of the Last Supper, Betrayal, Arrest, in: NTS 7 (1960/61) 77-85.

Thornton, Lionel S. The Common Life in the Body of Christ, (London, 1950³).

Thurian, Max. L'Eucharistie, Mémorial du Seigneur, Sacrifice d' action de grâce et d'intercession, (Neuchâtel-Paris, 1959).

Völker, Walther. Das Vollkommenheitsideal des Origenes, Eine Untersuchung zur Geschichte der Frömmigkeit und zu den Anfängen christlicher Mystik, (Beiträge zur historischen Theologie 7), (Tübingen, 1931).

Weiss, Johannes, Der Erste Korintherbrief, (KEKNT), (Göttingen, 1910⁹).

Wikenhauser, Alfred. Einleitung in das Neue Testament, (Basel, Freiburg, Vienna, 1961⁴).

Wiles, M.F. The Theological Legacy of St. Cyprian, in: The Journal of Ecclesiastical History 14 (1963) 139-49.

Wilson, R.McL. Gnosis and the New Testament, (Oxford, 1968).

BIBLICAL INDEX

Genesis	page		Exodus	page
2-3	30n		33,7-11	150n
3,1ff	55		34	8, 31
3,14-19	4		35-37	8
3,17	138			
4,10	23n		**Leviticus**	
6,1-4	9n			
9,9-17	5		5,1-5	192n
12,3	4n, 5		7,19	377
14,22	141		7,20	8, 377
15,9f	22n		7,21	8
15,18	141n		10,1f	253
21,23f	141n		11-14	8
26,28-31	141n		14,10	245
27,29	5		15	8
37,26	23n		15,16	343
			16	8
Exodus			16,15-19	22
			16,20-22	150n
3,5	317		17	84
6,4f	5		17,11-14	23n
6,8	141		18	84
6,12.30	35n		18,5	106
12,43-48	8		18,8	85n
19	31		18,24-30	19, 96
19,5f	5		19,12	141
19,15	323n		19,23	35
20	31		19,26	23n
20,4	292		20,9-16	82
20,7-11	141		24,5-9	320
20,13	275		24,16	7
22,20	102		26,14-43	5
24,3-8	106n		26,41	35n
24,8	22n			
29-30	8		**Numbers**	
30,29	8			
31	8		5,11-31	102
31,13.17	141		5,21-27	43n
32	8		15,22-36	140f
32,26	135		15,30	141f, 230n
33	8		16	161, 400

The letter "n" after a page number indicates that the reference is found only in a footnote on that page.

Numbers	page
16,33	253
19,22	398, 400
22	5, 160n
23-24	160n
24,9	5

Deuteronomy	
3,23ff	56
4,21f	56
5,11	141
6,5	364
12,15	23n
13,6	5, 44, 96
13,13-19	6
16,16	262n
16,21	335
17,1-7	5
18,15.18	86
19,11-13	55
19,15	353n
22,5	367
23,6	139
23,11	343
24,16	354
27	7
27,26	106, 154, 347
28,15ff	106n
29,1.9ff	106n
29,11	141n
29,18(17)	143n
29,19f	5
30,1-20	106n
30,7	5
32,34	55
32,40	141

Joshua	
6,17-21	6
7	79
7,19ff	79

Joshua	page
9,15	141n
15,63	328
16,10	329
24,9f	160n

1 Samuel	
14,44	141
20,12f	141
20,15	44
20,26	343
20,42	141n

2 Samuel	
1,16	82
24,14	146n

1 Kings	
3,6	142
8,33-35	156
14,10	253
16,31f	185

2 Kings	
4,42-44	26n
9,22	185
13,21	350

2 Chronicles	
34,24	5

Ezra	
10,8	6
44,19	8

Nehemiah	
9,3-5	156
13,2	139

Tobias	page		Sirach	page
3,7ff	9n		(Ecclesiasticus)	
6,7f.14ff	9n		24,21(28)	31n
8	9n		Isaiah	
Job			3,1	368
33,27f	192n		5,6	47n
			5,26f	368
Psalms			10,3	157n
			22,19	75
6,6	362		22,22	75
6,8	16		24,5f	5
17,6	317		29,13	364, 404n
23	25n		30,15	379
25,4	316		40,3	104n
28,4	125		42,6f	22n
31,3	73n		43,1	184
32,1-6	192n		48,22	256
33,9	368		53	22n
41,10	49n		53,4ff	56
51	193		53,13	32
62,8	73n		55,3	142
62,12	125		62,2	184
69,25(26)	78		65,13	368
83,13ff	4		65,15	6, 184, 368
89,4	142		65,16	368
95,5-11	134		Jeremiah	
103,30	248n			
106,26	141		5,4	220
108,7	334		6,10	35n
109,8	78		6,15	157n
129,8	256n		8,13	15
144,8.11	141		9,25	35n
			11,19	280
Proverbs			12,5	319n
			23,10	5
2,16	9n		31,33f	32
6,24.29	9n		34,18	22n
7,5.10	9n		Ezechial	
9,16-18	271			
24,12	125		14,12-14	354
			20,12	141
Wisdom			24,7	23n
			34,5	363
4,19	78		41,9	35n

Daniel	page		Matthew	page
9,4-20	156		2,2	72n
13	379		3,11	176n
			5,3	74n
Hosea			5,8	335
9,4	400n		5,17	32n
			5,19	154
Joel			5,23f	66, 262n, 357, 442n
3,1-5	414		5,28	275
			5,30	331
Micah			5,44	13
6,5	160n		5,45	138
7,1	15		6,3	226n
			7,6	10, 195, 281
Habakkuk			7,15	76, 246
2,4	106n		7,16-20	76
			7,21	16, 76
Haggai			7,23	16, 89n
2,12f	8		8,5f	156
			8,10	155
Zechariah			9,1-8.18	156
3,4	322		9,20	342, 350
4	180		9,21	350
9,11	22n		9,22	155, 350
			9,28	350, 414n
Malachi			9,29f	414n
1,10-12	245		10,2-4	39
1,11	193, 260, 414, 422		10,5	18f, 389
1,12ff	422		10,6-14	18f
1,14	193		10,15	18f, 109n
3,1	104n		10,32	131
			10,40	76
1 Maccabees			11,3	176n
1,47[50]	9		11,6	73n
5,5	6		11,18f	56
			11,20-24	19
Matthew			11,22.24	109n
2,2	72n		12,24.30	173n
			12,31	362
			12,32	174n, 327n, 362
			12,43-45	330, 349

Matthew	page	Matthew	page
13,16f	74n	26,28	22n, 145n,
13,29	328		314
13,30	138	26,31-33	73n
14,23.26	27	26,47-50	40
14,28f	29	26,63-66	71n
15,8	364	26,69ff	73n
15,17	324	27,3-10	43f
15,26f	196	27,25	61, 82
16,13-20	69, 71-76	27,42	72n
16,18	392	28,16	26n
16,23	39n	28,18-20	76
18,8	291		
18,15-17	236, 353,	Mark	
	430	1,1-11	20
18,15-18	17, 69-71,	1,34	39n
	91	2,16f	355
18,17	355	3,16	72n
18,18	76	3,22.30	173n
19,9	84	4,3-9	167n
19,22	305n	5,21ff	317
19,26	72n	5,27	342n
20,28	414n	6,13	155
21,18-22	14f	6,37.39-41.43.45	29
23,13	76, 173n	6,47f	27, 29
23,19	98n	6,49	27
23,23-28	18	6,52	28
24	159n	7,1-12	18
24,4f	76	7,13	18, 404n
24,11	76, 180,	7,15	18
	246	9,2-9	317
24,12	180	10,21	72n
24,24	76	10,45	414n
24,48	254	11,2	71n
24,51	44	11,12-14.20-26	14f
25,28b	22	12,30	364
25,40	61n	14,17-21	40
25,41	16	14,24	22, 23n
25,45	61n	14,32-42	27n
26,14-16	39	14,34-36	56n
26,20-25	40	14,71	13
26,26-28	199	15,2	72n
26,27-29	248n	15,9.12	26

Mark	page		John	page
15,32	72n		1,9	176n
16,7	27n		1,36.42.49	72n
16,16	76		3,5	20
16,19	27n		3,22	408
			4,21-24	54
Luke			5	24
1,21	135		5,8.14	156
2,43	135		5,26	34
3,16	409		6	24-34, 169
6,28	13		6,12	129n
9,34	135		6,14	176n
10,1-12	19n		6,27-33	149
10,13-16	19		6,31ff	31
10,16	76		6,35	368
10,22	56		6,38.41	31
10,27	364		6,45	32
10,30-35	167n		6,48-52	369
10,38-42	414n		6,53	368, 370
12,9	173n		6,53-56	33, 166
12,50	20n		6,54	49n
13,6-9	15-17		6,54-57	23
13,16	94		6,56-58	34
13,25	16		6,58	49n, 324
15,11-31	281		6,60	33n
17,3	353n		6,64	39n
18,13	321		6,69	88
18,35	135		6,70f	39n
19,44	157n		7	24
21,5	13		7,27	31
21,24	77n		7,37f	368
22,14-23	40		8,44	39n
22,15	21		9,22	7, 129n
22,19	67		9,34	17, 177n
22,24-26	60		9,35	177n
22,25	414n		10,17	26
22,27-30	45		10,30	396
22,31f	73n		11,3	156
22,39	41		11,24	321
22,61	72n		11,27	176n
23,34	13		11,48-50	71n
24,36	27n		11,52	171
24,37	28		12,2	321n
24,39	27n		12,4-6	39n

John	page	John	page
12,13	26, 72n	21	29n
12,42	7, 129n	21,1	28
13	42	21,1-14	29
13,1	29n, 56n	21,15-19	29n, 73n
13,1-20	45		
13,2	42n	**Acts of the**	**page**
13,2-30	39n	**Apostles**	
13,4-8	414n		
13,4-16	18	1	27n
13,10	37	1,6-8	77
13,11	42n	1,15-20	43f
13,18	49n	1,18f.21f	78
13,19	27n	2,1-4	86
13,21	42n	2,17-20	414
13,26-30	37f	2,38	54, 88
13,31f	26	2,39-41	54
13,34f	29n	2,42	58, 65
14,6	56	2,44f	58, 192
14,6-9	276	2,46	58
15,1-17	34-37	2,47	55, 129
15,6	139	3,12-26	86
15,8	167n	4,27.30	23n
15,9.12	29n	4,32.34f	192
16,2	7	5,1f	12
16,5-15	51	5,1-11	78, 96, 412
16,7	398	5,11	79n
16,10.16.22f	26	5,17	128n
17,1.4f	26	6,5	181
17,11.21-23	171	7,38	104n
18,2	41-42n	7,51	35n
18,5	42n	7,57	7
18,28	8	8,18-24	79f
18,36f	26	8,34	23n
19,7	7	9,4f	61n
19,12-16	71n	9,8f	81
19,19-22	26	10	65, 412
19,34	166, 170	10,15	18
19,35	166	10,28	8
20,22	69, 73n, 76f	10,44-48	408
20,23	69-70n, 73n, 76f, 392	11	65, 412
		11,3	8
20,29	74	11,9	18

Acts of the Apostles	page
11,15f	20n
13,6-12	80f
13,50f	81
15	286n
15,1	83
15,5	128n
15,12	167n
15,20	83-85, 174n
15,21	84
15,29	83-85, 174n
15,28	85f, 88, 412
18,5f	82
19,1-6	170n, 398n
19,3-6	397
21,25	83-85
21,28	105
23,12-15	105
23,12-21	141
24,5.14	128n
26,5	128n
28,22	128n
28,26-28	82
28,30	167n

Romans	
1,5.8	159n
1,18	109n
1,21	255
2,1.5	109
2,8	109n
2,17ff	108
3,23-26	176n
5,8-11	176n
5,12	55
5,12-6,1ff	95f
6,3f	55
6,3-11	21n
6,19	163
7	95f
7,5	93n, 163
7,6	163

Romans	page
7,7-12	107n
8,1-13	95f
9,3	104
9,22	129
10,4	32n
12,6	324
14,9	167n
14,22f	176n
14,23	323, 333, 343, 432
16,17f	109

1 Corinthians	
1,10	115n
1,12	100n, 110
1,12-15	21n, 115n
2,6	116
2,6-13	117
3,17	64n
5,1	84, 111
5,1f	85n
5,1-5	122
5,1-13	419
5,2	92, 96, 329
5,4	93, 96
5,5	44, 55, 93, 95, 102n, 121, 163, 417, 440
5,6	96, 288
5,7	96, 274
5,9-11	288
5,11	96n, 274
5,12f	119, 417
5,13	44, 93n, 96 289n
6,9-11	97, 274
6,13	274
7,12-14	289
7,14	17n, 21n, 421n
8,8	324

1 Corinthians	page	1 Corinthians	page
10,1-11	100	14,23f	419
10,3	149	14,26	117
10,14-22	97-100, 419f	14,26-40	419
10,14-33	59	14,30	117
10,16	99n, 420	14,34f	285n
10,16-21	97f	14,37f	89n
10,17	63, 99n	14,38	64n
10,18	97n, 149	15,5-9	75n
10,21	374, 377, 421	16,1-3	61n
10,22	100	16,20ff	64n
10,25-28	85n	16,22	64, 104
10,27-29	53		
11,17ff	97	**2 Corinthians**	
11,17-34	58-64, 416	2,4-10	111
11,18f	100n, 192	2,10f	112
11,19	100, 128n, 246	3,1	180, 373n
		5,16	110
11,20	194, 420	6,9	122n
11,20-22	160n	7,8.12	111
11,23	199	8,9	167n
11,24	22n	10	89n
11,24f	67, 199	10,1-13	110
11,25	22, 24	11	89n
11,26	57	11,6.13-15.22f	110
11,27	102, 137n, 377, 395	11,25	167n
11,27f	270f, 320	12	89n
11,27-29	375	12,1	117
11,27-30	194	12,7	94, 117
11,27-32	420, 439f	12,20f	112
11,27-34	100f	12,21	110
11,28	172, 193, 319n, 321	13	89n
11,29	316	13,1	110
11,30	102n, 270n, 318, 324	13,2	110f
		13,10	111
11,32	122n, 274		
11,34	194	**Galatians**	
12,3	104, 107n	1,1-4.6f	103
12,13	115n	1,8-10	104
14,6	117	1,9	105
14,20	116	1,11f	117
		2,2	117

Galatians	page		
2,10	83		
2,11-14	18, 107, 419		
2,14-16	88		
3,10	106, 154, 347		
3,1-14	105		
3,12f	106		
3,13	107n		
3,14	107		
3,19	104n		
3,27	398		
3,28	226n		
4,9	18		
4,21-31	108, 260		
5,1	18		
5,3	154		
5,10.14	108		
5,19-21	97n, 336		
5,20	129n		
6,1	108		
6,13	107		
6,15f	114n		
6,18	163		

Ephesians	
1,17	117
1,22ff	119
2,2	119
2,14	226n
3,3.5	117
4,4-6	284
4,5	394
4,11-13	116
4,15	119
5,5	97n, 289
5,5-7	119
5,8	120
6,16	120

Philippians	
1,28	113, 129
2,2-8	117f

Philippians	page	
3,1ff	113	
3,8	114	
3,12	115	
3,15	116f	
3,15f	114	
3,17	115	
3,18	113, 129	
3,19	114, 129	
4,1	113	
4,2	118	
4,2f	430	
4,8f	113	

Colossians		
1,6	159n	
1,13	93n	
1,16	118	
1,23	159n	
1,28	116	
2,4.8.10	118	
2,11-13	20	
2,12	21n, 55	
2,13	35n	
2,15	118	
2,16f	309n	
2,17	119	
2,18	118	
2,19	119	
2,23	118	
3,5-8	97n	
4,12	116	

1 Thessalonians	
1,8	159
4,7	289
5,14	91
5,20f	180
5,23	270n

2 Thessalonians	
2,1-4	91

2 Thessalonians	page		2 Timothy	page
3,6	92, 329		4,2	125
3,6-12	91		4,9f	121
3,6-15	419			
3,7-9	92		Titus	
3,14	91			
3,15	163		1,1	127
3,16	91		1,5	128, 179
			1,1-16	128
1 Timothy			1,10.14f	121
			1,13	128
1,1	122		2,12	122n
1,3	120f, 125,		3,8	128
	179		3,9	121
1,4.7	121		3,10	129n, 256
1,13	122		3,11	129-131, 335
1,19f	121		3,12	121, 127
1,20	125			
3,15	127		Hebrews	
4,1	127			
4,1-3	121		2,1-3	134
4,4	99n		3	136
4,5	323		3,7-11	134
5,17	123		3,13f	136
5,19	124		3,15	135
5,19-22	123		4	136
5,22	124, 288n		4,1-11.16	136
			5,11	133
2 Timothy			6,1-9	136
			6,4-6	137, 139,
1,1.8	125			145n, 327n
2,4	366		6,7f	138
2,12f	131		7,25	145
2,14-16	125		7,26	208
2,17f	127		9,9	193n
2,18f	125		9,14	22n, 143,
2,20f	126, 420			193n
2,21	126-128,		9,18-22	22
	138n		9,26.28	146
2,23	123		10,10	143
2,25	122n		10,17	143n
2,25f	125, 127		10,18	143, 146
3,1	127			152
3,6f.13	126		10,19-22	144n

Hebrews	page
10,22	193n
10,24f.29	133
10,25	430
10,25-27	142
10,26	140, 142f, 144n, 146, 152, 173, 174n, 223 230n, 233
10,26-30	417
10,26-39	139
10,27-29	145
10,28f	145n
10,29	144n, 327n
10,29-31	142
10,30f	145
10,31	146n
10,37	133
12,1	143, 152
12,6	122n
12,15	143n
13,4	144n
13,9	149
13,9-14	148
13,10	147, 196, 420f
13,11	149
13,12	22n, 134, 149n
13,12f	152
13,13	149
13,13f	150

James	
1,2-6.12.15	153
1,22	154
2,2-4	154
2,5	74n
2,9ff	154
4,1-4.7	153
4,17	154

James	page
5,1-6.9	154
5,14f	155
5,16.19f	156

1 Peter	
1,1	156
1,2	22n, 24n
1,14	158
1,22	157
2,11-13	157
2,13-19.21	158
3,1.5f.22	158
3,21	193n
4,3-5.7	157
5,1	158n
5,5f	158

2 Peter	
2,1	129n
2,1-22	159
2,3	160
2,9	109n
2,13	161
2,13f	159
2,14f	160
2,15	181
2,17	161
2,20-22	162
3,2f	162
3,7	138, 162
3,9	338
3,10.12	138

1 John	
1,6f.9	172
2,1	167
2,1f	172
2,3f	88
2,15f	175

1 John	page		3 John	page
2,18	164		3.5f.8	178
2,19	165, 178		9f	177
2,22	164		9-12	90
3,6.8.10	172		10	17
3,12	160, 173		Jude	
3,14	175n			
3,15	173		4	159f
4,1-3	165, 180		7	162
4,2f	164, 168		11	160f, 181
4,5	175		12	159, 161
4,6	165		13	161
4,8	173		17	159n, 162
5,4	176		18	162
5,6-8	165-171		22f	162
5,7	396			
4,14-21	173n		Apocalypse	
5,16	173, 176, 420		1,12	180
5,16f	417		2,1-7	179, 182
5,19-21	175		2,5	379, 420
5,21	174		2,7	184, 199n
6,6	170n		2,11	184
			2,12-17	182f
2 John			2,18-29	185f
			3,1-22	186f
5f	177		3,5	131
7	164		6,17	109n
7-11	176		7,13f	20n
10f	256		7,13-15	22n
			22,2.14	199n
			22,15	104n

abortion, 300n
Acts of Thomas, 381n
agape-meal, 60, 62n, 63, 97,
    159n, 161, 196, 199n, 201n,
    212, 302f, 425n
Agrippinus of Carthage, 295n,
    390
allegorical method, 269, 271f,
    275, 306f, 316, 320-23n,
    328f, 332n, 335, 341
analogia fidei, 255, 324
Anastasius (Pope), 307
anathema (see also curse, 13,
    104f, 107n, 308
Anicetus (Pope), 262f, 266-68
anthropology, 335
antipopes, 294, 386f
Apocalypse of Baruch, 30n
apokatastasis, 309, 327n, 435
apostasy, 13n, 36n-37, 98n,
    134-39, 141f, 144n, 146,
    173f, 200, 225, 229, 231f,
    234, 255f, 281n, 327n, 333,
    337-41, 350, 371-85, 403-04n,
    437, 448
Apostolic Constitutions, 46,
    345
Apostolic succession, 252-54,
    426, 428, 438
arcane discipline, 10, 196,
    202, 223f, 290, 299n, 422
Aristotle, 311
Ascension, 26n
atheism, 246, 297
Augustine of Hippo, 220n, 227,
    411
authority (ecclesial), 88-90,
    94, 96, 111, 121, 161, 178f,
    204n-15, 281, 284, 294n,
    296, 302f, 328n-29, 338f,

352, 359, 372, 374, 377n,
    378-80, 392, 423-38, 437f,
    447

Balaam (Bileam), 160, 181f
ban, 4-7, 13-17, 70, 76, 91f,
    97, 105, 122n, 127, 141,
    206, 299, 306, 430
Baptism (Christian), 19-22,
    55f, 61, 65-68, 88, 93n,
    95, 97, 99n-100, 115n,
    128n, 133n, 137n, 143,
    145n-46, 170f, 195-98, 200,
    212f, 228-31n, 269, 273,
    281-86, 292, 298, 303,
    312n-13n, 323n, 325, 342n,
    347-49, 355, 357f, 371n,
    384, 387f, 392-99, 401-10,
    414, 418, 421f, 429-38,
    441
baptism (non-Christian), 12,
    20, 136, 164n, 168-70, 397,
    421n
baptismal oil, 399
baptismal water, 398n
Basilides, 240, 246
Bellarmine, Robert, 415n
Benedict XII (Pope), 405n
bishops (episcopacy), 120,
    123n, 125, 178f, 203n,
    206f, 209-28, 251, 257,
    266, 284f, 292n, 294n,
    296, 298, 302f, 317, 328n,
    338, 351f, 358-60, 365f,·
    374, 376, 379f, 384, 386,
    391f, 398n, 400f, 402n,
    423-28, 436-38, 442, 449
blasphemy, 122, 219, 226,
    231-34, 252, 297n, 301,
    335, 350, 353n, 361f, 394

The letter "n" after a page number indicates that the reference
is found only in a footnote on that page.

Blastus, 266
blessing, 4, 13, 107, 136n,
  138, 139n, 184, 256, 397n,
  414
blood-drinking, 23, 33, 83,
  85, 202, 214

Cain, 160, 173
Callistus (Pope), 294-300,
  390n
Canaanites, 329
Catacombs, 299n
catechumenate (catechuems),
  65, 228, 281, 287, 299,
  301n-02, 305, 312n, 325f,
  336, 344n, 387, 434
Catiline, 202n
censure (see ban)
Cerdon, 258
Cerinth (Cerinthianism), 164,
  168, 235, 256
Chiliasm, 337
Chrysostom, John, 303n
Church
--as body of Christ, 23, 33
  51, 59n, 61-68, 99, 119,
  220, 369-71, 414-20, 426-
  29, 436, 439
--as pilgrim, 67f, 147-53
--as sacrament, 51-53, 65n,
  391, 415n, 419
--relationship of one church
  to another, 180f, 268, 415n,
  420, 439, 443, 448
--relationship to sinners,
  234f, 258n, 271f, 295, 312n,
  322, 352-59, 361, 363, 379,
  389, 394-96, 400f, 409, 417,
  419-23, 429f, 433, 437
--relation to Judaism and the
  world, 238, 300n, 353n,
  356f, 363n, 368
circumcision, 8, 20, 35, 83,
  107f, 113-14n, 145n, 335,
  421n

clean (see purity)
Clement of Alexandria,
  254, 268-76, 305, 435
Clement of Rome, 133, 159n,
  178n, 204-10
clergy, 203f, 285, 302n,
  316n, 366f, 386, 423,
  372-76
confession of sins, 156,
  172, 192-94, 198, 224,
  227f, 245, 287n, 328n,
  375n-76n, 423, 429
Confirmation (Sacrament of)
  292n, 387f, 397n, 408f
Constantine the Great, 238,
  279, 411
Cornelius (Pope), 298n,
  386-89
Councils (Synods)
--of Africa, 378, 383-85,
  387, 389, 394, 404, 407
--of Constantinople (543)
  307f
--of Elvira, 260n, 390n,
  411n
--of Iconium, 396
--of Jerusalem, 83-86
--of Nicea, 405n
--of Synnada, 406
--of Vatican II, 415n
Covenant (New), 22f, 32-34,
  52-57, 130, 136, 142, 146,
  255, 260f, 275n, 415f,
  422
Covenant (Old), 5, 11, 14,
  22f, 32n, 56, 106n, 130,
  134, 141f, 255, 260f,
  275n, 323n
curse, 4-7, 13-17, 64, 79,
  101, 105-07, 125, 130,
  138f, 141, 154, 160, 163,
  202n, 205, 347, 367n,
  389, 414
Cyprian of Carthage, 49n,

123n, 194n, 207, 251n,
260n, 273, 292n, 303n, 337,
339, 343, 365-407, 411,
436-38, 442-45, 448f
Cyrillonas, 47f

deacons, 203n, 209f, 212f,
215, 258, 303, 351, 356,
358, 374, 378, 402n, 424
Demetrius of Alexandria, 305f
Devil (demon, Satan), 9n, 12,
16, 39n, 45, 53, 81, 93-95,
97f, 102n, 110, 112, 121f,
126, 153, 172f, 175, 182,
213f, 221, 230n, 240f, 257,
283, 291, 292n, 302, 309,
319n, 329f, 348-50, 357f,
368, 374, 377n, 387, 394,
402n, 434, 440f
Diatesseron, 40, 46, 49
Didache, 10, 61n, 64n, 163n,
172, 179, 191-204, 222n,
224, 245, 261, 345, 421f,
431, 434
Didascalia Apostolorum, 46,
265n, 345-64, 430f
dietary laws, 9f, 275, 358
Dionysius of Alexandria, 336-
44, 350n, 406, 435f
Dionysius of Corinth, 201
Dionysius of Rome, 406
Docetism, 164, 210, 212, 214,
221, 242, 279f, 432
doctors (of the Church), 203n
Donatism, 207, 391, 398, 436

Easter controversy, 219, 235n,
262-68, 427f, 441f, 448
Ebionites, 170n, 251, 255,
271, 393
ecumenism, 3, 412, 439, 443,
445-49
Ephraem, (Commentary on the
Diatessaron), 46f
Epiphanius, 242, 267, 307
Epistola Apostolorum, 235-37,
264
Esau, 143n
eschatology, 16f, 19, 30n,
35, 44, 51f, 55-57, 64n,
77f, 89-92, 101, 109,
120, 127, 129, 136, 138,
145n-46, 157, 159f, 162,
180, 186f, 199, 214, 216,
222, 226, 236, 309, 349-
51, 354n, 358, 362, 382,
413f, 416, 429
Essenes, 10-12, 17, 44, 91,
94, 97n, 120, 170n
Eucharist (in general), 10,
20-37, 38, 40, 42, 58-68,
97-103, 104n, 107, 137,
144n, 148-53, 160n, 165-72
183, 187, 193-203, 207-09,
213-17, 223, 235, 243-55,
259-61, 268, 270-72, 279-
82, 285, 290-94, 303, 308-
24, 340-44, 349-51, 355f,
364, 366-71, 374-78, 387-
89, 414-43, 445
--exclusion from, 3, 37-50,
97, 99, 149, 196, 281, 288,
293, 302-03n, 321, 337-39,
344n, 348, 351, 356, 364,
374, 379n-80, 412, 419-22,
430f, 434, 437, 439-44
--private, 212, 425
--right to, 149, 380n, 393,
422
--valid or worthy reception
of, 49, 61-63, 101-03, 137n
194, 198, 245, 249-51, 270,
281, 288f, 303f, 310-12,
315n-16, 318-24, 342n, 358,
374-77, 380-84, 388, 399,
402, 421f, 426, 435, 439f
eucharistic ecclesiology,
215, 267f, 303n, 315,
368-71, 388, 391, 393,
423
eucharistic words of insti-

tution, 198-203, 402
Eusebius of Caesarea (History
  of the Church), 49n, 201n,
  239n, 262-64, 279, 305, 337-
  40, 386-91, 406, 411
excommunication, 6n-7, 11, 16f,
  23, 35-38, 40, 42-51, 53f,
  64n, 69-86, 89-94, 96-97n,
  99, 104n-05, 110f, 122, 124-
  26, 128n-29, 131, 144n, 160,
  165, 177f, 181, 194, 204n-
  06, 217, 223, 230n, 235f,
  242, 257-59n, 263n, 266f,
  273f, 282n, 286, 288f, 300f,
  302n, 306, 316f, 321f, 325-
  33, 340, 351-61, 367, 369-
  72, 378-80, 391, 398, 404n,
  406, 416-20, 426, 429-31,
  435-37, 441-43
exorcism, 136n, 301f, 394,
  397n, 434, 441

Fabian (Pope), 298n, 386
Fabius of Antioch, 387, 338-
  41
faith, 14, 27n, 61, 64-66,
  72-75, 88, 103, 106-107n
  118, 120-22, 128, 134, 137,
  148, 154f, 161, 165, 173-
  76, 211n, 226, 236, 239,
  242, 251, 253n, 257, 268,
  270, 276, 281n, 283, 290,
  292, 304, 307, 315, 323,
  333-35, 342n, 351, 387,
  394, 396, 398f, 408f, 413f,
  416, 418, 426, 432f, 448f
fasting, 264f, 290, 293f,
  363
Felicissimus, 378n, 380n
Firmilian of Caesarea, 395,
  397, 402-04, 438, 443f
food and drink (see also
  dietary laws), 11, 30n,
  83, 85, 91, 98n, 102, 121,

147-52, 182f, 200f, 214,
  244, 280f, 309n, 311,
  323f, 358, 377
forgiveness (see also re-
  pentance), 13f, 22, 55f,
  69, 76f, 111f, 131, 152,
  155, 172, 220, 228-35,
  258n, 269, 272f, 295-
  96n, 303, 326f, 340, 349,
  361f, 372, 379, 383, 395,
  397f, 408, 422
Fragmentum Muratorianum,
  228

Gaius, 300n
Gnosis (Gnosticism), 49n,
  80n, 100, 103n, 109f,
  114, 118, 121, 126, 158,
  165, 181, 228, 235f,
  238-43, 246-49, 255-60,
  266, 268-70, 277, 309,
  346, 416n, 447
Gregory Thaumaturgus, 343n

Hellenist influence, 153,
  157
Heraclas of Alexandria,
  306, 336
heresies and factions (see
  also schism), 100, 105,
  107, 110, 113, 115n, 119,
  121f, 125, 127-29, 158-
  65, 168, 170-72, 174,
  176, 178, 180-87, 192,
  201n, 209-19, 225, 236,
  238f, 246-60, 263, 266f,
  271f, 274-84, 297, 300,
  303, 333-36, 346, 351,
  361-64, 384, 387-410,
  415n-16, 420, 423, 426-
  28, 432f, 438, 440
hierarchical system, 158,
  203n-17, 254, 285, 298f,
  302n-03, 306n, 312n, 341,

423-28, 432f, 436, 442
Hippolytus, 242n, 266, 278,
    294-304, 390n, 428, 434,
    441
Holy Spirit, 85f, 88, 96,
    137, 142, 165f, 168f, 171,
    173n-74n, 251n, 313n 347-
    50, 355, 361f, 381, 387f,
    391-93, 397f, 400n, 408-10,
    414, 438, 446
Honorius I (Pope), 428
hypostasis, 313n

Ignatius of Antioch, 163n,
    179, 209-19, 225, 247, 249,
    425f, 428
Illiad, 144n
immanence of Christ (see also
    unity with Christ), 34-37,
    56, 59
imprisoned Christians, 359
infallibility, 425
intercommunion, 304n, 438f,
    445f, 448f
Irenaeus of Lyon, 49n, 181,
    219, 240, 246-61, 268, 345,
    428
Israel (old and new contrast-
    ed), 14-16, 79, 81f, 86,
    108, 129, 135, 147-53,
    175, 180f, 289n, 335, 346f,
    412-22, 435f

Jebusites, 328
Jerome, 308, 333n
Job, 94
Johannes Damascenus, 13n
Josephus, Flavius, 11n
Judaizers, 83, 103, 105, 107,
    109f, 113, 128, 145n, 210,
    216, 264, 266, 277, 346f,
    376n
Judas Iscariot, 13n, 37-50,
    78, 194n, 319, 354, 387,

404, 435
jurisdiction (see author-
    ity)
Justin Martyr, 202n, 241,
    243-46
Juvenal, 300n

Kingdom of God, 18, 39n,
    54, 57, 89n, 97, 104n,
    119f, 225f, 309n, 336,
    338
kiss of peace, 293f, 302
Korah (Dathan and Abiram),
    161, 253, 350, 400

laity (layman), 203n, 208,
    285, 302n, 305, 363,
    372-73n, 378n-79, 402n,
    423
Latinization of the Church,
    266f, 296n
laxism (see rigorism)
Lazarus, 321
Leo II (Pope), 428
letters of recommendation
    and reconciliation, 338f,
    373, 385
libellus, (libellatici,
    sacrificati, lapsi),
    365f, 372-86, 437, 448
Logos (Word), 24f, 31-33,
    243, 248-51n, 259n, 269,
    310n, 312-15, 319n-20,
    322, 324, 326

magic, 6n, 80f, 102f, 126,
    202n, 257n, 290, 301,
    303
Marcion (Marcionites),
    201n, 221, 241f, 246,
    255, 257f, 279f, 282n,
    285n-86, 299
marriage, 17n, 21n, 228f,
    282n, 289f, 300, 323n,

348, 351, 358
maturity and perfection, 116
Minucius Felix, 202n
Monarchianism, 295
Montanus (Montanism), 49n,
    133n, 191n, 230n, 234, 278f,
    281n, 285n-86n, 288, 296n,
    299, 393, 432, 436
morality and ethics, 84-85n,
    87f, 92, 95, 101, 107, 109f,
    119, 121, 154, 157f, 171,
    177, 191f, 194, 198, 200,
    204n-05, 207, 218, 224-26,
    233, 269-72, 312, 315, 320,
    322, 332, 352, 416-19, 430-
    32, 438
Mystery (Mythric) Cult, 263n,
    283n, 422
Mystici Corporis (encyclical),
    415n

Nadab and Abiud, 253
neo-Judaism (see also Juda-
    izers), 221, 341-43, 346-50
    368f, 375, 435
Nicolaites, 181-83
Novatian (Novatianism), 49n,
    133n, 294n, 296n, 336, 345n,
    385-90, 401, 406, 428

oath, 106n, 141, 200
occupations (see professions)
Ordeal (trial by), 102f, 440
ordination (Holy Orders,
    priesthood), 123, 136n,
    203n, 207, 213, 302n, 305-
    06n, 375, 388, 390n, 392,
    394, 396-97n, 400f, 428,
    438
Origen, 49n, 241n, 273, 305-
    36, 342-43n, 397, 435f
orthodoxy (Christian), 88f,
    201n, 210, 212, 215, 226,
    249, 252, 277, 308, 334f,
    351f, 413, 418, 424-27n,

429, 443

paententia secunda (see
    also forgiveness), 227-
    30, 268-70, 273, 287,
    326, 354n, 429, 431f,
    434
Pantaenus, 269
Papias of Hieropolis, 43n
Passover (Jewish), 25, 38n,
    45, 303n, 388, 427
pastoral functions of the
    church (see also Peter),
    417-19, 446-49
Paul of Samosata, 426
penitential system, 123f,
    133n, 136n, 155, 228,
    234f, 272-74, 287n, 318-
    20, 322, 325-28n, 331f,
    337-41, 343, 354f, 360,
    369n, 373n-74, 376, 379f,
    405, 429, 431
Peter, 13, 18, 29, 69, 71-
    75, 78-80, 107, 392, 419
Philo, 11n, 25n, 130, 307,
    332
philosophy, 119, 125, 241,
    243, 298, 311-14, 325-27,
    336, 371n
Pius I (Pope), 228
Pius XII (Pope), 415n
Plato (Platonism), 306n-07,
    311f, 314, 449
Plinius, Gaius, 11n, 200-
    02n
Plotinus (neo-Platonism),
    312n, 314n
pluralism, 427, 433
Polycarp of Smyrna, 49n,
    209, 219-21, 247, 257,
    259n, 262f, 267
Polycrates of Ephesus, 263
Pontianus (Pope), 295
posthumous condemnation,
    307f

prayers for the dead, 350

pre-existence and nature of
Jesus Christ, 334f

presbyters (presbyterate,
priest), 155f, 158n, 177,
205, 209-13, 215, 220, 253f,
257-58n, 294, 298, 300, 302n-
03, 316, 373n-74, 378f, 402n,
424, 437

priesthood of all Christians,
285, 322, 428, 432f, 435f,
441, 445

professions (prohibited to
Christians), 290-92, 301,
367

prophets (Christian), 178,
203f, 206, 233, 252, 255,
279, 431

Purgatory, 269

purity (impurity; purification), 7-11, 17-23, 35, 37,
56, 82, 96, 105, 123f, 175,
193f, 198, 208, 215f, 218,
245, 268f, 275f, 290, 302n,
311, 316-18, 320, 323, 328,
330, 336, 342f, 349f, 354,
357f, 375-77, 379-83, 392n,
395, 398, 400, 414, 422,
434f, 448

Pythagoreans, 326

Quartodecimans, 263-68, 304n

Qumran (see Essenes)

readmission to the Church, 99,
122-24, 132, 137, 174n, 193,
218, 223f, 229f, 258, 281n-
82n, 286-88, 295, 313f, 319n-
320, 322, 326, 328n, 331-33,
336-41, 354, 359f, 362, 369n,
372-86, 390n, 417, 422, 429-
31, 434, 436f, 448

real presence (in the Eucharist), 32-34, 46-48, 62,

103, 195n, 280n, 302,
310n-11, 313n, 369-71,
377, 389, 437

rebaptism, 272, 336, 343,
390-410, 421n, 434, 437f,
442, 444, 448

reconciliation (see read-
mission)

Reformation, 445

repentance, 13n, 17, 19,
88, 99, 105, 110, 112,
124, 130, 132-33n, 136-
39, 144n, 173n-74n, 183,
186f, 194, 197, 218, 220,
222-37, 259, 270, 272f,
286f, 320, 330, 337n-38,
341, 354f, 358-64, 372-
73n, 390n, 417f, 429,
431, 433, 436f, 440f, 448

revelation, 116f, 134n, 306n

rigorism and laxism (see
also Montanus), 133, 237n,
273, 277, 296n, 303, 327n,
333n, 337, 341, 352, 354,
363f, 372, 378n, 380,
385f, 406, 431-33

Rufinus of Aquileis, 308

sacrifice, 8f, 22, 53, 55,
59, 83, 98f, 139-53, 182f,
185, 192n-94n, 208, 243f,
251n, 260f, 294, 338-40,
364-66, 376f, 380-85,
389, 393, 400, 403, 421f,
437f

Sallustius, 202n

Saturnilians, 246

schism (schismatic), 178n,
205f, 208f, 216-18, 253,
255, 285, 294-300, 336,
350, 376n, 378n-79, 384,
386-90, 398-401, 404,
415n-16n, 423, 433

Scholasticism, 415n

Sebellianism, 297
self-condemnation, 129-31, 141,
    216, 256, 389
Serapion of Alexandria, 339f
Servant of Yahweh, 22n, 56
sexual matters, 9n, 19, 84, 92,
    95, 121f, 124, 126, 144n,
    159, 163, 172, 177, 181,
    183, 185f, 201f, 220n,
    223f, 226, 229, 240, 258,
    274f, 288f, 294, 296n,
    300f, 322-23n, 329, 348,
    435
Shepherd of Hermas, 227-35,
    258, 270, 273, 345, 431
sin (sinners)
--against the Holy Spirit,
    173n-74n
--categories of, 97, 162, 174n,
    186f, 230-34, 273, 275f
    286, 288, 292n, 295, 316,
    319n, 326, 328, 330, 333,
    339, 352, 361f, 380, 416n,
    420, 430
--unto death, 173-74n, 176,
    230f, 272, 327n, 361, 417
--willful, 130, 140-47, 173-
    74n, 223, 230-33, 430
slaves, 300f
Soter of Rome, 224
Stephen I (Pope), 343, 391,
    397, 403-06, 442
Stoicism, 241
substance, 310n-311, 313n
syncretism, 118, 183, 239,
    258n, 298, 419

Tacitus, 202n, 300n
Tatian (see Diatessaron)
Tertullian, 202n, 231n, 242n,
    266, 273, 278-96n, 299n-
    300, 302n, 307, 309, 312n,
    351, 390, 431-33
tests for orthodoxy, 164f
    176, 180, 203f, 215, 283,
    351, 391n, 418, 423-28, 432f

Thomas Aquinas, 313n, 415n
Torah, 30-32
tradition (Apostolic and
    ecclesial), 58, 89n, 112,
    121, 252-55, 267f, 277,
    284, 297, 378n, 390, 403-
    05, 410, 427f, 438
trinity, 335, 337, 391,
    396f, 414

unity of Christians, 115n,
    117-19, 171f, 181, 208,
    211f, 215, 217, 226n,
    251f, 255, 263, 267f,
    282n, 284f, 316, 318-20,
    333, 371n, 377, 387, 390-
    94, 396, 401, 415n-16n,
    418, 422, 437-39, 442, 449
union with Christ and God,
    (see also immenence), 66-
    68, 95, 97-99, 115n, 148f,
    171f, 175, 181, 211n, 214f,
    217, 251, 319n, 393, 441

Valens, 219f
Valentinus (Valentinianism)
    239f, 246, 255, 259, 300
validity of sacraments (see
    also Eucharist), 58, 213,
    267, 272, 282-84, 287,
    303f, 377n, 379, 390-410,
    422, 426, 428, 432f, 436,
    438, 440
Victor I (Pope), 263, 266-
    68, 427
virgin birth, 334
Wisdom (personified), 31n,
    271f
women (esp. in relation to
    the Church), 284n, 300,
    341f, 348-51, 467f, 402n
Xystus (Sixtus, Pope), 263n,
    406f
Zephyrinus (Pope), 266, 294-
    96n

29